HARVARD ECONOMIC STUDIES

PUBLISHED UNDER THE DIRECTION OF
THE DEPARTMENT OF ECONOMICS

VOL. V

WOOL-GROWING AND THE TARIFF

A STUDY IN THE ECONOMIC HISTORY OF THE UNITED STATES

BY

CHESTER WHITNEY WRIGHT, PH.D.

INSTRUCTOR IN POLITICAL ECONOMY IN THE UNIVERSITY OF CHICAGO
SOMETIME AUSTIN TEACHING FELLOW IN HARVARD UNIVERSITY

AWARDED THE DAVID A. WELLS PRIZE FOR THE YEAR 1907–08, AND PUBLISHED FROM THE INCOME OF THE DAVID A. WELLS FUND

CAMBRIDGE
HARVARD UNIVERSITY PRESS
LONDON: HUMPHREY MILFORD
OXFORD UNIVERSITY PRESS

To My Father

PREFACE

In the whole history of the tariff, probably no schedule has excited more attention and controversy than the wool and woolens schedule. The granting of protection to both the grower and the manufacturer, whose interests ordinarily are so opposed, has furnished an excellent example of the working of the policy of protection in some of its phases. The results of protection in both industries afford unusually interesting problems in economics, and also in politics. The protection of wool has long been the chief bait which the manufacturers could hold out to the farmers of the country to secure their support for the protective system. Wool has been the most widespread and important single agricultural product a protective duty on which could be held to benefit the farmer generally. An attempt to estimate the results which the farmers have obtained from this duty should thus be worth while.

My chief interests in the subject, however, have centered in somewhat broader aspects of the problem. To determine the extent to which the tariff moulded the fate of this pursuit, and whether its effect had or had not been exaggerated, it became necessary to inquire into all the other factors that influenced, in one way or another, the development of the industry. The study has thus become one of the intricate interplay of economic forces and the complicated working of economic laws. The effort to untangle a perplexing situation, such, for instance, as arose during the Civil War with the arrival on the scene of action of a group of new and unfamiliar factors, should prove instructive as illustrating the complicated character of economic problems and the errors which may be committed when such complexity is unrecognized or ignored. The investigation, furthermore, may serve to throw light upon certain characteristics of agriculture and, perhaps, add a chapter to that neglected part of our economic history. Finally, a study of the development of the wool-growing industry in the United States affords an admirable illustration of the working out of certain fundamental influences which have largely dominated the economic history of the country.

The subject of wool and the tariff is not a new one, nor is there any lack of writing upon it. The justification for this addition will have to come, if at all, through new methods of attacking the problem. As is intimated above, approach is through the past. It is hoped by means of a careful examination and analysis of that past to discover what were the forces that shaped the growth of this industry, how they operated, which of them were dominant and which subordinate, how potent a factor the tariff was, — in short, just why the industry followed the course of development that it did, and what determines its present position.

This does not pretend, therefore, to be a narrative history of the industry; that the reader can find elsewhere. Here an attempt has been made to follow general outlines and broad movements. Details are given only where they serve to intensify the outline or sharply to characterize some movement. The general outline once traced, the aim has been to determine the underlying and the dominant forces. Any matter which on investigation proved to have a direct bearing upon the fate of the industry, however remote from the subject it might at first appear, has been treated. If a great deal of space and attention has been devoted to such matters, it is because of the belief that to attain the desired goal a thorough knowledge of them was indispensable. The treatment of these topics, however, does not pretend to be complete, those phases only having been touched upon which had some direct bearing upon the growing of wool. Thus, the manufacture of wool for certain periods has received considerable attention, and for others little, according to the varying importance of this factor; but in no case does the account of it pretend to be complete. A similar assertion may be made as to general agricultural conditions. Although the United States has been preëminently an agricultural country, this phase of its economic history has suffered from the most amazing neglect. The lack of obtainable information on this topic has been a decided handicap for the writer, and has obviously made it impossible to cover that field satisfactorily.

The end to be obtained by this study of economic history is a knowledge of the forces which are at work determining the course of the wool-growing industry. The practical application of that knowledge, aside from such broader insight into the problems of the country's economic development as it may afford, would come: first, from the light which it throws upon the question whether this industry should be protected; secondly, from the ability thus obtained to point out, in case protection were deemed advisable, just what forces would have to be contended against and what line of action followed to secure most readily the end desired. Whether the industry should in fact be protected is a question upon which it is not attempted to pass judgment, since it is believed that the present study may be made more effective by letting the reader draw his own conclusions.

An economic question which, in this country, has been the source of more controversy or upon which prejudices are stronger than that of the tariff, it would be difficult to find. Whether I have succeeded in the endeavor to maintain an impartial attitude in undertaking a scientific analysis of one phase of this vexed topic will have to be left to others. I can only say that such an effort was sincerely made.

To Professor F. W. Taussig, under whom the study was undertaken, most grateful acknowledgment is due for constant encouragement, friendly interest, and painstaking revision of the manuscript, as well as for supervising its passage through the press. I am also indebted to Professor Edwin F. Gay for scholarly criticism and suggestions for improving the manuscript, which he most kindly consented to read, and to Professor Thomas N. Carver, the editor of the series in which it is published.

CONTENTS

LIST OF CHARTS

WOOL-GROWING AND THE TARIFF

CHAPTER I

WOOL-GROWING BEFORE 1800

ALTHOUGH the growing of wool did not receive sufficient attention before 1800 to deserve the name of an industry, nevertheless a review of this earliest period is desirable, in order not only to understand the conditions that existed when the industry actually came into being, but also to comprehend better the causes which led to its birth.

Wool-Growing in Colonial Times.

The earlier explorers or settlers found no sheep[1] in the colonies, and from the start they had to depend entirely on such as could be imported. Columbus is said to have brought some from Spain in 1493,[2] and the flocks brought over from time to time by the earlier explorers and conquerors from that kingdom of the fleece are to be regarded as the progenitors of the sheep which later were found scattered through the southwestern part of the country, to some extent in the piney woods of the Gulf states, but mainly to the westward in New Mexico and southern California. There they wandered for centuries, neglected and almost unnoticed, occasionally supplying the native tribes and the few settlers with mutton and with coarse wool for blankets and clothing. In time, by the slow process of evolution, they became adapted to climate and soil, and eventually were the sturdy basis of an important branch of our wool-growing industry.

The first sheep introduced into the colonies of the Atlantic coast appear to have been those brought to Virginia by the London Com-

[1] Throughout this study, emphasis is placed on the number of sheep rather than on the quantity of wool; the latter being a joint-product, its amount is fundamentally determined by the number of sheep.

[2] *Census*, 1900, vol. v, p. ccii.

pany in 1609.[1] These, of course, were of the English breeds, but came before the improvement in that stock, as was the case with all the colonial importations. Sheep were brought to New Netherland by the Dutch as early as 1625,[2] these presumably being of their own Texel breed. In New England there appear to have been sheep by 1631, when, it is stated, there were four hundred in Charlestown, besides "some store" in Watertown.[3] Sheep were brought to Connecticut with the first settlers, and in Rhode Island they were more numerous than anywhere else.

The lot of the innocent sheep in these struggling colonies was indeed a hard one. They proved to be the only domestic animals which did not multiply freely,[4] and it was by constant work and effort alone that the race was kept from extinction. The wolf was its deadly enemy, but the severe winters, combined with lack of care on the part of the owners, also depleted the flocks. The colonists seldom made any effort to protect their sheep against winter storms, and, accustomed as these animals were to a milder clime, they suffered greatly. The wolves were such a serious danger that, so far as possible, the sheep were herded on small islands just off the coast, where, the wolves once exterminated, they were safe; or else on peninsulas, where protection was comparatively easy. Thus we find that the sheep around Boston were kept on islands in the harbor, or on such necks of land as Nahant. The origin of the flocks which were so long a feature of the island of Nantucket is thus explained. Flocks were to be found — to mention the more important — on the island of Rhode Island, Long Island, Staten Island, Fisher's Island, as well as on the numerous necks of land along the Virginia coast. When no such naturally protected spot was available, the sheep, in New England at least, were generally kept in one herd on the common lands or sheepwalks of the town, under the care of a town shepherd.

Under such conditions it is easy to see why the colonial flocks increased but slowly. They were as numerous in New England as

[1] Bishop, *History of American Manufactures*, vol. i, p. 304, note.

[2] *Ibid.*

[3] Johnson, *Wonder Working Providence*, pp. xvi, 46. This number is thought an exaggeration. Bishop says that sheep were first brought to Massachusetts about 1633.

[4] Eggleston, "Agriculture in the Colonies," in *The Century Magazine*, January, 1884, pp. 445-446.

anywhere, but even there growth proved difficult. In 1642 there were only a thousand sheep in Massachusetts, and wool was being imported.[1] By about 1652 the number had crept up to some three thousand.[2] It is evident, however, that wool was by no means plentiful at this time, for the General Court was frequently passing measures intended to increase the flocks.[3] In 1654 the colony was "in great straits in respect to clothing," and the exportation of sheep from Massachusetts to other colonies (with one exception) was forbidden, while measures were also taken to prevent their slaughter and to stimulate the manufacture of cloth.[4] Apparently these efforts met with success, for within fifteen years the value of sheep had so fallen that the rate at which they were assessed was reduced three separate times.[5] It is even stated that in 1675 wool was exported, but the quantity[6] was probably insignificant, though sufficient to lead Massachusetts to prohibit the practice.[7] The people of Rhode Island seem to have had more and better sheep[8] than any other colony. As early as 1648 they were sending sheep to Connecticut, where the situation was reversed. The records of that colony, notably between 1660 and 1673, show constant efforts to increase this stock.[9] As early as 1661, one writer reported that New England had nearly one hundred thousand sheep, and was soon likely to supply the Dutch.[10] Though this zealous supporter of English wares doubtless exaggerated the facts, it is clear that by 1675 the worst of the early struggle of the sheep to get a foothold on this inhospitable shore was over.

In New Netherland, during Dutch rule, the supply of sheep seems to have been meagre. After the first importation in 1625 there

[1] Winthrop, *Journal*, vol. ii, p. 154.

[2] Johnson, *Wonder Working Providence*, p. 175.

[3] See *Records of the Massachusetts Bay Company*, vol. ii, pp. 105–106; vol. iii, pp. 133–134.

[4] *Ibid.*, vol. iii, pp. 355–356, 424.

[5] *Ibid.*, vol. iv, part i, p. 367; part ii, pp. 42, 564.

[6] Weeden, *Economic and Social History of New England*, vol. i, p. 305. It is also stated that wool was then being imported (*ibid.*, p. 238).

[7] *Records of the Massachusetts Bay Company*, vol. v, p. 28.

[8] *Calendar of British State Papers*, Colonial and West Indies, vol. ix, p. 221; vol. v, p. 343.

[9] *Public Records of Connecticut*, vol. i, p. 349; vol. ii, pp. 34, 51–52, 139, 197.

[10] *Calendar of British State Papers*, Colonial and West Indies, vol. v, p. 25.

had been another in 1630, yet in 1643 there were not, it is stated, over sixteen in the colony.[1] In 1650 there was much complaint about the scarcity of sheep, and the refusal of the English colonies to sell them.[2] But after New Netherland came under English control the number evidently increased, for by 1708 it was reported to the Board of Trade that three quarters of the woolen goods used were made among the people.[3]

Again, in the colonies to the south of New York sheep were less numerous than in New England. In 1663 the Swedes were reported to have but eighty sheep.[4] Pennsylvania, too, was slow in introducing them, but by 1698 had established fulling mills, and in 1700 was declared to possess rapidly multiplying flocks. In Maryland in 1663-64 the export of wool was forbidden.[5] The early history of sheep-raising in Virginia shows a very slow advance. Not only were the same difficulties met here as in the other colonies, but there was less necessity for woolen clothing, and the energy of the farmers was largely devoted to tobacco. In 1649 the sheep in this colony numbered three thousand.[6] Various measures were taken to increase them, and about 1676 exportation of them was prohibited.[7] But in spite of their small number, sheep, and wool also, were cheap, showing how slight was the demand.[8] In the last quarter of the century, however, they spread more rapidly, and by 1690 flocks of sheep had become "objects of common observation in Virginia."[9]

It is thus evident that, when the eighteenth century opened, sheep had secured a firm foothold in the American colonies. The physical difficulties incident to the introduction of the race had by that year been completely overcome, and the supply seems to have been sufficient to meet the needs of the time. These needs, it is true, were limited to the wants of each farming household: the growing of

[1] *Bulletin of the National Association of Wool Manufacturers*, vol. xxix, p. 120. Hereafter cited as *Bulletin*.

[2] *Documents Relating to the Colonial History of New York*, vol. i, p. 368-369.

[3] *Special Report on the History and Present Condition of the Sheep Industry of the United States*. United States Department of Agriculture, Bureau of Animal Industry, D. E. Salmon, Chief, 1892. Hereafter cited as *Sheep Industry*.

[4] Bishop, *History of American Manufactures*, vol. i, p. 315.

[5] *Calendar of British State Papers*, Colonial and West Indies, vol. v, p. 163.

[6] Bruce, *Economic History of Virginia in the Seventeenth Century*, vol. i, p. 336.

[7] *Ibid.*, p. 376. [8] *Ibid.*, pp. 484-485. [9] *Ibid.*, p. 481.

wool was simply a part of the general household economy. But since the chief physical obstacles to the increase of sheep had been removed and a foundation upon which to advance had been laid, it only remained for the colonists to go ahead and build.

In the eighteenth century, however, there appeared another class of difficulties — the economic ones. These, to be sure, had existed and had doubtless exercised some influence before, but now that the more immediate obstacles were either lessened or removed, those of economic character became of much greater relative importance.

The chief of these, the one which from 1700 on proved to be the greatest enemy of the colonial sheep, was the British woolen manufacture. If there was one industry which the British government was guarding with greater care than another, it was the woolen manufacture. To prevent any encroachment on its domain was the constant endeavor of the government, and of this domain the wool industry in the American Colonies was considered a part. In 1660 England had prohibited the export of sheep and wool,[1] — her first blow at the colonies. In 1699 Parliament forbade the colonies to export wool and woolens either to one another or to any other country whatsoever, — a second blow. There is no reason to believe that if the export of wool from the colonies to foreign countries had been permitted, it would ever have amounted to anything. Shipments of woolens from one colony to another did sometimes occur,[2] but they do not appear to have been at any time very extensive. The chief sheep-raising districts, according to the report for 1704 of the surveyor of the customs in New England, were Nantucket (where there

[1] *Calendar of British State Papers*, Colonial and West Indies, vol. i, p. 481. When the Virginia Legislature, in 1684, passed an act to encourage textile manufactures, it was annulled by Parliament (see Lord's *Industrial Experiments in Colonial America*, p. 128).

[2] We find reports that in 1720 druggets and stuffs from New Hampshire were sold in the Boston market (see Lord's *Industrial Experiments in Colonial America*, p. 136). In 1746 the country people of New York, though partly supplying their own needs, were also buying from Massachusetts. In 1756 a cargo sent from Boston to Albany had 200 homespun jackets (*ibid.*, p. 136). In 1715 the Governor of New York wrote that the people of New York and Albany wore no clothing of their own manufacture, but that was not so of the rest of the population. He did not know of any homespun ever having been sold in shops (see *Documents Relating to the Colonial History of New York*, vol. v, p. 556).

were between 20,000 and 30,000 head), Martha's Vineyard, Block Island, Canonicut Island, and some of the small islands in Massachusetts Bay. Since so few sheep were kept on the mainland that the towns were supplied largely from the islands, there was considerable difficulty in enforcing this law.

A natural but unexpected result of the law was to hasten the spread of sheep. As the surveyor reported: "The act has had the effect that those towns which cannot be supplied but by stealth nor without great charge and hazard involved in smuggling are now endeavoring to raise sheep and keep them by shepherds."[1] He adds that in a recent journey to investigate the situation he found that towns which formerly had not a hundred sheep would shortly have a thousand.[2] A year or two later a surveyor noted "the dangerous growing manufacture of wool in New England," and in 1708 he wrote that this growth had been such that not one in forty but wore "his own carding and spinning," and in 1719 scarcely a countryman came to Boston but "clad in his own manufacture."[3]

The failure of England to keep the colonies continually and sufficiently supplied with woolen goods was a frequent cause of distress. In many instances it was this distress alone that led the colonists to grow and manufacture wool for themselves. Thus in 1654 the scarcity of English cloth, of frequent occurrence in time of war, was the cause of measures to increase the sheep.[4] Again in 1715 a letter to the Board of Trade declared that, nine years before, the great scarcity and dearness of woolen goods, which sold at 200% advance, had forced the colonies to set up "a very considerable manufactory, still in being," by which the importation from Great Britain had decreased £50,000 a year.[5] Thereafter the supply of woolen goods

[1] Lord, *Industrial Experiments in Colonial America*, p. 129.

[2] *Ibid.* [3] *Ibid.*, pp. 131–133.

[4] *Records of the Massachusetts Bay Company*, vol. ii, p. 105–106; vol. iii, p. 355.

[5] Bishop, *History of American Manufactures*, vol. i, p. 330. In 1709 Governor Dudley of Massachusetts reported that the woolen trade with England had greatly abated and that people were clothing themselves with their own wool (see Lord's *Industrial Experiments in Colonial America*, p. 132). A report from New York stated that three quarters of the linen and woolen used was made at home, especially of the coarser sort (see *Documentary History of New York*, vol. i, p. 712).

from England seems to have come with sufficient regularity and in adequate quantity so that the colonies were no longer compelled to manufacture for themselves on this account. The scarcity of commodities which could be used to help pay for English goods remained an important factor in inducing the colonists to manufacture their own cloth.[1] About 1717 England is said to have exported to the colonies, on an average, some £147,438 worth of woolen goods.[2] A very complete report from the various colonies, made in 1731, indicates that the British woolens were not losing ground as they had been in the period just preceding, and that there was almost no manufacturing except for household use.[3] Certainly at this period we find fewer attempts than formerly to stimulate the sheep industry. In 1748 the Swedish traveler, Kalm, declared that all the woolen manufactures came from England.[4] Apparently these conditions remained unaltered down to 1770. Outside of the towns, the farmers continued to supply a large part of their own wants with woolen of household manufacture, yet, as the Governor of New York reported, "without the least design of sending it to market." [5] Virtually all those who were not engaged in some agricultural pursuit depended on English woolens.

Though this influx of British manufactures was the greatest hindrance to the advance of the sheep industry between 1700 and 1770, it was by no means the only one. No sooner had wolves begun to disappear than dogs harassed the flocks. As early as 1730 New York was passing acts to prevent the destruction of sheep by this new foe.[6] Another trouble appeared as a result of the gradual taking up of the common lands, and the abolition of the common flock; for the individual could not afford a shepherd for his small band. Again, the sheep still suffered very severely from the neglect of their owners, especially in winter. In 1717, it was reported that on Fisher's Island

[1] Lord Cornbury noted that this scarcity "sets men's wits to work, and puts them on a trade which I am sure will hurt England in a little time, viz., the woolen manufacture on Long Island and Connecticut." Lord, *Industrial Experiments in Colonial America*, p. 131.

[2] Beer, *Commercial Policy of England*, p. 81.

[3] Bishop, *History of American Manufactures*, vol. i, pp. 339–341.

[4] Kalm, *Travels*, vol. i, pp. 58, 257.

[5] *Documents Relating to the Colonial History of New York*, vol. vii, p. 888.

[6] *Ibid.*, vol. v, p. 909; vol. vi, p. 160.

alone, over eleven hundred sheep died by being buried in the snow,[1] and in a single hard winter a little before the middle of the century a third of all the sheep in the northern colonies perished.[2] There was, to be sure, an increase in the number of sheep at this period, but after about 1715 it was rather incidental to the increase in population than the result of any real and determined general effort to increase the supply of domestic wool and woolens for the colonists' needs. Aside from this, wool-growing as an industry, in the first three quarters of the eighteenth century, made no advance.[3]

From 1770 *to* 1800.

How largely dependent on foreign sources for their woolens the colonies really were, is best illustrated by the effects of the Revolution, which largely cut off this supply. The gradual increase in the restrictive measures of Great Britain, combined with the better enforcement of those measures, first led the colonies to shake off their dependence on English woolen goods. Moreover, as a mark of patriotism, many of those living in the towns now used homespun and other domestic cloths in place of the finer British goods. The extent of the decline in the consumption of British woolens is indicated by the following table: —

[1] *Niles' Register*, vol. xlviii, p. 188.

[2] Eggleston, "Agriculture in the Colonies"; in *The Century Magazine*, January, 1884, p. 445.

[3] The author of *American Husbandry*, writing just before the Revolution, describes the situation in regard to sheep as follows: "Sheep also they have in great numbers, and though the wool does not equal the best in England or Spain, yet it is much better than is produced in many of our counties, and makes cloth that answers exceedingly well for the general wear of the province, fine as well as coarse cloths, and accordingly almost all the farmers with their servants with the lower classes of other sorts are clad in it; they have no lands in the whole province but what do excellently for feeding sheep, even the very worst tracts maintaining great numbers. Sheep are kept in such numbers that wool might be a valuable article of exportation unwrought and by a proper policy in the mother country wool might become as good an import from the colonies as any other" (vol. i, p. 167). The author later proposes to give a bounty on imports of colonial wool into Great Britain, thus raising the price in the colonies and burdening American manufacture while helping the British manufacturer (see vol. ii, pp. 268–269). This description considerably exaggerates the extent of the wool-growing industry in the country at the time, as the scarcity of wool during the Revolution makes plain.

Exports of all Woolen Goods from the United Kingdom to the American Colonies.[1]

1772	1773	1774	1775	1776
£925,643	£549,030	£775,424	£49,769	£15,657

The Revolution increased the demand for domestic wool, not only by cutting off the supply of foreign woolens, but also by creating new needs, those of the army, for which the existing stock of sheep was utterly inadequate. Hitherto the flocks had been limited to the wants of each household, and were so scanty that Otis declared there was not enough wool raised in all America to make each person a pair of stockings.[2]

In an endeavor to meet the new demand, the Congress of Deputies and various conventions and assemblies from Massachusetts to Virginia passed resolutions calling upon the people to use their utmost endeavors to improve the breed and increase the number of sheep.[3] The Continental Congress made frequent appeals to increase the supply of woolens for the soldiers, much of whose clothing was of linen. All these efforts proving, however, insufficient, the country found itself obliged to buy woolens in an indirect way of its enemy,[4] and to such an amount that France entered a protest.[5]

Nevertheless, the Revolution did not pass without some effect upon the sheep industry, though the resulting growth was neither so great nor so lasting as might have been expected. During the war, many sheep had been slaughtered or had degenerated from lack of care. Then, when peace came, the British woolens poured in as of old. In the case of the coarser goods, however, the country supplied a greater proportion of its own needs than formerly. For the higher grades of cloth, since no fine wool was to be found in the country, it was still entirely dependent upon Great Britain. In Massachusetts, soon after the war, the importation of foreign manufactures was less by a half than twenty years earlier.[6] In the South too there was seen an increased attention to manufactures: in Virginia, it is said, three fourths of all the clothing was now manufactured by the people,

[1] The value as rated in the Inspector's books. For the figures by groups of colonies, see Bishop's *History of American Manufactures*, vol. i, p. 176.

[2] Sheffield, *Observations on the Commerce of the American States*, 6th ed., p. 25.

[3] See Bishop's *History of American Manufactures*, vol. i, pp. 380–381.

[4] *Ibid.*, p. 395.

[5] Sheffield, *Observations*, p. ii.

[6] Bishop, *History of American Manufactures*, vol. i, p. 414.

whereas before the war seven eighths of it had been imported.[1] The struggle for political freedom had awakened a spirit of independence which now sought a new field of activity in industrial life.

From the close of the war we find increased effort to improve the sheep of the country. Numerous societies to promote agriculture and manufacturing were formed, with Tench Coxe as a leader in the movement. In 1785 the Philadelphia Society for the Promotion of Agriculture was organized, and in the same year a similar society in South Carolina.[2] The latter is noted for having offered a medal to the person who would first establish and keep in that state a flock of sheep of pure merino blood, — the earliest known effort to secure that breed for America. Yet all this was important, not because of actual results obtained at the time, but simply as an indication that a handful of people had become aware of a deficiency in this industry and were making a real effort to supply the lack. The movement was led by a lonely few and lacked the requisite numbers for lasting effects. The great body of farmers took no interest in it, and the absence of fine wool still continued the most striking deficiency in the industry of wool-growing.

After 1790 the sheep seems to have received rather less attention than in the preceding decade. As more prosperous times dawned, and an opening appeared for the export of agricultural produce, the desire to have the country supply itself with wool was forgotten. The result is reflected in the increased importation of British woolens: for the years 1790–94 the imports averaged £1,400,000 in value; for 1795–99, £2,300,000.[3] It was easy to secure woolens from abroad and to pay for them from the proceeds of the merchant marine and the exports of agricultural produce; therefore sheep were neglected, and, with one or two exceptions, such a thing as an improved sheep was unknown. Washington had one of the finest flocks in the country. He had given it much personal attention, and after his death it was well cared for by Mr. Custis, whose Arlington long-wool sheep, as they were called, were far famed. The flocks on Smith Island in Virginia were also much above the average, as were one or two in New England. Yet the premium offered by the South Carolina Agri-

[1] Bishop, *History of American Manufactures*, vol. i, p. 413.
[2] *Ibid.*, pp. 416–417.
[3] Brothers, *Wool and Wool Manufactures of Great Britain*, p. 144.

cultural Society as early as 1785 was still unclaimed: there was not a pure-bred merino sheep in the land. Nothing could better indicate the general attitude of the time towards the industry of wool-growing than the fact that when some of the precious merinos actually reached Boston in 1793, and were given to a man in Cambridge, he calmly ate them. Years later, when buying similar sheep for a thousand dollars each, he first realized what a luxury he had enjoyed.[1]

In short, the pursuit of wool-growing in the United States in the year 1800 was in virtually the same position that it had held a century before. In but few cases did it pretend to be anything but a part of the general farm economy of each agriculturist. The wool produced was of good strength, and in quality neither fine nor coarse. The situation was well described by a writer of a later date: "For coarse domestic clothing and their own immediate wants the common coarse-wooled sheep were reared by most of the farmers, as they had been from the first introduction of sheep into the country, and occasionally a trifle over was sold at the 'stores' in the country. Beyond that the flocks were seldom allowed to enlarge, and of course it was too inconsiderable an interest with individuals to attend much to the care of the sheep or the quality of the fleece." [2]

[1] *Sheep Industry*, p. 133.

[2] *Niles' Register*, vol. lxvi, p. 386.

CHAPTER II

THE ADVENT OF THE MERINO, 1800–1815

THE average flock of sheep in 1800 was no better than in 1690. The great improvements in the breed of sheep which, after 1750, took place in England under the care of Bakewell and Ellman had had no influence on the flocks of the United States. The efforts made during the last quarter of the eighteenth century to introduce the Spanish merino into England, France, and Germany[1] had not been followed by any corresponding move on this side of the Atlantic. Not until the first decade of the nineteenth century did this country secure a good breed of sheep. Nor was it until then that wool-growing can fairly be said to have become an industry on a commercial basis.

From 1800 *to* 1807.

The causes of this development are to be found in the conditions which at the time led to the rise of the woolen manufacture in this country. A review of these, then, will be desirable before turning to wool-growing itself.

There had been some efforts to establish the woolen manufacture in the United States outside of the household before 1800, but the results had been slight. During the Revolution an unsuccessful attempt was made to establish an independent factory at Philadelphia. In 1788 the Hartford Woolen Company was formed in Hartford, Connecticut, and it continued the manufacture of cloths for several years. At about the same time, mills were started in Stockbridge and Watertown, Massachusetts, but they proved to be very short-lived. Finally, in 1794, there was set up at Byfield, Massachusetts, by John and Arthur Scholfield, what is called "the first American woolen factory in which the attempt was made to manufacture woolens by modern machinery and power."[2] It was several years, however, before power was applied to either spinning or weaving.

[1] See Youatt, *The Sheep*. See also Toynbee, *Industrial Revolution*, pp. 43–44.

[2] North, "History of the Woolen Manufacture in New England"; in Davis's

During the earlier years of the new century carding machines introduced by the Scholfields were set up in a number of places, being used to card the wool for the household manufactures. In a few localities also there were attempts to establish factories, among which may be mentioned one at Peace Dale, Rhode Island, in 1801, one at Seymour, Connecticut, in 1806, and two started by the Scholfields, one in 1799, the other in 1801, at Montville, Connecticut, and Pittsfield, Massachusetts, respectively.[1]

The chief obstacle to the success of the factories was that at this time the imports of woolens from abroad supplied the whole demand for fine cloth, while other fabrics were supplied by the household. For the years 1790 to 1799, the imports of British woolens to the United States had averaged nearly two million pounds sterling in value.[2] Figures for later years are not available, but it is evident that the output of the few little mills in the United States was infinitesimal in proportion. To be sure there was a tariff on woolens, which, starting at 5% ad valorem in 1789, had risen to 10% in 1792, 15% in 1794, and 17½% in 1804; but it was not till it reached 35%, on the outbreak of the War of 1812, that it afforded any substantial aid to the infant industry.

The manufacturers complained that the scarcity of wool was a great hindrance. Domestic wool of the desired quality was certainly scarce, but such wool could be imported, and at this time there was no duty on it.[3] There is no doubt that it would have been of some advantage to have had a domestic supply, yet there is no less doubt that the manufacturers could have had such a supply if they had offered the farmers a sufficient inducement. This they could not

New England States, vol. i, p. 197. See also Taft's *Notes on the Introduction of the Woolen Manufacture*. For more detailed accounts of the early woolen manufacture, see the above two references and Bagnall's *History of the Textile Industries in the United States*. A somewhat more detailed account by North will be found in *Bulletin*, vols. xxix–xxxiii. For a claim to an earlier factory, see *Bulletin*, vol. xxix, p. 214.

[1] See Taft's *Notes*, pp. 32–40.

[2] See Brothers' *Wool and Wool Manufactures of Great Britain*, pp. 143–144.

[3] Since wool was specifically excepted in the clause levying a five per centum ad valorem duty on all unenumerated articles, in both the tariff of 1789 and that of 1790, it came in duty free till 1816. The Tariff Act of May 2, 1792, has a section exempting from duty all articles exempted by the tariff of 1790 and *adding* to those theretofore exempted, among others, "unmanufactured wool." I can find no record of the exemption of 1790 having been repealed and am unable to explain this "addition."

do; and the simple truth at the bottom of it all was that they could not compete with the English goods. Such were the conditions which the wool-grower had to face during the first seven years of the nineteenth century, and the natural result followed.[1]

The first merino sheep to aid directly in the improvement of the wool of this country arrived in the year 1801, when the ram Don Pedro was brought from France to New York by Dupont de Nemours and M. Delessert.[2] Four animals had been embarked, but only this one survived. In the same year Seth Adams imported a pair of Spanish merinos, and was awarded the premium which had been offered by the Massachusetts Society for Promoting Agriculture for the first merino brought into the state.[3] The following year Robert Livingston sent from France to his home in New York state two pair of merinos selected from the flocks of the French Government at Rambouillet. These, like the ram Don Pedro, were descended from Spanish stock brought into France during the last of the eighteenth century. But by far the most significant importation of the time, both as regards size and results, was that of David Humphreys, who in 1802 returned from Spain to his Connecticut home with seventy-five ewes and twenty-one rams, all of pure merino blood.[4] These furnished a solid foundation upon which to start a lasting and far-reaching improvement in the flocks of this country. In recognition of the great service Humphreys had thus rendered, the Massachusetts Society for Promoting Agriculture voted him a special gold medal. During the next few years we find several notices of the arrival of a pair or so of fine-wooled sheep. In 1803 two pair

[1] Michaux, traveling westward from Philadelphia in 1802, says: "Sheep being very scarce, the wool is very dear; at the same time they reserve it to make stockings." In Kentucky he notes that "they bring up very few sheep in these parts; for although I went upwards of two hundred miles in this state I saw them only in four plantations. Their flesh is not much esteemed, and their wool is of the same quality as that of the sheep in the eastern states. The most I ever observed was in Rhode Island." *Travels*, pp. 30, 191. *Cf. Niles' Register*, vol. xli, p. 218.

[2] A full account of these early importations may be found in the *Sheep Industry* or in Randall's *Fine Wool Sheep Husbandry.*

[3] For the best account of the award of this medal, about which there has been some confusion, see *Bulletin*, vol. xxxv, p. 238.

[4] It is now generally agreed that these were Spanish sheep known as Infantados, which have a thick fleece with considerable yolk. See *Sheep Industry*, p. 161. See also Randall's *Fine Wool Sheep Husbandry*, p. 37.

of the black-faced variety reached Philadelphia from Cadiz. In 1807 six merinos arrived at the same port from the flocks of the Prince of Hesse Cassel. In the same year Robert Livingston secured another ram, and in 1809 General John Armstrong imported nineteen merinos.[1] In 1807 a Massachusetts farmer seems to have succeeded in smuggling at least one pair of the improved Bakewell sheep from England.[2] These make up all the importations worthy of notice up to the year 1810. Insignificant as was the total, it at least supplied the germ from which greater things might grow. An opportunity such as never before existed was now open.

Nothing could be more indicative of the position then held by the industry than the way in which this opportunity was treated. In the few localities where the imported sheep were to be found, they were not altogether neglected, — at least the owners, unlike the Massachusetts owner of 1793, did not send them to the butcher, — but there is no evidence that the agricultural community as a whole showed any recognition of the importance and value of the new breed. "I have been extremely mortified," wrote David Humphreys in August of 1802, "to find that the breeding of sheep has been much neglected for some time past. It is but too evident a vital impulse is wanted to give new vigor to it."[3] "I was astonished," said Livingston, "when I found upon my return in 1805 that the introduction of merino sheep had excited so little attention, — that, although the Legislature of Connecticut had very properly noticed the patriotic exertions of Col. Humphreys, none of his sheep had been sold in this state. I had also the mortification to find, that notwithstanding my injunction, mine had been less extended than I expected. Nay, I learned with surprise, that a flock of near one hundred of half and three quarters bred merinos from a ram sent out by M. Delessert to his farm at Roslindale, near Kingston, had been sold at vendue at a price inferior to that of common sheep, and that above half of them had perished from neglect the following winter. I knew the importance of the object, and I resolved to leave no means unessayed to convince my fellow-citizens of it."[4] To accomplish this

[1] *Sheep Industry*, pp. 163–170.
[2] Bishop, *History of American Manufactures*, vol. ii, p. 119.
[3] *Bulletin*, vol. xxxv, p. 247.
[4] Livingston, *Essay on Sheep*, 1810, p. 7.

end he began purchasing the scattered remnants of Delessert's flock at prices which amazed their negligent owners.

The ignoring of these sheep seems the more strange in that they did not degenerate on American soil, but on the contrary improved. Humphreys, writing in 1807, says: "The attempt to propagate the pure merino in this country has been attended with complete success. . . . The identical sheep which I brought to this country yield on an average about half a pound more of wool apiece than they did at the first shearing after their arrival. . . . It is the opinion of all farmers in Connecticut acquainted with the original flocks and their descendants, both pure and mingled blood, that they are better adapted to our climate, and more easily nourished both in summer and in winter, than the common breed of American sheep. . . . Further, they preserve the entire character, shape, and qualities of the best merinos in Spain."[1] Under such conditions — and the facts amply bear out this opinion — there would seem to be even less justification for the common neglect of the merinos.

One explanation of it, however, was the natural conservatism of the farming class. Their tendency was to follow in the old ruts, and it took something very unusual to turn them into a new track. The "vital impulse" of which Humphreys spoke was lacking. It was just this that Livingston endeavored to supply by paying high prices for Delessert's sheep. Another drawback was that there had been some difficulty at first in carding the fine merino wool with the machines at hand, but this was soon overcome.[2] The fundamental difficulty, however, was the one we have already seen: there was no demand for the finest wool in the household manufacture, and the product of the woolen mills was insignificant in quantity, foreign manufactured goods supplying all the fine woolens used in the country.

From 1808 *to* 1815.

The Woolen Manufacture and the Household Industry.

After 1807 all this was changed: the factories began to multiply with rapidity, the price of merino wool soared skyward, and the farmers started a veritable stampede for the hitherto neglected fine-wooled sheep.

The cause of the change was the cutting off of foreign commerce

[1] *Bulletin*, vol. xxxv, p. 253. [2] *Ibid.*, p. 253, "Humphreys' Letter of 1807."

following the Embargo, the Non-Intercourse Act, and the hostile tactics of Great Britain and France. Just how far this reduced the imports of foreign woolens it is impossible to say, yet there can be no doubt that the reduction was very considerable, probably a half.[1] To appreciate what this meant to the half-dozen or so woolen manufacturers of the country we must remember how slight was their total output in proportion to the volume of imports; to understand what it meant to the grower of fine wool we must recollect that a generous share of these imports were of a fine grade of cloth, and that in 1807 there could not have been, at the most liberal estimate, over 50,000 pounds of pure merino wool in the country. The restriction of commerce was somewhat less and the imports were a little heavier in 1810 and 1811, but the War of 1812 followed, cutting off the supply of foreign woolens. Thus from 1808 till the end of the War of 1812, the growers and the manufacturers of wool in this country had the benefit of what was almost a prohibition of imports of both the raw material and the manufactured article.

The effect upon the woolen manufacture was immediate. It is very noticeable that several of those who had been the leaders in securing fine-wooled sheep were among the first to establish woolen mills. Humphreys had started one in 1806, Livingston had one by 1810 at least, Du Pont had opened one near Wilmington by 1812, Rapp's communistic colony at Harmony in western Pennsylvania was manufacturing broadcloth from the clip of its merino sheep in 1810,[2] and Wells and Dickinson, who had the best flocks in the West, had erected a mill at Steubenville, Ohio, by 1814. The Census of 1810, admittedly incomplete, returned twenty-four woolen mills.[3] Fourteen of the mills manufactured annually some 10,000 yards of

[1] The value of the imports paying 17½ % duty, among which manufactures of wool were included, averaged $8,700,000 from 1804 to 1807, while for the years 1808 to 1812 it was $4,050,000. Blodget states that the value of British woolens consumed in the United States in 1807 was $4,500,000 (see *Economica*, 1810, Appendix, p. 6). A return to the House of Commons in 1809 put the "real value" of woolens exported to the United States at £4,894,008 in 1806, £4,288,866 in 1807, and £1,994,902 in 1808. The "official value" for these years is given as £2,966,809, £2,502,929, and £1,134,940 respectively. This is exclusive of the trade of Scotland. A considerable portion, possibly a third, was reëxported to the West Indies. (See Pitkin's *Statistical View*, 1835, p. 294.)

[2] Bradbury's *Travels*, Thwaites's ed., vol. v, p. 315.

[3] See also *Parliamentary Papers*, 1812, "Orders in Council," pp. 446–462.

cloth each, selling at from one to ten dollars a yard.[1] The total output of all was estimated at 200,000 yards of cloth. It is believed that only four or five of the mills were engaged upon fine cloths;[2] most of the others were working on army and navy cloths, negro cloths, and blankets, and used the common wool of the country. "The great obstacle to the extension of the manufacture," said Gallatin, "is the want of wool, which is still deficient in quantity and quality."[3] It seems more likely, however, that this applied only to the manufacture of fine cloth: the output of other cloths did not increase faster because the household products, which mostly met this need, were so strongly intrenched.[4]

By far the greatest stimulus received by the woolen manufacture came from the War of 1812. The duty on woolens was raised to 35% ad valorem in that year, but the really effective check to importation was the shutting out of foreign goods — more complete than ever before — which the war entailed. There were also two other favoring factors: the manufacturer of fine woolens was aided by heavy importations of merino sheep in 1810 and 1811, and the owner of a mill putting out coarser goods found an extensive, new, and unoccupied market in the wants of the army. This demand far exceeded the supply of the household industry and even, it seems, of the manufacturers, for the government was once more obliged to buy woolen goods, in a roundabout way, from the enemy.[5] Broadcloth was selling easily at from eight to twelve dollars a yard, and is said to have risen at one time to eighteen dollars.[6] So high were the prices that the manufacturers were accused of extortion, a charge of which Bishop[7] seeks to clear them, though even he admits that the profits were very great.

No wonder that the woolen manufacture attracted the eyes of

[1] Gallatin's Report, *American State Papers*, "Finance," vol. ii, p. 427.

[2] *Report on Wool and Manufactures of Wool*, 1887, p. xlix. See also Davis's *New England States*, vol. i, p. 207.

[3] *American State Papers*, "Finance," vol. v, p. 427.

[4] The total value of the factory product at this time has been put at $4,000,000 by Hayes (*The Fleece and the Loom*, p. 42). If the estimate of 200,000 yards for their total output is anything like correct, — and such evidence as is obtainable makes it appear reasonable, — then this figure for the value should be cut down more than one half.

[5] In 1813 some $600,000 worth of army and navy cloths, blankets, etc., was purchased abroad. See Bishop's *History of American Manufactures*, vol. ii, p. 195.

[6] *Ibid.*, pp. 194–195. [7] *Ibid.*, p. 195.

many, and that factories sprang up as if by magic.[1] Twelve charters for woolen mills were granted in New York in one year.[2] Nor was the activity wholly confined to the East. One man built in western Virginia or in Ohio a new woolen factory each year of the war.[3] In 1816 it was stated that $450,000 capital was invested in the woolen mills of Connecticut alone, their capacity being 275,000 yards of narrow or 125,000 yards of broad cloth. The total capital of the woolen manufacture of the country was even put at $12,000,000, and the value of the product at $19,000,000.[4] Whatever the true figures were, there can be no doubt that the period between 1810 and 1816 witnessed a marvelous growth in the woolen manufacture, and that its output at the end was at least three or four times what it was at the beginning.

Though the rise of the manufacture of woolens was an event that had the greatest influence on the wool-growing industry, yet the quantity of wool which it consumed was not to be compared, at least in the beginning, to that used in the household industry. The estimated output of the woolen factories in 1810 was 200,000 yards of cloth,[5] while the incomplete Census returns give the amount of woolen cloth manufactured in families as 9,528,266 yards;[6] that is, at least twenty-four out of every twenty-five yards of woolen cloth manufactured were made in the household. Gallatin, in 1810, referring to textile fabrics in general, declared it probable that "two thirds of the clothing worn, including hosiery, and of the house and

[1] Cf. Bishop's *History of American Manufactures*, vol. ii, pp. 194–195, 233. See also Taft's *Notes*, pp. 41–42.

[2] Taft, *Notes*, p. 55.

[3] This was the grandfather of W. D. Howells, who had just come from the English woolen industry. See Howells's *Life in Ohio*, 1813–1840, pp. 8–19.

[4] *Niles' Register*, vol. x, p. 82. These were the figures presented by a congressional Committee on Commerce and Manufactures, on March 6, 1816. The value of the product was made up of cost of raw material, $7,000,000; increase of value by manufacturing, $12,000,000. This latter figure seems very high, for it has generally been estimated that the raw material makes up not over half the value of the finished product. There is no specific statement that these figures do not include the establishments engaged simply in carding and fulling, though that is certainly the natural inference.

[5] See *ante*, p. 18. The actual figure given in the Census is 71,020 yards.

[6] Coxe, *Arts and Manufactures*. Among the states for which the Census gives no return of the household cloth output are Massachusetts, Maryland, Kentucky, and North Carolina. The figures are simply suggestive.

table linen used, by the inhabitants of the United States who do not reside in the cities, is the product of family manufactures."[1] Woolen products, however, were even more completely confined to the household than were other fabrics, for in referring to them he says, "Almost all wool is spun and woven in private families, and there are yet but few establishments for the manufacture of woolen cloth."

During this period, a good share of the household product passed, at one time or another, through the separate carding and fulling establishments which were then so common.[2] The Census of 1810 returned 1776 carding machines, through which were passed some 7,400,000 pounds of wool, and 1682 fulling mills, which finished 5,450,000 yards of cloth.[3] Flannel, homespun, and some other kinds of cloth, apparently about one half of the total, were not fulled. Judging again from the proportion indicated by these returns, something like three quarters of the wool was carded in the mills. Fulling, which required the most elaborate outfit, had long been carried on

[1] Gallatin's Report, *American State Papers*, "Finance," vol. v, p. 427. "In the lower counties of Virginia and the upper counties of South Carolina and Georgia and generally in North Carolina almost the whole summer clothing of all classes was of household manufacture and slaves were entirely clothed in that manner. The scarcity of wool alone prevented winter clothing being made in the same way" (Bishop, *History of American Manufactures*, vol. ii, p. 150, footnote). When the first settlers went to Ohio "whole households were clad in dressed deer-skins." Sheep were not introduced until about 1797–98. Then "for more than twenty years nearly all cloth worn in the families of farmers, and of many in town, for every-day dresses, was made in the households of the wearers" (Hildreth, *Pioneer History of the Ohio Valley and North-West Territory*, 1848, p. 392–394). Hall, writing about 1820, said: "A very large portion of the western people manufacture their own clothing; among the farmers the practice is universal: and it extends so far to other classes that it is not at all unusual to see professional gentlemen in affluent circumstances and men of high official rank clad in plain domestic fabrics. I could name several of our most distinguished public characters who make it a rule to wear no cloth which is not manufactured in their own families" (*Letters*, p. 68).

[2] "Besides the knitting and sewing, which was the work of the older women, the wool of the few sheep each farmer kept was spun in the family. So also was the flax which grew in the flax patch. . . . The wool was sometimes carded at home, but usually it was sent off to one of the carding machines that would be put up in a mill for the purpose of preparing the wool for spinning by carding and making it into rolls." (Howells, *Recollections of Life in Ohio*, 1813–1840, p. 124.)

[3] Probably these figures, which are very incomplete, include the small amount carded and finished for the manufacturers as well. There are 108 carding mills out of the above number for which no output is given, and the same is true of 257 of the fulling mills.

under a separate roof. Carding, which required only the simple hand cards, had been easily pursued in the household; but the application of power to this process, and its rapid introduction after 1800,[1] soon brought it out from under the family roof.[2]

The carding and the fulling mill, both seeking a location on the bank of some stream, were frequently united. The same sort of location was sought by the grist mill and the lumber mill. They all tended toward a common point, and the clearing thus made gradually widened. It was from just such little beginnings in the river valleys that the manufacturing towns of New England and the Middle States sprang. It was from the combination of the carding and the fulling mill there taking place (though more immediately from the carding mill), that the woolen manufacture finally emerged.

The advance of the woolen manufacture during the war was not, however, at the expense of the household industry. One of the main reasons for the growth of the factory was that the household industry, by nature not readily adjusted to rapidly changing conditions, proved unequal to the vast demands so suddenly imposed upon it. Nevertheless, it rose to the occasion as best it could. A person writing in 1816 says, "The vexations of our trade and the subsequent war chiefly originated, or at least established, them [the household manufactures] as a part of our rural economy, and they have become as much a business with the female part of our family as the raising of grain, tobacco, and cotton is of the male part." Four fifths of the laboring class were then clothed in domestic manufactures.[3] As power was not applied to the weaving and spinning of woolens till after the close of the war, the household industry at this time had little to fear from the factory.

A very substantial impetus to household manufacture came from the innumerable premiums and awards offered by the various societies then formed for the promotion of industry.[4] Thousands of yards of woolen were each year displayed in competition at the annual fairs. Some of the states adopted the same policy. New York

[1] *Ante*, p. 12.

[2] Taft, *Notes*, p. 37.

[3] *Niles' Register*, vol. x, p. 323. It was added that their total value could not be less than $120,000,000. In 1815 Jefferson wrote, "I make in my family 2000 yards of cloth a year which I formerly bought from England."

[4] See pp. 24–25.

in 1808 passed a law offering an annual premium of $80 in each county of the state for the best specimen of woolen cloth made in any household, and other premiums were open to competition from the state at large. The law was slightly changed in 1810, and, "proving eminently beneficial," was renewed in 1812 for three years longer. During the period from 1808 to 1815, a total of $21,000 was so distributed.[1] The rivalry thus engendered was of no slight aid in increasing the quantity of the household product, as well as in improving its quality.

In fact, at this period the household industry seems to have become distinctly aggressive. Formerly its output — except, perhaps, in the case of hosiery,[2] which had always been an important branch of this domestic industry — had been pretty closely confined to the needs of each household. But now the farmers began to pay more attention to the outside market then open to them, and increased their flocks accordingly. This growth of the household industry, together with the rise of the woolen manufacture from almost nothing to one of the important industries of the land, revolutionized the pursuit of growing wool. The "vital impulse" which Humphreys had in 1802 found wanting was now supplied.

Wool-Growing becomes an Industry.

The first indication of the change which was about to come over this pursuit was the phenomenal rise in the price of fine wool and merino sheep. In 1807 a full-blooded merino ram lamb was valued at $100.[3] By 1809 and 1810 these rams had risen in value to $1000 or $1500, and ewes went at $1000.[4] At the same time the price of

[1] In 1812 there was no distribution. For the laws and more details, see *Transactions of the New York Society for Promoting Useful Arts*, vol. iii; vol. iv, part I, Appendix.

[2] For instance, the Germantown hosiery. In 1810 Martha's Vineyard was exporting 9000 pairs of stockings annually (see *American State Papers*, "Finance," vol. v, p. 427). Michaux remarks that, in Tennessee, as early as 1802, the legislature was awarding premiums for the best piece of cotton cloth manufactured in the family in each county. He adds that "here, as well as in Kentucky, the wealthiest people, as much from patriotism as economy, wear garments of the stuffs fabricated in the country. They also find this the only method of keeping among them the little money which they have in circulation and preventing it from passing to England" (*Travels*, p. 296).

[3] Bishop, *History of American Manufactures*, vol. ii, p. 119.

[4] Randall, *Fine Wool Sheep Husbandry*, p. 45.

pure merino wool rose from seventy-five cents a pound to two dollars.[1] By 1810 Livingston had sold four full-bred ram lambs at $1000 apiece, not to mention the sales of his grade merinos, while the fleece from his pure merinos went at two dollars a pound and that from his half-blood merinos at seventy-five cents.[2] Common wool, however, was bringing only about thirty-seven and a half cents. Livingston in his *Essay on Sheep*, published at this time,[3] pointed out that ten common sheep would yield wool worth in all $15, while the clip from an equal number of merinos was worth $70. By crossing a merino ram with the common ewes the value of the fleece from their offspring could be doubled. This was sufficient to arouse the most backward of farmers. Coming at a time when the foreign market for his other products was being steadily diminished, these hitherto neglected sheep appeared to bear a veritable fleece of gold, and the demand for them soon became as unreasoning as it was insatiable.

Just at this juncture affairs in Europe took a turn most opportune for the wool-grower of this country. Spain had long been the home of the merino sheep, and her flocks were superior to any others in the world.[4] It was to Spain that England looked for a supply of fine wool. There the sheep had been guarded as one of the treasures of the kingdom, and their exportation prohibited. It had been impossible to obtain them except by smuggling or by special royal gift. England, France, and Germany had obtained a few by this latter method, and it was from these that their fine-wooled flocks were descended. Hence the world was not slow to take advantage of the opportunity, when, during the convulsions of the Napoleonic Wars and the invasion of Spain by two hostile armies, the Junta then in control of the government, sore pressed for money, and fearing that in any case the flocks would be scattered or slaughtered, offered many of the most famous for sale. There was thus open to the United States, in the hour of its greatest need, an opportunity to secure in abundance some of the finest sheep in the world.

[1] Bishop, *History of American Manufactures*, vol. ii, p. 135.

[2] *Transactions of the New York Agricultural Society*, vol. ii, xxii, p. 66.

[3] See pp. 120–126.

[4] For a description of the different flocks of Spain see Youatt's *The Sheep*, or Randall's *Fine Wool Sheep Husbandry*, p. 7.

Fortunately the lifting of the Embargo had come just in time, so that when the cabañas of Spain were despoiled there were American vessels in the harbors of Spain and Portugal ready to seize with avidity upon this golden chance. Fortunately, also, there was then as American Consul in Lisbon, one who was thoroughly alive to the needs of his country, — William Jarvis, of Vermont.

The first successful shipment from Consul Jarvis, consisting of forty-five rams of the Escurial stock, reached Boston April 13, 1810. Such was the rage for these sheep that eleven of them sold for nearly $1000 apiece.[1] Other shipments followed immediately, till Jarvis had sent over in all some four thousand sheep. Of these about fifteen hundred went to New York, one thousand to Boston and Newburyport, and the rest were scattered among seacoast towns from Portland to Norfolk. Many other men became interested, and nearly every ship that touched at Spanish ports was glad to turn an extra penny by bringing back to America a few of the highly prized animals. It has been estimated that, between April 1, 1810, and August 31, 1811, some twenty thousand of these sheep were landed in the United States.[2]

Against such a deluge as this the high price at first obtained for these sheep could not hold, and soon they were selling at from $100 to $300 or less.[3] This, together with the hostile attitude of England, and the increased danger to commerce, virtually put an end to the movement in 1811. But by that time the United States had an ample foundation for a fine-wool industry. It could not be built in a day, to be sure, but there was no longer any physical obstacle in the way. The same had in a measure been true in 1802, but the infinitely larger supply of merinos in 1811 greatly facilitated matters. Once more it was left to the farmer to do as he chose about advancing, and now there was no uncertainty in his action.

Another factor of no little importance in the dissemination of the improved breed of sheep is found in the societies for promoting agriculture and industry which became so numerous just at this time.

[1] *Sheep Industry*, p. 173.

[2] For a detailed account of these events, and an elaborate table of each importation into the United States, giving the port of entry, number of sheep, the shipper, consignee, etc., see *Sheep Industry*, especially pp. 193–197.

[3] *Ibid.*, p. 197.

It is interesting to note that one of the leaders in the movement to start these societies, Elkanah Watson, got his original suggestion from the interest shown in a pair of merinos which he exhibited for a while in the public square of Pittsfield, Massachusetts, in 1807.[1] The following winter he addressed the farmers of the locality on the advantages of these sheep, especially for the hill regions of New England, and eventually, as a result of his efforts, the Berkshire Agricultural Society was organized. The Society held an annual fair and cattle show, at which numerous premiums were awarded.

This system was quickly introduced into other localities. In 1809 the Pennsylvania Society for Improving the Breed of Cattle was formed.[2] It held its first annual show in the autumn of that year, and awarded many premiums on sheep. The same year saw the organization at Georgetown, D. C., of the Columbian Society for Promoting Domestic Economy, which held its first fair a year later.[3] About this time, also, there came into being the Merino Society of the Middle States.[4] Its first meeting was held at Haddonfield, N. J., in 1811, when "several hundred full-blooded merinos were exhibited." [5] The following year the Society offered several premiums for the best essays on "Merino Sheep." A general interest in the new breed was indicated by the publication of two books on the subject which were translated from the French,[6] as well as two contributions by American writers.[7]

Some of the states also took a hand in the movement. New York passed a law giving a premium of fifty dollars for the first merino buck introduced into each county of the state.[8] The similar encouragement given to the household woolen industry, which has already been mentioned, was felt of course by the wool-grower as well. All this was of the greatest aid in improving the flocks of the country. It was at the annual shows that many of the farmers first saw the merino sheep. There also they always had an opportunity for acquiring some of this stock, if they desired to do so. To induce them to acquire it every incentive was offered.

[1] Watson, *History of Agricultural Societies*, p. 116. [2] *Sheep Industry*, p. 76.

[3] Bishop, *History of American Manufactures*, vol. ii, p. 140.

[4] *Ibid.*, p. 135. [5] *Ibid.*, p. 171.

[6] *Ibid.*, p. 171.

[7] Livingston, *Essay on Sheep*, 1809. Bard, *The Young Shepherd's Guide*, 1811.

[8] See Bishop's *History of American Manufactures*, vol. ii, p. 135.

Under these favoring conditions something had been accomplished in extending the improved breed of sheep even before the importation of merinos in 1810. Humphreys' flock began to spread through Connecticut and Rhode Island, and soon reached southern Vermont.[1] From southern Vermont a few had spread to Washington County in New York, which also eventually produced a large supply of fine wool. By 1809 Livingston's flock had increased to 645 sheep of from one half to full merino blood, besides 310 "native ewes." [2] The annual sales from his flock spread the breed through Dutchess County and the adjoining regions of New York. It was from this stock that Elkanah Watson secured the pair which he brought to Pittsfield, Massachusetts, in 1807,[3] and there started what was long a centre for the growing of fine wool. By 1805 or 1806, Rapp had carried merino sheep to his communistic settlement in western Pennsylvania, and by 1811 had a flock of one thousand, at least one third of which were merinos.[4] In Delaware, whither Du Pont had moved his merinos, was one of the biggest flocks in the country, a large proportion of it of merino blood.

Nor was this breed entirely confined to the eastern states. In 1807 Seth Adams had moved to Muskingum, Ohio, with from twenty-five to thirty sheep descended from his importation of 1801. Some of these, it is said, were the first merinos to reach Kentucky.[5] Again, in 1810, Adams, who had formed some arrangement with Humphreys, drove 176 of the latter's flock to Kentucky and Tennessee, where they were sold.[6] Although all this relates to the growing of fine wool only, it must be borne in mind that such wool formed but the smallest fraction of the domestic supply. Greater attention is devoted to it because it was largely from this side that there came the first and most effective stimulus to improve the country's flocks.

As to the total number of sheep in the country, the best estimate

[1] Bishop, *History of American Manufactures*, vol. ii, p. 135.

[2] *Sheep Industry*, p. 143.

[3] Watson, *History of Agricultural Societies*, p. 116.

[4] Bishop, *History of American Manufactures*, vol. ii, p. 194.

[5] *Sheep Industry*, p. 136. A correspondent writing from Chillicothe, Ohio, in 1814, said: "Four years ago, I believe, there was not a merino sheep in this state, and very few of any breed, nor was there a manufacturing establishment of any kind in this section of it" (*Niles' Register*, vol. vi, p. 209).

[6] *Sheep Industry*, p. 137.

available puts the figure for 1810 at seven million.[1] These were calculated to shear from twelve million to fourteen million pounds of wool.[2] During the two following years the flocks were rapidly increased, receiving especial aid from the great influx of merinos in 1810–11, and notwithstanding the fact that this caused a temporary depression in value. The author of *The Shepherd's Guide*, published in 1811, declared [3] "that in spite of the fall in the price of sheep and the glut of wool," the merino sheep industry was still the most profitable business the farmer could engage in, and the glut would soon pass.[4] In fact the temporary decline in the price of sheep probably favored the spread of merinos by enabling the less prosperous farmers to secure stock to improve their flocks, something which the previous prices had rendered quite impossible. Then, the moment it became plain that war with England was inevitable, the scramble for sheep increased. Tench Coxe, writing in 1812, declared that the manufacturer's demand for wool continued to exceed the farmer's ability to supply the various qualities.[5] He expressed the belief that in that year the amount shorn in the United States had increased to 20,000,000 or 22,000,000 pounds.[6] The

[1] Coxe, *Arts and Manufactures of the United States*, 1810, pp. xiv-xv. If anything this figure is too high.

[2] The higher figure is probably nearer the truth and quite probably an underestimate. The total quantity of wool wrought up into fulled goods in the United States in 1810 was put at 12,000,000 pounds, an estimate which may reasonably be reduced by one third (see *Niles' Register*, vol. ii, p. 8). The number of sheep indicated by the Census "so far as returned," and the return from Pennsylvania, which, it was stated, "is probably reasonably accurate," were as follows: —

	Pure Merino	*Grade Merino*	*Tunisian*	*Common*	*Total*
Pa.	357	4,071	759	613,036	618,223
U. S.	431	6,133	759	726,330	1,584,652

In some states the total only is given. The figures for Vermont and Connecticut, also "thought reasonably accurate," were 450,000 and 400,000 respectively (see Coxe's *Arts and Manufactures*, p. 46).

[3] Pp. 18–19, 25.

[4] The price of stock sheep was much more affected than that of wool. This is the only mention of any glut of wool at that time that has been found. Baltimore quotations for September, 1811, were, full-blood merino wool, $1.50, $2.00 a pound; crossed, $0.75–$1.00; common, $0.37 (see *Niles' Register*, vol. i, p. 32).

[5] Coxe, *Arts and Manufactures*, p. xiv.

[6] *Ibid.*, pp. xv, xxx. Though many thought this figure too low, an even lower one seems more reasonable.

rapid increase was due, he says, to the improvement in the breed of sheep, the greater care and attention given them, and the cutting off of the export for slaughter.[1] "It is probable," he adds, "that no country has ever effected so great a change in the value and extent of its stock of sheep as the United States within a very few years. . . . Sheep were formerly a mere matter of domestic economy and convenience, but have at length become a great universal object of agricultural profit and wealth." [2] The last sentence strikes the keynote. Formerly there had been no market for wool, and the farmer simply grew enough for his household wants; now there was a steadily growing market, the supplying of which occupied an important part of the farmer's attention. This establishment on a commercial basis marks the real birth of wool-growing as an industry.

As has been seen, the War of 1812 not only cut off the hope of an increased supply of woolens from abroad, but also created an extra demand for coarse wool to supply the needs of the army. The price of pure merino wool advanced once more, reaching the highest point in 1814, when it sold for between $2.00 and $3.00 a pound.[3] The wool from a full-blooded merino wether sold in Boston at the following prices per pound:[4]—

1813	1814	1815	1816
$1.42	$2.00	$1.08	$1.00 (pulled)

At the factory at Steubenville, Ohio, the following prices were paid:[5]—

	Full blood	*7/8 blood*	*3/4 blood*	*1/2 blood*
1814	$2.75	$2.50	$2.00	$1.35
1815	1.35	1.15	1.00	0.85

Common wool remained at between thirty and fifty cents, the supply being more nearly equal to the increased demand than in the case of the fine wool. Since the difference in the cost of growing the two grades was comparatively slight, the farmer naturally preferred to

[1] The average number of sheep annually exported in 1800–07 was 9711. For the years 1808–11 it fell to 2693. This factor was relatively insignificant.

[2] Coxe, *Arts and Manufactures*, pp. xiv and xv.

[3] Bishop says it went as high as $4.00 a pound (vol. ii, p. 195). Some allowance should be made for the state of the currency.

[4] *Massachusetts Agricultural Repository and Journal*, vol. iv, p. 160.

[5] *Niles' Register*, vol. xxxvi, p. 399.

keep the merino if he could, for at the price at which this wool sold he could not but make a profit, no matter how reckless or ignorant his management.

The interest in the new industry rapidly spread through the country from Maine to Virginia and westward to Ohio and Kentucky. The movement is well characterized by a farmer who, writing from western Virginia, says, "Heretofore throughout Virginia, Kentucky, and Tennessee . . . sheep were only considered as an useful appendage to the farm, incurring no expense, generally very little attention, and affording supplies for the table and a little wool for the slaves. . . . Since the war, the raising of sheep has become an object, and very many gentlemen in the western country have increased their flocks to incredible numbers, — three, five, and six thousand." [1] In 1814 what seems a very reasonable estimate placed the number of sheep in the country at ten million, but the calculation of the clip as thirty million pounds is excessive; 22,000,000 to 24,000,000 pounds is more probable.[2]

A bird's-eye view of the industry of wool-growing in 1815, at the end of the period marking its first struggle for existence, would show in almost every state north of the Carolinas some district particularly noted for the number and quality of its sheep. In Vermont, Windsor County was a famous centre. Here, among others, Consul Jarvis kept his flock of several hundred pure merinos, picked from those he had sent over from Spain.[3] In Massachusetts, Berkshire County was the chief seat. In 1815 there were reported to be within a mile of Pittsfield over eight thousand sheep, at least half of which were three quarters merino or better.[4] In Rhode Island, the islands of Narragansett Bay held many a valuable flock. Humphreys' was the most noted in Connecticut. New York probably had more sheep than any other state, Dutchess County and Long Island being the homes of the best stock. In New Jersey, the returns to the state

[1] *Niles' Register*, vol. vi, p. 335.

[2] *Ibid.*, p. 173. Certainly the average fleece at that time was not so heavy as three pounds, in spite of the improvement in the breed, though statements to the contrary are to be found (*ibid.*, p. 335). Another correspondent in the same year says, "It would not perhaps be overstraining the fact to say that the number of sheep in the United States has been trebled, and the quantity of wool quadrupled within the last five years" (*ibid.*, p. 333). This, however, is certainly a gross exaggeration.

[3] *Sheep Industry*, p. 283.

[4] *Niles' Register*, vol. viii, p. 311.

authorities in 1814 showed that out of a total of 285, 049 sheep, 3,807 were pure merinos, while 25,826 more were grade merinos. In Pennsylvania, the prominent sheep districts were the locality about Philadelphia in the east and Washington County in the west. In Delaware and Maryland, they were to be found about Wilmington and Hagerstown respectively. In the West, there were excellent flocks in the blue-grass region of Kentucky, and a band of merinos had been carried to Indiana when Rapp moved his colony to New Harmony in 1814. The chief centre, however, was about Steubenville, Ohio, where Wells and Dickinson had a large and valuable flock in connection with their woolen mill. The neighboring parts of Virginia and Pennsylvania, as well as Ohio, abounded in fine-wooled sheep. Thus the end of this period shows a remarkable advance in the industry of growing wool, as regards both the quality and the quantity of the product. Flocks of a thousand or so were by no means uncommon, though ten years earlier such a thing was unknown. There were probably few districts in the country north of the Carolinas in which a merino sheep was not to be found, although fifteen years before there had not been a single one in all the United States.

The main causes which underlay the rapid rise of the wool-growing industry between 1808 and 1815 are now evident, and need but be summarized. The events of the period shut out the supply of foreign woolens upon which the land had so greatly depended. The country was thus compelled to meet its own wants.[1] Woolen mills sprang up like mushrooms in the night, and farmers lost their senses in the rush for the scarce merinos. Throughout the period it was the fine-wooled sheep that attracted most attention and led in the rise of the industry. This was owing to the fact that all the fine cloth consumed had formerly come from abroad, while the larger part of the coarser goods used had been supplied by the household industry. With the outbreak of the war the demand for fine

[1] We find occasional mention of the importation of wool during these years, but no indication of the amount, which was probably slight. Texas wool was received at Pittsburg in 1812 (see *Sheep Industry*, p. 167). Coxe (*Arts and Manufactures*, p. xiv) says, "There has been a considerable importation of wool." During the war some Spanish wool was captured and brought home (see Taft's *Notes*, p. 42). The grades most needed were the finest and the coarsest. In 1814 one house in Pittsburg imported 13,246 pounds of Spanish wool (see *The Navigator*, 8th ed., 1814, p. 65).

goods was further supplemented by an unusual demand for the coarser cloth. This, together with the exclusion of foreign goods, not only stimulated the lower grades of the woolen manufacture, but led the household industry, in its attempt to supply this market, to shake off the shackles which had formerly confined it to the needs of each individual family. Based on this developed household industry and the rising woolen manufacture, but chiefly on the latter, there came into existence the industry of wool-growing.

There remains, however, another point for consideration. As will be seen throughout the history of this industry, its course cannot be understood without some knowledge of contemporaneous conditions in general agriculture. It must be borne in mind that there was a double reason why the country did not grow fine wool earlier: it was able to get woolens from England with ease, and it was able to pay for them by the proceeds from the export of food stuffs. But the conditions which shut out the woolen goods must also have cut into the trade which gave the country an outlet for its surplus agricultural products. How greatly this suffered is indicated by the following tables:[1] —

	Exports of animals and animal and vegetable food. Average annual value.	*Total domestic exports. Average annual value.*
1803–07	$20,000,000	$44,000,000
1808–11	12,000,000	32,000,000
1812–15	14,000,000	27,000,000

Average annual exports of domestic agricultural products.
(*In thousands.*)

	Pork bbl.	*Beef* bbl.	*Corn* bu.	*Wheat* bu.	*Flour* bbl.	*Butter* lbs.	*Cheese* lbs.
1803–07	68	106	3312	418	986	2097	979
1812–15	13	30	1104	90	940	766	409

It is clear, then, that the farmer must have had to look for some new product for export. At the same time that the old market was closing upon him, the market for wool was rapidly developing. A combination of circumstances offering unusually bright prospects

[1] Based on Evans, *Domestic Exports*, 1790–1850.

in this direction,[1] the farmer now for the first time turned to sheep as really worthy of serious attention.

Before leaving this period, a word should be said about the competitors of wool, — a word that is all the more necessary in that during just these years a new fibre was entering upon the scene, which was destined to play no unimportant part in the future of wool. This new rival was cotton.

Prior to 1790 very little cotton had been grown in the United States. It was used to some extent, but was for the most part imported.[2] Between 1790 and 1799 the production of cotton in the United States rose from one and a half million to twenty million pounds, and by 1816 had reached one hundred and twenty-four millions.[3] The consumption of the United States, placed at five million pounds in 1790, had increased to eight million in 1800, sixteen million in 1810, and thirty-one million five hundred thousand in 1815.[4] The rapid increase in consumption was greatly stimulated by the steadily falling price during these years. The average price of middling upland cotton, in New York, was: —

1790–99	1800–09	1810–16
32.45 cents	22.75 cents	17.10 cents

Up to 1809 the price of cotton did not fall materially below the price of the common wool of the United States. Still, many uses were found for which it was better suited than wool. The extent to which it was supplanting other fibres is indicated by the amount consumed in the household industry. Its use here, it should be borne in mind, was impeded in most places by the fact that it had to be brought

[1] A similar cause diverted much of the capital at one time invested in commerce and shipping into the woolen manufacture.

[2] The average importation of raw cotton 1790–99 was 2,500,000 pounds.

[3] These and the following figures come from Hammond's *Cotton Industry*, Appendix. The years end August 31st.

[4] The figures for consumption given by Hammond appear not to include the cotton imported in the form of manufactured goods. Hence the figures for the years 1800 and 1810, when the imports of cotton manufactures were falling off, cannot be accepted as indicating an actual doubling in the total consumption of cotton. This correction makes less difference in the case of the increase between 1810 and 1815, for presumably the greater share of the falling off in the imports of cotton manufactures had come before 1810. There was thus probably an even greater proportionate rate of increase between 1810 and 1815 than the figures indicate.

from some distance.[1] This was not true of either wool or flax. Nevertheless it sometimes found its way to the most remote districts. Coxe observed in 1810 that the surplus energy of the new settlements in western Pennsylvania was applied to the manufacture of cotton.[2]

Some idea of the relative importance of cotton goods as early as 1810 is to be had from the Census returns for that year. There were then made in the families of the country sixteen million yards of cotton goods, twenty-one million yards of flaxen goods, and nine million yards of woolen goods, besides twenty-six million yards of mixed, blended, and unnamed cloths and stuffs. The absolute figures are unreliable, but the relative quantity of each kind of cloth is probably indicated with fair accuracy.[3] Cotton seems already to have forged ahead of wool in the household industry, in spite of the recentness of its appearance. Flax, however, led them all. Two fifths of the spinning-wheels in Pennsylvania and Vermont were probably employed on flax, said Coxe,[4] and added that "flax is the most general and the most familiar of all the family operations relating to the threads and cloths for apparel and furniture in the United States."[5] It was not, however, from flax that the wool-grower of this country met serious competition. Cotton could generally be substituted for wool as well, if not better, than flax. In fact it soon nearly vanquished flax in its own domain.

The competition of cotton first had an important effect during the War of 1812. Conditions were then so unusual that this was

[1] One good New England farmer's wife, who found some difficulty in securing the cotton which she desired to mix with her wool, is said to have suggested to her husband, with more Yankee ingenuity than learning, that he procure a cotton ram to cross upon his ewes so that they could get their cotton and wool already mixed.

[2] See Coxe's *Arts and Manufactures*, p. vi. The figures given for four newly settled counties in western Pennsylvania in 1810 are very instructive as indicating the proportion in which the three important fibres were then used in the farming communities. These four counties, with a total population of 2005, had 1256 sheep, 64 looms, and 355 spinning-wheels. They manufactured in the households 412 yards of woolen cloth and 5272 yards of mixed and hempen cloth. No doubt the easier access to the cotton supply somewhat increased the proportion of that fibre. Cf. note, p. 33.

[3] The only important states from which there were no returns were Massachusetts, Maryland, Kentucky, and North Carolina. Twelve million yards of the cotton cloth came from the South, but almost no flaxen cloth.

[4] *Arts and Manufactures*, p. xv.

[5] *Ibid.*, p. xxxiv.

wholly disguised. But that the facts were such as to bring this result there can be no doubt. In the first place the country had by this time become a heavy exporter of cotton. Yet the very conditions which shut out the foreign woolens and sent the price of wool soaring skyward, shut in the domestic cotton and depressed the price of that staple. It was from 1809 to 1814 that the price of cotton was lower than in any of the other years between 1791 and 1820, and the very lowest prices came just at the time of the war.

	Average annual production of cotton in the U. S.	*Average annual exports of cotton*	*Left on domestic market*[1]	*Av. annual price, Middling Upland cotton, N. Y.*
	thousand lbs.	thousand lbs.	thousand lbs.	cents
1809–11	82,000	69,757	12,243	15.8
1812–14	73,000	22,053	59,947	12.8

Foreign cotton manufactures, of course, were shut off at this same time. Nevertheless the quantity of domestic cotton thrown upon the market was so enormous — the table indicates the increase of the amount available for 1812–14 over 1809–11 to be 317% — that the price sank to the lowest level in years. Now this was exactly the period when the demand for wool was the greatest. It was, then, inevitable that cotton should be substituted for wool wherever possible. It could not well be used for the needs of the army, nor in the place of broadcloth, but there were many other opportunities to substitute cotton goods for woolen, or at least to mix cotton with wool. That such an increase in the use of cotton did take place is indicated by the statement made in 1816 that cotton yarn "is now as regularly found on the memorandums of country storekeepers as any other article whatsoever, *and is entirely a thing of a few years' date*."[2] None the less, to all outward appearances, this rivalry from cotton made no impression upon the industry of wool-growing. The phenomenal advance of the latter in the face of all this, only shows how great a stimulus was applied to the industry during the first years of its growth.

[1] The imports of raw cotton averaged 424,177 pounds greater during the latter period and slightly increased the large domestic supply.

[2] *Niles' Register*, vol. xi, p. 177. The italics are mine.

CHAPTER III

WOOL-GROWING FINALLY ESTABLISHED ON A COMMERCIAL BASIS, 1815–1830

THE most important factor in the history of wool-growing during the years between 1815 and 1830 is to be found in the crisis which the woolen manufacture of the country was then passing through. Without the woolen manufacture further advance in the production of wool, under the conditions then existing in the United States, was not to be expected.

For the woolen industry of the country these years brought a desperate struggle. When the prop of restricted commerce, by means of which it had maintained itself from 1807 to 1815, was suddenly taken away upon the close of the War of 1812, the artificiality of its growth was relentlessly exposed. The fostering nation did its best to provide another support in the form of a tariff; but in face of a most unusual combination of forces this proved of slight avail, and for the next dozen years the nursling suffered sadly. Eventually, however, with pluck and enterprise, the industry emerged, still in its early stages, but at last able to stand alone.

The State of the British Woolen Manufacture.

To comprehend the peculiar situation which confronted the American manufacturer at this time, it is essential that one should have some knowledge of what was then taking place in the woolen industry of Great Britain.

The British wool manufacture was divided into the manufacture of worsteds, or stuffs, and the manufacture of woolens, or cloths. The former used chiefly the long and rather coarse wool of such English breeds of sheep as the Leicester and the Lincoln; the latter employed the fleece of the short-wooled English breeds like the Southdown, or the still shorter and far finer wool of the Spanish merino. A large number of merinos had been imported in 1792, and the King, who had received a few of the breed as a gift from the King of Spain, sold at auction some of his flock (which had been carefully managed by Lord Western,[1] the English champion of this breed), in order to help disseminate the species. But these attempts to introduce the merino into England failed, for the breed was not suited to English agricultural conditions. Thus there was no merino wool grown in the country. Furthermore it happened that at this time the fleece of the short-wooled English breeds was increasing in length and coarseness.[2] Under these circumstances England was forced to import wool if she wished to manufacture any of the finer grades of cloth.

Up to about 1814 nearly all of the wool imported into Great Britain came from Spain.

Imports of Wool into the United Kingdom.[3]
(Thousands of pounds.)

	Spain	*Germany*	*Australia*	*S. Africa*	*S. America*	*Total*
1800	6,062	412				8,608
1810	5,952	778				10,873
1820	3,536	5,113	99	29	69	9,776
1830	1,643	26,073	1,967	33	19	32,313

The highest point of these imports had been reached in 1807, when ten million pounds of Spanish wool was brought from there. But the flocks of Spain never recovered from the devastation of the Napoleonic Wars, and under the neglect which followed they steadily declined. The German States, on the other hand, were then producing a large quantity of fine wool, and England turned in that direction for her supply. By 1820 the imports from Germany surpassed those from Spain. They continued to rise, and for the next twenty years Germany was the source of most of England's foreign wool supply. The supply from the Southern Hemisphere, which later became so important, was then of little account.

The necessity of going abroad for fine wool was more than com-

[1] Bischoff, *History of the Woolen and Worsted Manufactures*, vol. i, p. 256. Hereafter cited as "Bischoff."

[2] *Ibid.*, pp. 141–149, 378. This was due to the improved system of agriculture, which brought in turnips and roots on which the sheep were fed; also to the frequent crossing of the New Leicester on the Southdown.

[3] *Journal of the Royal Statistical Society*, vol. xxii, p. 10. For a complete table giving the imports from all important countries yearly, 1796–1869, see *ibid.*, vol. xxxiii, pp. 502–505.

pensated by the virtual monopoly of wool suitable for worsted goods or stuffs, commonly known as combing wool, which the United Kingdom then possessed. In the hope of retaining at home the manufacture of these goods, the government had early restricted the export of combing wool, and, since the middle of the seventeenth century, had prohibited it. About 1780 the growers of long wool, seeing a chance to gain by the higher price which their product would bring abroad, if exportation were permitted, began an agitation with that end in view.[1] At the time little was accomplished, the worsted manufacturers naturally opposing it. During the first part of the nineteenth century the worsted manufacture was developing very rapidly, and little further was heard of this cry.

The rising importance of the worsted industry was one of the features of this period, and its continued advance ever since has exerted no slight influence on the growing of wool. An important aid in the advance was the introduction of machinery. This, says James, entirely transformed the aspect of the worsted manufacture.[2] "With the year 1818 a new era commenced in the preparing and spinning of worsted goods."[3] A new era began, too, for Bradford, which after 1819 was the centre of the trade.[4] The improvements also led to the use of shorter and finer wool for worsteds. Southdown, and even grades of merino, were frequently used, and it thus became possible to meet the demand for a finer quality of worsted goods.[5]

The general introduction of machinery, in England as well as in the United States, proceeded much more slowly in the manufacture of wool than in that of cotton.[6] The attempt to use power looms in England in 1822 resulted in their destruction by the weavers. In

[1] James, *History of the Worsted Manufacture in England*, p. 300. Hereafter mentioned as "James."

[2] *Ibid.*, p. 331. [3] *Ibid.*, p. 384. [4] *Ibid.*, p. 387.

[5] For a detailed description of this change, see James, pp. 415–421. See also Bischoff, vol. ii, p. 274.

[6] As late as about 1835, Baines wrote: "The power loom has hitherto been principally employed in weaving cotton goods, particularly calicoes and fustians, for although this machine has for more than ten years been well adapted for weaving all kinds of plain silk, linen, woolen, and worsted goods and all patterns of those fabrics not requiring more than 12 heddles and 12 sheds, and in some patterns upwards of 30 sheds, and of working with one or two shuttles, yet it is comparatively little used in any of those manufactures" (*History of the Cotton Manufacture*, p. 239).

1826, however, they were rapidly being installed. Nevertheless, as late as 1830 power looms had not been applied to any extent in the manufacture of goods made solely from wool.[1] The low rate of wages made hand labor comparatively inexpensive. Combing machines were not generally adopted until the long strike of the combers in 1825.[2] Spinning by power came in some time before this.[3] No doubt the delay in bringing machinery into use in the woolen manufacture was due to its strongly intrenched position as a household industry. For centuries the growing and manufacture of wool had been one of the staple industries of the kingdom. Whole districts of families had been brought up in its ways, and it had become thoroughly organized on this basis. Such a long-standing order of things was not to be overthrown at a moment's notice by the appearance of machinery.

The cotton manufacture, on the other hand, led the way in the introduction of machinery. Being a comparatively new industry, unhampered by custom and tradition, it readily adopted the new methods, and became as a result an even more powerful rival of the woolen manufacture. This competition was further intensified by the low price of cotton between 1820 and 1830. A witness before a committee of Parliament in 1828, said that the practice of weaving cotton had greatly increased during the previous six or seven years, adding that "nine tenths of the peasantry of England are clothed in cotton, whereas they used to be clothed in woolen. . . . It has caused a diminished demand for English wool, and has, I think, been one main cause of the low price."[4] The competition from cotton will be further considered when we take up conditions in

[1] Bischoff, vol. ii, p. 273. They had been used for narrow goods, chiefly bombazets, and also for flannels, but were not much employed in the woolen cloth manufacture of Yorkshire.

[2] James, p. 297.

[3] *Bulletin*, vol. xxxi, p. 255.

[4] Bischoff, vol. ii, pp. 178–179. MacPherson, under as early a date as 1785, says: "Neither was a cotton gown attainable by a woman in humble circumstances; and thence the cottons were mixed with linen yarn to reduce their price. But now cotton yarn is cheaper than linen yarn, and cotton goods are very much used in place of cambrics, lawns, and other expensive fabrics of flax; and they have almost totally superseded the silks. Women of all ranks, from the highest to the lowest, are clothed in British manufactures of cotton, from the muslin cap on the crown of the head to the cotton stocking under the sole of the foot" (*Annals of Commerce*, vol. iv, p. 81).

America. There can be no doubt that it was important among the many causes which oppressed the British woolen industry during these difficult years.

The declining price of wool led to further trouble for the manufacturer. Between 1804 and 1814 the price of English short wool had been abnormally high,[1] owing to a combination of factors, including the inflated currency, the extra demand of war times, and the imposition in 1803 of an import duty on wool of 5s. 3d. a hundredweight, which by 1813 had crept up to 7s. 11d.[2] After 1814 the price of short wool began to decline, though long wool was advancing. This led to a strong demand upon the part of the agricultural interest for more protection, and in July, 1819, the remarkable advance in the duty to 56s. a hundredweight, or 6d. a pound, was secured.

This heavy duty at once aroused the cloth manufacturers, and a sharp contest sprang up.[3] The conflict was only increased when the Government coupled the proposal to rescind the import duty with a clause repealing the prohibition of export, thus setting cloth and stuff manufacturers at odds. The price of short wool continued to decline in spite of the duty, but the English manufacturers said that it depressed the price abroad still further, thus giving the Continental manufacturers a chance to undersell them. To prove this, they pointed to the decline in the production and export of cloths. Between 1815 and 1824 the number of pieces of cloth exported from Great Britain fell off nearly one half, while the number of pieces of stuffs doubled.[4] At length a reduction of the wool duty was secured. In 1824 it was lowered to 1d. a pound. The following year it was fixed at ½d. a pound, if valued at one shilling or less, 1d. if above; and colonial wool was admitted free. At the same time the prohibition on the export of English wool was repealed. Thereafter the British wool manufacturer had free access to the wool markets of the world. How much this must have meant is indicated by the refusal, in 1828, to increase the duties, in the face of one of the most distressing periods the British wool-grower has ever known.[5]

[1] For table of prices, see Appendix. The price of English long wool showed no marked advance until 1814–20, though higher than before 1800.

[2] For a convenient table of import duties for 1803–44, see Senkel's *Wollproduktion und Wollhandel*, p. 29.

[3] For a full account of this struggle, see Bischoff.

[4] For figures, see Bischoff, vol. ii, Appendix, table 7.

[5] *Ibid.*, pp. 212, 252.

Trade in general was very much upset throughout this period. With the close of the Napoleonic Wars an adjustment to the new conditions had to be made. Then there was the heavy drag caused by the falling prices, as the period of inflation was passing away. This was not over before the high import duty on wool was imposed. No sooner was the duty reduced and the prohibition of export removed, than there came, in 1826, one of the severest crises that England has ever experienced. A prolonged business depression followed, from which the wool trade hardly recovered before 1830. The course of events is best reflected by the fluctuations in the price of wool.

Average Price of Long and Short Wool in England.[1]

	1804–14	1815–18	1819–24	1825–26	1827–29	1830–32
Southdown	28d.	23d.	17⅔d.	12d.	9d.	13d.
Lincoln	14	18¾	13⅔	15¼	10¾	11⅓

The Lincoln combing wool, it will be noticed, suffered less throughout the period than the clothing wool, thus indicating the greater prosperity of that branch of the manufacture. Even in the years of depression, the worsted manufacture fared much better than the cloth manufacture.[2] Immediately after the close of the European wars England found an outlet for her surplus stock in the reopened markets of America. This was short-lived, and the depression in the woolen trade which followed was so great that, in spite of the increase of over 5d. a pound in the duty, the price of wool fell. The fall in Southdown wool immediately after 1824 is accounted for by the removal of the duty, but even with the permission to export, long wool still declined. The culmination of the depression came in the years 1827–29, when wool reached an unprecedentedly low figure. At length, in 1830, conditions began to mend.

The importance of all this for our subject is that the many troubles of the English woolen manufacturer served to make his competition with American rivals the fiercer. The ups and downs of the British woolen trade resulted in the shipping of vast quantities of English goods to the American market which frequently sold at a price that did not even cover cost. Further it was the cloth and not the stuff

[1] See table of prices in Appendix. Cf. James, pp. 316, 317, 382, 422.

[2] James, pp. 267, 378, 428.

(worsted) trade which suffered most in England; and the American manufacturer did not make stuffs, but was entirely engaged upon cloths. In the course of the American woolen manufacture during these years, this English competition was the fact which counted for most.

The Final Establishment of the Woolen Manufacture in the United States.

From 1816 *to* 1820.

Though available information as to the state of the woolen manufacture in the United States between 1816 and 1820 is very meagre, all that we have indicates that it was then passing through one of the severest trials in its history. Within a year or two after the end of the war, many establishments had been closed and no new ones seem to have been set up. Some of the mills struggled through the period, but even for the few so fortunate as that, the profits were next to nothing.

The immediate cause of the trouble was the influx of foreign goods. It was this flood that led to the enactment of the tariff of 1816, which, however, did not go into effect until July 1st of that year, when the deluge was almost over.[1] This tariff levied on woolen goods a duty of 25% ad valorem, to be reduced after three years to 20%; but before the three years had passed, the reduction had been indefinitely postponed. Figures of the imports for these years show that a phenomenal importation took place in 1815. The amount fell off somewhat in the two following years, though still very large; it rose again in 1818, but by 1819 had once more declined.[2] How hard the industry was hit and how slight was the pro-

[1] This came in in spite of the relatively high war duties, which were still continued. The official value of all exports of British woolens in 1815 was £10,000,000, or double the normal quantity. The following year it had fallen back. For figures, see Bischoff, vol. ii, Appendix, table vi.

[2] See James' account of the trade conditions (pp. 378–385). The declared value of British wool and woolen manufactures exported to the United States for the years ending January 5 was:—

1816	£4,378,195	1820	£1,768,295	1823	£2,362,846	1826	£1,961,677
1817	3,029,671	1821	1,073,484	1824	1,577,734	1827	1,227,728
1818	2,234,653	1822	1,980,001	1825	1,768,004	1828	1,566,673
1819	3,160,406						

(*Journal of the House of Lords*, vol. lx, 1828, Appendix 3, p. 907.) Bischoff says that

tection afforded is evinced by the numerous petitions for an increase of duties which began to pour in on Congress.[1] These proved sufficient to prevent the contemplated reduction in 1819, and only missed securing an increase in the duties by the failure of the tariff bill of 1820. With the pressure under which the foreign manufacturers were then laboring, the tariff of 1816 proved to be of little avail.

Another difficulty from which the American manufacturers suffered was poor technical equipment. Their industry had sprung up under hot-house methods. They had been able to sell their goods at a price which paid a handsome profit, even with the most shiftless and ignorant management. But, when commerce was reopened after the war and an unusually keen rivalry was felt, for the first time by most of them, it was at once found that the former lax methods would not serve.

The first necessity was for more and better machinery. Delay in securing it had no doubt been due in part to an act of the British Parliament forbidding the exportation of machinery, plans, or models. This Act had been passed in 1774 and was in force, virtually without interruption, until 1845.[2] Some plans were with difficulty smuggled in, but eventually the act stimulated Yankee ingenuity. During the War of 1812 power-cards were in very general use in the woolen mills of New England,[3] but at the end of the war it yet remained to apply power to spinning and weaving. Weaving by power came in a little ahead of spinning. In 1812 T. R. Williams, of Peace Dale, Rhode Island, had invented a power-loom for weaving saddle girths and webbing. Four of these machines were being successfully operated by Rowland Hazard in 1814. But it was not until after 1820 that they were applied to the making of any important fabrics.[4] Spinning-jennies run by power did not appear in this country till 1819, although they were common in England by 1800.[5] Except for this appearance of a germ of better things, these years saw no advance in the equipment of the American woolen mill.

in 1819 the value of goods made of short clothing wool and sent from Great Britain to the United States was declared to be £2,130,408. The following year this figure was cut in half, and in 1821 stood at £684,949 (vol. ii, p. 13).

[1] *Bulletin*, vol. xxx, p. 119.

[2] Hayes, in "American Textile Machinery," gives a good account of this matter (*ibid.*, vol. ix, pp. 3–6).

[3] *Ibid.*, vol. xxxi, p. 255. [4] *Ibid.*, p. 278. [5] *Ibid.*, p. 255.

A few clues as to the general condition of the industry in 1820 are to be obtained from the Census of that year, though the returns were so incomplete and unsatisfactory that at first it was not intended to print them. At that time most of the establishments returned were using less than ten thousand pounds of wool each. It is evident that they produced for a small local market only. The number of concerns which used over ten thousand pounds of wool, and (so far as the returns enable one to judge) did more than merely card wool or finish the cloth, was thirty-four.[1] The industry was engaged chiefly in the manufacture of broadcloth, narrow and plain cloths, cassimeres, and satinets. A few mills were turning out kerseys, kerseymeres, flannels, blankets, carpets, and stockings. The hat manufacture was to be found nearly everywhere, and, as formerly, seemed to thrive where no other branch did.[2] Easy access to the fur required seems to explain this fact. Virtually all the concerns in the West which used wool were making hats. Apparently there were almost no establishments south of Virginia which turned out any product of wool, and the few that are mentioned made hats. In cases where comments on the state of trade accompany the returns, they indicate that the business yielded little or no profit, and a number of the establishments had shut down. This year, to be sure, was one of general trade depression, following the crisis of 1819; but the trouble in the woolen manufacture had been continu-

[1] This does not include the hat manufactures, nor the cases in which no distinction was made between the quantity of wool and of cotton, where both were used together. Of the latter there were probably three using over ten thousand pounds of wool. The 34 concerns were located as follows: New Hampshire, 1; Vermont, 2; Massachusetts, 4; Rhode Island, 3; Connecticut, 5; New York, 6; New Jersey, 3; Pennsylvania, 2; Maryland, 5; Ohio, 2; Kentucky, 1.

[2] In the report on the wool trade, in Parliament, in 1828, we find that the hat manufacture seemed to be the only branch of the American manufacture that could compete with the British in foreign markets. One witness declared: "Until the last few years they used to have all their hats from England, now they have not any; they now not only manufacture their own but export largely to South America. This largely diminishes our export" (*Journal of the House of Lords*, vol. lx, 1828, Appendix 3, p. 766). Another testified as follows: —

Q. "Do the North Americans meet you in the markets of South America?"

A. "Not as a manufacturing nation except in the manufacture of hats. They export more hats to South America than we do. Preference is given them."

Q. "But that is not the case with cloth?"

A. "No." (*Ibid.*, p. 767.)

ous since the end of the war, and it is evident that at this time the industry had reached a very low ebb.

From 1821 to 1824.

Beginning in 1821 there were distinct signs of a revival in the woolen manufacture. Money was actually being invested in the industry, and for the first time since 1815 new mills were erected.[1] One of the most hopeful signs was the more general adoption of power-machinery. In 1822 the first power-loom for weaving broadcloth was started in Rhode Island. The following year the Hamilton Woolen Company at Southbridge, Massachusetts, the largest wool manufacturing concern in the country, replaced its hand-looms with those run by power.[2] Bishop states that a manufacturer of power-looms who made seventy a week was unable to supply the demand.[3] It was in these years also that the first spinning-jennies run by power were introduced.[4] That improvements were sought is indicated by the invention of the Goulding carding machine, patented in 1824. This is said to have decreased the number of men employed in carding and spinning nearly one half, and it proved among the most notable of American contributions to woolen machinery.[5] Although its advantages were not generally recognized till a year or two later, it indicated a movement to establish the industry on a sound basis.

The importation of woolen manufactures still continued, but it was far less than before 1819. Beginning in 1821 we first have complete figures of the commerce of this country, and these show that the average value of the manufactures of wool annually imported from 1821 to 1824 was $8,767,000, the heaviest importation coming in 1822. By far the larger part of the imports was of cloths and cassimeres, the average value of the goods coming in under this head being $6,354,000. Worsted stuff goods made up $1,924,000 of the

[1] See Bishop, vol. ii, pp. 270, 294, 297. See also *Niles' Register*, vol. xxii, p. 225.

[2] *Bulletin*, vol. xxxi, p. 278.

[3] Bishop, vol. ii, p. 270.

[4] *Bulletin*, vol. xxxi, p. 256.

[5] One of the chief improvements it applied was the endless roving. Among other things it allowed an increase in the number of spindles from 120 to 200, the replacing of the old 24–28 inch cards by 40 inch cards, and an increase in the revolutions of the cylinder of the carding machine from 75 to 85 @ 100 a minute. See North, *ibid.*, vol. xxxi, p. 267.

remainder, and the rest was blankets. Thus over three quarters of the imports competed with the product of the American mills.

Moreover, this competition was still severely felt. By no means must it be thought that the American woolen manufacture was really prosperous at this time. Many manufacturers were still meeting with nothing but loss. Petitions still asked for more protection.[1] In 1823 the woolen manufacturers about Boston organized, for the first time, and presented to Congress a petition in which they declared that many had been compelled to suspend or change their operations, and others feared a like fate; that they were unable to compete with foreign nations because of the more perfect machinery, the lower wages of labor, and the cheaper wool of the latter.[2] They asked for 12½% additional duty. Eventually in the tariff act of 1824 an increase was granted.

Nevertheless there can be no doubt that the years from 1821 to 1824 saw the woolen manufacture slowly gathering strength. At least four mills had been started at this time, and manufacturers later agreed that the period just before 1825 had been better than any since 1815.[3] Further evidence to this effect is seen in the imports of raw wool, which then began to assume some importance. Before 1822 the imports had been so insignificant that wool was not included among the separate items in the schedule of imports, but by 1825 over two million pounds were brought into the country.[4] In fact the woolen manufacture was slowly but steadily gaining ground, and seemed to be on the point of firmly establishing itself, when once more a great wave of goods swept across the Atlantic, and again imperiled its very existence.

From 1825 *to* 1830.

The sudden increase in foreign competition came in spite of higher duties. The tariff of 1824 granted the advance so long sought by the manufacturers. The duty on woolen goods was raised to 30% till 1825, and 33⅓% thereafter. At the same time the duty on wool was increased so that after 1826 it was 30%, except that costing ten cents or less, which still remained at the old rate of 15%. The

[1] See *Bulletin*, vol. xxx, p. 145. See also *Niles' Register*, vol. xxiv, p. 148.
[2] *Niles' Register*, vol. xxiii, p. 190.
[3] *American State Papers*, "Finance," vol. v, pp. 792–832. [4] See *post*, p. 63.

higher duties, however, had little effect in stopping the flood of goods from abroad. The year 1825 showed a growth of 50% in the value of imports, and the average for the years 1825–28 was $9,600,000. Of this amount $4,600,000 came in under the head of cloths and cassimeres, $1,500,000 as worsted stuff goods, and about $500,000 each under carpets, blankets, and flannels.

The effect of this pressure from abroad is not to be judged simply by the increase in the value of the goods imported. The chief trouble came from the abnormally low prices at which the goods were sold. These years, it will be remembered, mark a period of unusual depression in the British woolen trade. Many firms had to throw their product upon the market at any price, and undoubtedly goods were frequently sold below cost.[1] Large quantities were sent over and sold at auction for whatever they would bring. Most of these were consigned to agents of the British manufacturers stationed in this country, and invoiced, it was claimed, at a value considerably below their actual worth.[2] That there was much evasion of the tariff duties seems beyond question, though the depressed actual value exaggerated the impression of the extent of this practice. Furthermore, just at this time England removed her high duty on wool,[3] which, combined

[1] *Niles' Register* for November, 1826, says that a friend of the editor recently purchased at an auction sale in Boston about $1000 worth of British woolens, "the stock and materials for the making of which, he believes, must have cost more money in England. . . . He . . . laid them aside under a perfect assurance that they must greatly advance in value, for the very good reason that labor and capital can't be employed, or duties paid, out of less than no product" (vol. xxxi, p. 177).

[2] "The records of our custom houses show that more than four-fifths of the woolen goods sent to this country are imported by, and on account of, foreigners" ("Memorial of the New England Woolen Manufacturers," *ibid.*, p. 185).

[3] It has been said that the repeal of the duty on wool by Great Britain in 1825 was expressly to offset the effect of the American tariff of 1824. It is true that the English manufacturers noted with alarm the increased amount of wool imported into the United States, the growth of manufactures there, and the decrease of British exports thither, especially between 1819 and 1821 (really due to a glut of the market by British goods, combined with the business depression). See Bischoff, vol. ii, pp. 12–13, 15, 157, 216. But it was the Continental manufacturer that was feared as much if not more, and the further fact that Spain and other countries had passed retaliatory acts which cut off some of the markets for English wares (see *ibid.*, p. 216). As it was then stated, "The quantity of wool forced by the tax on foreign markets at reduced prices has enabled foreigners to undersell the English manufacturers, and given great encouragement to the manufacture of the United States" (*ibid.*, p. 13). Trade with

with the trade depression, sent the price of the raw material "to an unprecedentedly low figure." The situation is well summed up in a "Memorial of the Growers and Manufacturers of Wool," of Woodstock, Vermont, dated December, 1826 (p. 4): "Partly from England having glutted the South American market, partly from the repeal of the English duty on foreign wool, partly from the commercial and manufacturing distress which for eighteen months past has pervaded that kingdom, reducing the price of manufacturing labor to less than one half the former rate, and partly from frauds committed on our revenue by English agents in this country invoicing their goods far below their cost, and rendering the protection given by the tariff of 1824 a perfect nullity, our country has again been deluged with British goods." The tendency under such conditions was to throw the burden of the American tariff upon the British manufacturer. So far as the American manufacturer was concerned the situation was such that the duties were of little avail.

The effect of all this upon the woolen manufacture of the United States is best set forth in the testimony given before the Committee on Manufactures of the House of Representatives in January, 1828.[1] There was virtually unanimous agreement among those who testified that since the beginning of 1826 the industry had met with nothing but losses. "I do not know of anybody in the woolen manufacture who has made anything in that period," exclaimed one who had already lost $30,000.[2] Another declared, "I don't know of one who has been doing a profitable business since 1824." [3] No one seems to have contradicted these assertions. Six out of the thirteen men stated that their factories had never paid a dividend, or had never been profitable. One of the others, whose business had started in 1810, had paid a dividend of two dollars a share in cloth, and possibly one other dividend. Still another, testifying for the years from 1813 to 1825, had not returned two per cent on the capital. Only four ad-

the Continent was declining, and under the Warehousing Act of 1824 foreign cloths were given free transit through England to the foreign markets of South America and the East Indies (see *ibid.*, pp. 107–108). There is no reason to doubt that the repeal would have come even if there had been no tariff in the United States. To have retained such a duty on raw material would have been the very reverse of the policy of free raw materials towards which England was then turning.

[1] *American State Papers*, "Finance," vol. v, pp. 792–832.

[2] *Ibid.*, p. 816.

[3] *Ibid.*, p. 820.

mitted, or left one to infer, that at some time their establishments had been profitable, and even these had been losing since 1825.[1]

Similar conditions were shown by the petitions for more protection, and especially for specific duties, which were then pouring in on Congress.[2] The petition of the manufacturers about Boston in 1826 asserts that "in most of the large manufactories in New England at least half of the machinery is idle. . . . Those who continue a portion of their former business do so under great embarrassments, and without any hope of successful competition unless some laws are enacted for their relief." [3] A memorial from the wool-growers of Berkshire County, Massachusetts, in the same year, says that "there is not at this day a single woolen establishment in N. England in full

[1] These manufacturers who were seeking higher protective duties should not be taken too literally, but that their distress was serious cannot be doubted. During these years, however, their chief difficulty was due to market conditions, and was of a temporary character. Quite a different point of view, also strongly biased, is found in the testimony of the British woolen manufacturers at this same time (see *Journal of the House of Lords*, vol. lx, 1828, Appendix 3, pp. 746–938). One witness declares: "Other countries are making rapid strides to compete with us, particularly North America. . . . They are now making very rapid strides and I have no hesitation in believing that in a very few years they will be as independent of us for coats as they are now for hats" (p. 766). Another says: "Yes, they are increasing to an extraordinary degree, for I know many respectable merchants at New York, Baltimore, and Boston who used to be importers as merchants from this country of what we call English Dry Goods, which they have completely given up importing, and have turned the capital to manufacturing in their own country" (p. 767). It is evident, however, that it was only in the coarser cloths that the American manufacturer was much feared. "In a certain description of cloths of almost every description under 12s. a yard they are now successfully competing with us" (p. 767). "The low articles are of necessity, they will manufacture them, but by no means the great bulk I conceive. . . . We send [our superfine cloths] very largely to the United States; they will have great difficulty in interfering with any of our cloths that are worth more than 10s. a yard; I do not think they can manufacture them" (p. 886). "The United States . . . from the low price of cotton and other of their own products have, in place of buying the coarse middle cloths of this country to the extent they formerly did, manufactured for themselves many of the articles they formerly used to import from this country" (p. 881). "Blankets are an article they have not got on so fast in the manufacture of" (p. 847).

[2] Stanwood explains the difficulty of the American manufacturer after 1824 as due to lack of skill and to inexperience, higher cost of labor, and preference of the consumer for foreign goods. The manufacturers, instead of giving these sound reasons for a higher duty, relied, he says, on the more popular one of the reduction of the duty on wool by England. See *American Tariff Controversies*, vol. i, p. 280.

[3] *Niles' Register*, vol. xxxi, p. 186.

operation." [1] The Harrisburg Convention of 1827, got up mainly in the interests of the woolen manufacturers, declared in its memorial to Congress that the value of the capital in this manufacture had been cut in half, owing to lack of adequate protection.[2]

How powerful the causes of this distress must have been is even better appreciated when we remember that it did not follow a period of hot-house growth under artificial conditions, as was the case in the difficulty between 1816 and 1820. In fact it had been preceded by a period of slow advance under fairly normal conditions. Nevertheless the woolen manufacture was now greatly depressed.

It should be pointed out, however, that not all branches of the industry suffered alike. It seems to have been the broadcloth manufacture that suffered most severely. The decline in the price of this fabric between 1823 and 1824 was from $33\frac{1}{3}\%$ to 40%, according to the testimony of one of the manufacturers in 1828, who added that "the best investments in broadcloth manufactures in the country are not worth over fifty cents on the dollar." [3] The fall which took place and the long period of time over which it extended, are indicated by the following prices: [4]—

	1825	1826	1827	1828	1829
Broadcloth per yard	$4.00	$3.75	$3.00	$3.25	$2.25
Washed full-blood merino wool per lb.	.60	.60	.40	.45	.35

Broadcloth being made from merino wool, its low price is reflected by the fall in the price of that wool. The lower grades of wool, on the other hand, did not suffer so great a fall as the fine wool.[5] This indicates that the distress in the lower grades of the manufactures was not so extreme. In fact, we find some signs that the manufacture of flannels was actually increasing at this time. "American flannels are rapidly driving the foreign article out of the market," is the word in 1827.[6] A flannel mill was erected in that year, and the flannel manufacture was mentioned as the only one making a profit in 1827.[7]

[1] *Niles' Register*, vol. xxxi, p. 289.
[2] *Ibid.*, vol. xxxii, p. 296.
[3] *American State Papers*, "Finance," vol. v, p. 826.
[4] *Niles' Register*, vol. xxxvi, p. 147.
[5] See table of prices and charts in the Appendix. See also page 74.
[6] *Niles' Register*, vol. xxxii, p. 290. See also vol. xxviii, p. 166.
[7] "In 1827 the flannel manufacture made some profit, but I don't think any of the

Flannels were made from domestic wool, and had gained by the increased duty on cloths in the tariff of 1824, while not suffering so much from the duty on wool. In the satinet manufacture, an important branch of the industry, one of the troubles was nothing less than domestic competition. At least, two of the manufacturers so declared, saying that there was comparatively little foreign competition in this line.[1] Satinet, the demand for which was rapidly increasing, had a cotton warp and generally used a medium or low grade of wool. Both this grade of wool and cotton were to be found within the country; hence the greater development of this branch. Moreover, the imports of raw wool were slowly rising in amount, and this rise could hardly have taken place if the woeful tales of some of the manufacturers held true of all branches of the industry. These imports, however, were in the main of the inferior qualities. Thus, although the mills making the lower grades of goods and employing the domestic wool or cheap imports suffered least, there can be no doubt that the whole industry was hard pressed.

A strong but vain effort was made in 1827 to pass the woolen bill, which was to increase the duties on wool and woolen manufactures. The increase was finally secured by the tariff of 1828, but hardly in the form desired by the manufacturer, as the wool and woolens schedule was one of the "abominations" for which this tariff was noted. In the first place there was imposed on wool a mixed duty of four cents a pound and forty per cent ad valorem, the ad valorem rate being raised to forty-five per cent and fifty per cent for the two following years. The duty on woolens was put at forty-five per cent ad valorem. But the chief feature was the introduction of the system of minimum valuation on woolens, which had proved very effective in the case of the duties on cotton goods. The lowest minimum was fifty cents a yard, the other points were one dollar, two dollars and a half, and four dollars, the duty on goods whose value fell between any two of these points being assessed as if they were valued at the higher.[2] Had it been possible to enforce the

other woolen manufacturers made anything" (*American State Papers*, "Finance," vol. v, p. 820). Still, the business had not been generally profitable since 1824.

[1] *American State Papers*, "Finance," vol. v, pp. 813, 821.

[2] The dollar minimum had been omitted in the plan of the woolen manufacturers. A large share of the goods imported were valued at about that point, and its insertion was directly hostile to the woolen interests. See Taussig, *Tariff History*, pp. 94, 95.

act, the chief advantage gained by it would have come from this system of minimums. But, in fact, it led to much fraud and undervaluation. Moreover, the increased duty on woolens was largely offset by the advance in the duty on wool, especially by the effect of the specific duty on the cheaper grades.

The revival of the industry, which was expected to follow the passage of this act, failed to come. Some investments in woolen mills were made in anticipation of beneficial results, and a temporary rise in the price of wool took place; but 1829 proved as poor a year as any of the others, if not poorer. A manufacturer in the interior of Massachusetts wrote at this time: "I believe there is scarcely a woolen manufacturer in New England making a cent at present."[1] Though the imports of manufactures fell off somewhat in this year, the price of wool was very low, and that of broadcloth lower than ever before.

It was not until the year 1830 that signs of awakening life appeared. But when once started, the industry seemed to be trying to make up for lost time. Within that year the prices of all grades of wool virtually doubled. Mills opened at once, and new ones were constructed as rapidly as possible. The prosperity was felt in England as well. The imports of goods into the United States rose to twice the previous amount, but this seemed to make no difference. At a meeting of the manufacturers held in New York in 1831, except for the protests against undervaluation and other frauds,[2] hardly a complaint was uttered. At last the woolen manufacture seemed to be firmly established.

To what extent was the tariff of 1828 responsible for this result? So many factors enter into the problem that it is difficult to solve, but a few clues to the answer may be found. The average value of the imports of manufactures of wool for the years 1829–30 was $6,546,000; for the two following years $11,819,000.[3] The explana-

[1] He continues, "Indeed the factory at which I am engaged has been continually losing since 1825, and, although in that year we paid 60 cents for wool and 25 cents per yard, we made money; but now at the low price of wool [33 cents for the best, he previously states], and paying only 6 cents per yard for weaving by power, we are losing" (*Niles' Register*, vol. xxxvi, p. 298).

[2] An act had been passed in 1830 to remedy these difficulties, but apparently without success.

[3] Flannels and carpets were the only classes of goods in which the imports fell off noticeably under this act.

tion of this difference is to be found, not in the tariff, but in the depressed condition of trade during the first two years and the sudden revival of prosperity during the other two, though a part of the difference in values is accounted for by variations in the price of the goods. The state of the woolen trade during the first years that the tariff was in operation indicates that of itself the tariff could accomplish little. Niles pointed out[1] in 1829 that, although the duty on foreign wools was nearly 50% higher, their price had fallen 7% between 1827 and 1829, while American wool had declined 25%, adding, as a notorious fact, that both wool and woolen goods bore an average price of from 15 to 20% less than in the years from 1825 to 1827. To be sure, the tariff had not had much time for its effects to work out, yet later it certainly showed little power to stop the rapid increase in the inflow of foreign goods. Thus far, certainly, there is no indication of any particular efficacy for the wool manufacturer in the tariff of 1828.

Furthermore, the very way in which the bill was concocted, as well as the contemporary views of the woolen manufacturers on the measure, would not lead one to expect much aid from this tariff. That the bill was purposely designed to be so obnoxious to the northern manufacturers as to lead their representatives to vote against it, is well known. Indeed, it is said that they would have killed it[2] but for the increase in the ad valorem duty on woolens by the Senate. That, even as passed, it was very unsatisfactory to the woolen interests is made plain by contemporary opinion. The editor of *Niles' Register*, who had been a most ardent champion of the woolen manufacturers' cause, proposed to call the act "A bill for the slaughter of sheep, and to prevent the growth of wool in the United States, and for other purposes."[3] The New England manufacturers had vigorously protested against the bill while it was under consideration, because the increase in the duty on woolen goods was frequently more than offset by an advance in the rates on the raw material.[4] In the Free Trade Convention of 1831, a

[1] *Niles' Register*, vol. xxxvi, pp. 82–84. [2] Taussig, *Tariff History*, pp. 95–101.

[3] *Niles' Register*, vol. xxxvi, p. 83. In later years, when memory of the "abominations" had dimmed, and they looked back on the high rates of duty, this opinion was changed. In 1844, the same journal, speaking of the tariff of 1828, declared that it arrested the slaughter of sheep (no. lxvi, pp. 386, 387).

[4] *Ibid.*, vol. xxxiv, p. 3.

manufacturer declared that, when the duty on wool was taken into account, this tariff did not give the manufacturer more than 25% protection.[1] Another agreed in putting the actual gain at that figure, because of frauds and the effect of the wool duties, adding that the manufacturer could do better under the tariff of 1816.[2] Whether the tariff of 1828 was or was not better for the wool manufacturer than the preceding acts, it is certain that it was not looked upon with great favor by the manufacturers of the time. Probably it was at least as helpful to them as the preceding tariffs. But it is unquestionable that it was not enough better to be a factor of more than very minor importance in the final establishment of the woolen manufacture which then took place.

To get at the underlying causes of this change from instability to stability requires a glance at the advance then made in the technical side of the industry. First of all it is important to note that it was just in these years between 1825 and 1830 that there came the greatest progress in bringing power-machinery into common use. Though spinning and weaving by power began to come in after 1820, it was some time before their use was really widespread. Further, it was not until the years we are considering that the benefits derived from Goulding's invention began to be greatly felt. The woolen manufacturers in 1828 agreed in their testimony that there had been a very great advance in mechanical methods during the three or four years immediately preceding, and there can be no doubt that the severity of the competition they were then meeting had greatly hastened the introduction of these improved methods. Seven out of the thirteen manufacturers who testified said that they could carry on the actual process of manufacture as cheaply as in England. Most of them thought our labor as cheap as that in England, and one, who declared English labor cheaper, said we had compensating advantages. There was general agreement that the raw material cost considerably more, five of them giving specific estimates which put the price in this country at 50 to 75% higher than the London prices.[3] It was the very finest and the coarsest

[1] Henry Lee, *Exposition of Evidence*, no. iv, p. 8. [2] *Ibid.*, p. 8.

[3] *Niles' Register*, March 8, 1828, said that wool in the United States cost 80% more than in England (vol. xxiv, p. 23). The petition of the Boston manufacturers in 1826, likewise declared, "Wool is now sold in Europe at 50% below its prices in the United

grades of wool which were most deficient here. No doubt the duty on wool was a handicap, but it was more than offset by that on the finished product.[1] By 1828–30 the use of power in the chief processes of the woolen manufacture may be said to have been generally introduced. As Hayes says, "The period of 1830 we may fix upon as that of the completed and successful introduction of the woolen manufacture in this country, substantially with the principal appliances and machinery of the present day."[2] Almost all of this advance had been made since 1820. By 1830 the American manufacturers were certainly very nearly, if not quite, as well equipped, so far as machinery went, as their British rivals.[3] Since their protective duty was largely offset by the tax on their raw material, this was essential for further advance. And with the general introduction of an effective mechanical equipment, one of the chief steps in the way of advance had been taken.

In addition to poor technical equipment there was another cause for the depressed state of the woolen manufacture during this period, the removal of which greatly aided in its final establishment. This was the constant fluctuations in the home market, and the resulting continued uncertainty from unceasing upheavals of the industry, frequently referred to in the testimony of the manufacturers in 1828.[4] Often some one particular cause of the fluctuations was singled out, but many pointed to the fluctuations as in themselves disturbing.

States." "Some of your memorialists," it adds, "have recently purchased bills at 12½% premium and remitted them to England for the purchase of wool which will cost them less, delivered at their doors with all the charges of exchange, freight, duty, &c., than the price of the article here. Merchants in this country have imported large parcels of wool from England the last year, paid the duties and all the charges, amounting to 50%, and sold it here at an advance" (*ibid.*, vol. xxxi, p. 185). No doubt the rapidity of the drop in England following 1825 had increased the margin somewhat beyond the normal difference, the market not having had time, under the disturbed conditions, to adjust itself.

[1] In 1831 a manufacturer said: "We can and *do* make cloths for less money per yard than it costs to make the same qualities in England. This we have tested by experiment. . . . The difference is in the stock." Henry Lee, *Exposition of Evidence*, no. iv, p. 8.

[2] *Bulletin*, vol. ix, p. 20.

[3] For this year, it is difficult to agree with the conclusions of North that the American woolen manufacture has always been twenty-five years behind the British in the matter of its mechanical equipment.

[4] *American State Papers*, "Finance," vol. v. pp. 829, 830.

One correspondent of *Niles' Register* declared that these were the sole reason for the trouble.[1] Though not the only obstacle, they unquestionably formed a large part of the difficulty under which the industry suffered at the time. Not only does this apply to the years from 1825 to 1830, but we find here the main clue to the course of the woolen manufacture throughout the period which led to its final establishment.

The chief explanation for these fluctuations, as has been indicated, is to be found in the unusually disturbed condition of the British wool manufacture. The woolen industry of the United States emerged from the War of 1812 in an unhealthy and overgrown condition. At that juncture the country was flooded with British woolens, and this infant of artificial growth, totally unaccustomed to such competition, was suddenly paralyzed. Even if the imports had been perfectly normal, a reaction and readjustment would have been inevitable and necessary. But before the industry had even begun to recover from one blow, another was struck, one originating in the widespread industrial depression in the United States. The prostration was thus continued until the year 1820. By 1821, however, the situation had become less unfavorable and signs of reviving life began to appear. Both in England and the United States conditions were more nearly normal, except that the British manufacturer suffered from a heavy duty on wool. Under these circumstances a very slow but steady advance is to be marked in the American woolen manufacture. The tariff of 1824, with the increased duties on the raw material as well as on the finished product, did not improve the situation of the manufacturer much, if at all.[2] Nevertheless, at the time there appeared no reason to doubt that the industry was just on the point of establishing itself in a modest but independent way. Events most needed to accomplish this end were then taking place. Power machinery was beginning to come into general use, and the domestic wool supply of the grades in which the deficiency was the greatest was increasing. Everything looked favorable, when suddenly the industry was engulfed in

[1] *Niles' Register*, vol. xxxi, pp. 226–228.

[2] One manufacturer testified: "I have considered that the tariff of 1824 put the woolen manufacturer in a worse position than before" (*American State Papers*, "Finance," vol. v, p. 821).

another trade upheaval, and its final establishment was still further delayed.

The situation was peculiarly difficult. Against such conditions as then existed in England no reasonable tariff could be of the slightest avail. With a large stock of goods on hand, the raw material for which had been bought before the drop in prices, and with the country in the midst of a great industrial depression, many English manufacturers were bankrupt.[1] They had to sell at any price. The burden of the tariff under these circumstances tended to fall almost entirely upon them, and in consequence their goods sold in the United States so much the lower. Such an event coming at the crucial period in the history of the woolen manufacture of this country, at the moment when, after having carefully adjusted itself to normal conditions, it was attempting once more to get upon its feet, was enough to undo any industry. When we consider the critical stage which the industry had just reached, and the temporary character of this disturbance, we cannot but conclude that the special circumstances were of such a nature as to offer justification for an even higher tariff than that which was actually granted.[2]

During the years between 1825 and 1830 the industry was submitted to the very fiercest competition. In a desperate effort to meet it, every possible improvement was made, but in vain: there was nothing but loss. Still, the remnant of the industry which survived was found hardened, tempered, and well prepared. In the final

[1] For a letter describing the conditions in Yorkshire in 1826, see *Niles' Register*, vol. xxxi, pp. 266–268.

[2] This could not be said of the case just following the War of 1812, when the English manufacturers, though overstocked, were in no such depressed state as after 1825, and the distress of the American manufacturer was largely due to the necessity of adjusting his methods to meet foreign competition under purely normal circumstances. There would, of course, be many practical difficulties in securing the adjustment of a higher tariff to changing conditions. A point generally overlooked in discussing the question of protection during the period following the close of the War of 1812 is the fact that the infant manufactures *had already been started* during the period of restricted commerce. Consequently the problem of the applicability of protection then was not simply the usual question of starting up a new industry, but of helping to sustain one already started, one which if not aided was likely to fall and thus result in a heavy loss. This possible loss from free trade is a feature which does not ordinarily enter into the question, but during these years it was one argument in favor of protection, an item helping to offset any disadvantages that such a policy might involve.

establishment of the industry which then took place, the tariff of 1828 counted for little. It had not shown power to stimulate manufacturing during the first years of its existence, and when the industry did revive, it was in the face of a rising tide of imports, which this tariff failed to keep back any better than previous acts. Some aid above that required to offset the duty on raw material the tariff did afford, but to one who knows the state of preparedness of the manufacture at the time, it does not seem improbable that the industry would have started up even without the tariff. The only thing then needed was a few years of favorable trade conditions. When these came, beginning in 1830, the woolen manufacture at once became firmly and finally established. Thereafter, however severe the crisis or slight the tariff, there was never a time when its stability was in the slightest doubt.

The Household Industry.

While the woolen manufacture of the United States was being so roughly buffeted about by the varied events between 1815 and 1830, the household industry fared much better. Its economic basis as a by-product of the farm was such that it suffered little from the troubles which beset its rival in the factory. The ups and downs of the market had a comparatively slight effect upon its output. Even when the household product was intended for sale, — a situation which, as has been seen, was very common by 1815, — its market was likely to be in the more remote country districts, where foreign woolens did not easily penetrate.

Information and data as to the household woolen industry are so very difficult to obtain, and at best so vague, that the trend of events has to be followed very largely through evidence which is circumstantial. The most satisfactory statistics are those for the state of New York. In 1820 some ten million yards of woolen, linen, and cotton cloth — or seven and a quarter yards a person — were manufactured in the families of that state.[1] At this time there were 991 fulling mills and 233 carding machines. The returns of the state Census for 1825 and 1835 were: —

[1] Goodenow, *Topographical and Statistical Manual;* quoted in *Niles' Register,* vol. xxii, p. 226.

Yards of Goods Manufactured in the Households of New York State.[1]

	Fulled cloth	*Flannel and woolen cloth not fulled*	*Cotton and other cloths*
1825	2,918,233	3,468,001	8,079,000
1835	2,183,951	2,790,069	3,799,953

In the latter year, there were made in the factories of the state 6,626,058 yards of woolen cloth, 686,203 yards from cotton and wool mixed, and 24,175,257 yards of cotton cloth. It is interesting to note the predominance, over all other classes, of factory-made cotton goods. As compared with the figures of 1820 there were, in 1835, 965 fulling mills and 1061 carding machines.[2] An agent of the Secretary of the Treasury reported in 1832 that in one hundred and twenty-five towns of New Hampshire, "something more than one half" of the clothing for the inhabitants was made in families, the greatest part of it being woolen.[3] All this would seem to indicate that in the years between 1815 and 1830 the household industry held its own, though no doubt the factory product was gaining relatively.

The agricultural societies continued their activities through this period, offering a constant incentive to increase the household product, both in quantity and in quality. Some idea of the surprisingly large amount that could be made by one family is obtained through the accounts of the awards given at some of the agricultural fairs, where almost invariably a premium was offered for the best piece of cloth or the largest amount made by one person or family. At the Pittsfield (Mass.) Cattle Show and Fair of 1821, one family exhibited 438 yards of fulled cloth, 171½ yards of raw flannel, 53 yards of carpeting, 142¾ yards of table cloth and other linen goods, — in all 805¼ yards, made by the mother and four daughters within a year.[4] In 1822 the Susquehanna [Pennsylvania] Agricultural Society awarded its premium for the greatest quantity of domestic manufactures pro-

[1] The figures for 1825 are taken from Pitkin's *Statistical View*, 1835, pp. 490–491.

[2] The state then held 234 woolen factories and 111 cotton factories. That is, the average product of the woolen factory of New York was 31,249 yards of goods, while that of the cotton factory was 217,797 yards, a most significant commentary on the position of each. This assumes that the woolen mills made all the cloth in which wool and cotton were mixed.

[3] Pitkin, *Statistical View*, 1835, p. 491.

[4] *Niles' Register*, vol. xxii, p. 266.

duced in a single family to one which had made upwards of 1600 yards of different kinds of cloth, besides stockings and yarn that had been sold.[1]

Some idea of the quantity and variety of goods made in this manner is conveyed by the following list of goods manufactured in 1822 by a single family in the state of New York: 319 yards of linen cloth, 25 yards of kersey, 42 yards of skirting, 35 yards of diaper, 52 yards of cotton and linen, 199 yards of woolen cloth, 16 yards of kersey for blankets, 24 yards of plain flannel for blankets, 28 yards of cotton and wool, 34 yards of cotton, and 22 yards of worsted, — in all 796 yards, — besides socks, pantaloons, frocks, aprons, blankets, sheets, and skirts.[2] When such a quantity and variety could be supplied by a household, there was little occasion for the farming community to resort to the product of the factory.

The frontier and the more remote farming districts were of necessity self-sufficing: the product of the factory, whether domestic or foreign, was hard to obtain. But in the whole agricultural community, even where it was obtainable, few families could afford broadcloth or the better grades of cloth such as they themselves were unable to produce. In the other lines they could supply their own wants. Nearly every one had a small flock of sheep; one such as could be kept with little extra trouble or expense. The women of the family employed their spare time in spinning or in weaving, while the carding and finishing, if the latter were needed, could be done at one of the mills that were to be found in every neighborhood. These products were a regular part of the farm economy.

In localities near the cities, on the other hand, the consumption of factory-made goods was slowly increasing. There lived the large body of those who desired and could afford fine cloth. At this time, too, the unusually low price of cloth of all kinds increased the consumption of these goods. But the factory product did not then invade and capture the territory of the household industry in anything like the manner in which it did during the next twenty years. This industry began to suffer seriously only when the cost of manufacturing had been lowered by the complete introduction of power machinery, and when improved transportation facilities gave the manufacturer

[1] *Niles' Register*, vol. xxiii, p. 144.

[2] *Ibid.*, p. 181. This gives several similar examples.

easy access to the agricultural districts and at the same time gave those districts a market for their produce. Up to 1830 these changes had not taken place, and until then the household woolen manufacture fairly held its own.

The Growing of Wool.

Nothing could better testify to the importance of the woolen manufacture as an aid in starting the industry of growing wool than the blight which fell upon the latter when the former was in distress. Throughout the period from 1815 to 1830 the ups and downs of the manufacture were closely reflected in the fluctuations in the course of wool-growing. These were more exactly indicated by the state of the fine, wool industry, which suffered severely, while the common sheep passed a comparatively uneventful period, their mainstay, in fact the mainstay of wool-growing in general, at this time, being the household industry. Since the relation was so close, we may divide the period into sections similar to those made in the review of manufacturing.

From 1816 *to* 1820.

With the close of the War of 1812, the inflow of British goods, and the prostration of manufactures, the price of wool at once dropped. As it had been the fine wool which experienced the greatest rise in the preceding period, so it was this grade which now suffered the greatest fall. Having sold at $2.00 a pound or more in Boston in 1814, the wool of full-blooded merinos now sold there for from 60 to 85 cents. In the West, at Steubenville, it fell from $2.75 in 1814 to $1.10 for the years 1817 to 1820. The drop in the wool of half-blooded merinos was from $1.35 to $0.55 for the same period.[1] Common wool suffered less, the price in Boston during these years ranging from $0.20 to $0.55 a pound. The greater depression in the case of fine wool was due to the fact that the common wool was mainly used in the household industry. The use of the latter in factories was increasing, but fine wool had to depend entirely on the factory for its market.

Nothing can better indicate how artificial was the stimulus re-

[1] See quotations in *Hunt's Merchant's Magazine*, vol. iv, p. 287. See also *Niles' Register*, vol. xxxvi, p. 399.

ceived by both the growing and the manufacture of fine wool, during the period of restricted foreign commerce, than the reaction which now set in against fine-wooled sheep. The wrath vented on the innocent merinos was in proportion to the speculative craze which had just brought them into popular favor. For two or three years following the end of the war the mere mention of this breed to the irate farmer was enough to provoke an outburst of abuse. Some intimation of the popular feeling on the subject is to be found in contemporary papers. In 1818 the Secretary of the Massachusetts Society for Promoting Agriculture, in venturing to utter a plea for the persecuted merino, said: "The writer would observe that he knows it to be vain to attempt to bring merino sheep soon again into favor; all that he aims at is to prevent the entire destruction, or the utter neglect of them, which would eventually come to the same point." [1] In addressing the Massachusetts Agricultural Society at the Brighton cattle show that same year, he said: "Shall we dare to mention the merino sheep, or shall we awaken recollections of an unsuccessful experiment and individual loss, which will more than compensate for the pleasure derived from this invaluable accession to our own domestic flocks? . . . May we not take the liberty to plead the cause of this unoffending race of animals? . . . We ought not to be discouraged by calamities which have fallen upon individuals who entered it like a South Sea speculation. . . . Let us not then despair of the ultimate success of the breed of merino sheep. I hold those in high honor who have continued to encourage this unpopular race of animals, with a conviction that their country would be ultimately benefited, and that a temporary depression would be followed by a just and reasonable estimate of their value." [2] The tone of abject apology at being so bold as even to plead for the merino, which appears throughout the address, gives the best conception of the place which this breed then held in the eyes of the general public.

Many of these valuable animals were sent to the slaughter-house. Half-blood merinos were sold to the butcher for $1.25 a head.[3] It is even said that full-blooded merinos, such as formerly sold for $1000, were now to be had at $1.00.[4] However this may be, it is certain that

[1] *Massachusetts Agricultural Repository and Journal*, vol. v, p. 167.

[2] *Ibid.*, pp. 230–235.

[3] *Ibid.*, vol. iv, p. 140.

[4] Randall, *Fine Wool Sheep Husbandry*, p. 48.

all along the coast, where the merino had formerly been most welcome, the breed now met the same hard fate. The more noted flocks usually escaped, but the common farmer's contempt for the breed was as great as his previous craze had been senseless. Where the merinos were not sold for slaughter, they were neglected, or mixed with the common sheep.

Except for this outbreak against the merino, which continued unabated, there was little to note in the wool-growing industry of the country except its continued westward extension. In the trans-Alleghany region, where British broadcloth was less abundant, the merino fared much better than to the eastward; and many sheep escaped slaughter by being driven to the valley of the Ohio.[1] Then, too, the westward movement of population, which assumed such large proportions after the close of the war, carried many sheep in its train. In 1817 the first merinos reached Illinois, brought by George Flower, who settled, with Birkbeck and other Englishmen, at Albion.[2] The increase in the flocks of the West was due to the necessity which confronted the pioneer farmer of supplying his own needs.

We should remember that in 1816 there was levied the first duty on wool. It is significant that this was imposed by the clause of the act which fixed a duty of 15% ad valorem on "all articles not free, and not subject to any other rate of duty." This together with the fact that there was almost no discussion of the duty, except for a proposition to lower it to 7½%, indicates how little demand for it existed and how unimportant it was then thought.[3] As events at first turned out, this proved the correct view: during the first few years of its operation it had no effect whatever. In fact, the influx of foreign manufactured goods was so great, and the collapse of the home manufacture so complete, that little or no wool was imported during the first four or five years under this tariff. When the House of Representatives called for a statement of the imports of wool for the years 1817–21, the Secretary of the Treasury replied, under date of January 28,

[1] In 1817 several hundred merinos were taken to Meadville, Pennsylvania, from New Jersey. See Bishop's *History of American Manufactures*, vol. ii, p. 246.

[2] See an account of his flock written by Flower, in Hall's *Statistics of the West*, 1836, pp. 147–149.

[3] *Bulletin*, vol. xxx, p. 65. This doubtless explains why more than one writer speaks of the tariff of 1824 as the first to levy a duty on wool. Cf. Lewis's *Our Sheep and the Tariff*, p. 94, table; Bogart's *Economic History of the United States*, p. 153.

1822, "It is my duty to state that at the time the forms were prescribed under the Act of 1820, it was not known that wool to any considerable extent was imported." [1] Not only were there no imports worth mentioning, but the country seems to have been actually exporting at this time. Between 1817 and 1819, from 24,000 to 269,000 pounds of wool were yearly exported to Great Britain.[2] That all of this was grown in the United States is improbable, but some of it unquestionably was, for we have contemporary testimony to that effect.[3]

On the whole the years from 1816 to 1820 mark a retrograde movement in the wool-growing industry. To what extent the flocks were depleted it is impossible to say, but there can be no doubt that as regards quality, at least, there was a serious deterioration. The fine-wooled sheep suffered severely from the heavy importation of British manufactures, and the common flocks of the country found their only salvation in the household industry.

From 1821 *to* 1824.

With the reviving trade conditions after 1820, and the new signs of life in the woolen manufacture, the prospects of the sheep of the country became brighter. Wool advanced slightly in price, it began to be imported in large quantities, and there was no longer any thought of exporting it. By the year 1822 the imports of wool had become of such importance that they were included as a separate item in the commerce and navigation returns. For the three years 1822 to 1824, the average importation of raw wool was 1,563,000 pounds; its average value, 23 cents.

It was at this juncture that the wool-growers began to send to Congress memorials asking for further protection on wool.[4] They also very sensibly asked for protection for the manufacturer, without which, of course, a duty on the raw material was of slight avail. The

[1] *American State Papers*, "Commerce and Navigation," vol. ii, p. 612. Such returns as the Secretary was able to give, admittedly very incomplete, showed imports of 2000 to 9000 pounds a year in 1817–1819, some 106 pounds in 1820, and 384,333 pounds up to September 30, in 1821.

[2] *Journal of the Royal Statistical Society*, vol. xxxiii, p. 502.

[3] See *Massachusetts Agricultural Repository and Journal*, vol. v, p. 168. See also Memorial to Congress from Albany, New York, 1824; quoted in *Bulletin*, vol. xxx, p. 146.

[4] *Bulletin*, vol. xxx, pp. 148–149.

household manufactures had always used domestic wool, each family simply growing enough for its own needs. Under such conditions there was almost no importation of foreign wool and no demand for protection from the wool-growers. But with the advance of the woolen manufacture there appeared an increasing market for wool. This market the domestic growers now sought to supply, and the wool-growing industry acquired a commercial basis. When the domestic growers saw foreigners beginning to supply this market and thus undermining the new basis of their industry, they for the first time made an appreciable demand for protection. The consequences of the rise of the wool manufacture are thus clearly seen.

In fact it was still the importation of wool in the disguised form of manufactured goods which proved to be the most serious rival of the domestic clip. Probably something over one half of the imported manufactures of wool were made from grades of wool similar to those found in this country. On this supposition, the imports of directly competing wool in this form were from five to eight times as great as the imports of raw wool.

But by no means all the raw wool brought into the country was like the domestic product. The wool then grown in the United States on the ordinary flocks of the country, known as common wool, was of medium length and neither fine nor very coarse. It usually sold for between twenty and thirty cents a pound. This wool, most of which was still used in the household manufacture, made up the great bulk of the domestic supply. Then there was the wool of the merino sheep — such as were left — and of their grades, all finer than that of the common sheep. The quantity of the best, however, was very small. An experiment tried in Pittsfield indicated that only about one pound in seven hundred was fit to make the very finest cloths, and a test made in Dutchess County, New York, another fine-wool centre, gave scarcely four hundred pounds of that quality out of a total of eighty thousand.[1] But the finest wool of all was that of the Saxony sheep, and this breed only began to appear in the United States during the latter part of the twenties.[2] The coarsest

[1] *Niles' Register*, vol. xxxvii, p. 97. This was in 1829.

[2] Dickinson testified in 1828 that the region about Steubenville had merino wool as fine as the best Saxony he ever saw, but the quantity was very small, 3000 to 4000 pounds out of 80,000 to 100,000 (see *American State Papers*, "Finance," vol. v, p. 802).

wool, such as was used in "negro cloths," coarse blankets, and carpets, which sold at from seven to fifteen cents a pound, was also not to be found in appreciable amounts on the sheep of this country. Thus the deficiency came in the finest and coarsest grades.

A contemporary estimate divided the imports of the year 1822 into 700,000 pounds of superfine wool, 440,000 of common wool, and 590,000 of coarse wool.[1] Some idea of the general character, value, and source of these imports is given by the following table, which covers all the more important countries of shipment.

Average Annual Imports of Wool, 1822–1824.

	Spain	*Germany*	*Portugal*	*Turkey and Levant*	*South America*
Thousands of lbs.	148	166	220	339	174
Average value, cents	47	31	28	9	14

At least one third of the imports, it is clear, did not in the least compete with the native product. About one third was of the finer grades, of which our supply was very limited; the remainder was not very unlike the native clip.

Aside from the insufficient domestic supply of the desired grades of wool, there were other reasons which tended to increase the imports. Manufacturers found that the wool which they got from the American farmer was very uncertain in regard to its condition: some was clean and well put up, but more was poorly washed, and the fleece was full of tags and ends. And to the present day this difficulty confronts the buyer of American wool. The result is thus described by one who was familiar with the trade as early as 1816: "They know the value of Spanish wool and will purchase it, while they approach American wool as they would a lottery, under the just impression that the chances are against them."[2] Another fact which counted against the domestic product was that most of the manufacturers lacked the capital necessary for the purchase of domestic wool on such short credit as the growers usually demanded, whereas longer time and easier terms were given by the foreign wool-merchants.[3] The amount of wool imported in the raw state,

[1] *Treasury Report*, 1823; quoted in *Niles' Register*, vol. xxiv, p. 40.

[2] *Massachusetts Agricultural Repository and Journal*, vol. iv, p. 65.

[3] *Ibid.*, p. 66.

however, played but a very minor part in the competition met with by the American grower.

The first symptom of better times for the wool-grower was in an abatement of the unreasoning hostility to merino sheep. In April, 1821, it was noted that "the prejudice against them is now very much weakened, so that those sheep sell for double the price they did last year."[1] Although the general disfavor into which the breed had fallen was no longer marked, nevertheless they were still looked upon rather coolly, and by no means recovered their former exalted position. In the districts around the larger cities, such as Boston, New York, and Philadelphia, the merino was discarded for good, and people began to turn to the English breeds of mutton sheep, with mutton and lamb as their chief object rather than wool. But even where fine wool was sought, the Spanish merino was now passed by in favor of a newcomer, the Saxony.

The Saxony sheep were descended from the Spanish merinos, mainly of the Escurial stock, brought to Saxony about 1765.[2] There they were bred with the greatest care, all efforts being directed toward securing the finest possible fleece.[3] The fleece averaged one and a half to two pounds of washed wool for ewes, and two to three pounds for rams, the staple being an inch to an inch and a half in length. But fineness of wool was gained at the expense of other qualities. The carcasses of these sheep were very small and made poor mutton, and the great care which the animals received resulted in weak constitutions, and an unusually small number of offspring.[4] These latter characteristics, however, were overlooked by the American wool-grower, who, disregarding even the light weight of the fleece, saw nothing but its fineness and the higher price which it brought in the market.

Although the greater number of these sheep were imported in 1825 and 1826, yet their arrival may properly be considered here,

[1] *Massachusetts Agricultural Repository and Journal*, vol. vi, p. 364.

[2] They are sometimes called Electoral sheep, from the Elector of Saxony, who was presented with a large flock by the King of Spain.

[3] For a description of the breed, see Randall's *Fine Wool Sheep Husbandry*, pp. 24–26, 139–142.

[4] Randall says that, at the time of their importation into the United States, they had touched the bottom of their degeneracy, and that they improved later (*Fine Wool Sheep Husbandry*, p. 26).

for the impulse which caused it is to be found in the reviving state of the manufacture at this time. The first of this breed to reach the country came in 1822, when four were brought to Boston.[1] Nine followed the next year, and in 1824 they began to come in large numbers. At a sale in Boston in that year, 46 rams, 25 ewes, and 4 lambs sold at an average of $69.35.[2] At a similar sale in the following year, 138 sheep sold at prices ranging from $23 to $450.[3] Many of the purchasers came from New York, as well as from the New England states. These sheep were also being imported into New York and other ports along the coast, so that the breed became well scattered through the country.

Many of those brought over were, unfortunately, of a very inferior grade. Pure-blooded Saxons brought in Germany $30 or $40, while the grade sheep, selling there at $5 or $10, could be palmed off on the ignorant American farmer with nearly equal success.[4] The price of the Saxons was fairly maintained until about 1827. In New York, in the spring of 1826, bucks sold at $160 to $350 and ewes at $30 to $85,[5] but at a sale in Boston the following year the prices ranged from $8 to $64, averaging $27.[6] This decline was due to the demoralized state of the woolen manufacture at that time, and the importation of sheep at once fell off. The recorded arrivals of Saxony sheep at the ports of Boston, New York, Portsmouth, Philadelphia, and Baltimore, during these years were: [7] —

	1824	1825	1826	1827	1828
Number of sheep	77	164	2288	398	550

But the new cloud which appeared on the horizon of the wool-grower put a sudden check to the progress of the Saxony sheep, and for another period the whole industry was overcast.

From 1825 *to* 1830.

The price of wool, which had begun to fall in 1824, took a decided drop in 1826, and, except for a momentary rise when the tariff of

[1] *Sheep Industry*, pp. 231, 232. [2] *New England Farmer*, vol. ii, p. 314.

[3] *Ibid.*, vol. iii, p. 383. For individual prices, and list of buyers and their places of residence, see *ibid.*, p. 413.

[4] See the statement by Gove, who was the leading importer of the breed (*Sheep Industry*, p. 232).

[5] *Niles' Register*, vol. xxx, p. 138. [6] *Ibid.*, vol. xxxiii, p. 17.

[7] *Sheep Husbandry*, p. 235. For fuller details see *ibid.*, pp. 231–236.

1828 was passed, remained at a very low level until 1830.[1] This but reflected the movement in the price of wool in England, and was due, as has been indicated, to the unusual trade depression, particularly in the woolen manufacture, in that country, and the consequent sacrifice of British goods in the United States at prices which spelt ruin to the American manufacturer. The effect of this depression upon the importation of Saxony sheep has just been shown. The effect upon the industry of wool-growing in general, however, was not nearly so severe as the distress which followed the close of the War of 1812; for the decline we are speaking of, unlike the reaction following the war, had been preceded by a period of slow but steady advance under more nearly normal conditions. There was some distress among the farmers, and some slaughtering of flocks, but no such outbreak of wrath and general upheaval as appeared between 1816 and 1820, in the anti-merino crusade and the general neglect and destruction of flocks.

In response to the demand of the growers for further protection, the tariff of 1824 had raised the duty on the better grades of wool. All wool exceeding ten cents a pound in value paid twenty per cent in 1824, twenty-five per cent the next year, and thirty per cent from 1826 on; that valued at ten cents or less remained at the old rate of fifteen per cent. Under this tariff the imports increased somewhat, in spite of the depressed state of the manufactures of the country. For the years 1825 to 1828 they averaged 2,642,000 pounds, valued at nineteen cents a pound. For comparison with conditions during the preceding period the following table has been constructed.[2]

Average Annual Imports of Wool, 1825–1828.

	Spain	*Germany*	*United Kingdom*	*Portugal*	*Turkey and Levant*	*South America*
Thousands of lbs.	170	149	435	202	847	497
Value, cents	38	43	33	23	9	6

There is noticeable here a tendency to increase the imports of the

[1] For prices and chart, see Appendix.

[2] The quantity of wool is the official estimate. The country given is the country of export, which, except in the case of the United Kingdom and of Portugal, is probably the country of production.

cheap wool from South America and Turkey, which had been favored by the tariff for the reason that this grade of wool did not compete with the domestic clip, — a fact which was made clear during the debate on the bill.[1] The real competition from which the wool-grower suffered under this tariff, as under the previous one, was in the imports of wool in the form of manufactured goods. Again this manufactured wool was many times that imported in the raw state.[2] It was not, however, the increase in the quantity of raw and manufactured wool coming into the country — only two or three million pounds — which caused the trouble, but the ruinous prices at which it was sold on the glutted market.

Under this depression the flocks began to decline. Of the wool manufacturers who testified in 1828, seven declared that the number of sheep in their locality was decreasing, two that it was stationary, and none that it was increasing. In most cases the decline had been going on for three years or more; in one or two only, since 1826.[3] The cost of keeping sheep in the eastern states was put at not less than $1.12 a head, and from that price up to $1.50,[4] while the wool of an average flock was selling at less than $1.00 a fleece. This depression hastened the movement, which had started in the neighborhood of the larger cities, toward the mutton breeds; — a move-

[1] *Bulletin*, vol. xxx, pp. 153–155.

[2] Mr. Mallory of Vermont, in his speech of March 4, 1828 (*Congressional Debates*, vol. iv, part 2, p. 1739), submitted the following estimate of the amount of wool coming in, in the form of manufactured goods: —

Cloths and cassimeres worth	$5,000,000	6,500,000 lbs.
Flannels and baizes worth	500,000	1,000,000 lbs.
Carpeting worth	500,000	1,000,000 lbs.
Blankets worth	600,000	1,500,000 lbs.
	$6,600,000	10,000,000 lbs.

This is certainly an underestimate. The average value of imported manufactures of wool, 1825–28, was $9,600,000, while his estimate foots up to but two thirds of this sum, showing that much was omitted (notably worsted-stuff goods, though to be sure combing wool was not grown here). Further, the figures for the amount of raw wool in the cloths and cassimeres seem very low. It is reasonably safe to put the quantity of wool imported in the form of manufactured goods at not less than 18,000,000 pounds, nearly two thirds of which competed with our native clip.

[3] A Genesee River farmer was butchering his flocks and feeding their meat to the hogs, with pork selling in Rochester at 2½–3 cents a pound. See *New England Farmer*, vol. vi, p. 245.

[4] *Niles' Register*, vol. xxxvi, p. 347.

ment that was further quickened by the fact that the coarse wool of these breeds did not suffer as much in price as the fine wool. By 1830 the merino sheep had pretty nearly vanished from the flocks of New Jersey, Delaware, and the eastern parts of Massachusetts and Pennsylvania, their place being taken by the Cotswold, Leicester, and Southdown breeds.[1]

In the West, however, there was rather a tendency to increase the flocks. Many sheep from the East were driven to this region. In the fall of 1827, from 5000 to 6000 passed through Frankfort, Kentucky, on their way West.[2] Some 20,000 were said to have been sold in Kentucky at prices ranging from 37½ to 75 cents a head, averaging about 50 cents, and this in spite of the fact that many were grade merinos. As early as 1824, 10,000 sheep were sent in one year from Washington County, Pennsylvania, to Ohio.[3] In 1826 sheep were reported as "rapidly increasing" in Indiana.[4] Further, fine wool was in greater demand in the West than in the East, and hence both merino and Saxony sheep fared better there. The increase in the flocks of the western states was due partly to the increasing population, but even more to the protection from foreign goods obtained by reason of geographical situation and the heavy cost of transportation.

For this period there are sufficient data to give us some notion as to the distribution of sheep in the country, and their total number. In 1825 the number of sheep in New York, according to the state returns, was 3,496,539. In 1819, when the industry was at its ebb, the number had been placed at 1,500,000.[5] This state was now supposed to have about one quarter of all the sheep in the country. As formerly, Dutchess was the leading county, with 350,000, — a figure which had increased to 450,000 by the summer of 1827.[6] The number of sheep in Pennsylvania was about 2,000,000.[7] Of these 110,451 were to be found in Washington County, where the flocks were of an unusually fine grade and sheared 400,000 pounds of wool. In New England, Vermont held the lead as a wool-growing state, with about 1,000,000 sheep, its flocks being generally noted

[1] *Sheep Industry*, p. 427.
[2] *Niles' Register*, vol. xxxiii, p. 277.
[3] *Sheep Industry*, p. 499.
[4] *New England Farmer*, vol. v, p. 150.
[5] *Niles' Register*, vol. xvi, p. 271.
[6] *New England Farmer*, vol. vi, p. 89.
[7] *Niles' Register*, vol. xxix, p. 88.

for their fine quality.[1] Maine also had a great many flocks.[2] In Massachusetts, Berkshire was the leading county, with some 200,000 sheep.[3] For the South we have no figures, but there sheep were comparatively scarce. In western Virginia many excellent flocks were to be found, and also in Kentucky. In Jefferson County, Ohio, — the county in which Steubenville is situated, — there were said to be 25,000 sheep by 1825.[4] Messrs. Wells and Dickinson, who owned the woolen mill there, each had a flock of from 2000 to 2500, mostly merinos, and admittedly among the best in the country.[5] In Clermont County, in the southwestern part of the state, the number in 1828 was put at 33,000.[6] At the same time flocks were spreading in Indiana and Illinois. As to the total number of sheep in the whole country in 1825, the most probable figure is about 12,000,000.[7] They produced about two and a half pounds of washed wool a head. It is unlikely that the number changed much before 1828. If anything it declined, but the falling off in the coast region was not very marked, and presumably was fairly offset by the advance in the interior.

The industry, however, was simply holding out in hopes that eventually its petitions for relief would be heard. On the passage of the tariff of 1828, which went into effect on July 1st of that year, it was thought that aid had at last been obtained. The act imposed a specific duty of four cents a pound on all wool, and in addition an ad valorem rate of 40%, to be increased in 1829 to 45%, and the following year to 50%. Discrimination in favor of cheap wool was done away with. As far as these duties went, the grower certainly could not complain. Though they were particularly well calculated to shut out the wool most needed by the manufacturer and least dangerous to the grower, they were heavy enough on all grades. In truth, how-

[1] *New England Farmer*, vol. vi, p. 155.

[2] The figures 800,000–1,000,000 for the winter of 1826–27 and 1,300,000 for the following winter (*New England Farmer*, vol. vi, p. 155) are certainly too high.

[3] *Niles' Register*, vol. xxxiii, p. 207.

[4] *New England Farmer*, vol. iv, p. 144.

[5] *Ibid.*, p. 144; also *Sheep Industry*, pp. 522, 529.

[6] *Niles' Register*. vol. xxxiv, p. 252.

[7] An estimate in *Niles' Register* puts the number at 15,000,000 (vol. xxix, p. 402). In 1827 a Boston memorial of those opposed to protection on wool and woolens, speaks of the current estimate as 12,000,000 to 15,000,000 (see *Bulletin*, vol. xxxi, p. 170). The lower figure seems the more probable.

ever, the satisfaction obtained from this act by the grower was not much greater than that secured by the manufacturer.

In the first two years of the operation of this tariff, the average imports fell off to about 1,000,000 pounds, but with the reviving prosperity of the next two years, rose to nearly 5,000,000, which was almost double the amount for any previous year. The average quantity for the whole period was 2,957,000; the average value, 18 cents a pound. Thus — as in the case of manufactured goods — when the test came, this act proved unable to stem the flood of foreign wool. How much more would have come in under the previous tariff, it is impossible to say. Still, as the following table indicates, when compared with the similar one for the years just preceding, the importation of cheap, coarse wool fell off relatively to that of better grades, which leads one to infer that the new tariff actually did exercise special restraint on cheap wools.

Average Annual Imports of Wool, 1829–32.

	Spain	*Germany*	*United Kingdom*	*Portugal*	*Turkey and Levant*	*South America*
Thousands of lbs.	186	270	714	132	953	503
Value, cents	31	37	31	20	12	4

The average importation of manufactures of wool under the act was, as has been seen, slightly lower than during the years immediately preceding. Further, in spite of this decline in the total, the imports of worsted stuff goods, the wool in which did not compete with the domestic clip, increased. The net result of this was to decrease the imports of directly competing manufactured wool between two and three million pounds. This much more than offset the slight increase in the importation of raw wool. Hence it may be said that the grower was slightly better off because of the tariff of 1828. But when we remember earlier conditions, and the vast amount of wool coming in in the manufactured state, it is evident that this is not saying much. As it was phrased at the time, the real difficulty lay in the fact that "the domestic *growth* of wool is amply protected, but the domestic *consumption* of it is not." [1]

The wool-growers had expected great things of the tariff of 1828, and its passage alone was sufficient to advance the price of wool, and

[1] *Niles' Register*, vol. xxxiv, p. 266.

give a forward impulse to the industry. But their faith received a severe test when in 1829, despite the unusually small imports of wool and manufactures of wool, the price of this staple fell to as low a point as before. For several years the country had been fairly smothered with cheap woolens, and there was no market left. Most of the growers, however, seem to have kept up their hopes, and they were eventually rewarded when, in 1830, the price of wool soared upward, and a period of prosperity dawned at last.

Before turning to a general view of the situation in the industry at this time, it will be desirable to glance at a change of conditions which took place during the last few years of this period. Up to 1825 virtually no wool from the Ohio valley had reached the eastern markets. All the wool used in the seaboard states was either grown in the East or imported from abroad. Massachusetts, the great wool manufacturing state, grew, according to the estimates, from one third to one twelfth of the wool consumed within her borders.[1] About one fourth was imported, but the remainder came from the surrounding states, mainly from New York and Vermont. It is in 1825 that we first find mention of the fact that western wool was being regularly sent across the Alleghanies. In that year, in Washington County, Pennsylvania, — excellently situated for easy access to the East, — out of a total of 400,000 pounds of wool raised, three fourths was consumed in the household manufacture, and of the remainder but 33,000 pounds went to eastern markets.[2] In 1828 the manufacturers testified that some quantity of Ohio wool had been seen in Boston during the years immediately preceding.[3] In 1827 it was said that "large parcels . . . [were] received from Pennsylvania, Ohio, Kentucky, and western Virginia," and a single house in Steubenville had forwarded about 150,000 pounds to Boston in one year.[4] In 1828 Dickinson declared that during the last three years he and his partner had annually shipped from Steubenville to the eastern markets from 30,000 to 50,000 pounds of wool, most of which went to Boston.[5] It is to be noted that throughout these years fine wool was

[1] *American State Papers*, "Finance," vol. v, pp. 794, 796.
[2] *Sheep Industry*, p. 499.
[3] *American State Papers*, "Finance," vol. v, pp. 794, 805.
[4] *Niles' Register*, vol. xxxiii, p. 155.
[5] *American State Papers*, "Finance," vol. v, p. 801.

selling at better prices in Steubenville than in the East. On the other hand, coarse or common wool, at least during the latter years, sold at a higher price in the East than in the West.[1] Thus we find a statement that, about 1822, merino wool had actually been sent to Steubenville from New Jersey.[2] Conversely the wool which Dickinson sent East was of the coarser grades. In two years out of the three, however, Dickinson lost on these shipments. But even in 1830 the amount of wool which reached eastern markets from the Ohio valley was very meagre.

One difficulty was that means of communication between the East and the West were only just beginning to be opened. A second difficulty was that the buying and selling of wool did not become a distinct branch of trade until about 1830.[3] Up to 1825, or thereabouts, manufacturers bought most of their wool direct from the farmers. But very soon commission merchants, who accepted consignments, appeared in the important markets. Still, in the increased activity in manufacturing after 1829, mill owners had to scramble round the country to get wool; and it is said that, as it could be bought for cash only, the manufacturer frequently had to mortgage his mill and ma-

[1] The prices paid at the Steubenville mill were: —

	Full blood No. 1	*Full blood* No. 2	$\frac{7}{8}$ *blood*	$\frac{3}{4}$ *blood*	$\frac{1}{2}$ *blood*	$\frac{1}{4}$ *blood*	*Common*
1825	125	95	60	45	35	30	30
1826	125	95	50	40	35	30	30
1827	85	60	45	35	30	25	20
1828	70	50	40	35	30	24	24
1829	70	45	37½	31¼	31¼	25	25

For the complete figures 1814–1829, see *Niles' Register*, vol. xxxvi, p. 399. This should be compared with the prices in the East given in the Appendix. The grading at Steubenville may have varied somewhat, and the terms of payment there probably required longer credit, but the difference here noted was a real one. The explanation for these differences seems to be, in the case of the higher grades, the greater protection given to fine wool manufacture in the West because of the difficulty of marketing British goods there. The higher price of coarse wool in the East was due to the greater attention given there to coarser goods, partly because they offered more profit under the existing state of manufacturing, partly because in the West the household product supplied all needs for these goods, whereas in the East an increasingly large number of persons depended on the factory for such fabrics.

[2] *Niles' Register*, vol. xxii, p. 267.

[3] This and the following is based on the account of Geo. W. Bond, in the *Report on Wool and Manufactures of Wool*, 1887, p. lxvii.

chinery in order to procure it.[1] At the same time the manufacturers united and sent an agent to Europe to buy wool, which was sold at auction on its arrival.[2] In 1831–32 they again had to resort to this method to obtain the wool wanted. Usually, importations were made by the merchants and ship-owners engaged in foreign commerce. When the wool trade once became established, however, much less difficulty was experienced in obtaining both domestic and foreign supplies.

The total number of sheep in the country in 1830 was probably not much greater than in 1825, — about 12,000,000 or 13,000,000. The average fleece weighed two and a half pounds, washed, producing a total clip of 30,000,000 to 32,000,000 pounds of wool.[3] What, then, was the proportion of foreign wool consumed in the country to this domestic supply, and how was the latter used?

The quantity of wool used in domestic manufactures is not easy to determine. In 1826 it was said that more than one third of the wool manufactured here was obtained from Europe.[4] In 1828 the testimony of wool manufacturers, so far as they touched on this point, indicated that about one quarter of the wool consumed by manufacturers was of foreign growth. Assuming, then, as is reasonable, that all imported wool was used in the mills, the average imports for these years of 2,500,000 pounds would make the amount of domestic wool consumed in the mills some 7,500,000 pounds. But the estimate that one fourth of the wool used was foreign was given mainly by the

[1] *Report on Wool and Manufactures of Wool*, 1887, p. lviii. [2] *Ibid.*, p. lxvii.

[3] The Committee on Manufactures of Wool, of the Convention of Friends of Domestic Industry, which met in New York in 1831, put the probable number of sheep in the United States at 20,000,000, producing 50,000,000 pounds of wool. Although the number of sheep increased very rapidly after 1829, it could not have been nearly so high as this estimate puts it. Even in 1840 the Census returns gave but 19,000,000. For the proceedings of the Convention and further data, see *Niles' Register*, vol. xli, Addendum, pp. 53, 54.

[4] Petition of the Boston Wool Manufacturers, 1826. See *Niles' Register*, vol. xxxi, pp. 185, 186. A Boston memorial of 1827 from those opposing protection put the domestic clip at 37,500,000, and, adding to this the total imports of raw wool, put the total consumption at 40,000,000 pounds. They thus pointed out that only from four to five per cent of the wool used was from abroad, instead of from twenty-five to fifty per cent, as some declared. This, of course, neglected foreign wool consumed in the form of manufactured goods. Very likely the figures 25–50% had reference simply to factory-used wool, and in that case the memorial erred in not deducting the wool used in the household industry before obtaining the proportion of foreign wool used.

larger manufacturers, located in the East, particularly in Massachusetts and Pennsylvania, and would not hold for mills located in the interior, where the quantity of foreign wool consumed was probably smaller. Hence a rough guess, for it cannot pretend to be more than that, would put the total amount of domestic wool consumed by the manufacturer at between 10,000,000 and 12,000,000 pounds.[1] And since the total domestic wool supply was between 30,000,000 and 32,000,000 pounds, we are led to the conclusion that from one half to two thirds of this supply was used in the household woolen manufacture.[2]

We are now in a position to get some idea of the proportion between foreign and domestic manufactures of wool then consumed in the country. The total amount of wool, both domestic and foreign, consumed in the factories of the country, is placed between 12,500,000 and 15,000,000 pounds. The total importation of manufactures of wool during these years averaged about $9,000,000 in value. At what seems a very reasonable estimate, this contained at least 18,000,000 pounds of wool. We are thus led to infer that the foreign goods made up between one half and two thirds of the total amount of manufactures of wool then used in the United States.[3] Last of all we come to the conclusion that the wool brought into this country, in both raw and manufactured states, was at least equal in amount to two thirds of the total domestic production. If we deduct from this the part consisting of wool unlike that grown in this country,[4]

[1] The only excuse for resorting to such uncertain ground is the belief that it is of value to know whether the manufacturer's consumption was nearer one fourth or three fourths of the domestic clip. It is thought that we have sufficient data for a reasonably accurate answer to that question. To greater certainty this answer does not, and could not, pretend.

[2] In 1831 it was estimated, at the Convention of the Friends of Domestic Industry, that the proportion of wool used in the factory to that used in the household was as three is to two. Although the factory product was just then increasing rapidly, and although this estimate includes foreign wool used in the factories, still it is believed to be too high.

[3] North maintains that "the most careful investigation of all the data at hand warrants the conclusion that fully one half of the consumption [of woolens] (exclusive of the products of the household industry) was of foreign origin" (*Bulletin*, vol. xxxi, p. 207).

[4] This includes all that was imported as worsted stuffs, carpets, and blankets, an allowance for the fine wool in the finest broadcloths, and about half the imports of raw wool.

we find that the total amount of imported wool which directly competed with the domestic clip was equal to about one third of that clip. About four fifths of this came in the form of manufactures of wool.

The Influence of the Competition of Cotton and General Agriculture.

A factor already once noted, the influence of which on both the growth and the manufacture of wool, it is believed, has been too little recognized, is the competition of cotton. As early as 1810 the effect which this competition was destined to have was foreseen by Coxe, who then said, "Cotton is the only redundant raw material, adapted to the manufacture of cloths for apparel and furniture, produced in the United States; and being the most susceptible of labor-saving operations, the cotton branch will probably, nay, certainly, become very soon the most considerable of our manufactures. It is adapted to all seasons in its various forms, and to a greater variety of uses than any other cloth or stuff. While sheep's wool continues to be much more wanted than cotton wool, the latter will be proportionately used as a substitute for sheep's wool in blankets, corduroys, velvets, and the chain and warp of goods with woolen woof or filling. They are substituted for worsteds or stuffs of combed wool. Further, cotton cloth can be printed, an operation seldom performed on woolens."[1] This process of substitution was just what did take place during the War of 1812, as has already been pointed out. But the process did not end with the war. The ground gained by cotton at that time, under circumstances which exerted great pressure in its favor, was not lost when the pressure lessened. Advances once made were held, and the invasion of new fields continued.

In the period between 1815 and 1830, however, progress was not so rapid as during the years immediately preceding. Still, though the manufacture of cotton suffered somewhat just after the war and again in 1822–23, the period, which for the woolen manufacturer had brought a life and death struggle, was for the cotton manufacturer, on the whole, one of prosperity.[2] In 1830, when the

[1] Coxe, *Arts and Manufactures*, 1810, p. xxviii.

[2] For further information on the cotton manufacture, see Stanwood's "New England Cotton Manufacture," in Davis's *New England States*, vol. i. See also White's *Memoir of Slater*.

woolen manufacture was first firmly established and was as yet inferior to the household woolen industry, the cotton manufacture was carried on almost entirely in the factory.[1] But much of this advance was at the expense either of the household cotton industry or of the foreign manufacturer, and did not mean an equally great increase in the actual consumption of cotton.

After the war, the price of cotton rose, and for the years 1815-19 averaged twenty-five cents a pound, as compared with seventeen cents for the preceding years. This, of course, put a check upon its use, and tended to favor wool, which was then low. But this high level for cotton could not be maintained: for the years 1820-26 the price sank to 14.3 cents, and for the years 1827-32 it averaged but 9.8 cents. Thus for the period between 1820 and 1830 cotton was considerably lower in price than at any previous time since it had come into widespread use. But wool also was depressed at this time, particularly so during the very years when cotton was at its lowest. This is one reason why the use of cotton did not increase faster. Nevertheless, it gained somewhat, and the consumption of the United States, which had been 31,500,000 pounds in 1815, averaged 43,276,000 for the years 1827-30.[2] Though most of this increase was probably either natural growth or at the expense of flax, cotton, we know, was stealthily invading the woolen manufacture. There the greatest progress was being made in the manufacture of satinets and other goods using a cotton warp. For the wool manufacturer of the country this proved a great boon, but so far as the grower of wool was concerned it had no redeeming feature: it all meant simply so much the less demand for his wool, and a lower price. Still, it appears that on the whole, for the period from 1815 to 1830, the depressed state of the wool and woolen trade proved sufficient to stave off any serious new increase in the use of cotton. The most significant point of all is that the advance made by cotton under the unusual conditions during the War of 1812 was even more than maintained.

Nothing has as yet been said about the influence, during this period, of general conditions in agriculture. This factor was not without importance in the wool-growing of the preceding period, and in later years it sometimes directed the whole course of the industry.

[1] See *Bulletin*, vol. xxxi, p. 205.

[2] These figures are from Hammond's *Cotton Industry*; see *ante*, p. 50, note.

Why, then, should it be neglected now? The truth is that the agricultural situation at this period happened to be such that it exercised almost no control over the course of wool-growing.

To understand the reason for this rather unusual state of affairs — for such in fact it was — we must remember the economic changes that had been wrought by the period of restricted commerce and the War of 1812. Before 1808 agriculture and foreign commerce were the chief economic activities of the country. Manufacturing hardly existed, and such goods as were not made by the household industries were imported from abroad and paid for by the exportation of food stuffs. After the war all this was changed. Agriculture and commerce were no longer the all-engrossing pursuits they had once been, and manufacturing began to receive more attention. Internal development and a national economy were the cry of the day, and the "American system" arose. Except for the two or three years preceding 1819, the foreign markets declined, and, in spite of the growth of the country, exports of food-stuffs fell off as compared with the years before 1805. In fact this was the time when the foreign commerce of the United States was relatively of less importance than at any other period of peace in the history of the country — a natural consequence of the movement towards economic independence and national self-sufficiency which characterizes this epoch in our economic development.

The years just preceding 1820 are the only years of this period in which we find any signs whatever that general agricultural conditions had an effect on wool-growing. In 1817 and 1818 the prices of flour and other food-stuffs had been unusually high, but in the two following years they underwent a precipitous decline. No doubt the high prices before 1819 induced some to turn away from wool-growing, but the industry was already so depressed that probably those who were willing to abandon it at all had previously done so. Then, when the crisis came, in 1819, wool was as much affected as anything else. Beneath these reasons, however, were more fundamental ones. In the first place, by far the greater part of the domestic wool supply was produced for the household industry. There the market fluctuations had comparatively little effect. Furthermore, the great wool-producing region was New England and the Middle Atlantic states. In New England, at least, there was little grain or meat produced except for the local markets, and the low prices consequently had slight influence. They were doubtless felt more in the Middle States, but even there the surplus produce was small. The region which really suffered most was the Ohio valley, where food-stuffs were virtually the sole resource, and distress was consequently greater.[1] This did lead a few farmers to turn toward sheep,[2] but there are no indications that the movement was at all noticeable. Nor was it likely to be, for there was no appreciable local market for wool. At this time wool-growers generally had not begun to ship wool to the East, and their market was strictly limited by the needs of each locality. Hence there was little inducement to turn to the growing of wool. After 1820 prices for agricultural produce were fairly normal, and under a continuance of the situation as regards agriculture which has just been described, where the economic organization was so largely local in scope, this factor left the course of wool-growing quite undisturbed.

Summary.

In looking back over the years between 1815 and 1830, we find that they mark a period when the wool-growing industry of the United States, quantitatively at least, made little advance. The number of sheep fluctuated somewhat from one series of years to another, but at the end of the period did not greatly exceed the number at the beginning. Similarly, the quality of the flocks changed little either for better or for worse. In the rage against merinos after 1815 the best flocks were saved, and where the general farmer merely neglected these sheep, they at least helped to improve the common stock. The actual loss at this time was in a measure offset by the importation of Saxony sheep before the period closed. From one point of view, however, the situation in 1830 was notably better than that in 1815. At the close of the war, the industry was in an overgrown and unhealthy condition; its basis was artificial and unstable. At the opening of the year 1830, on the other hand, this was no longer true. It had passed through many years of depression, and had finally emerged in a sound condition on a sure foundation. This was the greatest gain that the period brought.

[1] *Niles' Register*, vol. xx, p. 96.
[2] *Ibid.*, p. 86.

The factors which determined the course of the industry of wool-growing at this time are unusually simple and clearly defined. Complicating effects of the general conditions of agriculture are not observable. There was no new or unusual development in the competition of cotton. The tariff, in the final outcome of events, played but a minor part. The gain from the duty on the importation of foreign wool was largely nullified by the imports of foreign woolens, the protection against these proving of little avail under a combination of circumstances which tended to cast the burden of the duties on the foreign manufacturer. Throughout this period the disturbing influence was felt of the many difficulties of the British woolen manufacture. The inevitable reaction in America after the War of 1812 was combined with the heavy sale of English goods in this country. This was followed quickly by the domestic crisis of 1819–20. Recovery had hardly begun before there set in the unusually distressing period following the English crisis of 1825. All this proved doubly hard for the American wool-grower, because of its serious effects upon the manufacturer. In the general distress consequent on such fluctuations, whatever aid the tariff may have afforded at one period was forgotten in the greater losses resulting from its failure at other periods. The mainstay of the wool-grower during these years was the household industry.

CHAPTER IV

THE PERIOD OF THE EAST'S SUPREMACY, 1830–1840

BEGINNING with 1830 the wool-growing industry of the United States entered upon a new era. The country was prosperous, the woolen manufacture was well established, and the price of wool was high. The period between 1830 and 1840 brought to the eastern wool-grower the reward of his persistence, and saw the fruition of his hopes. These years mark the heyday of the fine-wooled sheep, and the height of the wool-growing industry in the East.

The Wool and Woolen Markets Abroad.

Since conditions in the foreign woolen trade played so important a part in the previous period, it will be desirable to note the change in the situation abroad at this time. As was to be expected, the rise in the price of wool in the United States but reflected the rise in the world's market. Quotations in London, it is true, did not advance so precipitately as in Boston and New York, but the upward movement which began in 1830 was continued up to 1837.[1] At the beginning of the period wool was scarce and the demand active, partly because of the preparations then being made in fear of an outbreak of war. A London letter of June, 1831, says, "This country has not been so bare of wool for thirty years as within six months past."[2] As the high price of wool would indicate, the manufacture was generally prosperous. "The years from 1830 to September, 1836," says James, "may be regarded as among the most prosperous periods in the history of the West Riding stuff trade."[3] The cloth manufacture also seems to have fared well. The export trade, as well as the home market demand, was strong, particularly that in stuffs. Between 1837 and 1840 there was some depression, the causes of which lay in the United States. During this decade, too, improvements were being made in the process of manufacture, such as the introduction of the Jacquard fancy loom and the use of cotton warp in worsted goods.

[1] See price tables in Appendix.

[2] *Niles' Register*, vol. xl, p. 421.

[3] *History of the Worsted Manufacture*, p. 450.

They, however, will be considered in connection with events of the next period, when their effects began to be generally felt.

In the wool trade, also, there now appeared the beginnings of a movement the results of which did not really become appreciable until after 1840. This was the rise of the Southern Hemisphere as an important contributor to the world's wool supply. It was in this decade that Argentina and other sub-tropical countries began to pay serious attention to the development of their resources for wool-growing. At the time, however, the only appreciable increase in the clip from any of these regions was in that from Australasia. Exports from there to Great Britain, virtually the whole production, rose from two million pounds in 1830 to ten million in 1840.[1] The bulk of Great Britain's wool supply at this time came from Germany, the highest point ever reached in the German imports — thirty-two million pounds — coming in 1836. Notwithstanding these advances, it was the failure of the world's wool supply to keep up with the rising demand of the manufacturers which caused the high prices of this period. These high prices, however, sowed the seed from which the next period reaped a most abundant harvest.

The Prosperous State of the American Wool Manufacturer.

It has generally been found true that whenever one of the protected industries of this country was in distress, it did not hesitate to let the fact be well known. Hence, if we can judge anything from absence of outcry and scarcity of information, this period was, upon the whole, one of prosperity for the American wool manufacture.

The industry began to revive in 1830. The question how much the tariff of 1828 had to do with this has already been discussed. Certain it is that the unusually heavy importation of goods in 1831 and 1832 had no visible ill effects upon the industry. The "Tariff of Abominations" was replaced by the Act of 1832, which went into effect March 3, 1833. Perhaps the chief benefit derived from this change was the removal of all duty upon wool costing eight cents a pound or less. That costing over eight cents paid a duty of four cents a pound and 40% ad valorem. In the case of manufactured goods, the whole system of minimums was done away with, ad valorem duties

[1] See *post*, p. 97. For a complete table of the imports into Great Britain at this time, see *Journal of the Royal Statistical Society*, vol. xxxiii, pp. 502–505.

being generally substituted. On most goods the rate was fixed at 50% ad valorem. Carpets and blankets, with some exceptions, came in at 25%, flannels at 16 cents a square yard, and worsted stuff goods at 10%. This act, however, remained in force less than a year, and was superseded on January 1, 1834, by the "Compromise Act" of 1833. This latter provided for a cutting down of all duties over 20%, one tenth of the excess to be taken off in each alternate year until December 31, 1841, when one half of the remainder was to be dropped, and six months later the other half. Aside from this, the only important change was the transfer of worsted stuff goods to the free list.

Under this act the importation of manufactures of wool made a decided advance: their average annual value for the years 1835–41 was over sixteen million dollars. But it is significant of the gain to the manufacturer under this tariff that whereas the imports of manufactures increased but 75%, the imports of raw wool increased 250%. Almost one half of the gain in the manufactures of wool came in the worsted stuff goods, now admitted free, and forming nearly one third of the total. The rest of the gain was in cloths and cassimeres and blankets. In the importation of flannels there was a marked falling off. Despite the declining rate of duties, there was no increase in the imports during the latter years of the operation of the act,[1] and there can be no doubt that it proved to be as favorable a tariff as the manufacturers had yet enjoyed.

Up to 1837 there seems to have been almost nothing but prosperity for the woolen manufacturer:[2] his only trouble was the high price of wool. The best general view that we have of the industry at this period is contained in a little book by Messrs. Benton and Barry describing it in 1836.[3] The table which follows is, for the New England states, so far as it is possible to judge, fairly accurate: for the rest of the country it is not much more than an estimate.

[1] Partly owing to the business depression then, and partly to the fact that the decrease in duties was not very marked till the very last.

[2] In 1834 some manufacturers were reported as selling their machinery (*Niles' Register*, vol. xlvi, p. 423), but the following year it was stated at a meeting in Worcester, Mass., that new machinery, capable of using two million pounds of wool annually, had been set up in that vicinity within a year (*ibid.*, vol. xlviii, p. 242).

[3] Benton and Barry, *A Statistical View of the Number of Sheep and an Account of the Principal Woolen Manufactories*, 1837.

Number of Sets of Machinery engaged on Each Fabric.[1]

	U.S.	*Me.*	*N.H.*	*Vt.*	*Mass.*	*R.I.*	*Conn.*	*N.Y.*	*Pa.*	*O.*
Broadcloths	344	3	—	37	150	4	17	100	19	6
Cassimeres	178	15	10	23	59	—	4	60	1	3
Satinets	574	5	19	37	195	16	93	100	58	5
Flannels	158	—	10	3	77	—	9	40	19	0
Linseys	210	—	—	—	18	60	15	51	21	16
Blankets, hats, and yarn	24	1	4	—	10	—	9	—	—	—
Carpets	61	—	—	—	10	—	37	—	6	—
Total	1549	24	43	100	519	80	184	351	123	30

It is interesting to note that by far the most important fabric of the industry at this time seems to have been the cheap cotton-warp satinet. The broadcloth probably used all the fine wool of the country, and it is safe to say that the satinets, cassimeres, linseys, and flannels were generally of a low grade, employing either the common wool of the country or the cheap imported fibre. One great difficulty in the way of using the cheap wool from the River Plate region had been the peculiarly obnoxious burr which was found in it. This difficulty was greatly lessened by the invention, about 1833, by M. H. Simpson, of Boston, of a burring machine for extracting these troublesome particles.[2] The tendency of the manufacture in this country, furthered by the tariff, was toward a greater use of these cheap wools. The total consumption of the woolen manufacture was estimated at:[3]—

Number of Sets of Machinery engaged on Each Fabric.

1400 sets using 22,000 pounds of common or fine wool each	30,800,000
150 sets using 50,000 pounds of coarse foreign wool each	7,500,000
Total consumption	38,300,000

Probably this figure was a trifle high, but it cannot have been much out of the way. Of the total, about ten million pounds was of foreign

[1] The figures for New York are estimates. The total for the United States includes, besides those given above, the estimated numbers in New Jersey, Delaware, Maryland, Virginia, and Kentucky. See *Statistical View*, p. 126.

[2] *Bulletin*, vol. ix, p. 44.

[3] Benton and Barry, *Statistical View*, p. 125. The first figure as there stated is called "within a fraction of 31,000,000."

origin. From this we are led to conclude that since just before 1830 the woolen manufacture had at least more than doubled. Nothing could better substantiate our conclusions as to the final establishment of the industry, after a long struggle, in 1830, and its thorough preparedness to advance the moment a favorable opportunity was given, than the rapid strides made in these few years.

Between 1837 and 1840 there was no progress, — possibly there was a retrograde movement. When the panic of 1837 broke over the country, the woolen manufacture suffered with everything else. In September, 1837, it was said that nine tenths of the factories of the country had closed.[1] In 1838 the outlook improved, but the business depression was long drawn out. In 1839 some woolen manufacturers were reported to be selling their machinery and turning to cotton,[2] and even in 1840 it was stated that half of the machinery in New England was idle.[3] In fact the country did not fully recover from the crisis of 1837 and the consequent trade upheavals until after 1841; hence the continuation of this depression in the woolen manufacture is not strange.[4]

As to the condition of the industry in 1840, at the end of the period under review, the Census of that year — the first which makes any pretense to completeness — gives little insight. There were then returned 2585 fulling mills, and 1420 woolen manufactories. The total product of these factories was valued at twenty million dollars. Probably the woolen manufacture was about where it had been just before the outbreak of the panic, but, even so, this would mark the decade as one of most satisfactory progress.

Part of this advance was at the expense of the household industry, for at this time we first see frequent signs of its approaching dissolution. The product of the household industry of New York state was: —

	Fulled cloth	*Flannel and cloth not fulled*
1835	2,183,951 yards	2,790,069 yards
1845	1,664,366 yards	2,650,115 yards

[1] *Niles' Register*, vol. liii, p. 34. [2] *New England Farmer*, vol. xvii, p. 397.

[3] *Niles' Register*, vol. lviii, p. 304.

[4] To attribute this depression wholly to the tariff of 1833, or to say that the tariff "virtually destroyed the woolen manufacture" (Stanwood, *American Tariff Controversies*, vol. ii, p. 33), is absolutely unwarrantable. The imports for 1840, 1841, and 1842 averaged much lower than during the preceding six years.

That the household manufactures were still of considerable importance is shown by the large number of fulling mills, as compared with the number of manufactories, returned by the Census. But general application of power in the processes of manufacture had now been made, and the first blow struck. Steps were already being taken to deal the death stroke by overcoming the inacessibility of the localities where the industry had its stronghold. The beginning of the end was in sight.

Wool-Growing at the Period of the East's Supremacy.

Among the various circumstances which conspired to mark this period as the one when the industry of wool-growing reached the zenith of its development in the East, we may first take up the nature and extent of the competition met with from abroad. The striking change here is in the character of the raw-wool imports under the tariff of 1833, which, it will be remembered, admitted free of duty wool valued at eight cents or less. As a result the imports of wool tripled in amount as compared with those of the preceding period, the average for the years 1835 to 1842 being 10,026,000 pounds; but their average value was cut in half, now being nine cents a pound. As this would indicate, most of the wool imported came in free, as valued at eight cents or under. The average amount so imported for the years 1835–41 was 9,103,000 pounds, while the average of imports with a higher value was 923,000 pounds, — about one tenth as much. The coarse wool came from South America — chiefly the River Plate region — and from Turkey and its Mediterranean dependencies. The better grades of wool came from Germany, Spain, Turkey, Great Britain, South America, and Australasia. For comparison with the foregoing tables the following is of interest: —

Average Annual Imports of Wool, 1835–1841.[1]

	Germany	*Spain*	*United Kingdom*	*Turkey & Levant*	*South America*
Thousands of pounds	113	127	770	2557	3429
Value, cents	40	17	19	7.7	6.4

[1] France sent annually 212,000 pounds valued at eight cents, Austria 220,000 pounds valued at twelve cents, and Italy 327,000 pounds valued at seven cents. Probably most of this was grown in Asia Minor or in northern Africa.

In the imports of free wool from South America and Australasia, we have the first signs of the wool-grower's future great rivals. At this time, however, they were puny enough. During these years, in spite of prosperity, the quantity of those raw-wool imports which directly competed with the domestic clip was as low as at any previous time since wool had been imported at all, and much lower than at any later date.

In addition to this, we find, on turning to a view of the imports of wool in the form of manufactured goods, that even here conditions were relatively less unfavorable than usual. The absolute quantity of competing wool imported in this form did increase somewhat: but owing to the greater share of the total made up by worsted stuff goods, not more than half of the whole quantity, or a smaller proportion than usual, consisted of the directly competing grades of wool. The amount was perhaps sixteen million pounds. Summing up the imports of both raw and manufactured competing wools, we find an absolute gain in their amount of from three to four million pounds. Relatively, however, in view of the favorable conditions and the high price of wool, this meant a gain for the American grower.

The prosperous days of the wool-grower which dawned in 1830 mark the height of the fine-wool industry in this country. The cause was the phenomenally high prices for fine wool which ruled from 1830 to 1837. Never since those years has anything like so high a level been reached.[1]

The first result was to revivify the craze for Saxony sheep, which, when it originally started, had been nipped in the bud. The merino was passed over entirely: only the Saxony would satisfy most of the owners of fine-wooled sheep. Just after 1825 Wells and Dickinson had added a band of Saxony sheep to their flocks at Steubenville. In September, 1830, these sheep were sold. The prices were low, eight of the best bucks averaging $22.50, yet a year earlier, we are told, it would have been impossible to dispose of them.[2] Their very cheapness gave everybody an opportunity to secure some of the much desired breed, and this band proved to be the origin of most of the fine-wooled flocks established in Ohio and neighboring states during

[1] In the speculation of 1872 it was attained for a few months, but the Civil War prices, when reduced to a gold basis, were not nearly so high.

[2] *Niles' Register*, vol. xxxix, p. 92.

the years immediately following. Many of the finest pure merino flocks in the country had Saxony blood introduced at this period. Only a few of the fine-wool growers, much to their later joy, held back. The movement was not so wild or unreasoning as the earlier craze for merinos, but, being one phase of the general speculation engendered by the prosperity of the period, it was widespread and went to the extreme. As Randall describes it, "bigger barns were built, and more costly preparations made for growing wool; and then farmers sent a hundred or a thousand miles to buy Saxony sheep at $100 or $500 a head. . . . The public was in the midst of a fine-wool cyclone." [1]

But the stimulus of high prices had its effect upon the common sheep of the country as well as on the fine-wooled stock. Sheep of any kind were welcomed by the farmer. Flocks increased everywhere, and under this advance the wool-growing industry of the East attained its maximum growth.

In New England, Vermont made the greatest progress. A report to the Legislature stated that between 1832 and 1837 there was a heavy decrease in cattle and increase in sheep, the latter amounting to a million.[2] The interest in sheep was intense, and in 1835 a society was formed at Montpelier to promote and improve sheep-breeding.[3] In the same year the raising of wool was reported as fast becoming the great business of the section around Claremont, New Hampshire, on the other side of the Connecticut River.[4] The editor of a Springfield (Massachusetts) paper of 1834 heard of such an unprecedented increase in the production of wool in the previous ten years — an increase which for the immediately preceding two or three years was estimated at 20% annually — as led him to conclude that inside of fifteen years wool would be as important an export as cotton.[5] In western Massachusetts, in 1835, wool-growing was considered one of the most lucrative pursuits the farmer could follow.[6] In New York there were reports in 1832 and 1834,[7] that some sheep were being sent to the boiling-down establishments, yet even this was ascribed to over speculation and too great haste in

[1] *Fine Wool Sheep Husbandry*, p. 56.
[2] *Hazard's Register*, vol. i, p. 48.
[3] *Niles' Register*, vol. xlvii, p. 410.
[4] *Ibid.*, vol. xlix, p. 220.
[5] *New England Farmer*, vol. xiii, p. 90.
[6] *Niles' Register*, vol. xlix, p. 68.
[7] *Ibid.*, vol. xl, p. 5. These establishments rendered the carcass into tallow, etc. Some boiling down of aged animals was inevitable. For additional information as to this process see footnote, *post*, p. 119.

increasing the flocks. In 1833 there came from one county of that state a story that the sheepwalks had absorbed the cow pastures so extensively as to raise the price of butter nearly 100%!

Most of the increase came before 1837. The crisis of that year brought a sudden drop in the price of wool, and in spite of a gain in 1838–39, it fell back again in 1840. Even then, however, prices were much better than before 1830, and the only result was to lower the rate of increase in the number of sheep. At the end of 1836 the number of sheep in the country was probably about sixteen or seventeen millions.[1] By 1840, according to the Census, it was 19,300,000. The total clip was then set at 36,000,000 pounds. This, however, is too low, — assuming the number of sheep to be correct; — for the average fleece was certainly over two pounds in weight, even when washed. A more probable figure for the total domestic wool supply would be between 45,000,000 and 50,000,000 pounds.[2]

In 1840 the New England and the Middle Atlantic states held nearly 60% of all the sheep in the country, about one third of these being in New England. In the South there were 4,500,000 sheep, two thirds of which were to be found in the states of Kentucky, Tennessee, and Virginia. In the Northwest there were 3,500,000, of which Ohio alone had 2,000,000; in fact, outside of Ohio, there were

[1] The estimate of Benton and Barry (*Statistical View*, p. 106) was about 13,000,000. In the states for which they aim to give more than an estimate the distribution was as follows: —

	Me.	*N.H.*	*Vt.*	*Mass.*	*R.I.*	*Conn.*	*N.Y.*	*Pa.*	*Ohio*
Thousands of sheep	622	465	1099	373	81	255	4299	1714	1711

The total included, besides the above, estimates for New Jersey, Delaware, Maryland, Virginia, and Kentucky. So far as those states are concerned for which the figures are intended to be more than estimates, it is believed that those given are reasonably correct. The deficiency would come in the regions for which there are estimates only, or no figures at all, mainly the latter.

[2] In the first place, there is every reason to believe that the total number of sheep returned by the Census is, if anything, rather low. The Census returns for the wool clip generally are admittedly too low (cf. note, p. 366). In 1836 Benton and Barry estimated the total clip at 42,000,000 pounds on the basis of 3¼ pounds a head. Though the result was not far wrong, the average weight per fleece was too high. The Massachusetts assessors' returns of 1837 found the average fleece to be 2⅞ pounds, but the flocks of that state were far above the general run, at least two thirds being of improved stock. For the country as a whole the average fleece seems to have been about 2½ pounds of back-washed wool, — if anything, less. At that time virtually all the wool was washed on the sheep before going to market.

comparatively few sheep kept in this section.[1] But the real importance and overwhelming predominance of the East in the industry of wool-growing is not fully understood unless we bear in mind that very little wool from either the West or the South ever reached the eastern market. Almost all the wool from the Ohio valley which went east at this period, passed over the Erie Canal.[2] For 1833 and 1834 the average amount that passed Utica on the canal was 1,125,949 pounds.[3] But nearly all of this came from New York state, for the amount cleared from the canal office at Buffalo, most of which came from the states farther west, was very slight, being as follows, in thousands of pounds:[4] —

1834	1836	1837	1838	1839	1840
186	252	39	108	131	170

Not until after 1840 did the product of the Ohio valley become of any importance in the wool markets of the East. During the period under consideration, virtually all the wool grown in the Western and the Southern states was consumed at home, either by the household industry or by such small woolen mills as were found in those regions. The woolen manufacture of the country, which was almost wholly located in the East, thus had to depend entirely upon the wool-grower of that region for its raw material or else go abroad.[5] It was therefore at this period that the wool-growing industry of the East attained its greatest growth, and reached the height of its prosperity.

The consumption of cotton in the United States during these years increased somewhat faster than during the period immediately preceding. Just before 1830 it averaged forty-three million pounds; by 1840 it had mounted to over one hundred million. The average price for the years 1830–1839 was 12½ cents per pound, a little higher

[1] Peck, describing this section about 1831, says: "Sheep do very well in this country, especially in the older settlements, where the grass has become short, and they are less molested by wolves. But few are kept. The people from the South are more accustomed to cotton for clothing than wool. . . . Common wool is worth thirty-seven and one half cents in the fleece. Little is said or done to improve the breed of sheep, or introduce the merino or saxony breed" (*Guide for Emigrants*, p. 173).

[2] For further details as to the conditions, see *post*, pp. 145–146.

[3] Pitkin, *Statistical View*, 1835, p. 579.

[4] *Niles' Register*, vol. lxix, p. 54.

[5] Of these states, New York was far in the lead as a source of supply, Vermont coming next.

than for the years 1827–29, but lower than the average for the whole of the preceding period. Since wool at this time was high, it is obvious that there was a great incentive to substitute cotton for the more expensive fibre. This tendency was further favored by the movement, then first assuming importance, to replace the household woolen industry by the woolen manufacture. Although cotton was used in the household product, yet, for many obvious reasons, it was much more likely to be used, in connection with wool, in the factory. The important part which cotton was beginning to play in the woolen manufacture is best shown by the overpowering position, among the fabrics then made, held by satinets. By this time the chief effects of the substitution of cotton goods for woolen fabrics, such as followed the introduction of the former into general use, had nearly passed away. From now on the most dangerous form of rivalry assumed by the cheaper cotton was its steadily increasing use in the woolen manufacture itself.

As to the effect of the general conditions of agriculture upon wool-growing during the decade under review, the situation remained much the same as during the period preceding. Up to 1835 the prices for agricultural products were about normal. In that year harvests failed, and again in 1837 and 1838. As a result, prices of all farm produce advanced, and from then till 1840 remained at an unusually high level.[1] The exportation of food-stuffs during this period, as compared with the previous one, remained stationary.[2] In short, between 1807 and 1840 this trade made no progress. The eastern states were now even less exclusively agricultural than formerly. Still, in Vermont and New York, the chief of those growing wool, agriculture continued all-important; and no doubt the slower increase of sheep after 1837 was partly due to the high prices of other farm products, which offered better inducements than wool. But there is no evidence that this was really a factor of any importance. It was the deficiency of the grain crops that caused the high prices, and sheep pastures in many cases were not very suitable for cultivation. Moreover, though the price of wool had fallen from its very high level, it was comparatively high even to 1840. In the West, where food-stuffs were the great staples, the high prices which they brought had more effect, and those who had an accessible market bent every effort toward

[1] For relative prices see table in the Appendix. [2] In fact wheat was imported.

them. Later this concentration of attention on food-stuffs had important results. At the time, however, the wool-growing industry of the region was of such a nature that it does not appear to have suffered. If affected at all, it merely advanced less rapidly.

Summary.

Looking back over the conditions in the years between 1830 and 1840, we can now understand why this period proved one of such growth and prosperity for the wool-growing industry of the United States. In the first place there was the prosperous condition of the woolen manufacture, which caused a favorable demand for wool. The number of disturbing events was very few. But to meet the increased demand no new region appeared with an extra supply. As a result the demand was concentrated upon regions already growing wool. Naturally they throve. But in the United States the main seat of the wool-growing industry was in the East: almost no wool was received from the West. Hence the increasing demand from the manufacturer was centred on the older states. Some of it was supplied by importation, though foreign lands failed to respond readily to the increasing need. To prove this we need but look at the comparatively high price of wool during the years between 1837 and 1841, in spite of the demoralized state of the woolen manufacture, and contrast it with the low price which afterwards ruled, when the manufacture was prospering, but when new sources of supply were pouring their wool upon the market. The key to the course of the wool-growing industry of the United States in the period of its maximum growth and prosperity in the East, is to be found in the favorable state of the manufacture, and the absence of serious competition in the supply of wool either from the Southern Hemisphere or from the West.

CHAPTER V

THE RISE OF THE MIDDLE WEST, 1840–1860

THE history of wool-growing in the United States in the period between 1840 and 1860 is, from the point of view of the economist, of unusual interest. There was then disclosed in a most striking manner the great diversity of the economic forces that bear upon this pursuit, and the many and varied effects of their intricate interaction. In the West was to be seen the change which took place in the character of agriculture when the pioneer farmer, in his westward progress, emerged from the wooded sections upon the open prairies; in the East was to be noticed the effect produced upon the agriculture of that region by the growth of manufactures, and the rise of an urban population. There were also to be traced at this time the changes wrought by an increased growth of wool in the Southern Hemisphere, the rising European demand for food-stuffs, improvements in the processes of manufacturing, and the introduction of new fabrics. Finally, of special prominence were the results of westward expansion, and the striding advances in the whole system of transportation both by water and by rail; for with these advances came the extinction of the self-sufficing frontier community and the rise of a better national and international economy. These events resulted, during the earlier years of the period, in transferring the main seat of the wool-growing industry from the East to the Middle West, and during the later years, in seriously threatening its future.

Before taking up separately some of the factors just enumerated, let us view the net result of their interaction during these years as reflected by the price of wool.[1] The crisis of 1837 was severe and far-reaching in its effects. The northeastern part of the country suffered less than most sections, but the rest of the country hardly recovered from the shock until after 1841. The price of wool, which had ranged very high between 1831 and 1836, fell sharply in 1837. With but slight interruptions in 1839 and 1841, this decline con-

[1] For tables of prices and chart see Appendix.

tinued until 1843, when Ohio fine washed wool was selling at 33 cents a pound. The price remained at this low level, except for temporary recoveries in 1844 and 1847, until 1849. Then began a rise which culminated in 1853, when the price of Ohio fine wool was double what it was in 1843. From 1853 till 1860 was a period of general prosperity and high prices. The crisis of 1857, though sharp, and for the moment very severe in the woolen manufacture, was short, and it affected industry in general much less than that of 1837. Under these favoring conditions the price of wool, until 1860, fluctuated at a high level, though not so high as between 1830 and 1837. In London the general trend of prices was much the same as in this country, though as usual with less extreme fluctuations.

The Foreign Wool Supply.

During these years the world's wool supply was increasing with great rapidity. Though the production of Great Britain, France, Germany, and other European countries was rising, it rose slowly, and most of the increase was due to the entrance of new producers upon the field. It was at this time that Argentina, Australasia, Cape Colony, and the East Indies first appeared as important contributors to the world's wool market. These years mark the real beginning of serious rivalry from the Southern Hemisphere.

In Argentina, the chief wool-producing country of South America, the oppression of Spanish rule, and, later, constant internal strife and dissension, had discouraged all efforts to improve the native criollo sheep, the degenerate descendants of early Spanish importations. Between 1825 and 1840 there was some improvement, and by the latter year wool had become a considerable item of export,[1] though "the majority of owners of sheep of the poorer sort still left them unshorn, and it was on to 1860 before shearing became an annual and general operation throughout the country."[2]

The first wool exported from Australia reached England in 1803. Sheep were earliest found in New South Wales, and were soon carried to Tasmania. In 1800 the total number in all Australasia was 6,124; in 1810, 25,888; in 1821, 209,158. The sheep men did not turn to Victoria till about 1825, or to Western Australia till

[1] Commissioner of Agriculture, *Report*, 1864, pp. 225, 226.

[2] Gibson, *History of the Sheep Breeding Industry in Argentine Republic*, pp. 26–30.

later; while in New Zealand, though sheep were introduced at an early date, they were not numerous till about 1850.[1] Advance in these colonies was so rapid that in the early '40's heavy losses were avoided only by the introduction of boiling-down establishments.[2] Even the gold discoveries of 1850 do not seem to have distracted much attention from wool-growing, for the exports continued to increase rapidly to the end of this period.[3]

The same interest in wool-growing which was awakening in Australia seems to have infected Great Britain's other possessions. Sheep had been numerous in Cape Colony as early as 1804, numbering half a million then, and over a million in 1811.[4] They were of the fat-tailed variety, merinos being scarce till about 1833. Not until the following year did the exports of wool from this colony rise above 100,000 pounds, but seven years later they had passed a million pounds, and the growth continued unabated. In India a somewhat similar type of sheep was found. There, until 1835, when the government took steps to improve the flocks, "the keeping of sheep with a view to exportation of the fleece was scarcely thought of."[5] The European trade in Indian wool dates from 1834.

Until between 1840 and 1850[6] Europe seems to have been able to meet her own wants as regards a supply of wool.[7] England, apparently, was the only country importing any large quantity of wool, and up to 1840 nearly all of her imports had come from either Spain or Germany. But in the period under review a complete reversal of conditions was taking place, for by 1850 only a small fraction of her imports came from the Continent. Germany, instead of exporting wool, now began to reach out for imports. Before 1840, exports of wool by the German Zollverein had always exceeded imports, yet this happened but twice after that year, and never after 1850. France, though never a great exporter of wool, also began about 1850 steadily to augment her imports.[8]

[1] Southey, *Colonial Sheep and Wools*, p. 225. [2] *Ibid.*, pp. 41-43.

[3] For a detailed account of conditions here and in the other British colonies up to 1850, and for tables of exports of wool, see *ibid.*, *passim*.

[4] *Ibid.*, p. 195. [5] *Ibid.*, p. 235.

[6] *Consular Report*, vol. xxxix, p. 395.

[7] No doubt some was received from Asia Minor and Northern Africa.

[8] For a complete account of this change, see Senkel, *Wollproduktion und Wollhandel im XIXten Jahrhundert.*

Until this date, except for the exports to the United States, most of the world's wool supply produced outside of Europe had found its way to the London wool market. Indeed, the importance of this market was largely due to the rapidly mounting supply of wool from the British Colonies, almost all of which at this time passed through the London auctions, which were held regularly from 1835 on. Thus some idea of the changes in the world's wool supply can be gained from the following table.

Imports of Wool into the United Kingdom.[1]

(*In thousands of pounds.*)

	Total	*Spain*	*Germany*	*Russia*	*River Plate*	*India*	*Cape Colony*	*Australasia*
1830	32,313	1,644	26,787	203	119		33	1,967
1840	49,448	1,267	21,837	4,519	617	2,441	752	9,721
1850	74,327	441	9,196	3,556	1,862	3,473	5,710	39,018
1860	145,502	1,000	9,954	8,730	2,875	20,214	16,574	59,166

Argentina was the only country producing any large quantity of wool for export most of whose product did not pass through English markets. A generous share of her output went directly to the United States.[2] It was to South America, too, that both France and Germany turned to meet their increasing needs, and they secured wool from this region direct long before they obtained it from the British Colonies in that way.

The best available estimate of the total wool supply of Europe and North America at this time is as follows, in millions of pounds.[3]

[1] *Journal of the Royal Statistical Society*, vol. xxxiii, pp. 502–505.

[2] Exports of wool from Buenos Ayres were as follows, in pounds:—

	To England	*To France*	*To the U. S.*
1843	1,418,125	3,966,625	3,763,872
1844	2,806,900	2,016,875	8,534,691
1845	3,240,300	2,331,225	10,820,900

(*Niles' Register*, vol. lxx, p. 3.)

[3] Helmuth Schwartze & Co., *Annual Wool Reports*. Cf. footnote to a similar table on page 164. The figures of wool in the grease for North America include 10,000,000 pounds for British North America. The original figures for North America, 90,000,000 and 110,000,000 pounds in 1850 and 1860 respectively, seem to me too high, and I have accordingly reduced them, cutting down the clean-wool figures in proportion.

Wool in the Grease.

	United Kingdom	Continent	North America	Australasia	Cape Colony	River Plate	Others	Total
1850	130	470	70	39	6	19	36	770
1860	140	500	90	60	26	43	76	935
				Clean Wool after Washing.				
1850	98	313	37	23	4	6	22	503
1860	105	333	48	35	14	14	50	599

This sudden appearance upon the world's market of large quantities of wool from the Southern Hemisphere was, of course, an important factor in determining the price of wool, and thus in influencing the conditions of the wool industry in America. What would have happened in the United States had this increase not taken place it is vain to speculate. The important point is to remember, when we come to view events in the United States at this time, what the conditions were in other parts of the wool-growing world.

The Tariff and Foreign Competition.

The more direct effect of foreign competition is seen in the kind and the quality of the wool imported, both in the raw state and in the form of manufactures. The duty on wool levied by the tariff of 1842 was on all wool valued at less than 8 cents, 5% ad valorem; on all valued at 8 cents or over, 3 cents a pound and 30% ad valorem. Nominally at least, this gave greater protection than the wool-grower had had under the last few years of the tariff of 1833. In point of fact, however, the act of 1842 was quite without effect. The imposition of the 5% duty on the cheap wool which had formerly been free was not sufficient to produce any appreciable result. The lowering, from 8 to 7 cents, of the limiting price for wool admitted free or at a low duty was offset by the low range of prices which prevailed during the continuance of this act. The duty on the higher grades of wool would have given better protection than was given by the previous act during the latter years of its existence, had such wool been imported. But the imports of fine wool under this act were practically nil — the annual average for the years 1844–46 was 261,000 pounds.

Nor was this situation due to the fact that the duty was prohibitive. The truth is, as will be seen later, that the United States was then actually exporting such wool. To be sure the quantity was small (though greater than the imports of that class of wool), and there proved to be little or no profit in the undertaking; but the significant point is that it was entered upon at all. There is, then, little reason to believe that, in practice, the tariff on fine wool afforded any real protection to the wool-grower. Nearly all the wool imported came in under the low duty, the yearly average for the years 1844–46 being 17,872,878 pounds,—a far greater amount than ever before. Much of this came from Turkey and other Mediterranean countries, but the largest share from any one region was sent by Argentina, a country which up to 1840 had never sent us over 2,500,000 pounds. With the duty on these heavy importations of cheap wool a purely nominal one, and that on the high-grade wools inoperative, it is difficult to see how the American wool-grower gained at all from the tariff of 1842.

When the tariff afforded no protection on the raw material, it is obvious that the amount of the duty on the manufactures of wool could make little difference to the grower. Still some knowledge as to whether the quantity of wool coming in in a manufactured state was great or small is desirable. For the years 1844–46 the average value of the annual imports of manufactures of wool was $12,703,059, a falling off of about one quarter as compared with imports under the former tariff. A part of this is to be accounted for by the lower prices that prevailed. A larger part was due to the heavier duties, and also to the greater actual protection given the manufacturer because of the comparative cheapness of domestic wool. On most woolen goods the duty levied by this act was 40% ad valorem; on worsted stuff goods, which had been admitted free by the Compromise Act, it was 30% ad valorem. By far the largest share of the falling off in the imports of manufactures of wool can be accounted for by the decline in the imports of worsted stuff goods, which for the years 1844–46 averaged $2,144,336 in value, or less than half of what they averaged under the previous tariff, when admitted free of duty. If we offset the increase in imports of raw wool against the decline in imports of manufactures of wool, we find that in a rough way they nearly balance one another. Hence we conclude that under the act of 1842 there was about the same amount of foreign wool consumed in the country as under the previous act, although the consumption of wool was steadily increasing.

This conclusion, however, does not hold true of the next tariff act, that of 1846. Under this all wool paid a duty of 30% ad valorem, a considerable increase for the low grades of wool but a decrease for the higher grades. Although the increase was placed just where it would be most effective, still the average imports under this act during the years 1848–57, 19,437,763 pounds, were somewhat greater than under the previous act. The average value was 11.3 cents per pound, and as the price of wool had risen, this valuation would indicate that the wool then coming in was, like that of the preceding years, of a very low grade. Over 10,000,000 pounds, or more than half of the annual imports, came from South America, and the average value of this wool was but 9.6 cents. A large proportion of the remainder came from Turkey or neighboring countries on the shores of the Mediterranean, and was likewise of low value.

Turning to the wool imported in the form of manufactured goods under the tariff of 1846, we find an unusual advance in quantity. In fact, the rate of increase, as compared with the imports under the previous tariff, was greater than in any case either before or since for which we have statistics. The average value of the imports of manufactures for the ten years 1848–57 was $26,612,642, an increase of over 100% as compared with the years 1844–46, and of 64% as compared with the years 1835–41, under the tariff of 1833. These years made up one of the most prosperous periods in the history of the country, and in manufactures, as in the case of raw wool, some allowance should be made for the higher prices which ruled after 1851. No doubt a part of the increase in imports was due to the lowering of the duty: on woolens it was reduced from 40% to 30% ad valorem, flannels and worsteds were admitted at 25%, and blankets at 20%. Probably, however, the manufacturer suffered less from imports of competing manufacturers than from the increase in the duty on his raw material.

If we now combine the greatly increased imports of wool in the form of manufactured goods and the slightly increased imports of raw wool, the total foots up to an annual average nearly twice that which prevailed under the tariff of 1842. Neither the population nor the domestic clip of wool was increasing at such a rate, and it is evident that in these years the American wool-grower was falling behind his rivals in the race for his home market.

To conclude the review of the tariffs of this period there remains but the Act of 1857. In this tariff there was a reduction of duties all along the line. The most important change was in putting all wool valued at 20 cents a pound or less upon the free list, wool worth more than 20 cents paying a duty of 24% ad valorem. Duties on woolens were reduced from 30% to 24% ad valorem, those on worsteds and flannels to 19%. Under these favoring conditions the foreigner made still further inroads on the market of the American wool-grower. The imports both of wool[1] and of manufactured goods during this brief time increased about one third. Of the raw wool imports something less than one half came from South America, and about two thirds of the remainder was fairly evenly distributed between Great Britain, Asia, and Africa. In the case of the imports from Great Britain it is impossible, of course, to tell the country of production. Nearly two million pounds of wool were annually being brought in from Canada at this time, free of duty under the reciprocity treaty of 1854. As in previous periods, the imports of fine wool of high value were insignificant, the annual average for the higher (dutiable) class for the years 1858–60 being 842,900 pounds, valued at 26 cents a pound. On the other hand, the imports of wool valued at 20 cents or less, and so admitted free of duty, averaged 28,964,297 pounds.[2] In nearly every class of manufactured goods imported there was an increase, but by far the greatest advance came in the worsted stuff goods, which in the years 1858–60 averaged $12,700,000 in value, and then for the first time surpassed in amount the cloths and cassimeres, thus topping the list of imported woolen manufactures.

We have somewhat rapidly reviewed the effects of the tariffs between 1840 and 1860 on the quantity of wool imported; it remains to say something further of the character of this wool. Warning

[1] The figures for the number of pounds of raw wool imported are estimates based on the value, and in the case of a small proportion are estimates of the amount imported from Canada on the pelt.

[2] This is obtained by deducting from the estimated total imports of wool the known amount valued at over 20 cents.

must be given, however, that as information on this point is scarce and uncertain, conclusions are inevitably of a somewhat vague and general character.

Turning first to the wool imported in a manufactured state, we find that under the tariff of 1842 about one half the value of imports under this head was made up by the two classes designated as "cloths and cassimeres" and "worsted stuff goods," the latter amounting to about one third of this half. The remaining half was largely made up by imports under the headings of carpets, blankets, hosiery, and shawls. Under the two following tariffs the proportion coming in under the headings "cloths and cassimeres" and "worsted stuff goods" was greater, making up about two thirds of the total. The value in each of these two classes was about the same. But under the tariff of 1857 the value of the "worsted stuff goods" had forged somewhat ahead of that of the imports of "cloths and cassimeres": the former class had increased 500% since 1844–46 (though scarcely 170% as compared with 1835–41), while the latter had only a little more than doubled, the two classes together then making up nearly four-fifths of all the imports. The remaining portion of the total imports of manufactures was made up of the miscellaneous classes, carpets, blankets, etc., previously mentioned.

Of the total supply of wool coming into the country in the form of finished goods we may say, with reasonable certitude, that the third (under the tariff of 1857, the half) which came in the form of worsted stuff goods did not seriously compete with the wool grown in this country. In 1840 there was practically no wool grown here suitable for such fabrics, and even in 1860, at the end of the period, the amount of combing wool of domestic production was estimated at only 3,000,000 pounds. As to the third (under the Act of 1857 it was higher) imported in the form of cloths and cassimeres, it is more difficult to determine because of the variations in the quality of these goods. Under this head the broadcloths came in and, it is safe to say, virtually all the imports of goods requiring the finer grades of wool. At this period the manufacturers of the country, as we shall soon see, were devoting more and more of their attention to the coarser grades of all goods. The production of broadcloth nearly disappeared, and the output of cassimeres was mostly of the inferior sorts; so that the demand for the best quality of goods (such as it was, since this, also, was decreasing) had to be met by bringing in supplies from abroad. No doubt much of the wool imported under this head was a finer grade than any grown here in an appreciable quantity. On the other hand much of it must have been similar to that clipped from the better flocks of the United States, and there can be no doubt that the importation of wool in the form of cloths and cassimeres meant serious competition for the domestic growers of fine wool. As to the remaining third of the imports of manufactured goods, mostly made up of blankets, carpets, hosiery, and shawls, it is still more difficult to decide. Probably, however, except in the case of the coarse wool in the blankets and carpets, most of this represents wool that did compete with one or another grade of the native product. Thus of the total imports of wool in the form of manufactured goods it is probable that from one half to two thirds entered into fairly direct competition with the domestic clip.

In the case of the imports of raw wool our information is a little more definite, but by no means so complete as could be desired. As pointed out, there was little or no fine wool imported in the raw state at this time. During the first part of the period the country produced a sufficient supply of the medium fine grades to meet the needs of the manufacturers, and during the later years the manufacturers called for less and less of these grades. Up to 1857 at least, — after that the value is uncertain but apparently higher, — virtually all the imports of raw wool were valued at from six to twelve cents a pound; whereas throughout the period the price of Ohio coarse washed wool was never below twenty-two cents and was usually above thirty cents, and in one year only did the price of common washed wool fall below twenty cents in the New York market. Yet to infer from this difference in price that these imports were of a grade very inferior to the domestic product, and hence that they did not compete with the latter, would be a mistake. A portion of these imports were low in price because they really were of inferior quality. Such, for instance, seems to have been the case with much of the wool that came from Turkey, the Levant, and the East Indies. It had a very coarse fibre with a fairly long staple, and was used mainly for carpets, "negro cloths," and the lowest grades of blankets. This made up from one quarter to two fifths of the imports, and was unlike any wool grown in the United States.

On the other hand, in the case of another important share of the imports, the price was low as compared with that of American wool, not so much because of the inferior quality of the wool as on account of the inferior condition in which it came to market. This applies to a great part of the wool from Argentina, which came to occupy such an important position among our imports during these years. Not so strong, though perhaps of the same fineness and length of staple, as the lower and medium grades of American wool, it still sold considerably below the latter because it was so full of dirt, burrs, and other foreign matter that in washing and cleansing it lost about two thirds of its weight, whereas the common wool of the United States, it was said, lost only a little more than one third. The result is illustrated by the following contemporary statement: "I was shown imported wool last year [costing under seven cents], by a manufacturer, which cost him in the condition it then was, 13 cents a pound. Yet it was equal in appearance to American wool worth 35 cents per pound. Owing to the shrinkage of this wool, however, it took three pounds of it to make one pound when it was worked into cloth, which, therefore, was equivalent to 39 or 40 cents per pound. American wool worth 35 cents per pound will shrink about one third in its preparation for cloth, and therefore cost when in cloth about 43-44 cents a pound."[?] "It is therefore apparent that this filthy foreign wool, last year, had a material influence in ruling the market price of American wool of medium quality."[1] Another writer says:[2] "The native wool of Buenos Ayres in the fibre is much like our common wool, perhaps not quite so soft. It is generally dirty and burry, and wastes 40–50% in washing and 10–15% in burring. It is generally used for all purposes where our common and coarse wool would be used. . . . The fine wool (of Buenos Ayres) wastes 60–70 pounds per hundred in washing and burring, and comes to the cards 15 cents a pound cheaper than our own wools of the same grade. . . . The present tariff of

[1] J. B. Nott, in *Transactions of the New York Agricultural Society*, 1846, vol. vi, p. 257. See also a similar statement, by Horace Everett, M. C. from Vermont, in the *American Agriculturist*, January, 1843, vol. i, p. 300.

[2] H. C. Merriam, in the *Albany Cultivator*; quoted in the *Prairie Farmer*, January, 1851, vol. xi, pp. 13, 14. This article gives an excellent statement of the character of the various wools then imported.

30% on their wool amounts to 2 cents a pound, and about 15% on its value (all expenses being paid), compared with that of our domestic wool. . . . The conclusion to which I have arrived is that all wools grown in the United States are depressed in the market 6–10 cents a pound by the present importation of foreign *rival* wools, principally grown in eastern South America." It is thus evident that this new source of wool supplies was a powerful competitor.

It must not be thought that all the wool from South America, or even from Argentina, competed with our own clip. Most of the wool from Chili and the western coast of South America, as well as some of that from the River Plate region, was coarse and harsh. The better grade, called mestiza wool, came from the cross of the merino and the native sheep, and was the result of vigorous efforts, which began about 1835, to improve the flocks of the country. Mestiza wool, like much of that from the River Plate, was full of a peculiarly obnoxious burr, which greatly reduced its value. This fact, together with the opportunity for mixing such wool with the cheaper wool of the region, to secure a low average value, made it possible to import it free of duty under the tariff of 1833. Apparently also the same method was used to bring it in under the 5% ad valorem duty of the following tariff, in spite of provisions intended to prevent it.[1]

It is thus evident that the effect of the duties on wool in the tariff of 1846 was to give a greater protection than at first might appear — perhaps from 5 to 6 cents a pound. This would seem to explain one reason why the imports of wool from South America remained so nearly stationary under this act. In the Act of 1857 one of the main objects of the manufacturers in fixing the maximum value of wool admitted free at 20 cents, was to let in this wool, particularly the mestiza, without duty. It was upon the latter that the manufacture of fancy cassimeres was founded,[2] and some indication

[1] "The duty [of the Act of 1842] is evaded both by importing fine wool with coarse, and unwashed with washed; and though provisos appear to be inserted with express reference to such frauds, yet the practice of the custom houses, under the instructions of the Treasury Department, affords not the least check" (*Hunt's Merchants' Magazine*, vol. xiv, pp. 244, 245). See also *Report* of the Secretary of the Treasury, 1845, pp. 285, 319, 320.

[2] J. L. Hayes, *Bulletin*, vol. xiii, p. 97.

of its usefulness to the manufacturer is seen in the rapid increase in the quantity imported under this act.[1]

After deducting from the imports of raw wool those from South America and the Mediterranean, the amount remaining to be accounted for is but slight. The imports from Canada were used in worsteds, and did not compete with much of the native product. The wool coming from the middle and northern parts of the Continent of Europe was generally of a medium or fine grade, and did compete with the American clip, but was insignificant in amount. Wool was not imported from Australia direct at this time, and how much came from there indirectly it is impossible to say; but the quantity must have been small, for Australian wool then too nearly resembled that already most abundant in this country. The case of the wool from Cape Colony was somewhat similar to that of the wool from Argentina. At first this wool had been very coarse and harsh, — most of it of "no value except to masons," says one.[2] Later it greatly improved, and under the Act of 1857 considerable quantities of a fair grade were imported, undoubtedly competing in the market with the medium and lower grades of the domestic clip.

We are now in a position to summarize the results of the tariffs during this period from 1840 to 1860, and to view the extent of the foreign competition encountered under these acts by the grower of wool, so far as that is indicated by the importation of wool, either raw or in a manufactured state. In the first place we are struck with the overwhelming predominance of the competition coming in the disguised form of imports of manufactures of wool, perhaps from two to four times that met with from the imports of the raw

[1] *Hunt's Merchants' Magazine* (vol. xliii, p. 345) quotes the following from a circular of G. W. Bond & Co.

Imports of Raw Wool into Boston (thousands of pounds).

	Carpet	*Common*	*Fine*
1854	9149	2635	1609
1855	5775	1207	264
1856	6656	835	931
1857	9281	4443	4217
1858	6291	1369	2890
1859	7724	2597	6856

[2] H. C. Merriam. See reference on page 104.

product.[1] The importance of this form of competition was probably seldom realized by the growers themselves. It is also a point of interest that the importation of manufactures of wool either lost, or made the slowest gains, under the tariffs of 1842 and 1857, when virtually all the raw wool was coming in free of duty. This raises the very tempting but hopelessly complicated question whether, in fact, the wool-grower gained more from the prosperity of the manufacturer under free wool, with the resulting increase in demand for the native product to mix with the foreign varieties, or from the duty on wool, under which the manufacturer suffered and the imports of goods increased. There is further to be noted that the wool imported in manufactured form competed mainly with the better grades of the domestic product. The directly competing raw wool imports, on the other hand, came into rivalry with the lower grades. This difference in competition, it should be remembered, first made its appearance within this period, and gained in strength throughout these years. Finally, and most important of all, we find that the domestic wool-grower was falling behind in the race with the rest of the world for his home market. From 1840 to 1860 the domestic clip increased but 68%,[2] and two thirds of this gain occurred before 1850. The increase in imports of all forms of competing wool was over 100%, and of all kinds of wool still greater. Between 1840 and 1850 the

[1] If we assume, as above, that from one half to two thirds, say seven twelfths, of the imports of wool in the form of manufactured goods, and one third to one half, say five twelfths, of the imports of raw wool, competed directly with the domestic clip, we have the following table: —

	Average annual imports of directly competing raw wool.	*Average annual imports of directly competing wool in the form of manufactures if $1.00 in value = 3 lbs.*	*Average annual imports of directly competing wool in the form of manufactures if $1.00 in value = 2 lbs.*
	millions of lbs.	millions of lbs.	millions of lbs.
1835–41	4	29	19
1844–46	8	22	15
1848–57	8	47	31
1858–60	12	64	42

Based as they are on such broad generalizations, these figures are only suggestive. The general conclusion arrived at, however, is believed to be beyond reasonable doubt. The estimate of 2 lbs. of wool to 1 dollar in value was, at this time, probably the more accurate. For the years 1835–41 the above proportions exaggerate the imports of competing wool. See page 88.

[2] Census figures.

domestic producer more than held his own, but the last decade of the period shows his foreign rivals fast supplanting him in his own market. By 1860, in fact, as will later appear, the proportion of foreign wool in the total consumption of the country—60 to 66⅔% —was decidedly greater than in any of the years immediately preceding, and very much greater than at any time thereafter.[1]

The State of the Wool Manufacture.

The necessity of surveying the state of the wool manufacture before being able to understand the conditions confronting the grower of wool is well illustrated in the years under review. The period was marked by a far-reaching change in this manufacture, the final effects of which are still being felt. It was, says one,[2] "an epoch in the cloth industry of the world and of the century." This change was the decline in popular favor of the broadcloth, and the usurpation of its position by the coarser worsteds and the more showy products of the fancy power-loom.

The immediate cause for this turn of affairs was to be found in the new inventions and improved methods of manufacture which came into use at this time. In France, in 1834, the Jacquard loom was introduced to manufacture the fabric called fancy cassimere. In this country, in 1840, a similar result was secured when Wm. Crompton, at the Middlesex Mills, in Lowell, turned out the first fancy woolens ever woven by power.[3] The loom used in these mills was rapidly introduced elsewhere, and proved especially useful in the manufacture of fancy cassimeres, which at once sprang into great favor. Between 1850 and 1860 styles ran to extremes, and these goods were in such vogue that at the end of the period there appears to have been more machinery engaged upon this fabric than on any other made in the country. It was made in varying grades from fine to coarse, but even the best did not call for such fine wool as had been used in the better broadcloth. Soundness, length, and strength of fibre were the qualities now sought instead of softness and fineness, which had been necessary when broadcloths were in demand. The effect of this on the grower of fine wool is easily seen.

[1] See table on page 225.

[2] J. H. Hayes, "Report on the Centennial Exhibit," in *Bulletin*, vol. vii, p. 109.

[3] Mudge, *Report on Wool and Manufactures of Wool*, 1887, p. xliii.

Another change was taking place at this time, the results of which were somewhat similar. This was the rapid advance of the worsted industry. In Great Britain this branch had been making greater progress than the cloth manufacture ever since the first of the century.[1] But from 1837 its growth was especially stimulated, first by the invention of processes leading to the introduction of cotton warp into worsted stuff goods, and a little later by the great improvements made in the machinery for combing wool.

About 1840 Bischoff [2] declared that "none of the combing machines yet invented are very perfect, and the finest wools are combed by hand." The Platt and Collyer machine, patented in 1827, was the one most used at the time. About 1843 Lister, in connection with Donisthorpe, succeeded in being the first to comb fine wool by machinery. Both Holden and Noble added improvements, and by the latter years of this period the hand-comber had disappeared.[3]

But the greatest change, the one most seriously affecting the grower of wool, was that wrought by the introduction of the cotton warp in 1837. Although some cotton had been used at an earlier date, in goods like Orleans cloths, not till that year were cotton warps used to any extent in worsteds.[4] It had been found difficult to dye the two fibres together, and also to secure the kind of warp needed. Writing in about 1847, Southey says, "Wool and cotton have been successfully mixed in the last few years, and have added a new feature and fresh importance to the woolen trade. Cotton now constitutes a very principal part in the manufactures in which formerly wool only was used," and he further adds that this has "created quite a new era in the stuff trade."[5] James declares that "the introduction of cotton warps in the weaving of worsted stuffs is incalculable in its importance. It gave a new character to the industry.

[1] The extent of the change is indicated by the following table of the export of cloths and stuffs from Great Britain in different years: —

	1816	1826	1840	1842
Cloths, pieces	636,368	384,508	215,746	161,675
Stuffs, pieces	593,308	1,138,588	1,718,617	1,979,492

(McCulloch, *Dictionary of Commerce*, 1856, p. 1429.)

[2] Bischoff, *History of the Wool and Woolen Manufactures in Great Britain*, vol. ii, p. 403.

[3] For a detailed account of this, see Burnley's *History of Wool and Wool-Combing*.

[4] James, *History of the Worsted Manufacture in Great Britain*, p. 473.

[5] Southey, *Colonial Sheep and Wools*, pp. 8, 14.

. . . The trade now assumed a new and broader aspect, and showed a power of adaptation for all classes of goods, and a capability of expansion, which, a few years previous, could not have been conceived." [1] The first product of this change was the fabric called mousseline de laine.[2] Cotton warp was also introduced into the mohair goods then coming into the market and very popular in the '50s. Many other new fabrics followed, generally characterized by less weight and durability than broadcloth, though more delicate, showy, and attractive — qualities which exactly met the growing taste of the time. The introduction of these fabrics struck another serious blow at the manufacture of broadcloth.

In the United States the results of this change were felt in the rapid increase in the importation of worsted goods rather than in any great development of that branch of manufacturing. In fact, the worsted industry did not exist in this country before 1840, and it never rose to any importance till after the Civil War. That this situation was generally recognized is to be seen in the lower tariff duties, or, as in the Act of 1833, the absence of any duty, on worsted goods. The primary reason for this was that the wool grown in the United States was not of the sort suitable for worsteds, which required, at that time, a comparatively long and coarse fibre of good strength. The wool clipped from our domestic flocks was too short in staple, besides being finer than that generally used for the purpose. About 1840 more long-wooled sheep were being raised in the eastern states, and the wool of these sheep, with such imports as were necessary, plus the aid of improved combing-machinery, enabled the country to make a start in manufacturing this line of goods.

What is reported to be the first worsted yarn spun since colonial days[3] was made in 1842. Worsted delaines soon followed, and in 1844 Samuel Lawrence said that several hundred looms were engaged on this fabric, and more were being erected.[4] The delaines first received attention here because they were made from the finest grade of combing wool. The high duty of the tariff of 1846 cut off the supply of coarser grades until 1854, when the Canadian re-

[1] James, *History of the Worsted Manufacture in Great Britain*, p. 471.

[2] As at first made in France, this cloth had been all wool, but in England and the United States it usually had a cotton warp.

[3] S. N. D. North in Davis's *New England States*, vol. i, p. 239.

[4] *New England Farmer*, vol. xxii, p. 257.

ciprocity treaty admitted Canadian wool (which was mostly combing wool) free of duty. This gave the worsted manufacture a new impulse,[1] yet even in 1860 the Census returns showed but three establishments, using in all only 3,000,000 pounds of wool. The increasing demand for these fabrics was almost entirely supplied by Great Britain.

We are now in a position to understand the course of the broadcloth manufacture during this period. In 1840 it was one of the most important branches of our wool manufacture; in 1860 it had very nearly disappeared. "In 1837," says one, "when our woolen manufacture was in its infancy, 344 sets of cards were at work on broadcloth alone, . . . yet to-day (December, 1856) there are not forty sets of cards at work on broadcloths in the United States — in fact this branch of industry is nearly blotted out."[2] This writer, like everybody else, put the whole responsibility for the loss upon the tariff of 1846. "When that tariff [1846] went into operation," says another, "there were 1800 looms, chiefly in New England, weaving broadcloth. Within a few years every one of them had stopped, or had been diverted to the production of an inferior grade of goods."[3] That the broadcloth industry did improve during the years when the tariff of 1842 was in force is generally acknowledged. But it should be remembered that at that time business was reviving from the prolonged depression following the crisis of 1837, and some improvement was to be expected in any case. Still, an important share in this prosperity must be credited to the tariff. Under it the importation of cloths was less than during the preceding years, and this in spite of the greater prosperity. The tariff raised the duty on cloths, and a combination of events minimized the disadvantage caused by the duty on raw wool. The schedules of the Act of 1846 were undoubtedly less beneficial to the broadcloth manufacture, and because of this some decline was to be expected. And yet, under the Act, there was no great increase in the imports of that class of goods until at least 1853. They rose somewhat, but no higher than during the operation of the Act of 1833, under which this branch

[1] J. L. Hayes, *Bulletin*, vol. ix, p. 180.

[2] The New York correspondent of the London *Daily News;* quoted in Tooke's *History of Prices*, vol. v, p. 664.

[3] Stanwood, *American Tariff Controversies*, vol. ii, p. 92. See also *Report* of the Ohio Board of Agriculture, 1862, p. 509.

of manufacture had easily survived. If, then, the broadcloth manufacture disappeared at this time, it would seem that its disappearance could not have been entirely owing to the competition of foreign broadcloth admitted under the tariff of 1846. There must have been some other more powerful force at work.

This conclusion is strengthened by our knowledge that a force calculated to do this very thing did exist. It was found in the competition of the new fabrics then coming into favor — in the growth of the manufacture of fancy cassimeres and delaines in this country, and of the worsted stuff goods abroad. The broadcloth manufacture of England was suffering from the same cause, and exports of English cloths were declining. There is, then, every reason to believe that this, and not the tariff of 1846, was the main reason for the falling off of the broadcloth industry in this country. No doubt the tariff alone would have caused some decline, but the almost total eclipse of this branch of the woolen manufacture was due in the main to the rivalry of these new fabrics.

Besides the changes in the more important branches of the woolen manufacture, there were also some developments in the minor branches of the industry which deserve mention. Most prominent among these is the growth of carpet manufacture. Here again Yankee ingenuity was the cause, this time taking the form of the first power-loom successfully used for the weaving of ingrain carpets, — the invention of E. B. Bigelow, in 1823. This was followed, in 1848, by the application of the power-loom to the weaving of Brussels carpets. The carpet manufacturers were somewhat hampered by the lack of a domestic supply of their raw material, yet they persevered, and by 1860 were using some 9,000,000 pounds of wool. In this period, too, the knit-goods manufacture attained its first growth. Knitting by power had been accomplished in 1832, yet in 1841 the whole product was estimated at but $41,000 in value. A circular knitting machine invented in 1851, and other improvements, gave further aid, and between 1850 and 1860 the value of the product of this branch of the manufacture increased from $1,000,000 to $7,000,000.

In the household manufacture of wool, this period witnesses only a rapid dissolution. Whatever may have been its extent in 1840, there can be no doubt of its virtual disappearance by 1860. In that year the total amount of wool passing through the simple carding establishments of the country was 5,000,000 pounds.[1] Three fifths of this was used in the North-West, and most of the remainder in the South. In the state of New York the number of yards of woolen cloth and flannel made in the family declined from 4,314,000 in 1845 to 578,000 in 1855.[2] In Ohio "from this time [1840] forth the carding machines and fulling mills which depended on custom work rapidly declined, and in 1850 scarcely a single one could be found that did custom work."[3] The household industry faded away before the spreading system of transportation, the consequent widening of the manufacturer's market, and the growing national economy.

The decline of the household manufacture was followed, particularly in the West, where the wool supply was rapidly increasing in the '40's, by the rise of a large number of small factories.[4] Here we see the industry in its process of evolution from a household basis to a town or small community basis. The introduction of the carding and fulling mills was the first step in the woolen industry away from the self-sufficing economy of the household. Then came the gradual addition of other machinery and processes, till finally the completed woolen mill or factory emerged. This was a small concern, the number of sets of condensing cards per factory in 1845 averaging about one and three quarters,[5] and few of the establishments supplied more than a local market.

[1] *Eighth United States Census.* [2] *New York State Census.*

[3] *Report* of the Ohio State Board of Agriculture, 1862, p. 503.

[4] In 1844 *Niles' Register* reports five woolen factories erected in Michigan during the past year, and an equal number going into operation in Maine (vol. lxvi, pp. 16, 256). The *Prairie Farmer* mentions several that were starting in Illinois at this time (vol. v, p. 156; vol. vii, p. 327).

[5] [Graham,] *Statistics of the Woolen Manufactories in the United States*, 1845. If Massachusetts, where the sets of cards averaged nearly four per factory, be omitted, the average for the country would be almost exactly one and one half per factory. Graham's list shows the following situation: —

	Me.	N.H.	Vt.	Mass.	R.I.	Conn.	N.Y.	N.J.	Pa.	Del.	Md.	Va.	Ky.	O.	Ind.
Sets of cards	42	81	113	483	80	220	470	19	147	12	27	24	12	98	6
No. of establishments	26	58	76	140	40	120	326	10	102	4	16	18	9	79	6

Other states, for which the number of sets of condensing cards is not given, had the following number of mills: Michigan 6, Illinois 6, Wisconsin 7, Missouri 3, Iowa 2, Tennessee 2, South Carolina 1, North Carolina 4, Georgia 3. Doubtless this enumeration is not complete, especially in the South and the West, but it gives a reasonably accurate conception of the general situation.

The woolen mill, together with the grist mill, the lumber mill, and the various establishments of similar mill type, all supplying simply a local market or a small community, were a part of that town economy which appeared in this country in the East and the Middle West for a brief period in its industrial history; in the South, the scattered population, the absence of towns, and the dominance of the plantation gave the household or plantation economy a much longer life. In many older countries, this town economy had existed in fully developed form for centuries. In this country, in the sections where it can really be said to have developed at all, its existence was timed rather by decades. In the New England and Middle States, phases of it appeared in the eighteenth century. In the Middle West, increasing settlement and the building of roads enabled it to supplant the household industry during the second quarter of the nineteenth century, but by the time of the Civil War it in turn was rapidly giving way before the improvements in the means of transportation (especially the railroads) which were expanding the markets to a more nearly national scope and ushering in a more extensive division of labor. In the sections of the West where the railroads preceded general settlement, affording egress for the staple products of the region to the outside markets and, at the same time, ingress for the products of other sections, town economy formed a scarcely perceptible stage in the industrial evolution.

On the whole these two decades appear to have been a fairly prosperous period for the wool manufactures. The waning of the household industry increased the market for them, and the favorable conditions that existed under the tariff of 1842 greatly encouraged the manufacturers.[1] The heavy duty on wool levied by the tariff of 1846 was undoubtedly a handicap. Yet we find Samuel Lawrence writing in February, 1847, "The business of manufacturing wool in this country is on a better basis than ever before, inasmuch as the character, skill, and capital engaged in it are such that foreign competition is defied. A few years and all articles of wool used here will be of home manufacture."[2] Nevertheless, the

[1] An account of the condition of a number of woolen manufacturing establishments, giving unmistakable evidence of prosperity at this time, is to be found in the appendix to Walker's *Finance Report* for 1845.

[2] Randall, *Sheep Husbandry*, p. 125.

industry did not progress so rapidly in the decade following 1850 as in the preceding one. Though the tariff of 1857 was favorable, the panic of that year bore severely on some of the mills, and there remained but little time to advance before 1860. For the period as a whole, however, the Census returns show steady progress.

Statistics of Manufactures of Wool in the United States.

	Capital	*Value of product*	*Wool consumed in condition purchased*
1840	$15,000,000	$20,000,000	
1850	32,000,000	49,000,000	70,000,000 lbs.
1860	42,000,000	80,000,000	98,000,000 lbs.

The amount of wool and cotton consumed in the various branches in 1860 was as follows in millions of pounds:[1] —

	Woolens	*Worsteds*	*Carpets*	*Hosiery*
Wool	86.3	3.0	8.8	2.9
Cotton	15.2	1.6	0.4	3.9

We thus find that even at this early date over one fifth of the raw material used in the woolen manufacture was cotton. Still during these years the competition of cotton was not so severely felt as before 1840, and its consumption does not seem to have gained much as compared with that of wool.[2]

Even more light as to the kinds of fabrics made at the close of this period and the relative importance of each is given in a table compiled by George W. Bond, showing the number of sets of machinery in the mills of New England and New York engaged upon each kind

[1] *Eighth United States Census.*

[2] The best available estimates of the total consumption of these two fibres in the United States for these years are: —

	Wool	*Cotton*
1840	76,000,000 lbs.	113,000,000 lbs.
1850	129,000,000 lbs.	263,000,000 lbs.
1860	213,000,000 lbs.	470,000,000 lbs.

The figures for cotton are from Hammond's *Cotton Industry*, those for wool are from the United States *Census* and include the amount imported in the form of manufactures. This item is not included in the figures for cotton. Here there was a relative gain for cotton — the imported cotton manufactures being valued at $6,000,000 in 1840, $20,000,000 in 1850, and $33,000,000 in 1860 — but the absolute amount is small.

of product.[1] Out of a total of 2537 sets for which he has returns, 677 were engaged on cassimeres, 410 on blankets and flannels, 374 on satinets, 161 on stock of yarn and hosiery, 151 on delaines, 134 on carpets, 113 on cloths with cotton warps, and the remainder on miscellaneous goods.[2]

It is now clear that the whole tendency of the woolen manufacture in this country from 1840 to 1860 was away from fine wool and towards the medium and coarser grades. Broadcloth had disappeared, and cassimeres, using a coarser wool, had taken its place. The output of satinets continued important, but that used a low grade of wool; the manufacture of blankets and flannels was advancing, but this used a medium grade of wool; and the new and popular delaines also required a wool of only medium fineness. The fibre used for hosiery was not fine, and that used for carpets was very coarse.[3] There was no longer any demand in this country

[1] For the complete table by states see *Boston Board of Trade Report*, 1860, p. 141. Graham also tells what kind of products each establishment was then turning out. Kerseymeres and satinets were by far the most important (see *Statistics of the Woolen Manufactories in the United States*, 1845).

[2] Broadcloths, it will be noticed, were not of sufficient importance to receive separate mention. This table should be compared with a similar one of Benton and Barry's for the year 1836 (*supra*, p. 85), but it should be borne in mind that theirs was supposed to cover the whole country. Another suggestive comparison is found in the following figures of the woolen manufactures of Massachusetts, by far the most important woolen manufacturing state, in 1845 and 1855:—

	1845	1855
Broadcloth	1,022,000 yds.	760,000 yds.
Cassimere	2,451,000 yds.	6,445,000 yds.
Satinet	3,559,000 yds.	6,736,000 yds.
Kentucky jeans	1,652,000 yds.	1,949,000 yds.
Flannels and blanketing	4,491,000 yds.	10,279,000 yds.
Not specified	702,000 yds.	

(Massachusetts State *Census*, 1845 and 1855.)

[3] The different grades of American wool, their relative value, and the kind of goods into which each entered, are well illustrated by the sorting in the wool depot at Kinderhook, N. Y., in 1847. No. 5, the coarsest, was used for making coarse satinets, baizes, and the coarser kinds of heavy goods, and was valued at 29 cents; No. 4, used for low flannels, satinets, and three quarters cloths, 32 cents; No. 4, delaine, used for medium kinds of worsted goods, 33 cents; No. 3, used for flannels, medium cassimeres, and satinets, and low-priced broadcloths, 35 cents; No. 3, delaine, used for mousseline-de-laines and other combing purposes, 30 cents; No. 2, 41 cents; No. 1, 44 cents; Prime 1, 46 cents; Extra, 52–65 cents. These high grades were used for

for the finest grades of wool. On the other hand, nearly all the fabrics manufactured were of a kind for which the domestic wool was well suited. The bulk of this wool was of middling length and good strength, neither very coarse nor very fine. And such wool the country was economically best fitted to produce. Here, at least, the course of events, from the point of view of the average wool-grower, was favorable.

The Growing of Wool.

The East.

Having reviewed the influences affecting the demand for wool and the extent of the foreign supply, we may now follow the course of the industry of wool-growing in this country. The pursuit had at this period become widespread, and as it was found in sections whose economic conditions were so varied as to produce very different results, it will be necessary to consider these sections separately.

In New England and the Middle Atlantic states after 1840, the industry of wool-growing, which until then had been mostly confined to this region, began to decline. This marks the turning point in the course of the pursuit in the East. Never thereafter did it recover the position it had then attained.

Number of Sheep in the East[1] *(in thousands).*

	Vermont	*Mass.*	*New York*	*New Eng.*	*Middle Atl.*
1840	1681	378	5118	3820	7403
1845		354	6443		
1850	1041	188	3453	2257	5641
1855		145	3217		
1860	752	114	2617	1779	4559

Vermont was then the great wool-growing state in New England, and had the finest flocks in the country. Addison County, near the

the finer qualities of cassimeres and broadcloths. The difference between No. 3 and No. 4 and the delaine qualities of the same numbers lay in the length and strength of staple, and not in the quality of the fibre. See *Transactions of the New York State Agricultural Society*, vol. vii, p. 540.

[1] The figures for 1845 and 1855 are from New York and Massachusetts State Censuses; others are from the United States Census.

middle of the western boundary of the state, was the renowned centre of the industry, though the neighboring county of Windsor also held some noted flocks. In 1840 the former county had more sheep in proportion to its area than any other county in the country, and the same was true of Vermont among the states. In this state were to be found the famous flocks of Hall, Robinson, Rich, Cutting, the Binghams, and, above all, the Hammonds.[1] Edwin Hammond was acknowledged as the leading American breeder of merinos. His sheep came from the Connecticut flock of Atwood, and Atwood's were descendants of Humphreys' early importations. It was sheep from Hammond's flock which, in competition with merinos from all over the world, won the highest award at the Hamburg Exhibition in 1861, and thus gave Vermont sheep a fame which survives to this day. Since it happened that during this period the Vermont or American merino, as it was called, was increasing in popular favor and taking the place of the Saxony, the Vermont breeders found that their sheep paid fairly well, more particularly after 1850. But their prosperity was due to the demand from the western sections of the country, where sheep were on the increase.

The breeders of stock sheep, however, formed[2] only a small part of the total number of sheep-owners, and others in the East, who kept sheep to grow wool, were having a different experience, and were consequently decreasing their flocks. The more rapid decline in the number of sheep in this region does not appear to have set in until 1845, but between that year and 1850 the fall was precipitous. About the latter date a well-known breeder in Vermont declared that within four years the number of sheep in the state had declined two thirds.[3] Just before 1850 high-grade merinos were selling at $.75 to $1.50, and even full-blooded merinos at $6 to $10.[4] In 1848 much wool was left on the hands of the growers, many of whom were disposing of their sheep for what the pelts and tallow would bring.[5] In New York, owing to continued growth in the western part of the state, the number of sheep actually increased

[1] For a detailed account of these see *Sheep Industry*, pp. 290–302.

[2] See Randall's *Fine Wool Sheep Husbandry*, p. 79.

[3] *The Boston Cultivator;* quoted in the *Prairie Farmer*, vol. x, p. 262. This is obviously an exaggeration, but it gives the contemporary impression.

[4] *Sheep Industry*, p. 320.

[5] *Transactions of the New York State Agricultural Society*, vol. viii, p. 381.

up to 1845. But it is significant that in both New York and Massachusetts, the only states for which we have figures in 1845, the flocks were diminished about a half between then and 1850. In Pennsylvania there was an increase between 1840 and 1850, but this took place in the trans-Alleghany region. The business of reducing sheep to tallow became important at this time, for many owners found that slaughtering their sheep for the pelt, carcass, and tallow offered better returns than growing wool.[1] Although conditions were somewhat more favorable when the price of wool began to rise in the '50's, yet in the eastern states it was the breeder of sheep rather than the grower of wool who gained by it. Maine was the only state to show an increase, and that only a paltry 1000. The falling off was much less rapid than during the five years preceding, but it was steady and general. So in 1860 we leave the wool-growing industry of the East in a state of decline.

Along with this decline there went another change, already foreshadowed, — a change in the character of the wool. The Saxony sheep with its superfine wool was forced to give way to the American or Vermont merino with its fleece of only medium fineness. Sheep of the latter breed, descended from Spanish merinos, were a little

[1] See the *American Agriculturist*, vol. iv, p. 212. In Buffalo the practice of boiling down sheep had existed at least as early as 1831 (see *Niles' Register*, vol. xl, p. 25). In 1847 it was a new industry in Chicago. $1.19 a head was there paid for a flock of 600 for this purpose (see *Prairie Farmer*, vol. vii, p. 334). This process had previously furnished an opportunity for the farmer to dispose of his aged sheep, but in the '40's it was evidently often reverted to as a means of getting out of the sheep business altogether without a total loss. Southey (*Colonial Sheep and Wools*, p. 314) quotes the following passage from a letter written by an American: "When wool and mutton are reduced to a low rate the inferior classes are slaughtered by thousands; the whole carcass except the legs, which are made into hams, is boiled down for tallow, and the residue thrown to the dogs or converted into pork. The latter assertion you may take to be a truly Yankee notion or an Irish bull, but it is, nevertheless, a practical fact." The relatively greater importance of tallow as a product of the sheep during these earlier years should not be overlooked. The following comparison of the situation in this country and in England is of interest in this connection. "In England the mutton sells for less than 12 cents a lb. while the best refined tallow is worth but 7 cents and wool 24 cents; hence there the farmer will keep the breed of sheep yielding the most mutton of a superior quality with the least consumption of food, while tallow and wool-making qualities will be minor considerations. In this country the case is reversed; wool of the same quality is worth more than in England, while tallow is usually worth twice as much as mutton" (*Genesee Farmer*, vol. xiii, p. 176). Cf. *infra*, p. 125.

larger in body than Saxony sheep, and their wool was of a somewhat longer staple, though still fine. Their fleece was at least a pound and a half heavier; besides, they were of a much stronger constitution, and thus required less care.

A controversy in regard to the relative merits of the merino and the Saxony broke out with vigor about 1835, and for the next decade the agricultural papers were full of it. Estimates of the cost of growing wool by each breed appeared in all sorts of guises, but it seems doubtful whether any satisfactory estimate could have been obtained. The conditions were so varied, the management so unequal, the items of cost so extremely difficult to determine, as the industry was then pursued, that however accurate the figures for one farm or locality, they could be of no value for another.[1] To judge of the relative profits of the two breeds is not quite so difficult. A very suggestive comparison of the most important item is made by Randall,[2] who points out that the Saxony sheep paid best between 1831 and 1837. After 1837 the price of Saxony wool seldom exceeded that of merino by more than five to eight cents. If the Saxony fleeece weighed three pounds and the merino four and a half pounds, then the former was worth $2.10 and the latter $2.70. Whatever the actual figures may have been, evidently the farmer was convinced that they favored the merino. Some, like William Jarvis, abandoned the Saxony even before 1835, others waited till after 1837, and the wholesale rout did not occur until after 1845. This is well indicated by the following table[3] of different breeds in Massachusetts.

[1] It is this belief which has led the writer to abandon the attempt to base any important conclusions on such data. The mere fact that wool was a by-product of the sheep, and the sheep (at the period here considered) a by-product of general farming, is sufficient to indicate the hopelessly complicated nature of the problem. Added to this difficulty is the almost total absence of any attempt at careful cost accounting — or even any accounting — among the farming class. These facts must be borne in mind, for they were not without their influence on the course of the industry in that they gave freer play to habit and inertia than would have been the case had a strict system of accouting been customary.

[2] See *Fine Wool Sheep Husbandry*, p. 92. The course of the average farmer is much more likely to have been determined by some such simple calculation, based on this all-important item, than on a more elaborate and detailed estimate. For several articles on the relative merits of Spanish and Saxony merinos, see *Genesee Farmer*, vol. viii.

[3] *Statistical Tables of Branches of Industry in Massachusetts*, 1837, 1845, 1855.

Number of Thousand Sheep.

	Saxony	*Merino*	*Other breeds*	*Total*
1837	47	200	127	374
1845	34	165	156	355
1855	7	66	73	146

Ohio was the only western state in which there was any amount of Saxony blood, and there it was not abandoned quite so early as in Massachusetts. Western Pennsylvania, particularly Washington County, proved to be the stronghold of this breed, but even there its popularity suffered. Thus ended the craze for the fine-wooled Saxony. As Randall remarks, "the fine-wool grower of this country seems ever to have fed on expectation, but never to have gained the fruition of his hopes."

The main cause of the downfall of Saxony sheep was the greater relative decline in the price of fine wool as compared with coarse, due, as has been foreshadowed, to the decline in the broadcloth industry and the increasing demand for fabrics of a coarser quality. In this change in relative prices the Saxony wool lost, as did even the merino, when compared with the common wool of the country. The change took place in the years between 1836 and 1844. This is interestingly brought out in the table[1] showing the index numbers for the price of common and merino wool from 1825 to 1860. In every year until 1836 the index number for merino wool is above that for common wool, and in every year after 1844 the situation is exactly reversed. The intervening years mark the turning point. The farmers did not seem to realize at first the nature of the change taking place. Agricultural papers were full of complaints that the buyers would not discriminate sufficiently in price between fine and coarse wool, or that they would not give a "just price" or "true value" for the former. This was one of the causes which led to the demand for wool depots. It was thought, no doubt with reason, that if a farmer could send his wool to such a depot and there have it sorted, he could get more for his fine wool; but it seems that he neglected this possible opportunity to gain as soon as the quotations for wool rose somewhat.[2] Yet the price of fine wool never fully recovered its former position.

[1] For table see Appendix.

[2] An actual case is cited where there were two clips from the same flock, cleansed

The change in the price of Saxony wool was certainly the chief and immediate cause of the disfavor into which sheep of that breed fell. But some farmers had never regarded them with favor, and still others had abandoned them even before their fleece had fallen in value and the general craze had subsided. The breed was hardly suited to the conditions which beset the average New England agriculturist. As compared with sheep of other breeds the Saxony required a great deal of attention and labor, and labor was scarce with the farmer. Then too, their offspring were not nearly so numerous as those of the coarser-wooled breeds, and lambs formed no small item in the profits. That Saxony sheep did not require so much to eat as the larger animals was a point in their favor, but this was offset by their lighter fleece. Finally, when the demand for mutton increased, as it did at this time, the small size of the Saxony and the poor quality of its meat became further objections. When to all these difficulties was added the decline in the price of fine wool, we find the reasons for the abandonment of this breed quite adequate.

Contemporaneous with the abandonment of Saxony sheep and the decline in wool-growing in the East, there appeared a complementary movement — that towards raising mutton. As wool, and in particular fine wool, became less and less an object in the keeping

by the same manufacturer, sold at the same time, and in all respects alike save that one had been sorted and the other had not, but the former sold for 10 cents a pound more than the latter (see *Transactions of the New York Agricultural Society* (1846), vol. vi, p. 260). It seems that in regions where there was little fine wool, and where, consequently, the fine-wool buyers did not go, there was not so much more allowed for fine wool above coarse as in other localities (see *ibid.*, vol. vii, p. 539). There was some agitation in New England in the '30's for more information and a better method by which the farmers could sell their wool. Fairs were then suggested (see *Niles' Register*, vol. xlviii, p. 137; *The New England Farmer*, vol. xiii, pp. 180 and 243). The first wool depot was not established till 1845, during the period of low prices. This was located at Kinderhook, N. Y. Wool was sorted into five qualities and sold, all charges being covered by a commission of one cent a pound and the insurance of one fourth of one per cent for three months. An advance on the value of the wool at seven per cent interest was made when desired. Soon afterwards a depot was opened at Buffalo, and in 1851 one in Chicago. In 1853 this was discontinued, owing to the high price of wool and the consequent difficulty in inducing farmers to send their wool to the depot. For further details see *The Prairie Farmer*, vol. vi, p. 378; vol. xii, pp. 149–153; vol. xiii, p. 205. *Transactions New York State Agricultural Society*, vol. vi, pp. 256–260, 265, 272, 273; vol. vii, pp. 538, 539, 553.

of sheep, mutton, and, incidentally, coarse wool, grew in importance. The movement towards mutton sheep found its initiative in the reaction against the merino after the War of 1812. At that time, however, little progress was made, and except in the immediate vicinity of Boston, New York, and Philadelphia, the mutton breeds were lost track of in the craze for the Saxony which followed the year 1828. But in the '40's, when fine-wooled sheep were discarded and the whole industry was sore pressed, those who still stuck by the sheep discovered in mutton an opportunity to make their flocks more profitable.

It was, of course, in regions nearest the markets of the large cities that mutton sheep received most attention.[1] Thus on Long Island or in the River counties of New York the English mutton breeds were preferred, whereas in western New York or Pennsylvania and in most parts of Vermont the merinos were more profitable.[2] In 1843 it was reported that on Long Island, during the few years previous, merinos were being crossed with English sheep, mutton being more of an object than wool.[3] In 1844 a visitor at Daniel Webster's farm in Marshfield found a flock of from 60 to 100 Southdown and Leicester sheep.[4] This tendency was more marked a little later. In 1850 sheep were kept in Rhode Island for lambs rather than wool.[5] A similar report came from Orange County, New York,[6] and it was said that even from Maine 17,000 sheep found a good market in Massachusetts that year.[7] In 1853 mutton had become a common article of transport from Maine to the Brighton market near Boston.[8] In 1854 word came from Oneida County in the centre of New York, that fine-wooled sheep could not be kept simply for wool, but that the mutton breeds must be resorted to.[9] Thus we see that the area which held mutton rather than wool as its object was rapidly spreading.

[1] In Massachusetts the growing importance of the mutton sheep is shown by the relative increase in the number of sheep under the heading "Other breeds" in the table on page 121, *supra*. Most of these were mutton sheep.

[2] See *Transactions New York Agricultural Society*, vol. iv, p. 257.

[3] *American Agriculturist*, vol. ii, p. 195.

[4] *New England Farmer*, vol. xxii, pp. 242, 243.

[5] Patent Office, *Report on Agriculture*, 1850, p. 477.

[6] *Ibid.*, p. 405.

[7] *Ibid.*, p. 425.

[8] Commissioner of Agriculture, *Report*, 1853, p. 40.

[9] *Ibid.*, 1854, p. 54. See also *Agriculture of Massachusetts*, 1853, p. 89; 1854, p. 360.

For raising mutton and lamb English breeds were the favorites, notably the Southdown, Cotswold, and Leicester. Their meat was of an excellent quality, and they were of good size, particularly the last two. Their wool was comparatively coarse, and in the case of the Cotswold and Leicester very long.[1] It was used for worsteds.

The demand for mutton sheep brought attention to another breed also — the Rambouillet, or French merino. Like the Saxony, these sheep were descended from flocks sent from Spain in the latter part of the eighteenth century. They had been bred with care on the stock farm of the French Government at Rambouillet, where they had developed a larger body than the Spanish or the Vermont merino, and a little coarser wool, yet neither so coarse nor so long as that of the English breeds, and particularly well suited for making delaines. A few of these sheep were imported into Connecticut between 1842 and 1846,[2] most of them eventually finding their way to the farm of the Bingham Brothers in Vermont.[3] These men had by far the best flock in the country, and the demand was such that between September, 1853, and May, 1854, they sold $43,000 worth of their stock, averaging $175 a head.[4] Most of their sales were shipped to western states. The French merino flocks, however, did not become very common at that time, and the farmer who had mutton in view turned to the English sheep.

The causes which led to this resort to mutton sheep were varied and numerous. They may be summed up under three heads: the relative gain in the price of coarse wool such as was grown on these sheep when compared with fine wool, the increasing demand for

[1] "Wool is a drug, and many, unwisely as we think, are slaughtering their sheep. The high price of mutton is drawing the attention of farmers to those breeds of sheep which mature early and afford mutton rather than wool. No one can question that the Leicester or South Down sheep or any of the breeds of long or middle wool sheep will fat easier and produce more, not to say better, mutton *for the food consumed* than the merino or other fine-wooled breeds. Mutton is in demand, but wool can scarcely be given away." *Genesee Farmer*, vol. xviii, p. 374 (Dec., 1857). For examples of the general discussion of "mutton versus wool" cf. *ibid.*, vols. xix, xx, *passim*. For full descriptions of the different breeds see Youatt's *The Sheep*.

[2] *Sheep Industry*, p. 276.

[3] For some account of this flock by A. L. Bingham, see *Genesee Farmer*, vol. xi, p. 182. For an estimate of its value by George Campbell, cf. *ibid.*, vol. xiii, p. 247. The paper remarks on "the considerable attention given to the subject of wool-growing of late" [1852].

[4] Swift, *History of Middlebury, and Addison Co.*, p. 104.

lamb and mutton, and finally the necessity then before the eastern wool-grower of finding some additional source of profit in his sheep. The first of these has already been dealt with, the second has not.

For some reason the meat of sheep had never been very popular in this country. No doubt this was in part due to the fact that the breed of sheep commonly kept did not give the best mutton. But there further appears to have been a sort of prejudice against mutton among the common people of the country. One person, writing in 1829, says, "The value of sheep is much lessened in our country, as compared with many others, because of the low estimation in which mutton is held by many of the laboring people — happily, in general, being able to make a choice of food, and prejudiced against 'sheep's meat.' For though it is found on the tables of the most wealthy, and by many such preferred — there is a notion that it 'looks poor' to purchase it, because it is the chief animal food of the poor in certain European countries."[1] Farmers generally ate pork, and beef being relatively plentiful, those who could afford a little more, ate that.[2]

At this period, however, mutton seems to have been rising in popular favor, aided no doubt by the improved quality of the meat breeds.[3] Further, beef and pork were in greater demand for export, especially after 1846. This fact, and the necessity of supplying the rapidly increasing non-agricultural element in the population, naturally directed more attention to the hitherto neglected mutton. It is not easy to obtain continuous market quotations for mutton in the period from 1840 to 1860, though there is no difficulty whatever as regards pork or beef. Thus under the heading "Sheep's Meat" in the table of index numbers of the Aldrich Report we find but two quotations between 1840 and 1851. The following are all the index numbers there given, the price for 1860 being 100.[4]

[1] *Niles' Register*, vol. xxxv, p. 401. Welby, traveling in this country in 1820, notes that "Americans little esteem" mutton. (*Visit to North America*, Thwaites' edition, p. 320). This helps to explain why "tallow is usually worth twice as much as mutton" (see *supra*, page 119, note).

[2] In the West, beef and pork sold at about the same price.

[3] "There has been a steady gradual increase in the demand for mutton and in a much greater ratio than the increase of population" (*Agriculture of Massachusetts*, 1860, p. 96).

[4] *Aldrich Report*, part i, p. 107.

1843	1846	1851	1852	1853	1854	1855	1859	1860
40	46	90	80	100	120	120	66	100

This indicates that the price of mutton in the decade between 1850 and 1860 was more than double that which prevailed between 1840 and 1850. The same conclusion is obtained from a somewhat fuller table also found in this Report.[1] This latter table gives six quotations for "good to choice sheep's meat, live weight" for four of the years between 1840 and 1850, the yearly average being $1.31 per head; while the twenty-eight quotations for the ten years 1851 to 1860 give an annual average of $2.89.[2] The impetus given to the production of mutton by this phenomenal and sustained advance needs no further comment.

The reasons which led the wool-grower to seek an additional source of income from his sheep were in many respects similar to those which led to the general decline of his industry, and as such will soon be taken up. For the moment they may be stated as the increasing cost of growing wool, and, between 1840 and 1850, at least, the low price obtained for this product. Had the advance in

[1] *Aldrich Report*, part ii, p. 31.

[2] See table in Appendix. Complete quotations might of course be found, but the omissions here, where full quotations are given for beef and pork, are certainly suggestive of the slight market for sheep's meat. That the sudden rise in the price of mutton in this period was a distinct and separate movement, and not due simply to the general rise in prices during the '50's, is borne out by the following table: —

		Average price decade ending 1830	*Average price decade ending* 1860	*Percentage increase*
Beef	per lb.	$.076	$.126	65.8
Ham	"	.095	.125	31.6
Lamb	" "	.059	.123	108.5
Mutton	" "	.064	.118	84.4
Pork	" "	.088	.114	29.5
Sausage	" "	.144	.115	0.9
Veal	" "	.075	.130	73.3

(Massachusetts Bureau of Labor, *Report*, 1885, Report on Wages and Prices 1752–1860, p. 195.) For a more complete table of prices, 1790–1860, *cf. ibid.*, p. 187. The prices for lamb and mutton as there given are as follows: —

For decade ending	1790	1800	1810	1820	1830	1840	1850	1860
Lamb (cents per pound)		7.2	7.2	6.9	5.9	7.6	7.8	12.3
Mutton " " "	4.3	5.6	7.4	6.9	6.4	6.9	7.8	11.8

It is interesting to note the relative prices of pork, beef, and mutton at this period.

the price of mutton come a little sooner, doubtless it would have at least postponed the extinction of many flocks. The conditions which tended to favor mutton sheep were well summed up by the report of a special committee in Massachusetts in 1860.[1] Therein were named as causes of the decline in fine-wool growing: the fluctuation in the price of fine wool, which in twenty years had sold anywhere from 54 to 28 cents; the uncertainty in disposing of the clip; the disproportionately increased expenses, trouble, and loss in a large flock of fine-wooled sheep over a smaller and more profitable flock of mutton sheep; the ready sale and quick return from mutton and lamb; the destruction of sheep by dogs; and the impossibility of competing with the sheepwalks of the West, the South, and Australia. With all these conditions hostile to fine-wooled sheep, it is easy to understand why the sheep-owner of the East who did not give up his flocks altogether, turned to the mutton breeds, whose product, both in flesh and in fleece, was so favored by the events of this period.

Several of these reasons help to explain the decline in the wool-growing industry in this region as a whole, and lead us directly to that subject. In the first place new competitors had appeared upon the field, and the price of wool was low. These competitors were to be found in the Southern Hemisphere and in our own West. Although the foreign wool consumed in the country did not increase till after 1846, it had its influence in lowering the price; and, in any case, as will later be seen, the supply of western wool reaching the East rapidly increased after 1840. The distressing thing to the eastern wool-grower was that these new competitors, seeming not to mind the low price, continued to increase their output. Apparently they could undersell him.

The actual cost of growing wool in the eastern states is hard to determine. The growers generally estimated it at from 25 to 40 cents a pound. Randall,[2] who was the authority of the time on growing wool, said that where the fleece did not exceed three pounds, $27\frac{29}{75}$ cents a pound was the lowest for which it could be produced in New York. The annual cost of keeping sheep was generally put at $1.10 to $1.50 a head. These figures were unquestionably much too high

[1] *Agriculture of Massachusetts*, 1860, p. 94.
[2] *Sheep Husbandry*, p. 58; see also p. 54.

for the new wool-growing sections. Certainly many conditions in the East were unfavorable as compared with these other regions. Thus, in states like Vermont and New York, it was necessary to provide shelter and fodder for the sheep for about five months of the year — an expense which was either very slight or non-existent in the newer wool-growing parts. Then, land in the East was becoming more and more valuable, — in 1859 the sheep lands there averaged $30 an acre in value,[1] — whereas in the West the public lands usually furnished free pasturage, and even if land were bought the cost was much less. Dogs, also, increased as the population of the East advanced, and their inroads among the flocks caused serious loss. Few could afford to keep a shepherd to guard their small band of sheep, and although dog laws were passed in most states, yet they seldom enabled the farmer entirely to recoup himself for the damage which he suffered from this source.

On the other hand there were some advantages possessed by the wool-grower of this region. The cost of transporting his wool to market was less, though at best this gain was slight, for the freight charge from the West or from Argentina was but two or three cents a pound.[2] His nearness to the market for lamb and mutton was a decided gain. In balancing these advantages and disadvantages against one another, the farmer of the East found, however, that the latter outweighed the former. Thus we must conclude that, in the period of low wool prices during the decade 1840–50, the competition from abroad and from the West led the eastern grower of wool to reduce his flocks.

But if this was the only reason, why was it that, when the price of wool rose after 1850 and remained at a level not far below that which prevailed when the flocks were being rapidly increased, there was not only no sign of even a slight addition to the number of sheep in this region, but a continued and steady decline? To be sure the value of land was presumably a little higher than at this earlier period, and the price of wool not quite so high, but these considerations were more than offset by the rise in the value of mutton. If, then, the flocks of this region continued to diminish after 1850, it is

[1] *Sheep Husbandry*, pp. 305–308. This would be a rather high average in a state like Maine or Vermont.

[2] See *The American Agriculturist*, vol. x, p. 97.

obvious that it must have been for some other reason than the competition of wool-growers from the West or abroad.

To understand what this other reason was we must remember the economic basis upon which the industry was then carried on. In the eastern states the growing of wool never was a distinct and separate occupation carried on for itself alone, as it is, for instance, in the Far West, in Australia, and in Argentina to-day: it had always been simply one side of the industry of general farming. Here the ordinary farming had from the beginning been of a general character and diversified. There never was a period of what could fairly be called one-crop farming, such as appeared in the West at a later date. The chief reason was that when the farms of this region were opened there was little or no market for their produce. They were of necessity largely self-sufficing, and hence their agriculture was diversified. Later, when markets were opened, the fertility of their fields had been impaired, and where any crop was cultivated, diversified farming was necessary. In the West, at least after about 1855, the farms had from the beginning a market for their staple product, and as long as the fertility of the soil remained unimpaired they could be devoted almost exclusively to one crop.[1] Under these conditions the importance of the share held by wool in the farm economy of the East varied greatly from time to time: at one period it was wholly incidental, at another it brought in a generous proportion of the farmer's income. At any time its relative importance was determined by two considerations, — the profits in growing wool and the profits in other products of the farm. Hence there were two main reasons either of which might cause a decline in the growing of wool, — a decrease in the returns from sheep, or an increase in the returns from some other farm product.

It is this latter reason which seems to explain the course of the industry of wool-growing in the East during the decade following 1850. The continued decline of the flocks, in the face of conditions

[1] See the account of "The One Crop Period," in Hibbard's *History of Agriculture in Dane County, Wisconsin.* The date at which the one-crop system developed in any locality depended largely on the period when an adequate market and transportation facilities became available there. It was not until after 1855, when the railroads crossed the Mississippi and began to extend ahead of settlement, that this system was general. Previously it was only possible for those so located as to have easy access to river or canal transportation.

which seemed to offer the former rate of profit, is to be accounted for by the increasing return from other products of the farm. The chief of these were dairy products. About 1847, just when the price of wool was low, there began a slight rise in the price of dairy produce, particularly butter. After 1850 this was very marked, and although wool was also advancing, the rise in the price of butter was relatively greater.[1] The extension of the railway system during these years also told in favor of the dairy as compared with the fleece, for dairy produce was not so well adapted to transportation as wool, being less valuable in proportion to weight, besides requiring greater care in carriage. The farmer was thus enabled to meet the needs of the growing urban population as well as the rising demand for export, this being still further facilitated by the introduction of the factory system of cheese-making early in the '50's.[2]

Reports from the farming districts at this time were full of remarks on this change.[3] In 1848 an agriculturist in Vermont wrote that the products of the dairy were increasing in the same ratio that wool was decreasing, in consequence of the low price of the latter and the enhanced value of the former caused by the foreign demand.[4] In that same year word came from New York state that the wool-growers there were turning to the dairy.[5] From eastern Pennsylvania came the report that sheep as a permanent stock had disap-

[1] See table of relative prices and chart in Appendix.

[2] George Geddes, writing of central and western New York, says: "When a country is first settled, the farmers will all try to raise grain; and, generally, they follow crop after crop, until the land is exhausted, and no longer yields remunerating returns. Flocks of sheep come next; and, if the land is really adapted to wheat raising, it is generally restored. But there is in fact but little wheat land in proportion to the whole quantity. Farmers who settled land having but little lime in it, and that was far from any market, thus, for a period, devoted it to sheep raising, looking for the sales from the wool to compensate them. As the price of wool declined these lands declined in selling value. The finding of a foreign market for our cheese, that has continued and grown, in our peaceful relations with Great Britain, made it possible to use these lands, that would not produce remunerating crops of wheat but did produce excellent grasses, for pasture and hay. This fact once understood, whole towns and counties sold their sheep and bought cows — and they did wisely, and are now reaping their reward. . . . Dairying profitably employs each member of the family" (*Bulletin*, vol. vii, p. 52).

[3] The reports on Agriculture issued during these years by the Patent Office and the Department of Agriculture give interesting notes on the various crops in different states.

[4] Patent Office, *Report on Agriculture*, 1848, pp. 368-369. [5] *Ibid.*, p. 404.

peared from the farms, "owing to the more profitable application of provisions and attention to the dairy." [1] In 1840, in Chautauqua County, New York, the dairy was said to be more profitable than wool-growing, [2] and from Kinderhook in the same state — the seat of one of the wool depots — came the assertion that "the high prices of butter and cheese for the past five years have led to substituting the dairy [for sheep-raising] in many districts." [3] In 1852 the reports of the various agricultural societies of Massachusetts frequently spoke of the dairy business as driving out the sheep, especially where there was a market for milk. [4] Further, the future prospects in dairying seemed brighter, as pointed out in 1850 by Randall, the noted wool-grower, who said, "Dairying is therefore regarded as not only as much or more profitable at present, but as holding out the greatest prospect of permanence in profit." [5]

The pastures of New England and of the Middle Atlantic states were found to be as well suited for dairying as for growing wool. This, however, was equally true of the grazing lands of the Middle West. But under the then existing conditions the West had, as we have seen, special advantages for growing wool. The dairyman, on the other hand, found that for him the East was more desirable. It was of much greater importance for him to be near his market

[1] Patent Office, *Report on Agriculture*, 1848, p. 450.

[2] *Ibid.*, 1849, p. 243. [3] *Ibid.*, p. 245.

[4] *Transactions of the Agricultural Societies of Massachusetts*, 1852, *passim.*

[5] Patent Office, *Report on Agriculture*, 1850, p. 139. An excellent summary of the conditions. Randall adds: "Causes . . . are rather diminishing than increasing [the sheep husbandry] throughout New York and New England. These are the extraordinary recent profits of dairying and the prospect that they will be continuous — the far better adaptation of the climate to cows than to sheep — the perfect knowledge of all sensible agriculturists that they cannot compete with the Southern or even the North-Western states in wool-growing, and the strong temptations which frequently occur to part with sheep. The comparative profits of dairying . . . have recently undoubtedly come to equal or exceed those of wool-growing, they are generally thought by farmers to exceed those of ordinary flocks of sheep." Elsewhere the same authority, the leading one of the time, writes: "Dairying is wholly driving out wool-growing in grazing portions of New York. It proved a steady and highly remunerative branch of husbandry. In proper situations it certainly can't be surpassed by any other pursuit. Besides the dairy region of the United States bears no proportion in extent to the wool-growing region." He insists, however, that while "dairying under the best circumstances is far more profitable than sheep husbandry with middling animals," yet the "best sheep are as productive as the best cows and require less labor" (*Fine Wool Sheep Husbandry*, p. 169). Cf. also pp. 170–171.

than it was for the wool-grower. Besides, butter and cheese, being more highly finished products than wool, required more labor and capital for their production, and these two things were scarce in the West. Thus it was not difficult for the cow to drive the sheep from the pastures of the East.

In the year 1860, consequently, we find the wool-growing industry in the eastern part of the United States suffering a steady decline, from two causes, — increased competition, from abroad and from the West, in the growing of wool, and greater profit offered by other branches of agriculture. A small proportion of such flocks as remained were kept for breeding purposes. An increasingly large proportion of the declining remainder was kept for mutton rather than for wool.

The South.

Some mention should here be made of the growing of wool in the South, for it was at this period that it received as much attention there as it ever did. Among the Southern states Virginia, Kentucky, Tennessee, and Texas were the only ones that had any considerable number of sheep.[1] At the opening of the century Virginia had had rather better sheep than most of the states, but latterly, except in the mountainous regions of the western part of the state, where there were some excellent flocks, they had been degenerating. Sheep reached Kentucky at an early date and soon spread to Tennessee. The rich blue-grass region was a favorite locality for them, and being specially suited to the English mutton breeds, which required a richer pasturage than the merino, it thus came about that from 1825 on many of these sheep were to be found there. In the '50's this region was the most important source of supply in the country for the long combing wool then sought by the manufacturers. Texas was of no importance as a wool-producing state until the last few years of this period. Small quantities of wool were exported while it was under Mexican rule, but as late as 1847 the demand for wool there was very slight.[2] A Corpus Christi paper of 1850 remarks on the first important shipment of wool grown in that vicinity, adding that "for years large

[1] Kentucky and West Virginia might more properly be classified with the northern wool-growing states, but for convenience they are taken up with these others now.

[2] *American Agriculturist*, vol. vii, p. 93.

flocks of sheep have been owned by citizens in this county, but no efforts have been made, we learn, heretofore, by the owners, to secure the wool."[1] During the following decade a considerable interest in sheep was aroused,[2] the flocks increased rapidly, improved breeds were driven to the state to cross on the native or Mexican stock,[3] and by 1860 Texas was sending some 3,000,000 pounds of wool to the eastern markets.

As for the other Southern states, they can scarcely be said to have had such a pursuit as wool-growing. Certainly they never sent any appreciable amount of wool to the market. Some sheep there were, to be sure, but their wool was all used in the household.[4] The domestic manufacture of wool, though never large in amount in this region, was continued here much longer than in the North. The wool was coarse, of fair length, and averaged about two pounds per fleece.[5] The sheep had no shelter, seldom any fodder, and were simply left to rustle for themselves. All the attention they got was a little salt and the annual clipping.[6] Though the cost of keeping

[1] *Prairie Farmer*, vol. x, p. 261.

[2] A Texas correspondent under date of February, 1860, says: "Many are now turning their attention to wool-growing in Texas, and wool will soon become one of the great staples of the state" (*Country Gentleman*, vol. xv, p. 108). A little later he writes that the cost of keeping 1000 sheep in Texas is estimated at less than thirty cents a head. Sheep lands are to be had at from $1 to $2 an acre (see *ibid.*, p. 156). "Sheep growing already enters largely into the husbandry of Texas, and this business is fast increasing" (*American Agriculturist*, vol. xviii, p. 77).

[3] Sheep costing $4 a head in Illinois could be driven to Texas and sold for from $8 to $10 a head. The cost of driving was about 10 cents a head for ferriage, bridges, etc., in addition to the cost of drivers, provisions, and outfit. Drivers were advised to drive only halfway the first season, wintering in Missouri on the way (see *Country Gentleman*, 1860, vol. xv, p. 284). Cf. *American Agriculturist*, vol. xviii, p. 77.

[4] See the Patent Office, *Report on Agriculture*, 1850, pp. 260, 365, 395.

[5] "There is in Georgia, South Carolina, Alabama, and other Southern states so much foreign matter in the wool that it shrinks nearly one half in cleaning and is regarded as no better than South American wool sold at New York for 7–9 cents" (T. C. Peters; quoted in *Genesee Farmer*, vol. x, p. 129).

[6] A Louisiana correspondent of the *American Agriculturist* in 1843 writes: "Sheep have only been considered valuable on account of their carcass. Food, except the pastures, they receive none, and no other care or attention except to salt them twice a week" (vol. ii, p. 204). In Georgia, says another, writing in 1849, "Sheep are generally kept not so much for the fleece as the meat and tallow" (*Genesee Farmer*, vol. x, p. 129). Still another writes in 1848, "The largest agricultural fair ever held in Georgia has just closed. Not a sheep was exhibited. The sheep is the most neglected animal in the South. John Randolph's statement that he would go

sheep and growing wool was put at the very lowest figure, — 50 cents a head and 3–8½ cents a pound,[1] — and though all the physical conditions seemed favorable, still the flocks did not increase and the neglect continued.

About 1845 Henry S. Randall began a series of letters to a southern newspaper pointing out the unusual advantages for growing wool which the South appeared to have, and endeavoring to induce the agriculturists of that region to follow what seemed to be their own best interests by adopting this pursuit. For a while considerable attention was aroused. Fortune favored the agitation in that it was just at this time that the flocks of the North were being so rapidly reduced. Many northern sheep were secured at a very low price, and shipped to Virginia or to other Southern states. Between 1847 and 1852 one dealer alone is said to have disposed of 13,000 sheep brought from other states to Virginia.[2] Such was the interest that, although between 1840 and 1850 there was a decline in the number of sheep in all the New England and Middle Atlantic states, yet those same years brought an increase in every one of the Southern states, the total there rising from 4,500,000 to 5,500,000. This increase, it should be borne in mind, was taking place when the price of wool was lower than ever before. But the advance was short-lived, for during the next decade the only states to gain were the newer ones, — Florida, Mississippi, Louisiana, Arkansas, and Texas, — the increase in the last-named state being the only thing that saved the group as a whole from a decline. This, too, was in the face of a decided rise in the price of wool. It is evident that the Southerner's actual experience with wool-growing did not prove so much to his advantage as the outward conditions had seemed to promise.[3]

One of the most obvious of the opposing forces was the ever-pre-

ten rods to kick a sheep but expresses a popular feeling that still prevails in all the planting communities that I have visited. The fleece of the sheep seems to be regarded as the competitor of cotton in clothing the people of all civilized nations" (*ibid.*, vol. ix, p. 216).

[1] See Randall, *Sheep Husbandry*, pp. 61, 308–9.

[2] *Sheep Industry*, p. 460.

[3] No doubt the low price of cotton from 1840 to 1850 and its high price from 1850 to 1860 had some influence on these temporary fluctuations. The causes for the general neglect of the industry lay deeper.

sent dog. Sheep interests were so unimportant that laws affording protection against dogs could not be secured, and where sheep received so little care as here, the losses suffered from this source were sure to be heavy. Other reasons for the slight attention given to wool-growing are less evident and more difficult to prove.[1] In mountainous districts, where cultivation was not easy and sheep should therefore have had a greater chance, the people engaged in farming, notably the poor whites, were very backward, ignorant, and of a shiftless character. They lacked the knowledge and initiative necessary to develop and carry on such an industry, for it was one in which care in a few details meant much. Further, these people formed a comparatively isolated community. They supplied most of their rather limited needs by their own effort, and produced little for outside markets. Few had any opportunity to sell wool, even if they had grown more than they themselves required. As for the cultivators located along the river bottoms, the coastal plain, or the neighboring uplands, their attention was given almost exclusively to cotton, tobacco, sugar, or rice. Aside from the unusual physical advantages for these crops there afforded, they found in slavery what was also of the greatest importance — plenty of cheap labor. In growing wool but little labor was required, and that of a kind which slaves were hardly prepared to give.[2] If wool-growing were resorted to, this unusual resource would be left idle. Moreover, these fertile lands of the South had no such great relative advantage over some of the newly rising wool-growing regions as they had over countries growing cotton, tobacco, sugar, and rice. Hence they clung fast to these staple products, and left the growing of wool to others.

The Middle West.

Turning to the West, we find that between 1840 and 1860 the industry of wool-growing was there undergoing a series of rapid and most interesting changes. These were due to the alterations then

[1] What follows applies only in a modified way to West Virginia and Kentucky, where, as has been noted, wool-growing was far more general.

[2] See a discussion of this point by the Editor of the *Prairie Farmer*, vol. viii, p. 271. "No sort of stock," he says, "requires anywhere near the amount of skill, care, and attention which must be used by the flock master. This skill and care are essential. There is no success without them."

taking place in the economic conditions confronting cultivators of that section of the country. Chief among these were the development of a better system of transportation, and the changes in the relative prices of wool and the other agricultural products of the region.

Before the opening of the Erie Canal, in 1825, the only market for the superfluous produce of the West was by boat down the Ohio and Mississippi Rivers to New Orleans.[1] The South-West, which was giving more and more attention to cotton, supplied a growing demand, and it was by this route also that the foreign market was reached. With the opening of the canal came an opportunity for such as could reach the shores of the Great Lakes to send their produce to the growing markets of the East. It was still some years, however, before any large volume of the products of western states passed through this canal.[2] The chief reasons were that population had first extended westward along the banks of the Ohio River and its tributaries, whence access was had to the New Orleans market, and that the East, which was largely supplying its own wants, had little need for western produce. The spread of population along the lake shores and through the northern part of the states came much later, and it was this region whose produce first fed the Erie Canal. The construction of other canals soon opened the interior districts. In 1834 came the opening of the water and rail route through Pennsylvania connecting the Ohio with the East, but this was never an

[1] For a description of these conditions, see Callender, "Early Transportation and Banking Enterprises of the States in Relation to the Growth of Corporations," *Quarterly Journal of Economics*, vol. xvii.

[2] In 1840 only one seventh of its tonnage came from other states than New York (see Ringwalt, *Transportation System*, p. 111). Some idea of its growth is indicated by the following table: —

Articles shipped Eastward from Buffalo (in thousands).

	1835	1840	1845	1850	1851
Flour, bbls.	86	633	717	984	1,106
Wheat, bu.	95	881	1,354	3,304	3,668
Corn, bu.	14	47	33	2,608	5,789
Provisions, bbls.	6	25	68	146	117
Butter, Cheese, Lard, lbs.	1,030	3,422	6,597	17,534	11,102

(Andrews, *Report on Trade and Commerce of the Great Lakes*, 1852, p. 92.)

important channel for through western produce.[1] In 1833 the completion of the Ohio Canal from Portsmouth on the Ohio River to Cleveland opened up the centre of that state and gave the Ohio valley a short water route to New York. Twelve years later the Miami Canal connected Cincinnati with Toledo. In 1840 the North-West was entirely dependent on these water routes, for it had in all but 89 miles of railroad. At that time most western produce still went down the Mississippi, the main articles being wheat, corn, pork, and beef. It was largely upon the market for these articles that the success of the farms depended.

Beginning about 1840 and continuing for five or six years there came a period of unusually low prices for agricultural produce. It was felt the more as during the preceding six years prices had ruled very high. The decline pressed with great severity upon the chief products of the West,[2] the prices of the staple products of that section falling in some cases to one half or even one third of their former level. Wheat sold below 50 cents a bushel and corn at 12 cents. The main use for corn was to feed hogs, and hogs sold for less than $1.00 a head.[3]

[1] Ringwalt, *Transportation System of the United States*, p. 111.

[2] See Semple, *American History and its Geographic Conditions*, p. 210. It is there stated that at this time "the Mississippi steamboats found in bacon a hot and cheap fuel." The situation in Dane County, Wisconsin, is described by Hibbard as follows: "In the early '40's . . . the 'home market' bubble had burst. Butter sold at five or even three cents a pound. Wheat was worth from 30 to 50 cents in Milwaukee, and the cost of hauling it there was equal to half or two thirds of its value. Hogs . . . were a drug on the market. . . . Pork was quoted at two and three cents, beef about the same" (*History of Agriculture in Dane County, Wisconsin*, p. 117).

[3] We have the following table of prices in McLean County, in the centre of Illinois, showing the changes which took place (*Publications of the Illinois State Historical Library*, No. 9, p. 537). More accurate figures can be found in the Aldrich Report, but they do not show the prices before 1840. Even in the eastern markets the general level of prices was low, though it was the West which suffered most. (See table of New York prices and chart in Appendix.)

	Sheep	*Corn*	*Hogs*	*Cows*
1833		$.33⅓	$2.81	$11.06
1834	$1.22		.72	7.08
1835		.20	1.83	10.87
1836	2.63	.30¾	1.52	18.50
1837			3.51	20.25
1838	1.91	.24½	3.33	12.60

In these years prices generally were low, because of the long-drawn-out depression after the panic of 1837; but in the case of the chief agricultural products of the West there seems to have been an even more fundamental difficulty. The great influx of population into the Middle West, where almost everybody turned to farming, resulted in an abnormal increase in the staple crops of that section. And the improvements in transportation which made it possible to market a larger portion of the crops had the same effect. Together these two factors produced a supply which far exceeded the demand. The eastern states apparently were able to meet their own needs, for it was not until after 1840 that any appreciable amount of the staple products of the West was shipped to the East.[1] The foreign market for food-stuffs failed to expand in the least. In fact in the thirty-year period from 1810 to 1840 the exports of wheat, flour, corn, corn meal, beef, pork, and bacon and ham, the great staples of the Mississippi valley, remained stationary, or, if anything, declined. Lard exports alone showed an increase. In short, those

	Sheep	*Corn*	*Hogs*	*Cows*
1839	$3.32	$.30⅓	$4.20	$20.09
1840	3.69	.20⅓	3.47	13.89
1841		.20½	1.76	13.54
1842	1.76	.13¾	1.00	7.50
1843	1.60	.12½		6.44
1844	1.40	.21½	.51	8.50
1845	1.50		.89	8.45
1846	1.14		3.17	7.75
1847		.14	1.45	10.50
1848	1.17		.62½	8.56
1849	.99	.14½	1.27	17.97
1850	1.40			11.07
1851	1.51		2.13	12.20
1852	1.62	.20	2.43	13.87
1853	2.25	.25	6.14	
1854	1.79	.25½	3.12	22.48
1855	3.64	.53	3.75	23.41
1856	1.86			27.15
1857		.21½	7.62	22.83
1858		.28	5.68	29.00
1859		.77	9.83	34.31
1860	2.76	.31	8.66	22.55

[1] Cf. the view of a western correspondent of the *National Intelligencer* in 1843, quoted in *Niles' Register*, vol. lxv, pp. 46–47.

years form a period when the country's exportation of food-stuffs, as well as its foreign commerce generally, was relatively of less importance than at any other equal period in its history. The failure of the foreign market to grow was due to the absence of any permanent European market for American produce, the temporary market of earlier times having been engendered by war. Moreover, the West India market, which had been the chief reliance, was now declining, owing to the falling off in the sugar industry consequent on the abolition of slavery in the British West Indies, and to the decreasing fertility of the islands generally, Cuba alone excepted.[1] Such being the situation, the chief market for the staple crops of the Mississippi valley was the cotton belt of the South. This one, to be sure, was expanding rapidly at the time, notably during the decade 1830–1840, yet hardly in the same ratio as the supply. Hence the period of abnormally low prices in the Middle West in the years 1840–45.

Under such a distressing drop in the prices of the staples of the West as took place after 1840 it is little wonder that the farmer of that section looked around to see what he could raise that might give a little better return. In his search he ran across the hitherto neglected sheep. Until then, as has been seen, very little wool had ever been sent to the eastern markets from western states. Such as had gone out came entirely from Ohio and Kentucky. But even in those states most of the wool grown was used by the farmers themselves, though it frequently passed through one of the small local woolen mills. About 1840, the farmers of Ohio for the first time (except in the district around Steubenville) began to sell wool for cash, and to purchase for cash or for produce such woolen goods as they required, instead of having the wool manufactured on their own account or on shares.[2] "Wool is comparatively speaking a new article on our market,"[3] said a Milan, Ohio, paper as late as 1844, in remarking on the interest in wool at that time; and it went on to say that probably 200,000 pounds would be shipped from there during the season, as contrasted with 30,000 for the preceding sea-

[1] Cf. Merivale, *Lectures on Colonization and Colonies*, part iii.

[2] Klippart, "Essay on Sheep and Sheep Culture in Ohio." Ohio State Board of Agriculture, *Report*, 1862, p. 503.

[3] Quoted in *Niles' Register*, vol. lxvi, p. 261.

son. The same year a Cleveland paper declared "We have in years past occasionally seen a wagon load of wool in our streets, but never before this year have our citizens seen the streets so frequently enlivened with them."[1] In 1841 there had been no wool market in Akron, Ohio, but in 1844 200,000 pounds of wool were purchased there.[2] The increase in the flocks of Ohio was rendered comparatively easy by the fact that, unlike the more western states, it already had many sheep within its borders. Thus in spite of the heavy drain on its flocks to supply the neighboring states to the westward, the number of sheep increased from 2,000,000 in 1840 to double that figure in 1850.

The greatest rush for sheep at this time was, however, in the more westerly states, particularly in Illinois. There cattle, hogs, and grain had previously received all the farmer's attention, while sheep were even more uncommon than in Ohio. To understand this we must remember the conditions which confronted the frontier farmer when he reached the prairie. Until then he had usually been obliged to clear his land before he could cultivate it. This necessity of making a clearing had been one of his greatest difficulties. The underbrush had to be removed, and the trees cut down or girdled and left to die, the stumps in either case remaining in the field. At length, after much toil, he could begin to plant. But in such a region sheep could be turned into the woods at once, and were of no little aid in clearing out the smaller undergrowth. Very little labor was necessary to grow wool, and the chief outlay of capital was that required to secure the original stock. Some fodder for winter scarcity and also a rough shelter were desirable, but were not always provided. Now this situation, though not so favorable to sheep that the cultivation of the land was much neglected on their account, was still distinctly less favorable to crops than the conditions on the open prairie. There all that the farmer had to do was to break the land and plant his seed. For this almost no capital was required, and capital was the thing that the pioneer farmer most lacked. When he finally decided to grow wool this need, as we shall see, proved to be his most serious obstacle. Further, he had always had a certain supply of labor in his family. To keep this fully employed in tending sheep

[1] Quoted in *Niles' Register*, vol. lxvi, p. 388.

[2] *Ibid.*, p. 388.

would require a large flock, and hence much capital; but in the growing of grain a small investment furnished full employment, and therefore the most economical use, for all the labor he could muster. He might, to be sure, raise grain and also keep a few sheep, as some did. Nevertheless it is evident that there was more inducement to cultivate the soil and less to grow wool than farther to the east.[1] Though this is but one reason among many,[2] it helps to explain the comparative scarcity of sheep on the prairie lands, shown in the following table: —

	Number of sheep per capita			*Number of sheep per acre of farm land*	
	1840	1850	1860	1850	1860
Vt.	5.76	3.23	2.40	0.246	0.176
N. Y.	2.11	1.11	0.67	0.181	0.125
Ohio	1.34	1.54	1.51	0.219	0.173
Ill.	0.83	1.05	0.45	0.074	0.037
Iowa	0.36	0.78	0.38	0.055	0.025

[1] When H. S. Randall, who lived in New York State, made a trip to the prairie region as late as 1847, he was amazed at the small quantity of all kinds of stock. "I saw one considerable flock of sheep, but elsewhere but here and there a score or two" (*Prairie Farmer*, vol. viii, p. 322–323).

[2] A fact which one might expect would have caused a more general adoption of sheep in this section where transportation facilities were so inadequate, was that wool had such relatively high value in small bulk when compared with the staple crops of the region. Evidently other considerations more than offset this advantage. Curiously enough, it was during these years, when the general attention happened to be turned towards sheep, but after the introduction of better transportation facilities was weakening the strength of the argument, that this advantage appears to have been emphasized. Thus it is noted that the early Wisconsin settlers "found about 10% of wool would pay its transportation to market while it took 50% of wheat" (*Country Gentleman*, vol. xxi, p. 349). "With wheat worth sixty-five cents per bushel it costs one bushel to send another from central Illinois to market. With corn at ten cents per bushel it takes over six bushels to carry the one to New York. It costs one cent and two thirds of a cent to send a pound of wool to New York, less than two cents will carry fifty cents worth of wool to market; to carry fifty cents worth of corn costs about three dollars. . . . A man can haul twelve to fifteen hundred dollars worth of wool with a pair of horses, and three or four thousand dollars worth with four yoke of oxen. . . . Such is the situation with respect to transportation of Minnesota, Iowa, Nebraska, Kansas, and Missouri; and on this account, if for no other reason, wool-growing is the best business for those states" (Department of Agriculture, *Report*, 1862, p. 286). The possibility of marketing grain in the condensed form of flour, pork, beef, whiskey, etc., should, of course, be taken into consideration.

Then, too, there seems to have been an impression, generally prevalent at first, that the prairie region, especially Illinois, was too warm for sheep, and also too level.[1] The notion that sheep could not thrive except in a hilly country apparently arose from the fact that in the eastern states they were generally found among the hills, the reason, of course, being that the level strips of land were cultivated. But when the prices of grain and meat dropped, the western cultivator seemed suddenly to see visions of great profits in the sheep industry. He looked out upon the vast prairies of government land where his flocks could graze, not only without cost, but, as some seemed to think, the whole year round. Even if hay had to be provided, there was plenty to be obtained at a dollar a ton.[2] The warm climate now appeared as an advantage, for no shelter would have to be constructed. In some localities wolves were troublesome, but they were fast disappearing. Sheep could be kept at from 30 to 75 cents a head, it was maintained, and wool grown at 12½ cents a pound.[3] Such tempting prospects could not be resisted, and everybody began to look for sheep.[4]

[1] *Prairie Farmer*, vol. xii, p. 35. [2] *American Agriculturist*, vol. i, p. 237.

[3] See *Prairie Farmer*, vol. v, p. 194. See also Patent Office, *Report on Agriculture*, 1845, p. 342.

[4] Still another difficulty is brought out in the following letter from an Illinois farmer: "The keeping of sheep on the open prairies is rendered more difficult than it otherwise would be by the existence of a law in this and other western states allowing cattle and horses to run free but obliging sheep to be kept in fenced pastures or watched if running on the open prairie. This is in consequence of the grain fields being generally surrounded with a fence which sheep could go under without difficulty. But many ample sheep pastures could be selected where no expense for fencing need be incurred yet for many years by the flocks being guarded at night and taken to their pastures early in the morning." He further adds: "We consider the reasons why sheep-growing has not been entered into as a distinct branch of business more extensively than it has, to be: (1) Money has been bringing such high rates of interest as to give little promise to capitalists of anything paying better; (2) The speculation going on in real estate has served like the *ignis fatuus* to blind all eyes to any other sources of gaining wealth; (3) The growing of grain has been so remunerative as to satisfy the desires of the farmer and attract all his capital and attention. These and no lack of profit in the investment are the causes why the farmers have not made of sheep and wool-growing a distinct business, as we hold they might, with as good or better results to themselves than from the growing of grain where it has to be transported at half its value to a distant market" (*Genesee Farmer*, vol. xix, p. 23). A later note says: "Sheep won't be found on the prairies till a different system of fencing prevails, speculation becomes less rampant, and farmers are forced to the adoption of mixed husbandry to keep up the fertility of the grain fields" (*ibid.*, p. 50).

The arrivals to supply this new demand began to reach Illinois about 1841. Most of those received in the next few years came from Ohio, where they could be bought for from $0.75 to $1.00 a head. These, of course, were simply the "common" sheep of the country, with no strain of improved blood. Some, however, came from farther East — from New York, Pennsylvania, and Vermont or other parts of New England — and these were sometimes of a better grade.[1] But only a few farmers could afford a good breed of sheep, and most had difficulty enough in securing any at all.

The obstacle to the extension of this industry, because of the amount of capital required, was strikingly illustrated at this time. An Illinois farmer, writing in 1841, complained that he had tried in vain all summer long to get some sheep, either to keep them from one to three years and deliver a certain quantity of wool yearly, or to take them to double in a certain time. His neighbors also were anxious to get into the business, and he thought that from 1000 to 2000 could be easily disposed of in this way in his locality; but to purchase sheep outright was, for most, impossible.[2] The editor of the *Prairie Farmer* corroborated this statement, saying,[3] "Hundreds of them are anxious to get sheep, but they are unable to pay for them at present." In the following year we find the assertion that "wool-growing is attracting much attention here, and farmers generally have not the means to send after flocks, but if a few could be bought, as the farmer's means permitted — 5, 10, 15, 20, or 50 — many would purchase. . . . All would not be able to pay down for them, perhaps most would prefer purchasing on a credit of one to two years."[4] This same lack of capital appeared again after the

[1] In 1841, 1000 merino sheep were reported as passing through Ohio on their way to Illinois, having been driven all the way from Massachusetts (see *Hazard's Register*, vol. v, p. 351).

[2] *Prairie Farmer*, vol. i, p. 67.

[3] *Ibid.*, p. 67.

[4] *Ibid.*, vol. ii, p. 17. A little later the same difficulty appeared in Iowa. J. B. Grinnell writes: "A new country is the paradise of *poor men*, and the high rates of interest, such as are unknown in the East, have rendered the purchase of stock an impossibility. The visitor, too, has coveted so many broad, fair acres which he found money to purchase, that the meeting of taxes and ordinary expenditures has made a demand equal to the full measure of his ability. And then flocks at hand were out of the question, and the driving of them 600 to 1000 miles from localities where they were to be found, seemed a forbidding, unprofitable journey. I should mention, too, that numerous and palpable failures alarmed the timid and put back wool-growing several years" (Commissioner of Agriculture, *Report*, 1862, p. 301).

Civil War, and also in more recent times, as a real difficulty in the way of the spread of the sheep industry.

In some cases the farmers associated together to send for sheep, but more often they had to depend on some eastern sheep-owner or speculator. The lack of ready capital frequently led to the practice of taking the sheep on shares.[1] In 1842 word came from Galesburg, Illinois, that extensive preparations were being made to go into wool-growing, and that citizens were on their way to Kentucky to purchase 1000 sheep.[2] In the same year over 10,000 were driven through Kane County for farmers in that and the adjoining counties.[3] Sheep were very cheap in Ohio just then, the common sort selling at 70 cents a head, with an additional cost of 25 cents a head[4] for driving them to Illinois in flocks of five to eight hundred. 1844 and 1845 seem to have been the banner years in the immigration of sheep to this region. Wool was then a little higher in price than for a year or so previous, and this gave an added stimulus. A correspondent writes, "I suppose there were never half so many sheep driven to Illinois in one season before this," and the editor adds "probably not a tenth."[5] One Illinois paper described the rush of sheep to Illinois, Wisconsin, and Missouri as "a perfect tornado."[6] A flock of 4000 sheep driven from Ohio to Illinois was said to have been preceded by others, amounting to 50,000, most of which were for Missouri, Iowa, and Wisconsin.[7] In Ohio the demand was such at this time that the price of sheep rose 100% in a few weeks. This

[1] As was true of the sheep driven to Wisconsin, 1850–55, to supply "the great demand without money if not without price. Farmers were informed now they could get a flock of sheep of their own in three to five years without a dollar of money. Their benefactors would let them sheep selected from the best eastern flocks from three to five years, only asking two pounds of wool per head per year and their number of good sound healthy sheep returned, — the farmer to have all the increase and all the balance of the wool just for the keeping. Most farmers were no judge of the age or condition of sheep, and these philanthropists were not long in disposing of their flocks. But they knew nothing about keeping sheep and made a wretched failure of it in many cases. There were thousands of such instances in Wisconsin" (*Country Gentleman*, vol. xxi, p. 349).

[2] *Hazard's Register*, vol. vi, p. 296.

[3] *Prairie Farmer*, vol. ii, p. 61.

[4] For a detailed account of the method and expense of driving, see *ibid.*, vol. iv, p. 215.

[5] *Ibid.*, vol. v, p. 49.

[6] *Niles' Register*, vol. lxviii, p. 80.

[7] *Prairie Farmer*, vol. iv, p. 231.

state also proved a convenient source of supply for the Michigan wool-growers, who were rapidly multiplying at this period.

Some measure of the extent of this increase in the wool-growing industry of the West, and its effect upon the East, is found in the shipments of wool from these states. The number of pounds of wool shipped eastward from Buffalo over the Erie Canal was as follows:[1]

1835	1840	1845	1850
140,911	107,794	2,957,007	8,805,817

The amount which went east over the other routes was comparatively slight, most of that going over the Pennsylvania canals coming from the western part of that state and the Pan Handle district of West Virginia. The receipts of wool over the two routes were as follows in thousands of pounds:[2] —

	1842	1843	1844	1845	1848	1849
New York canals	3,355	6,246	7,672	9,756	8,729	12,731
Penn. canals	1,268	2,500	8,166	3,763	2,930	5,113

At first all of the western wool received at Buffalo came from Ohio, and it was not until after 1840 that shipments were received from other states. Most of the exports from Ohio went out over the Lakes and the Erie Canal. Of the wool shipped over the Ohio Canal the quantity moving to the north and to the south was as follows:[3] —

	Received at Cleveland	*At Portsmouth*	*Total*
1839	32,176	49,926	82,102
1844	848,878	129,916	978,794

[1] Andrews, *Report on the Trade and Commerce of the British North American Colonies and the Great Lakes*, 1852, p. 92. Writing in 1849, the editor of the *Genesee Farmer* says: "Wool-growing is becoming an extensive business in the West. We have accounts of large and profitable clips the past season in various sections of Ohio, Michigan, Illinois, Wisconsin and other western and southwestern states" (vol. x, p. 211).

[2] Figures for 1842–45 are from *Niles' Register*, vol. lxx, p. 21; those for 1848–49 are from Patent Office, *Report on Agriculture*, 1849, p. 512. Much of this was not western wool. The amount coming over the Champlain Canal, presumably from Vermont, was: —

1842	1843	1844
640,000	1,426,000	1,297,000

(*Niles' Register*, vol. lxix, p. 54.) Between 1847 and 1849 Boston was receiving 3,500,000–4,700,000 pounds of wool by the Western Railroad.

[3] *Hunt's Merchants' Magazine*, vol. xii, p. 454.

The first shipment from Chicago is put down for 1841.[1] In 1842 the amount was 1,500 pounds, by 1851 it had reached 1,000,000, and in 1855 it rose to over 2,000,000 pounds, falling off, however, in the years immediately following.[2] The shipments from Detroit rose from 20,000 pounds in 1841 to 1,000,000 in 1847.[3] Wisconsin, a little slower in starting than the others, was also gaining fast. Little or no wool was sent down the Mississippi.[4] When in 1842 and 1844 a few bales of wool reached St. Louis they were unusual enough to attract special notice in the newspapers.[5] In the accounts of receipts of merchandise at New Orleans wool does not seem to have been of sufficient importance to receive separate mention. Thus the following table of the receipts at Buffalo of wool from western states fairly indicates the relative importance of these states as wool-growers, and the increase in the supply of wool coming from that region: —

Receipts of Wool at Buffalo on the Erie Canal.[6]

	Ohio	*Michigan*	*Illinois*	*Wisconsin*	*Indiana*	*Penn.*
1842	334	31	2			
1844	1720	256	71	12	12	15
1845	2250	352	162	37	35	79
1846	2775	521	225	38	48	137

The increase in the flocks of the West continued, though with somewhat abated force, until about 1855. In 1853–54, for instance, we find that sheep were still driven to Illinois from the East, 10,000 being reported as coming to Shelby County from Ohio.[7] But most

[1] *Niles' Register*, vol. lxii, p. 336.

[2] Andreas, *History of Chicago*, vol. i, p. 557.

[3] See *Sheep Industry*, p. 612. See also *Prairie Farmer*, vol. x, p. 31.

[4] Andrews, *Report on the Trade and Commerce of the British North American Colonies and the Great Lakes*, p. 707. In southern Ohio, while all the chief agricultural crops went down the river, tobacco and wool were shipped towards the lakes (see Ringwalt, *Transportation System of the United States*, p. 121).

[5] *Niles' Register*, vol. lxii, p. 384; vol. lxvi, p. 387.

[6] The figures for 1842 are from *Niles' Register*, vol. lxix, p. 54; those for 1844–46 are from Barton's *Brief Sketch of the Commerce of the Lakes*, folding table. The wool was, of course, not always exported from the state producing it, notably so in the case of Indiana. The amount going through the Welland Canal was very slight. None of the above tables can pretend to absolute accuracy. The original sources have not been accessible, and such tables as have been found do not always agree. It is believed, however, that the impression they convey is correct.

[7] *Prairie Farmer*, vol. xiii, p. 84.

of the additions to the flocks had been made before 1850. During the decade preceding that year, the flocks of the western states had doubled, or, if Ohio be left out of account, had advanced 150%. The sudden rise in the price of wool in 1852–53 gave the industry another impetus, but it proved to be of short life. The reaction set in about 1855. In Ohio the summit was reached in 1854 with 4,854,000 sheep, but by 1860 the number had been reduced to 3,546,000.[1] In that year Illinois and Indiana also showed a decline as compared with 1850.[2] Only the newer states showed gains in this decade, and they were slight, the net increase for the whole group being but five per cent, less than one twentieth of the rate for the similar period just preceding.

During the last half of this period, however, much more attention was paid to the quality of the sheep. Before 1850 the stock of these states was of a very inferior grade. Most of the farmers were ignorant as to the management of sheep or else careless. Randall, in describing a trip he took in about 1847, says that such flocks as he saw were decidedly inferior.[3] A Vermonter who had brought some merinos to Illinois in 1849, intending to buy sheep there and cross the merinos upon them, found the flocks of that region so inferior that he would not use them.[4] Even the sheep of Ohio, with the exception of a few large flocks, were described in 1844 as being

[1] The number of sheep in Ohio and their value was as follows, in thousands: —

	Sheep	*Value*		*Sheep*	*Value*
1840	2,028	$1,283	1854	4,854	$8,031
1846	3,141	1,758	1855	4,337	5,664
1848	3,677	1,988	1856	3,513	5,009
1850	3,942	2,060	1857	3,276	5,357
1851	3,619	2,060	1858	3,337	4,755
1852	3,059	3,581	1859	3,366	5,442
1853	4,104	6,448	1860	3,546	6,029

(From *Sheep Industry*, p. 574.)

[2] "About 1850–55 large flocks of sheep from the East were driven here" [to Wisconsin], but "in consequence of investing in sheep so unwisely and prematurely there was a great decrease in the number of sheep in the state, 1857–60." The writer, a Wisconsin wool-grower, adds: "The great difficulty in my opinion in the way of making wool-growing a success has been that the minds of the farmers have been so fickle respecting sheep — the sheep has been at times the most petted and best cared for thing on the farm, and at times the worst abused. Farmers have pursued no such course respecting any other product" (*Country Gentleman*, vol. xxi, p. 349).

[3] *Prairie Farmer*, vol. viii, pp. 322–323.

[4] *Ibid.*, vol. xii, p. 282.

mainly coarse "natives,"[1] and that year is declared to have "found Ohio with hardly a decent flock in the state." [2] The Saxony blood, which had once been common in the better flocks of Ohio, though it never got much farther west, was not given up quite so early there as in the East. Thus it was not until the '50's that the movement toward the Vermont merino had gained full headway. In 1854 it was reported that during the winter and spring from 2000 to 3000 blooded sheep, averaging $15 a head, had been sold in Chicago.[3] About this time also some French merinos were received from the noted Bingham flock in Vermont.[4] Thus improved blood became fairly well scattered among the flocks of the West, and was of no slight aid in increasing the returns from the industry at a time when they were beginning to look less attractive than formerly.

The states in which there was an advance in the number of sheep between 1850 and 1860 were those on the frontiers just being opened. The great influx of settlers was the cause of this growth, for among them there were always a few who brought sheep. This was particularly true of those who came from Vermont, New York, or Ohio.[5] They seemingly thought it a matter of course that sheep should form a part of the farm economy, and if they did not bring a few with them they soon obtained some. This helps to explain why sheep were most numerous in the more northern states, where the larger share of the emigrants from sheep states settled.[6] The greatest additions to the flocks at this time were, for instance, in Michigan. There, too, some households still supplied their needs with the clip from their own farms. But the significant and important point is that even in the newer states the increase in the flocks was by no means keeping pace with the increase in the population or in the farming industry.[7]

In the important wool-growing states of the West, where there appeared an actual decline in the flocks, we see the results of another economic change. This decline, it should be remembered, took

[1] *Prairie Farmer*, vol. iv, p. 321.

[2] Ohio Board of Agriculture, *Report*, 1862, p. 510.

[3] *Prairie Farmer*, vol. xiii, p. 212.

[4] *Ibid.*, p. 444.

[5] See Hibbard, *History of Agriculture in Dane County, Wisconsin*, p. 145. See also *Country Gentleman*, vol. xxi, p. 349.

[6] Conversely this gives an added reason for the scarcity of sheep in regions like southern Indiana and Illinois or Missouri, largely settled by people from the South.

[7] See table, *ante*, page 141.

place at a time when the price of wool was considerably higher than it had been since 1837; that is, higher than at the time when flocks were rushing into these states and every farmer was doing his utmost to secure a few sheep. On the face of it, this appears paradoxical. The explanation is similar to that which underlay the sudden rise of the interest in wool-growing about 1841,—another change in the relative prices of wool and other agricultural products.

The worst of the period of low prices for agricultural products came in the years 1843 and 1844. The two following years showed some improvement, and 1847 brought a decided jump upwards.[1] The Irish Famine, the modification and, finally, the abolition of the Corn Laws were the chief causes of this rise. From 1847 until 1852 there was a continuous though slow advance, but at that time the market for wool was improving as well. In 1852–53 there came another phenomenal rise in the prices of farm products. The main cause then was the Crimean War, though this was further enhanced by an increasing demand to meet the normal wants of Europe. The growth of exports at this time was as follows:—

Average Annual Exports from the United States (in thousands).

	Wheat	*Wheat flour*	*Corn*	*Corn meal*	*Bacon and hams*	*Cheese*
	bu.	bbl.	bu.	bbl.	lbs.	lbs.
1835–45	478	1,036	465	197	2,098	2,573
1846–58	4,483	3,014	6,945	347	32,045	8,584

The rise culminated in about 1855, just before the close of the war, yet prices were well maintained through 1857, and remained fairly high till 1860. Although there was also an advance in the price of wool during the years between 1852 and 1860, yet it was neither so great nor so well maintained as that which took place in the case of the chief food-stuffs. This once more altered the face of things for the western farmer. Wheat, selling in New York at $2.00 a bushel and in Chicago at from $1.00 to $1.75, seemed to open a veritable gold mine at the farmer's door. No wonder that he forgot all about his little flock, and speedily reverted to his first choice,—the wheat, corn, pork, and beef, for which his lands were so admirably suited.

[1] See Appendix for tables of prices and charts.

There was still another factor which militated in favor of grain and meat and against wool, — the growth of the railroads. It was just at the time when the prices of food-stuffs were so high that new railroads were being pushed out over the prairies with the greatest rapidity, thus opening a vast extent of fertile land. In 1850 there had been 1276 miles of railroads in the whole North-West; in 1860 there were 10,247 miles.[1] By 1855 railroads had crossed the Mississippi and stretched out into Iowa. Thereafter, it may be said, they advanced ahead of the main tide of western immigration. For the future the western settlers were provided with a means for sending their produce to the market, and one which did not eat up the whole value of the produce on the way. In 1853 Chicago secured a through rail connection with the Atlantic coast, and competition between water and rail routes for the higher class of goods began to be felt.[2] But the all-rail route to the East was not of so much importance to the farmer as was the network of lines which gave the vast interior tracts access to the water ways. In the comparatively large areas of the prairie region, where rivers were less numerous than to the eastward, and canals therefore of little avail, the railroad was the only hope. Most of the western produce struck the water ways sooner or later, but had it not been for these railroad feeders, much of it could not have been marketed at all.[3]

How comparatively slight was the gain obtained through the decreasing cost of shipping wool is seen by a glance at some of the rates recorded. The cost of carrying wool from central Illinois to the East in about 1843 seems to have been between two and two and a half cents a pound.[4] One quotation divides this as follows: Vermilion County, Illinois to Chicago, one half cent, Chicago to Buf-

[1] Based on figures in *Poor's Manual.*

[2] The removal of canal tolls on railroad traffic in New York and Pennsylvania in the '50's greatly increased this.

[3] The amount of wheat received and shipped at Chicago by these two methods in 1858 was: —

	Receipts	*Shipments*
By water	924,000 bu.	8,716,000 bu.
By rail	8,615,000 "	133,000 "

(*Chicago Board of Trade Report*, 1858, p. 18.) Wool at this time was mostly sent from Chicago by rail.

[4] See *Prairie Farmer*, vol. iii, p. 102. See also *American Agriculturist*, vol. ii, p. 109.

falo, one cent, Buffalo to New York, one cent.[1] In 1862 it was said to cost one and two thirds cents to send a pound of wool from central Illinois to New York.[2] Thus the cost of sending wool from Illinois to the East had fallen between 1843 and 1860, at a generous estimate, one cent a pound. Assuming the price of wool to have averaged twenty-five cents a pound, this meant a saving of four cents on every dollar's worth of the wool-grower's product. The freight and toll on a barrel of flour, over the Erie Canal alone, fell from 71 cents in 1841 to 34 cents in 1858.[3] These figures indicate a saving of 7½ cents a bushel in the cheapest form in which wheat was carried, and this was for only a part of the distance. With wheat selling at 75 cents a bushel in the West, this meant a saving of 10 cents on every dollar's worth of wheat-grower's product. Thus because of the improvement in transportation facilities between these two dates there was a gain on wheat of at least twice the amount (three or four times the amount is more likely) gained on an equal value of wool is certain.[4] The pressure which such a change would exert in favor of grain and against wool needs no further comment. This tendency, of course, had been at work all the time that sheep were being introduced. For a while other forces had been more than sufficient to counteract its effects. When these opposing forces had disappeared, the results were more plainly disclosed.

The wool-growing industry, it now appears, had never been so strongly intrenched in the western states, with the exception of Ohio, as in the East. It first rose to prominence because of a decline in the profits on the other products of the western fields, and when a little later, under the combined effects of a better system of transportation and a larger market, those products became more profitable,

[1] *American Agriculturist*, vol. i, pp. 176–177. In 1851 the rate on 100 pounds was given as follows: St. Louis to Chicago, 40 cents; Chicago to Buffalo, about 25 cents; Chicago to Albany, 75–80 cents; reduction possible on large shipments (see *Prairie Farmer*, vol. ii, p. 320). In 1849 wool was shipped from Fond du Lac to Buffalo for 50 cents a 100 lbs. (see *ibid.*, p. 300). In that year the cost of shipping wool from the Ohio or the Mississippi River to Buffalo was ¾ cents a pound, while to send a bushel of wheat cost 12 cents (see Patent Office, *Report on Agriculture*, 1849, p. 252).

[2] Commissioner of Agriculture, *Report*, 1862, p. 286.

[3] *Hunt's Merchants' Magazine*, vol. xlii, p. 118.

[4] In 1840 the difference between the price of wheat in New York and in Chicago was from 50 to 60 cents. In 1860 it had fallen to about 32 cents (see *Aldrich Report*, part ii, pp. 60–64).

it was soon given up. As we leave the wool-growing industry of the Middle West in 1860, it is slowly losing ground.

The Far West.

Although the wool-growing of the Far West had little effect upon the eastern markets, it should not be left without mention, for at the end of the period under consideration the Far West was the only part of the country which seemed to offer any promise for the future of this industry.

Sheep appear to have reached New Mexico and California originally under the Spanish rule. They received little care and for years simply degenerated. The greater number were, perhaps, in New Mexico, but there were also large bands in southern California, at one time held by the missions.[1] Here, however, the original flocks, unlike those of the East, seem to have been kept mainly for mutton, with little or no regard to the wool they might yield. Their wool was of the coarsest grade, but their meat was declared of excellent flavor. Mutton was to the people of New Mexico what pork was to the farmers of the rest of the country. It is said that from about 1825 to 1835 some 200,000 head of sheep were annually driven to the southern markets from this region.[2] On the other hand, the amount of wool carried over the Santa Fé trail, the natural outlet, was in 1845 "inconsiderable." "Formerly," says Gregg, who was writing at that time, "they sheared their flocks chiefly for their health and rarely preserved their fleece, as their domestic manufactures consumed but a comparatively small quantity."

On the discovery of gold in California and the influx of prospectors, a heavy demand for mutton had arisen, but the business of growing wool did not begin until about 1852. From 1852 to 1860 large flocks were driven to this state from New Mexico.[3] Eastern flock masters sent sheep round the Horn, and some even drove them across the plains. At first there were no woolen mills and all the

[1] As early as 1825 there were reported to be over 1,000,000 sheep in California (see *Census* of 1900, vol. v, p. ccxxiii).

[2] For a contemporaneous description of the conditions there, see Gregg, *Commerce of the Prairies*, 1845, vol. i, pp. 187–191, 307. In 1839 the traveler Farnham notes 200 Santa Fé sheep being driven to the Missouri market (see *Travels*, Thwaites' edition, p. 71).

[3] *Sheep Industry*, p. 948.

clip sold went to the eastern markets. Before 1860 two or three mills were started in Oregon and California, but most of the wool still went east. The California clip was reported as follows, in thousands of pounds:[1]—

1855	1856	1857	1858	1859	1860	1864
360	600	1,100	1,428	2,378	3,260	8,000

Thus by 1860 a start had been made in wool-growing in the Far West. It had received its initiative from the demand for meat, and as yet was of slight importance in amount. This, however, was the only large section of the country where at the close of the period the industry of wool-growing was not losing ground.

Summary, 1840–1860.

We may now review the years from 1840 to 1860 and form our conclusions in the light of all the facts presented. For the first half of this period the price of wool was low, owing to an increase in the supply both in the United States and elsewhere. The imports of wool in all forms remained about stationary under the tariff of 1842. In the East there was only a slight decline in the flocks; in the West, a phenomenal increase, with a still greater advance in the quantity of wool sent from there to the markets. The net result of these movements brought the country about 1845–46 to the verge of becoming an exporter of medium fine wool, though still a heavy importer of other grades.

At that time the impression was very general that a few years would see the country a great exporter of this staple. The *New York Evening Post* said: "We have already referred to the fact that is becoming every year more certain, viz: that this country is adapted by means of its extensive prairies to become in a few years a larger producer and exporter of wool than any other nation."[2] A person addressing the New York State Agricultural Society in 1848 said: "We shall soon have wool to spare, and we shall be called upon to aid in clothing the inhabitants of Europe as we now aid to feed them."[3] A national convention of wool-growers, assembled at Steubenville, Ohio, in 1847, resolved that it was of the utmost

[1] *Hunt's Merchants' Magazine*, vol. lii, p. 236.

[2] Quoted in *Niles' Register*, vol. lxvi, p. 387 (1844).

[3] *Transactions* of the Society, vol. vii, p. 547.

importance that a committee be appointed to ascertain the best foreign markets for their surplus wool.[1] The Nestor of the wool growers, H. S. Randall, wrote: "Our surplus wools can be exported to England at any time at a reasonable profit."[2] Numerous shipments were actually made — one lot even from Oregon — and the appearance of American wool on the London market attracted no little attention;[3] but the results fell sadly short of these brilliant hopes. The grade of this wool was either medium or fine, but the amount of dirt it contained and the poor condition in which it came to the market told against it. The exports were never important in quantity and frequently resulted in a loss.[4]

Conditions soon changed, and the notion of exporting at once vanished. The foreign production of wool continued to advance, and imports in the guise of manufactured goods came in ever-increasing amounts. The output from the western states also rose, and this in the face of the low price of wool. The East, however, could not continue the competition under these conditions, and soon relegated the industry to a position of very secondary importance.

During the last eight years of the period the price of wool was high, and general conditions were apparently favorable, yet the wool-growing industry declined. In the East it was simply a continuation of the previous fall: even better prospects failed to bring back the sheep. In the West the previous rise under low prices was now followed by a falling off under higher prices. In its main seat, the industry was losing ground, and no other region had as yet appeared prepared to take its place. Meanwhile the country's dependence upon foreign wool was rapidly increasing, attaining its maximum at

[1] *Prairie Farmer*, vol. vii, p. 242.

[2] *Sheep Husbandry*, p. 122; see also p. 296. A writer in *Hunt's Merchants' Magazine* says, "In medium grade wool, such as had ranged in our markets the past season at from 22 to 40 cents, we do not now, and probably never shall again, need protection. We can produce it as cheaply as any other nation, and shall export annually a constantly increasing amount. Yet, let it be remembered that we are exporters of this quality only, and large importers of others" (vol. xiv, p. 246).

[3] See *Niles' Register*, vol. lxix, pp. 162–163, 288; vol. lxxi, p. 192; vol. lxxii, p. 331. See also *American Agriculturist*, vol. iii, p. 329. It was said that Bishop Campbell, of Pennsylvania, actually went to Europe to seek a market for the finer wools of this country (see *Niles' Register*, vol. lxxiii, p. 16).

[4] See *Prairie Farmer*, vol. vi, p. 258. See also *Report of the Secretary of the Treasury*, 1845, pp. 471–472.

the close of the period, when it reached a point that has never since been equaled.

On the whole, the tariff does not seem to have been of much benefit to the wool-grower during this period. During the first few years the lower grades of wool were admitted at a purely nominal duty, while domestic medium and fine wool filled the home market. During the last few years the most dangerous competing foreign wools were admitted free. The intermediate period, when the duty on raw wool was fairly high and the actual protection afforded was the greatest (in spite of the imports of manufactured goods), was marked during the first years by the flocks of the East being cut in half and during the latter years by the beginning of a decline in the West. It is evident, then, that the actual course of the industry had little relation to the tariff. The first of the decline in the East was due to competition from other wool-growers, both domestic and foreign. The later decline in the East and both the rise and the fall in the West were mainly due to competition from the other products of the farm. For the whole period, this competition from other products was, therefore, the dominating factor in the course of the wool-growing industry of the United States.

CHAPTER VI

THE CIVIL WAR EPISODE, 1860–1870.

THE period upon which we now enter is unique in the history of wool-growing. It deals with a very distinct and separate episode in this history. The episode is peculiar in that it played no part in the real development of the industry. Had its events never taken place, had the whole period been omitted, the trend of affairs in the succeeding years, except in one region, would not have varied in any essential respect. To the record of permanent growth and development this chapter can add little or nothing. Nevertheless it presents an opportunity for studying the interaction of economic forces which is of more than usual interest. Thus we find here a striking example of how mistaken a calculation may govern the economic activities of a large group of people, and how widely at variance it may be with that assumed for the "economic man." The point of chief interest, however, is the record afforded of the manner in which a war, together with the abnormal conditions which it engenders, may upheave an industry, stop the natural course of its development, and stimulate abnormal forms of growth; only to have it found, when peace returns, that all these steps have to be retraced, while the industry goes through the wasting process of readjustment. Although the period thus serves to bring out one of the more commonly neglected sides of the widespread economic waste which follows in the train of war, it also adds a new set of factors to the great variety which have already been found to act upon this industry.

In studying this episode it will be best to divide the decade into two parts. The period of prosperity, covering the phenomenal rise of the sheep industry, continued to the end of 1866. The reaction which succeeded had practically run its course by the end of 1870.

The Period of Prosperity, 1860–1866.

The Course of Prices.

There were but few commodities the market for which was so altered by the situation arising out of the Civil War as was the case with wool. In the first place there was the unusual demand for wool which, as seen during the War of 1812, always arises in time of strife to supply the needs of the army — in this case an army of over a million men. In addition there now appeared the scarcity of cotton. For the previous half-century or more cotton had been slowly invading the domain of wool. By far the greater part of the world's supply of this fibre came from our Southern states. When the outbreak of hostilities virtually cut off the supply of cotton upon which so many depended, wool was called upon to make up the deficiency. This meant not only the substitution of wool for the cotton employed in the woolen manufacture, but also the use of woolen cloths for many purposes formerly met by cotton. On top of the increase in the demand for wool from these sources came the rise of prices due to the heavily inflated currency. According to all appearances, then, the price of wool might be expected to mount skyward, and the wool-growers' prospects of reaping a rich harvest were of the brightest.

In order to comprehend how the situation actually worked out during this troubled period it is necessary to clear the air of the deceiving effects produced by the inflated currency. It was the zealous wool-grower's failure to do just this which made it possible to lure him on by a vague mirage. For, as will later be shown, the one fact which the grower of wool saw during the period of the war was the steadily rising price of his product.

That this rise was so phenomenal as to hold his gaze very fixedly is not surprising when we compare the high prices of October, 1864, with the low prices of July, 1861, and find that the former show an advance for Ohio fine, medium, and coarse washed wool of 171%, 217%, and 355% respectively. But if we reduce the quotations for 1864 to a gold basis the increase is cut down by from two thirds to three quarters, the figures then being 31%, 53%, and 110% respectively.[1] Though these figures are of interest as showing the extreme extent of the advance which took place, it is of more importance to know the general level of prices maintained at this period, and how it compared with that for the preceding years.

[1] Wherever gold prices are given they have been calculated from the table of gold quotations in the *Bureau of Statistics, Finance, Commerce, and Immigration*, 1895, p. 518; also found in *Report of the Indianapolis Monetary Commission*, p. 562.

Average Price of Ohio Washed Wool per Pound.

	Fine	*Medium*	*Coarse*	*Av.* 3 *grades*
1852–1861	51.00 cts.	43.48 cts.	37.65 cts.	44.04 cts.
1862–1865 (currency)	75.63	73.94	70.89	73.49
1862–1865 (gold)	49.39	45.85	43.78	46.34

Increase or Decrease of Average Prices in 1862–65 *over* 1852–61.

Currency	+48%	+70%	+88%	+67%
Gold	− 3	+ 5	+16	+ 5

This table shows that during the Civil War the average currency price of wool in this country advanced between 48% and 88%, according to grade, over the level of the previous decade. The coarser the grade, the greater was the advance. But the most astonishing revelation is made when we look beneath the currency prices and reduce the quotations to the sound basis of gold. We then discover that the greatest rise in the average gold price of that grade of wool which advanced the most during the war was but 16%, while fine wool was actually lower than during the previous decade.[1] In brief, taking the average of all three grades, we find that *the Civil War advanced the gold price of wool but* 5%![2]

[1] Some of the advance, moreover, especially on the lower-priced wool, must be credited to the higher tariff duties.

[2] A study of price movements for this period shows that the upward trend of currency prices due to the premium on gold lagged slightly behind the rise of that premium until 1865, and was also slower to make the decline which succeeded (cf. Mitchell's *Gold, Prices, and Wages under the Greenback Standard*, p. 77). Thus using the premium on gold as the measure for reducing currency prices to a gold basis tends slightly to underestimate the real level before 1865 and to overestimate it after that date. The chance for error here is, however, so insignificant for the purposes of this study that it may safely be disregarded. The following table, on a somewhat different basis, by G. W. Bond, a careful authority of the time, shows substantially the same results. According to this, gold prices for coarse wool were higher during the three years after July, 1864, than for either the three years preceding or the four years before the war broke out, while fine wool was lower during the war than at either of the two other periods.

Average Prices of Domestic Wool per Pound.

	July, 1857–April, 1861	April, 1861–July, 1864		July, 1864–April, 1867	
	Gold	*Paper*	*Gold*	*Paper*	*Gold*
Fine	49.15 cts.	66.15 cts.	47.73 cts.	75.54 cts.	49.05 cts.
Medium	42.73	64.23	46.73	71.12	46.01
Coarse	33.69	57.15	38.20	65.00	41.63

(*Report of the Tariff Commission*, 1882, vol. ii, p. 2435.)

That this situation was not fully realized at the time by any large body of the people is evident from the tone of contemporary papers and from the action of the farmers. A great advance in prices had been expected as a result of the inevitable increase in demand which would follow from the needs of vast armies and from the scarcity of cotton. When the rapid rise in market quotations actually came, it was assumed that the expected had taken place. It is only too clear that the growers of wool seldom analyzed this rise in order to determine how much of it was real or how much fictitious and due entirely to the depreciated currency. To be sure, there were not lacking those who pointed out how illusory prices were: trade reports and, occasionally, agricultural journals made note of it. But actions speak louder than words, and further study only adds to the conviction that the basis of action for sheep-owners generally was the *currency* price of wool.

Further proof of the assertion that most of the increase in wool quotations was fictitious is obtained by a glance at the course of prices in the world's market — London. Comparing the average yearly prices of several grades for the two periods 1852–1861 and 1862–1865, we find in the latter period an advance or decline over the former as follows:[1] —

Lincoln middle wether	42%	advance
Down ewe	28%	"
Port Phillip superior fleece	5%	"
" " medium "	1%	"
" " grease	11%	"
Cape scoured	6%	decline
Cape grease	9%	"

The first two grades quoted — the only ones showing any marked rise in price — were the clip of English breeds of sheep, and were, the Lincoln especially, unlike any then generally grown in the United States. The other grades more nearly corresponded to the greater part of the clip of this country, but in these the rise was even less than here. It is thus clear that the market quotations in the United States when reduced to a gold basis but reflected those in the

[1] Calculated from tables in *Journal of the Royal Statistical Society*, vol. xxxiii, pp. 514–521. Quotations for Argentina mestiza wool would show a decline, for carpet wool an increase.

world's market. In that market the combing wools of the English breeds and the coarser wools were the only ones to enjoy any marked advance during the Civil War.[1] Certainly there can no longer be any doubt that the scarcity of cotton and the demands of the American armies did not, in fact, produce the rise in the price of wool which was expected. The quotations for the grades commonly grown in the United States did not advance appreciably, and the general expectation to the contrary proved but a delusion and a snare.

The Effect of the Cotton Famine.

To just what extent the scarcity of cotton affected the situation it is impossible to say, though it is clear that this factor was of much less influence than had been anticipated. The substitution of wool for cotton could take place, as has already been said, either by employing wool where cotton had been used in the manufactures of wool, or through the consumption of manufactures of wool in place of manufactures of cotton.

The first of these methods was not of much importance. In the United States in 1860 the total consumption of cotton in all branches of the woolen manufacture was 21,000,000 pounds. It was estimated that the quantity of wool substituted for cotton so used was 10,000,000 pounds,[2] an amount not likely to affect the price to any great extent. For Great Britain the figures are not available, but though they must have been larger they were probably of no greater influence relatively. Taken together, both amounts, while appreciable, were hardly sufficient greatly to disturb the market.

The question how far woolen goods were substituted for cotton goods is still more difficult to answer. The consumption of raw cotton in the United States during the war was less than half the ordinary figure.[3] Though Great Britain had formerly obtained from three quarters to seven eighths of her raw cotton from the United

[1] A Liverpool wool house circular of 1865, in comparing the prices of that year with those of 1860, declared that long-stapled English wool had risen 25% and coarse imported wools 20–50%, while Australian had not materially altered, and Cape, along with Buenos Ayres mestiza, had fallen 6% and 14% respectively. All this with a rise of 200% in cotton! Quoted in *Country Gentleman*, vol. xxvi, p. 237.

[2] *Boston Board of Trade Report*, 1863.

[3] Cf. Hammond, *The Cotton Industry*, pp. 254–277. The imports of cotton rose from 1,000,000 to 25,000,000 pounds.

States, the production in other regions was so stimulated that she managed to obtain in all about 50% of her usual total supply. The average annual consumption of raw cotton in that country for the years 1862–65 was 5,000,000 hundredweight as compared with 8,900,000 for the preceding four years.[1] The actual decrease in the supply of cotton, however, is not an altogether just criterion of the scarcity of cotton wares, since there appears to have been an overabundant supply of goods on hand at the opening of the war. A trade report, written in 1864, says: "Both in this country and Europe the large accumulation of cotton goods made before the war has only just been exhausted."[2]

The clearest light is thrown on this question by the statistics of the cotton and the woolen manufacture for 1860 and 1870. In the cotton manufacture the increase in the number of looms was the smallest in any decade for which we have figures, while the consumption of raw cotton actually declined — the only instance on record. Nor did the consumption in Great Britain between 1866 and 1870 show any advance over that for 1860, though an advance has been made in every decade since.[3] Such facts clearly indicate that the events of the Civil War resulted in the cotton manufacture's being set back fully a decade in its growth. In the woolen manufacture, on the other hand, the increase in the consumption of wool was more rapid than at any other period since the industry became firmly established in the country. A similar statement may be made as to Great Britain, where the consumption of wool by that manufacture increased at a greater rate than at any other period during the nineteenth century.[4]

[1] British Board of Trade, *Charts for the St. Louis Exposition.*

[2] *New York Chamber of Commerce Report*, 1863–64, part ii, p. 88. The Report continues: "Large amounts of cotton fabrics have been sold during the year in our markets that have been held by speculators ever since 1861 and 1862. England, too, has been exporting 65% of the amount of cottons that she shipped before the war, while she has been importing only 50% of her usual amount of raw cotton; showing that she, too, has been supplying her foreign market from old accumulations. This source of the supply of cotton fabrics it may be presumed is now exhausted, and the vacuum must be partially supplied by fabrics made of wool."

[3] British Board of Trade, *Charts for the St. Louis Exposition.* Cf. Table of consumption of cotton in Great Britain, the Continent, and the United States. *Census*, 1900, vol. ix, pp. 6, 12.

[4] The following table gives the statistics for the chief textile manufactures of Great

We learn moreover that at this time there was "a considerable change in the character of the textile manufactures worn or used: woolens, linens, and mixed fabrics largely taking the place of cottons. . . . Such was the hold which the rival fabrics obtained upon the public that it is only within the past few years [the later seventies] that cotton has made any decided progress toward regaining its former position."[1] Such evidence, together with the fact that this was the period of the greatest growth of the woolen industry and the smallest growth of the cotton manufacture in the course of the century, surely justifies the conclusion that the substitution of woolen goods for cotton goods was very considerable.

Still, as the above quotation reminds one, wool was not the only fibre which could be substituted for cotton. When cotton was first introduced, flax suffered even more from its competition than wool. It was but natural, then, that the scarcity of cotton should lead to a renewed and increased use of linen goods. Statistics show a rapid increase in the consumption of this fibre in Great Britain,[2] and an American trade report declares: "The consumption of this class

Britain, the second part covering in more detail the years immediately following 1860. The changes in these years were not due to any special development in the British export trade outside of the general increase or decrease in the use of these fibres. See Ellison's *Cotton Trade of Great Britain*, pp. 120, 129.

	Pounds consumed (in thousands)			*Increase % per annum*		
	Cotton	*Wool*	*Flax*	*Cotton*	*Wool*	*Flax*
1798–1800	41.8	109.6	108.6			
1829–1831	243.2	149.4	193.8	15.5	1.2	2.5
1859–1861	1,022.5	260.4	212.0	10.9	2.5	0.3
1880–1882	1,424.6	448.6	273.8	1.9	3.3	1.4
1860	1,083	270	211			
1864	561	343	246			
1868	996	356	259			
1871	1,206	421	318			
1877	1,237	435	305			
1883	1,510	455	257			

[1] Ellison, *Cotton Trade of Great Britain*, p. 129. He continues: "As respects clothing this was particularly observable amongst the artisan, operative, and laboring classes. Woolen and mixed fabrics superseded cotton for shirts, varieties of woolen or worsted cloths superseded moleskins and corduroys for outer clothing; cotton prints for dresses, frocks, and gowns disappeared, and in their place came worsted, alpaca, and mixed fabrics."

[2] Cf. the above table in footnote to previous quotation.

of goods [linen] during the last two years [1863–64] compares with the average as almost two to one. . . . Necessity has taught that linen goods may be very largely substituted for those of cotton."[1] Here we find one reason why the scarcity of cotton did not have an even greater effect upon the wool market.

Another fact, which should not be neglected, is the relative price of cotton as compared with wool. On the Liverpool market upland middling cotton averaged 21¾*d.* a pound for the years 1862–65; and the New York quotations reduced to a gold basis were almost identical — 44 cents a pound. The gold price of the three grades of Ohio washed wool for the same period averaged 46 cents a pound.[2] But owing to shrinkage it took from two to three pounds of washed wool to make a pound of scoured wool such as could be substituted for a pound of cotton. Thus Ohio medium scoured averaged 74½ cents in gold per pound, and Ohio fine scoured 95 cents in gold. These American prices were somewhat increased by the tariff, but in the London market medium and fine scoured wools ranged from 50 to 60 cents a pound or more. In fact only a few of the coarsest carpet wools actually cost less per pound scoured than cotton at Civil War prices,[3] and it was in these coarse grades of wool that the substitution of cotton was most difficult. It is thus evident that the great rise in the price of cotton was not sufficient, from the point of view of cost, to lead anybody to use wool in its place. But all this only serves to make the situation more puzzling than ever, for the facts previously brought out make it impossible to believe that wool did not in a measure fill the place left by the deficiency in cotton. The evident solution of the difficulty is that the superior qualities, for certain purposes, of wool over cotton led people to buy woolen goods in preference to cotton goods when the latter were no longer so far below the former in cost as to make cheapness outweigh superiority. Though cotton cost less than scoured wool per pound, still the rise in cotton proved sufficient in many cases where quality was considered to turn the balance in favor of wool.

What, then, is the final conclusion as regards the effect of the

[1] *New York Chamber of Commerce Report*, 1864–65, part ii, p. 80. Also *ibid.*, 1863–64, part ii, p. 90.

[2] See page 158.

[3] For additional series of wool quotations see North's *Wool Book*, 1895, pp. 34–35.

cotton famine upon the demand for wool? We have found, on the one hand, that this scarcity in the supply of cotton was met, in part, by the unusually large supply of cotton goods existing at the opening of the war and by the increased consumption of linen goods; and, on the other hand, that though this scarcity never proved sufficient to raise the price of cotton above that of scoured wool, yet as the difference in cost grew less and less the consumer bought woolen goods in place of mixed or cotton goods. While within the woolen manufacture the substitution of wool for cotton was not very appreciable, the substitution of manufactures of wool for manufactures of cotton was considerable. The absolute reversal, during these years, of the relative rate of increase in the consumption of the two fibres which prevailed throughout the rest of the century sufficiently proves this. Altogether, then, the effect of the cotton famine upon the wool market, though not so extensive as at the time people generally expected it would be, must nevertheless have been considerable.

Such being the case, how is one to explain the fact that no signs of such an effect were visible in the quotations on the wool market?[1] For the solution of this difficulty we have to leave the demand side of the market and look at that of supply.

The World's Wool Supply.

The main explanation for the puzzling course of events in this complex situation is at once made plain by an examination of the world's wool supply for these years.

Wool in the Grease (in millions of pounds).[2]

	United Kingdom	*Continent*	*North America*	*Australasia*	*Cape*	*River Plate*	*Others*	*Total*
1860	140	500	90	60	26	43	76	935
1865	150	500	165	110	33	137	86	1181
1870	150	500	176	175	43	197	69	1295

[1] "It is a singular fact and one very different from what most people anticipated that there has been in no part of the world any appreciable advance in wool traceable to the effects of the scarcity of cotton" (*Boston Board of Trade Report*, 1863).

[2] Helmuth Schwartze & Co., *Wool Circular*, March, 1887. The figures for the United Kingdom and the Continent are for washed wool; the others, for wool in the grease. The amounts for the first three divisions represent the production of wool, for the rest the imports into Europe and North America from the countries named.

The most noticeable fact revealed by this table is the remarkable rate at which three regions, the United States, Australasia, and the River Plate, were increasing their output. We have already seen that it was not until the period last reviewed that the countries of the Southern Hemisphere had become even recognizable contributors to the world's supply of wool. But by 1860 so good a start had been made that a continuance of such a rapid rate of growth as had marked the previous decade would mean a relatively enormous addition to the world's supply. Yet, during the next five years, that rate of growth was not only continued but immensely accelerated. In fact within this half-decade, while the wool grown in the United States nearly doubled, the clip of Australasia virtually did double, and that from the River Plate more than tripled. The net result of all this was that *the world's wool supply increased over 26% in five years.* This meant a rate of annual increase three times as great as for the preceding decade. In truth it is safe to say that the years of the American Civil War are marked by the greatest annual rate of increase in the world's wool supply in the course of the nineteenth century.

In this fact is found the key which solves the problem of prices in the world's wool markets at the time. Here is the explanation for the apparent failure of the cotton famine to affect the wool market. Knowing this, we understand why the demand for wool to meet the needs of the American armies had so little effect. Had these two abnormal demands not arisen, there is every reason to believe that the period would have witnessed a decline in the world's wool market. The cotton famine had its effect upon that market, but it was of a negative sort: it helped to prevent a decline. As it was, the abnormal increase on the demand side was met by an equally abnormal increase on the supply side, hence the comparatively unchanged level of prices.

The figures for North America give the product of the United States plus 10,000,000 pounds for British North America in 1860 and 1865 and 13,000,000 in 1870. The clip of the Balkan peninsula is not included under the Continent. As the original figures for the United States for 1860 and 1865 (100,000,000 and 115,000,000 respectively) were declared to be purely nominal, I have substituted others believed to be more nearly correct. Cf. footnotes, pages 174, 176.

Imports of Wool and the Tariff.

It will now be of interest to inquire how extensively the United States drew upon this increase in the foreign wool supply to meet the emergency which the country faced. But first it is necessary to examine the provisions of the new Morrill Tariff, passed March 2, 1861, and taking effect on April first, just as the war was breaking out. This act levied a duty of 5% on all wool valued at less than 18 cents a pound, 3 cents on that valued from 18 to 24 cents inclusive, and 9 cents a pound on all put at a higher figure. Sheepskins with wool on paid 15%. These duties on raw wool were not changed by the tariff of 1862, and thus remained in force until the close of the fiscal year 1864.

Under this tariff the average annual imports of wool for the years 1862–1864 were 70,000,000 pounds, an increase of 40,000,000 pounds over the period 1858–1860, though the average value, 17 cents a pound, remained unaltered. How much came in under the various rates of duty the available statistics, frequently changed at this time, do not tell. Some information on this point, and the facts as to the chief sources of the imports, can be obtained from the following table: —

Average Annual Imports of Raw Wool, 1862–1864.

	South America	*United Kingdom*	*France*	*Turkey*	*British N. America*	*Africa*
Thousands of lbs.	21,106	15,298	8,375	4,274	3,152	10,026
Value, cents per lb.	14.4	19.0	16.8	14.0	33.6	17.6

Evidently the Southern Hemisphere continued, as in preceding years, to be the main source of supply for raw wool, and by far the larger part of the increase was in imports which came from there.[1] The highest-priced wool was that from Canada, virtually all of which was combing wool, and at this time admitted free under the treaty of reciprocity. It is certain that no appreciable quantity paid the 9-cent duty, and it is unlikely that any large amount, certainly not more than a fifth, paid the 3-cent duty as valued from 18 to 24 cents.

[1] Much of the imports from the United Kingdom were of either Colonial or Russian origin.

We know at least that no considerable quantity of high-priced wool had been imported previously, and since the demand during the war was not of such a character as to increase its importation then, the average cost per pound did not alter. Thus it is evident that most of the dutiable wool did not pay over 5%, which meant less than a cent a pound.

But this hardly measures the amount of protection afforded except on the lower grades of the domestic clip. The mere fact that some wool came in under the 3-cent duty must be sufficient evidence that the medium grade of domestic wool benefited thereby. More was not imported because the native supply came nearer to equaling the home demand for this particular grade than usual. It is even probable that the growers of the best grade of wool benefited by the 9-cent duty, if we can judge by a comparison of the American gold price with the London quotations for a similar grade. The average New York gold price for fine Ohio scoured, 1862–65, was 94.9 cents. The London price for Australian average scoured was 62.5 cents. How closely these two grades resembled one another at this time it is hard to say, but estimating the shrinkage at about two thirds, this would indicate that the duty was fully operative on this grade as well.[1] This, however, applied to a comparatively small proportion of the domestic clip, the great bulk of which was of a lower grade. It cannot be said, then, that the protection enjoyed by the average American wool-grower during the first three years of the war was very great in amount.

In the case of manufactures of wool the tariff of 1861 was supposed to restore the level of duties in force under the act of 1846. In point of fact, however, most of the rates came out somewhat higher. The simple ad valorem duties were generally abandoned, and in their place a specific or mixed duty imposed. In many cases further complexity was introduced by subdividing different classes of goods according to value, and advancing the rate on the more expensive grades, while keeping that on most of the lower grades at least as high as before. In general the complex rates of this act tended to increase the protection afforded the manufacturer. The act is notable as being the first attempt to apply the principle of a scientifically adjusted compensating duty to offset the duty on raw wool, a principle which

[1] For further discussion of this method and question see pages 226–227.

became prominent in subsequent legislation, especially in the Act of 1867.[1] The tariff of 1861 had been in force but a year when it was superseded by the Act of July 4, 1862, which took effect the following month. The need for more revenue and the effort to offset the internal revenue duties on manufactures resulted in an increase of from 5 to 10% on most classes of goods. No change was made in the raw-wool duties.

The effect of these two acts upon the importation of manufactures of wool appears in the following table, which, for purposes of comparison, includes the figures for the two preceding tariffs.

Average Annual Imports of Manufactures of Wool.

	1848–1857	1858–1860	1862	1863–1864
Value	$26,000,000	$36,000,000	$15,000,000	$27,000,000
Average rate of duty	27%	21%	32%	39%

It cannot but cause surprise to find that during the first three years of the Civil War, when the demand of this country for woolen goods was so great, the average imports were valued at but $23,000,000, a third less than during the years 1858-1860, and even below the figures for 1848–1857. By far the greater part of the falling off occurred in dress and piece goods,[2] chiefly worsteds and delaines, and the remainder was largely in cloths and cassimeres. This is probably to be explained, to some extent by the general retrenchment of expenditure during the early years of the war and to some extent by the disappearance of the southern demand, both of which causes would chiefly affect these two classes of goods. The increased protection afforded by the tariff, augmented by the premium upon gold, in which the duties were paid,[3] and only in part offset by the newly imposed internal revenue taxes, also had its effect. Of equal importance was the fact that the war demand called for goods of the coarser grades, which were just the class that the domestic manufacturer was best able to supply. At this time, too, he was not hampered by a heavy duty on the raw material for these goods, being able to import it at a

[1] *Transactions of the National Association of Wool Manufacturers*, 1865–66, Statement of Committee to U. S. Revenue Commission, p. 8.

[2] The average annual imports were $10,000,000 less than during the years 1858–60.

[3] Cf. *American Agriculturist*, vol. xxiii, p. 71.

nominal rate. Were any further evidence of the gain of the manufacturer required, it would be sufficient to point with one hand to the unusual increase in the imports of raw wool and with the other to the decreased imports of manufactured goods. To the grower, however, the exclusion of manufactures was of no benefit so long as the manufacturer was able to import his raw material unhindered.

It but remains to determine the total amount of wool, both raw and manufactured, which came into the country during these years. If we adopt the usual estimate of three pounds of raw wool per dollar of manufactured goods, we find that the increased imports of raw wool were just offset by the decline in the imports in the form of manufactured goods, so that the total for the years 1862–64 was identical in amount — 140,000,000 pounds — with that for the years 1858–1860.[1] An estimate of the proportion of these imports which came into fairly direct competition with the domestic clip shows that there also no substantial change took place.[2] It would thus appear that, throughout the first three years of the Civil War, the country was able to meet, by the increased clip from its own flocks, such extra demand for wool as the war brought.

The raising of the tariff duties, either with the hope of directly increasing the receipts, or else to compensate the manufacturer for the internal revenue taxes imposed upon him, was a part of the regular plan by which the government financed the war, though it was very belated in effective operation. The expense of the war had been the primary cause for the enactment of the tariff of 1862, and it led to a further increase of duties under the tariff of 1864. This act, taking effect July 1, 1864, is chiefly notable for the very radical advance in duties then made, resulting in the return to a level unknown for many years. The rates of duty levied on raw wool, and the average annual imports under each rate for the years 1865–1866, were: —

[1] The imports for the years 1858–1860, however, had been rather high. The figures for 1848–1857 were 100,000,000 pounds.

[2] Assuming that the proportion for raw and manufactured goods remained the same (see page 107), and that $1 in value = 3 lbs. of raw wool, the figure is 68,000,000 pounds for the years 1862–64 as compared with 76,000,000 for the preceding period. Under this tariff the assumed proportions if anything somewhat underestimate the amount of competing wool, as the worsted stuff goods made up a much smaller proportion of the imports of manufactures than usual, a fact somewhat offset by the greater proportion of non-competing coarse grades in the raw-wool imports.

	12 c. or less	*Over 12 c. but not over 24 c.*	*Over 24 but not over 32 c.*	*Over 32 c.*
Duty, cents per lb.	3	6	10+10%	12+10%
Imports, lbs.	24,831,691	29,096,285	18,786	173,028[1]
Average value, cents per lb.	11.1	16.9	31.2	46.2

The total average annual importation was 58,000,000 pounds and the average value 16.2 cents a pound, both of these figures being a trifle under those for the years of the preceding tariff. Over three quarters of the wool in the class of lowest value was imported from South America. Of the class above that, one third came from the same source, a little less from Cape Colony, and most of the remainder from Great Britain, Russia, the British East Indies, and the shores of the Mediterranean. The two highest classes were nearly all combing wool, the falling off here as compared with the preceding years being due to the expiration of the Canadian treaty of reciprocity.

What a heavy increase in protection this tariff meant is best realized when we recollect that almost four fifths of the wool imported under the preceding act paid a duty of less than a cent a pound, and only about one fifth a duty as high as three cents, while now the very lowest grade imported paid three cents a pound, and over one half of the imports paid six cents a pound. Nor was the duty offset by internal revenue taxes, as were so many of the duties at this time. It applied to the grades of wool most widely grown in the country, and meant a real and substantial net increase in the protection which the wool-grower obtained. In fact, it proved to be but the beginning of an era of greater protection than the grower had ever known. This, furthermore, is a point to be kept in mind in connection with the movements of the price of wool at this period, for it certainly must have been of some aid in postponing or lessening the decline in price which was then just beginning.

The tariff of 1864 also brought a considerable increase in the duties on manufactured goods. Most of this was justified as compensation for the higher duties on the raw material and also for the increase in the internal revenue taxes.[2] Since the life of the act was short, it

[1] Omitting 47,524 lbs. of scoured wool.

[2] G. W. Bond says: "In 1864 for the first time duties were put on manufactures of wool over and above the amount required by the manufacturer to compensate for

is sufficient to note that the increase in duties was, roughly speaking, about one third. The average annual imports of manufactures for the years 1865–1866 was $40,000,000, an increase of nearly 80% as compared with the preceding three years, and the duties paid were 53% of the value. The net results of the increase in the imports of manufactures and the decrease in the imports of raw wool was an increase in the total imports of wool of 27% over those of the preceding years. The figures of imports for these two years, however, are misleading. The increase which took place came in 1866, and was entirely due to the rush to get goods into the country before a still higher level of duties, over which Congress deliberated for so long, should be put in force. For the year 1865 the imports of both raw and manufactured wool were less than during the earlier years of the war.

Considering the period of the Civil War as a whole, we may now feel fairly safe in saying that the protective tariff was only of very moderate aid to the grower of wool. The great growth of the world's wool supply did not result in any increase in the amount of foreign wool entering the country, the additions to the domestic clip proving adequate. That growth, however, did result in reducing the level of prices in the world's market lower than it otherwise would have been, and it was not until the last year of the war that the tariff duties began to afford the American wool-grower generally substantial protection against his foreign rival.

The Woolen Manufacture.

At the outbreak of the war the woolen manufacture appeared to be in a satisfactory condition. It had suffered sharply in the brief panic of 1857, but its rapid recovery betokened good strength. Additional evidence in confirmation of this belief is found in the attitude of the manufacturers towards the Morrill tariff. As the author of that bill himself said, "it was not asked for and but coldly welcomed by the manufacturers."[1] They appeared to be well satisfied with conditions as they were, and fairly prepared to meet the task which

the duty on raw material" (Mudge's *Report on Wool and Manufactures of Wool*, 1887, p. lx).

[1] *Congressional Globe*, 1869–70, p. 3295. Cf. also Taussig, *Tariff History*, p. 159, note.

now fell upon them. The demand for army clothing, the cotton famine, the war tariffs, and the stimulus of steadily rising prices all worked together to usher in a series of very prosperous years for the manufacturer, and for the industry a period of rapid growth such as has never been equaled since it was first firmly established.[1]

The chief demand, of course, was to supply the needs of the army, and to this task the mills at once turned. Factories were run day and night and even on Sunday. In Pennsylvania, where the woolen mills were more generally engaged on army supplies than in New England,[2] some of the cotton mills were converted to this purpose.[3] The result was that "more woolen goods were manufactured during the last quarter of the year [1861] for the army of the United States than were ever made during the same period for the whole population of the country."[4] The government soon found supplies crowding in too rapidly, and withdrew such orders as it could control, with the result of a set-back for the manufacturers in the early part of 1862. But the call for 600,000 more troops in the summer of that year gave a new stimulus, and from then on the machinery in the woolen manufacture was rapidly augmented. It was estimated that in the eighteen months from July of 1862 to January of 1864 the number of sets of machinery, including those ordered, had been increased by 1000, making the total at the latter date 4500.[5] All of this machinery, moreover, was run for a longer day than had been customary. The number of woolen mills increased from 1476 in 1860 to 1704 in 1865. The New York Chamber of Commerce Report for 1864–5 says, "The business has attained a magnitude which has far exceeded the most sanguine hopes, and in looking backward scarcely seems credible."

Accurate figures of the actual amount of wool consumed are not to be had, but at least a general idea can be obtained from various

[1] Cf. *Bulletin*, vol. xxv, p. 44. D. A. Wells has the following comment on this prosperity: "Now what was true of the cotton manufacture at that period was equally true of the woolen manufacture, and in a majority of instances the large profits realized by the woolen manufactures of the United States from 1863 to 1866 were due rather to the rise in price of their raw material than to any legitimate profits derived from the manufacture and sale of their productions" (Special Commissioner of the Revenue, *Report*, 1869, p. xciii, note).

[2] *Boston Board of Trade Report*, 1864.

[3] *Ibid.*, 1862.

[4] *Ibid.*, 1862.

[5] *Ibid.*, 1864.

contemporary estimates. *The New York Economist and Dry Goods Reporter* calculated that the complete outfit of a soldier represented about 25 pounds of raw wool, and that for an army subject to the wear and casualties of war the annual consumption of woolen material was equivalent to about 60 pounds of wool per man.[1] With an army of over 1,000,000 men in the field it concluded that this meant a total annual consumption of 60,000,000–70,000,000 pounds. This is in substantial agreement with the estimates of the Boston Board of Trade. During the year ending June 30, 1862, there were purchased for the army about 24,000,000 yards of kerseys and substitutes, and nearly 1,500,000 blankets, besides other minor articles, the total amount of wool required for these being estimated at 50,000,000 pounds.[2] The best available analysis of the situation as regards demand and supply under the new conditions in 1862 is as follows:[3]

Demand.

Demand for army		50,000,000 lbs.
Demand for navy		1,000,000 lbs.
To supply place of cotton		10,000,000 lbs.
Demand for civilians (heavy in spite of loss of South)	80,000,000 lbs.	
Less what army would have taken as civilians	15,000,000 lbs.	
		65,000,000 lbs.
Total		126,000,000 lbs.

Supply.

U. S. clip (Census of 1860)	60,511,343 lbs.
Less southern	8,597,805 lbs.
	51,913,538 lbs.
Domestic clip, say	52,000,000 lbs.
Domestic pulled	8,000,000 lbs.
Imports, say	60,000,000 lbs.
	120,000,000 lbs.

[1] Quoted in *Country Gentleman*, 1862, vol. xx, p. 145.

[2] *Boston Board of Trade Report*, 1863.

[3] *Ibid.*, 1863. The Census figures taken for the domestic clip are undoubtedly too small; 80,000,000 would be more nearly correct, increasing the total supply to 140,000,000. Cf. footnote, page 176.

For 1863 the estimated consumption for the army was 61,000,000 pounds,[1] and for 1864 about 75,000,000 pounds. The total consumption of wool in 1860 was 103,000,000 pounds, and for 1864 was placed at 214,000,000.[2] This substantially agrees with the statement of the Boston Board of Trade, made at the time, that the total consumption of wool in the country had doubled since 1860.[3]

Aside from the phenomenal growth of the woolen manufacture, the most important development which the Civil War wrought in the industry was the diversification and increased variety of output then introduced. The manufacture of bunting and of numerous other minor products began at this time. But the chief advance came in worsted goods, which were extremely popular just then. Half the imports of 1863 were said to be worsteds, and the American mousseline-de-laine manufacturers had already increased their consumption of wool by two thirds since 1860.[4] The growth of this branch of the manufacture was greatly facilitated by the improvements which had been made in combing-machinery during the preceding decade.[5] In the United States its growth had previously been retarded by the difficulty in securing an adequate supply of suitable wool, but during these years it was especially favored by the chance to import its raw material free under the Canadian reciprocity treaty. This helps explain the falling off in the imports of women's dress goods during the war. The demand for combing wool was rapidly increasing everywhere, but as nearly all of the increase in the world's supply of wool was from merino sheep, there was a general shortage of this grade. The same grade of wool was especially well adapted for use as a substitute for the cotton warp which had been employed in delaines and other worsted goods, and hence a further demand.[6]

[1] *Boston Board of Trade Report*, 1864.

[2] Census figures for 1860, including 5,000,000 lbs. of carded wool.

[3] Assuming, as I have done, that the clip of this country increased 62,000,000 pounds between these years, and that the average importations of raw wool advanced by 40,000,000 pounds, the total increase of 102,000,000 is in such close agreement with the above statements that it not only helps to substantiate them, but also increases my faith in the reasonable accuracy of the estimate for the domestic clip in 1860. Cf. footnote, page 176.

[4] *Boston Board of Trade Report*, 1864.

[5] Cf. Burnley, *History of Wool and Wool Combing.*

[6] Cf. *American Agriculturist*, vol. xxiii, p. 234.

So great was the need for this grade that the Chamber of Commerce of Bradford issued a special circular urging an increased production of long wools — 4 to 7 inches — suitable for worsteds.[1] These reasons furnish the explanation for the only considerable rise in the price of wool on the world's market during the Civil War. The absence of worsted goods had always been the weakest point in the American manufacture of wool. Though still in its youth, its rise at this time made it possible to say that 1870 "found the wool manufacture thoroughly organized, for the first time, in all branches of the industry, and able to supply the greater portion of the public needs in each," the chief exceptions being fine broadcloths and fine all-wool dress goods for ladies.[2] Such was the result of the Civil War stimulus upon the manufacture of wool.[3]

The Growing of Wool.

Having reviewed the course of the market and the operation of the tariff, we may now turn to the wool-growing industry itself and follow developments there during these eventful years. According to the Census of 1860 the total number of sheep in the United States was 22,000,000.[4] Of this total, 5,000,000 were to be found in the states which later seceded, and 2,000,000 in the Far West, but the great majority were in the North Atlantic and North Central states. In 1867 the estimate of the Department of Agriculture put the total at 39,000,000, but this did not include any for the Far West. Of this total, 3,500,000 were in the states which had seceded. The same authority puts the number of sheep in the loyal states, excluding the Far West, as follows, in millions: —

1860	1864	1865	1866	1867
15.1	24.3	28.6	32.6	35.8

These figures show the growth of the sheep industry in what was at that time the real wool-growing region of the country, and best

[1] Commissioner of Agriculture, *Report*, 1864, p. 243.

[2] North, *Bulletin*, vol. xxv, p. 44.

[3] For further information as to the state of the wool manufacture at this time, see *Transactions of the National Association of Wool Manufacturers*, 1865–66.

[4] The *Census* of 1900, vol. v, p. ccxiii, gives a table showing the estimate of an assistant marshal of the unenumerated sheep, by states, in 1860, the total being 1,505,810. No such estimates are available for 1840, 1850, and 1870. For the best discussion of the Census figures see this reference.

typify the effect of the war upon the industry. This effect was, in brief, to double the number of sheep.

In absolute numbers the greatest additions to the flocks were made in the older states, where the sheep industry already had a foundation upon which to build. Thus Maine, New Hampshire, Vermont, New York, Pennsylvania, and Ohio doubled their flocks during these years. Relatively, however, the greatest increase came in the states which were being settled at the time, or in those in which the original settlers had never paid much attention to sheep but had directed all their efforts towards the cultivation of the soil. Thus in Michigan, Indiana, and Illinois the flocks tripled, in Wisconsin they multiplied four-fold, and in Kansas six-fold, while Iowa and Nebraska stand at the head of the list with an increase of nearly nine-fold. The best data available indicate that in the Far West the number more than doubled.

Figures for the wool clip at this period are very uncertain, but the writer has finally chosen the following, believing them the most accurate available.[1]

	1860	1861	1862	1863	1864	1865	1866	1867
Millions of lbs.	80	92	106	123	142	155	160	168

We may fairly conclude that during the period of the Civil War the wool clip of the country doubled. Moreover it continued to increase till 1868. At the opening of hostilities, about 12,000,000

[1] The chief dispute is over the figures at the start in 1860. The Census of 1860 returned 60,000,000 pounds for the census year, and some persons have simply accepted this. The enumeration of the wool clip by the Census is admittedly too low (cf. footnote, p. 239) and G. W. Bond insists that 100,000,000 is more nearly correct (*Bulletin*, vol. xvii, p. 305). Mr. Bond also puts the clip for 1865 at 130,000,000 (*Bulletin*, vol. i, pp. 79–80). But the evidence of a great increase in the number of sheep between these two dates is too unmistakable to make it possible to accept both of his figures. I have chosen 80,000,000 as the amount best fitting in with such various bits of evidence as bear upon the point (see pages 164, 174). The estimate for 1861 is also my own, based on the probable rate of increase. The figures for 1862–67 are those of Special Agents Tichenor and Tingle from *Report of Tariff Revision*, 1886, pp. 238–239. If anything the series overestimates the rate of increase in the first year or two, and underestimates it for the last two years. Unless otherwise indicated, the figures of the wool clip for all years after 1867 are those of Mr. James Lynch of New York for the years 1867–85, those of Mr. J. P. Truitt of Philadelphia for the years 1886–91, and those of the *Bulletin* of the wool manufacturers, these being believed to be the most reliable, and also the more commonly accepted trade figures.

pounds of the clip came from the seceding states, and between 4,000,000 and 5,000,000 from the Far West. The wool of the South, however, had never been of much importance in the wool markets, for a large part of it had been consumed at home. So-called Texas wool was just beginning to reach the markets in some quantity, but much of it came from New Mexico. Hence the defection of the South had but slight effect on the domestic wool supply. The result, as appeared when we were studying the imports, was that in spite of the increased consumption of wool it was not necessary to resort to foreign sources, for the increase in the domestic supply proved equal to the emergency.

The East.

For the two decades preceding the Civil War the flocks of the New England and Middle Atlantic states had retrograded in numbers. Under the stimulus of the war the number of sheep in these two groups of states nearly doubled. In New England the increase continued until 1867, when these states held 3,500,000 sheep, a figure about 300,000 below the number in 1840. In Massachusetts the number of sheep in 1865 (169,442) was less than half that in 1854.[1] All the mania for sheep which raged at the time proved unable to restore the situation of twenty-five years earlier. In the Middle Atlantic states the highest point was reached in 1867 with 9,300,000 sheep, in this case higher by 2,000,000 than the figures for 1840. Here, as elsewhere, the greatest increase was found in the sections which had been the strongholds of the industry a generation earlier.

In these older parts of the country, moreover, the great stimulus to the industry given by the high price of wool was supplemented by that arising from the high prices to be obtained for good stock. In many cases this latter was even greater in effect than the former, as the demand for the best stock was so strong that it rose in price relatively higher even than did wool. The rush for sheep at this time was characterized by unusual attention to the quality of the animals bought, and the breeders of fine stock reaped enormous profits.[2] The heavi-

[1] *Agriculture of Massachusetts*, 1891, p. 115.

[2] "Sheep-raisers have found the business very profitable for the past few seasons. Fine-wooled sheep have been in great demand and immense numbers have gone westward from New York, Pennsylvania, Ohio, and Vermont" (*American Agriculturist*, Feb. 1865, vol. xxiv, p. 42).

est demand came from the Middle West, where the farmers were making the greatest effort to build up their flocks, till then comparatively neglected.[1] Doubtless the large majority of buyers were fairly well satisfied with the ordinary grade sheep or else were too poor to buy anything better, but there were not a few westerners who both appreciated the value of blooded stock and had money with which to purchase it.

The greatest gains from the rage for sheep which prevailed at this period fell to the breeders of Vermont.[2] Never before or since have the flock-owners of that state reaped such a rich harvest of profits. Many of them still owned sheep of the purest blood, descended from the first importations of Spanish merinos. By a long process of careful breeding, the stock had been greatly improved and a special type developed which became known as the Vermont or American merino. The Spanish merino had passed through various waves of popularity and neglect, but in 1860 was in the ascendant in the farmers' favor. The grand prize and gold medal of the Hamburg Exposition in 1861, awarded to the merino sheep of the Vermont breeder Edwin Hammond, in competition with sheep from all over the globe, attracted world-wide attention, and served to advertise the stock of this state just at the time when everybody was looking for the best sheep. The Civil War period proved to be the golden age of the merino in this country, and during that period no breed of sheep was in greater demand or could command a higher price through the country at large than the Vermont merino.

The prices obtained by Vermont breeders were from $100 to $200 for full-blooded ewes, the best easily bringing the higher figure, and from $1000 to $3500 for good rams. These prices moreover continued to be obtained after the war, till 1866.[3] As late as September, 1865,

[1] "There is an active sale of merinos throughout New York, immense numbers being purchased for western markets. For example, upwards of 1,100 have gone from two or three towns in Onondaga Co. this season. We hear of large sales in other counties." — *The Rural New Yorker;* quoted in *Country Gentleman*, Dec. 15, 1864, p. 385.

[2] "Sheep fever is raging to a high degree in Vermont." There follows a list of sales in which several sheep brought over $1000 apiece. (*Country Gentleman*, Oct. 15, 1863, p. 257.)

[3] An allowance must of course be made for currency prices. The highest price quoted is said to have been paid by an Illinois wool-grower, after having spent several weeks looking over Vermont flocks, for a Spanish merino ram bred by A. L. Bingham

a Michigan wool-grower paid $3000 for a yearling ram bought of Colonel Stowell of Cornwall, Vt.[1] The same issue of the paper that announces this sale also tells of the sale of two rams for $2500 each, and of five others for from $1000 to $1500 each.[2] The situation is admirably depicted in the following extract from a contemporary account written about February, 1865. "For several years there has been a gradually increasing interest in sheep-raising which seems now to have reached nearly its height in a mania for paying the most extravagant prices for fine-wooled sheep of different breeds. We have created a breed of our own, the American merino, which has attracted the world's attention by the prizes at Hamburg. This and the increased demand for wool in the Civil War and the inflation of prices have driven prices very high. We hear of sales of rams for $800, $1000 and $2500, and ewes and lambs in proportion. It is even reported that Mr. Edwin Hammond of Vermont refused to take $10,000 for his ram Golden Drop. Many people have taken to sheep-raising who were entirely ignorant of the business, and every animal which had the look of a merino and a greasy fleece has had a ready market."[3]

The last assertion was only too true, and it affords one of the best illustrations of the extent to which the mania for sheep was carried. The fleece of the Vermont merino, yielding a fine grade of wool, was very heavy, and was noted for its yolk or grease, which frequently made up two thirds or more of the total weight, and gave the fleece a dark brownish color. This well-known characteristic was very profitably utilized by Yankee ingenuity. Sheep of inferior blood, or more likely those of the French merino type, which had fallen into disfavor by 1860,[4] were covered with what became known as

and E. C. Eells. See *Country Gentleman*, Dec. 15, 1864, p. 385. Cf. *Paris Universal Exposition*, 1867, Report on Wool and Manufactures of Wool, p. 75.

[1] *Country Gentleman*, vol. xxvi, p. 205.

[2] For other records of prices and sales see *Country Gentleman*, vol. xxi, p. 177; vol. xix, pp. 236, 348; vol. xxii, p. 257; *American Agriculturist*, vol. xxiii, p. 330. The agricultural papers of the time are full of them.

[3] *American Agriculturist*, vol. xxiv, p. 43.

[4] A New York wool-grower says: "I agree with Mr. Randall in his estimate that between 80 and 90% of our northern and eastern wool-growers now thoroughly detest them. Mr. Randall thinks breeders have jumped off the bridge on the other side. I know that a French sheep could not be sold here to our breeders for any money, and there are but few who would take them as a gift" (*Country Gentleman*, 1860, vol. xv, p. 140).

"Cornwall finish" — a preparation of linseed oil and burnt umber — "so as to make the Spanish blood predominate," the result being a "nearly black external coating hardly to be distinguished from the natural gum by the most practised eye." [1] Such sheep, when sent to the western states, appear to have found ready buyers among the farmers there, who were little accustomed to judging this class of stock. But in many cases not even this amount of deception was necessary: the mere name of "Vermont sheep" was one to conjure with. Though there were known to be many excellent flocks in the neighboring state of New York, we are told that "not a few go to Vermont to be resold from that state."[2] A pamphlet issued by the Onondaga County (N. Y.) Wool-Growers' Association complained that sheep were taken from that county to the east for the sake of bringing them back or carrying them still farther west "*as pure* Vermonters." The imposture, it was explained, did not consist so much in misrepresenting the sheep — which were declared to be as good as nine-tenths of the Vermont sheep — as in obtaining an exorbitant price for them on a purely fictitious basis.[3] These incidents, unimportant as they may appear in themselves, are full of significance; for what could give better proof that a perfect mania for wool-growing possessed the American farmer at this time?

How unreasoning was the craze is further illustrated by the fact that the grade of wool which was advanced in price relatively more than any other by the Civil War was the long combing wool of certain breeds of English sheep, and that, of the grades commonly grown in this country, the coarse wool rose most, while the clip of the much sought-for fine merino was least affected.[4] The unusually heavy fleece of the full-blooded merino counted in its favor, though two thirds or more of the weight was nothing but grease.

Another curious fact is that the farmers continued to pay high prices for sheep through the fall of 1865, after the war was over. To pay high prices at the opening of the war was perfectly reasonable: everything pointed to a great increase in the demand for wool,

[1] *Country Gentleman*, vol. xv, p. 140. [2] *Ibid.*, Dec. 15, 1864, p. 385.

[3] *Ibid.*, July 7, 1864, p. 16.

[4] "Certain grades of coarse wool have brought higher prices than superior grades of merino and other fine wool, and have met with a much quicker and more advantageous market" (*American Agriculturist*, February, 1865, p. 43).

and they could hardly foresee the enormous increase in the world's supply which followed. The strange thing is that after the first year or two, when the actual course of events had belied their expectations, they still continued to pay these high prices, continued moreover when the war, the primary cause for the rise of those expectations, had come to a close.[1] The prospect of an increase in the tariff duties, which was being vigorously agitated then, had something to do with it, but is hardly an adequate explanation. The real power which sustained these prices was a blind but tenacious faith in hopes which, though originally not without some justification, had long before been shown to be illusory.

There was one tendency in the wool-growing industry of the East at this period which had little connection with Civil War events: this was the movement towards raising mutton sheep. The movement had received a decided impetus during the fifties, when the price of sheep's meat about doubled, as compared with the previous level. The advance of that decade was not only maintained during war times but even increased, though both pork and beef declined in value.[2] The increase in price was doubtless chiefly due to the great demand for sheep consequent on the high price of wool. There was, however, a steadily growing demand for mutton, as contemporary statements like the following bear witness. "The scarcity of mutton has, as would be expected, been aggravated by the rise in wool. We say aggravated because year by year before the breaking out of the war it had been more and more difficult to procure a supply of good mutton at reasonable prices. At present this article is one of the luxuries. Even if the wool market should return to its ordinary level or below it there is abundant encouragement for sheep-raising."[3] Randall, writing in 1860, said: "I am strongly impressed with the opinion that the production of mutton has been too much disregarded as a concomitant of the production of wool. A pound of well fatted mutton can be grown more cheaply than a pound of any other well fatted meat. Its consumption is rapidly increasing in the cities."[4] The scarcity of good mutton is surprising.

[1] See page 178.

[2] This statement is for gold prices. See table on page 192, and chart in Appendix.

[3] *American Agriculturist*, November, 1862, vol. xxi, p. 330.

[4] *Fine Wool Sheep Husbandry*, p. 152.

At this time much of the best mutton for Boston had to be obtained from Kentucky, the early centre of the mutton breeds of sheep in this country, and the best New York hotels imported their supply from England.[1] An English newspaper correspondent writes: "American mutton, even in the most expensive restaurants, is detestable. . . . Now and then in private houses, and as a great delicacy, you are regaled with a haunch or a saddle of English mutton imported by Cunard steamers." [2] Another says: "We are rapidly finding out too in this country that mutton of really good quality is not inferior as food to any other meat." [3] In 1864 a leading agricultural paper wrote: "There has been a great improvement in the direction of mutton within ten or fifteen years — an improvement which will undoubtedly extend in the future until it reaches restaurants and hotels as well as the private tables of fastidious purchasers. As a general rule we are only beginning to learn what good mutton is. . . . But the proportion of mutton eaten to other meats is showing a gradual increase which will undoubtedly continue as the quality of what is generally marketed becomes better." [4]

Signs of the interest taken in the improvement of mutton are seen in the demand for Southdown sheep. Some of this breed had been brought to New Jersey from the famous flock of Jonas Webb in England, and frequent notices of the sale of this stock are found in contemporary agricultural papers.[5] The prices, however, did not begin to equal those paid for merinos, $500 being exceptional for a ram, while ewes seldom brought $100. Other mutton breeds, such as the Cotswold and Leicester, were in better favor because of their long combing wool. In the United States the chief source of supply for sheep of these breeds was Kentucky,[6] but many were imported from Canada or England.

Another factor, which had before worked in favor of the mutton breeds but which was especially felt during the war, was the relatively greater increase in the price of the coarser-fibred combing

[1] *Country Gentleman*, vol. xxiii, p. 41.

[2] *Ibid.*, 1864, vol. xxiv, p. 290.

[3] *Ibid.*, 1864, vol. xxiii, p. 41.

[4] *Ibid.*, vol. xxiv, p. 289.

[5] *American Agriculturist*, vol. xxi, pp. 255, 303; vol. xxiii, p. 299.

[6] Hence we find the unusual spectacle of sheep not meant for slaughter moving eastward when, in 1864, a flock of 100 mutton sheep selected from Kentucky was sent to Concord, N. H., to be disposed of among New England farmers. See *Country Gentleman*, vol. xxiv, p. 336.

wool which they yielded than in that of other wool.[1] This advantage grew as the rising worsted manufacture of the country increased its consumption, and especially when the end of the reciprocity treaty with Canada shut off the free importation of combing wool from that quarter.

At this period, consequently, the discussion among the farmers as to whether they should keep sheep mainly for wool or for mutton became very vigorous.[2] The general conclusion was, however, that where a city market was easily accessible, if the land were fairly rich and only a small flock of sheep (say 50–75) were kept, the mutton breeds paid better. This virtually restricted these breeds to parts of the eastern section of the country, but occasionally flocks of mutton sheep appeared in the North Central states. In the East the practice of buying sheep (generally western stock) in the fall and feeding them through the winter in order to sell the lamb and mutton in the spring, was growing more common.[3] As population increased and cities grew, the area in which mutton sheep found favor steadily expanded. At this period, however, it was still very limited in extent. In the Middle West virtually all sheep-owners, and in the East a large majority of them, were primarily concerned, not with the raising of mutton, but with the growing of wool.

The Middle West.

The main seat of the wool-growing industry of this country at the time of the Civil War was in those states of the Middle West centring about Ohio, to which it had been transferred from the East during the previous period. But the six years or more preceding the war had witnessed a steady decline in the flocks of these states. Throughout the Middle West it was only in states then in process of settlement — such as Kansas, Nebraska, Iowa, or Michigan — that there were any signs of progress. The war-time stimulus, however, completely changed the face of affairs, and the rush for sheep in the forties, which had first generally introduced them into this region, was quite outdone by the stampede that now ensued.

Ohio was traditionally the great wool-growing state of this section.

[1] Cf. Commissioner of Agriculture, *Report*, 1862, p. 255.
[2] Cf. *Country Gentleman*, vol. xvi, p. 236; vol. xvii, pp. 108, 124, 225.
[3] *Ibid.*, vol. xvi, p. 44.

There the number of sheep, which had declined from 4,800,000 in 1854 to 3,500,000 in 1860, had by 1865 risen to 6,300,000, and in 1868 reached 7,688,845, the highest point ever attained in the history of this or any other state with the single exception of Texas.[1] In Illinois the flocks had fallen to 775,000 head in 1860, but by 1865 they had nearly tripled, and by 1867 nearly quadrupled.[2] An Illinois farmer wrote to the *American Agriculturist* in 1862, "We want 5000–10,000 sheep in this county immediately. Where can we get them and at what price?" and the editor remarked that similar inquiries were coming in from other points in the West.[3] Iowa, for which the Census of 1860 returned 280,000 sheep, had in 1863, according to the state census of that year, nearly 600,000. During the latter year, it was reported, the railroads alone brought in 63,000.[4] Michigan, much of which was still unsettled, became by the doubling of her flocks one of the leading wool-growing states. In the other states to the west of the Mississippi settlement was still rather sparse and, though the rate of increase in the flocks was phenomenal, the absolute clip was small. The growth of the industry for the two sections of this group is indicated by the following table, which also shows that here, as elsewhere, the advance continued for two or three years after the war had come to an end.[5]

Number of Sheep (in thousands).

	1860	1864	1865	1866	1867
North Central	6,628	11,496	14,301	16,530	14,620
Trans-Mississippi	1,224	1,875	2,409	2,967	3,662

[1] The number of sheep in Ohio each year was:—

1860	3,546,073	1864	5,560,318
1861	3,943,436	1865	6,305,796
1862	4,448,227	1866	6,966,028
1863	5,042,439	1867	7,555,507

(See *Sheep Industry*, p. 574.)

[2] These are Department of Agriculture figures. Others make the number nearly 3,000,000 as early as 1865. See *Sheep Industry*, p. 596.

[3] *American Agriculturist*, vol. xxi, p. 69.

[4] Commissioner of Agriculture, *Report*, 1864, p. 168. J. B. Grinnell, who owned or held on shares from 6000 to 7000 sheep, says: "The war stimulated wool-growing immensely in Iowa. I sold my wool for several years at $.75 to $1.05 a pound" (*Tariff Commission*, 1882, p. 1136).

[5] For 1860, Census figures are given; for the other years, estimates of the Department of Agriculture. These figures do not include the Far West.

Throughout the Middle West the farmers seem to have been suddenly seized with a conviction that their section was predestined to be a great wool-growing country. In comparing the conditions there, especially on the prairies, with those in the East, they calculated that the cost of keeping sheep was far less in the West. In the *Report* of the Commissioner of Agriculture for 1862 it was concluded, on the basis of a thousand letters from farmers in the northern states, that the average annual cost of keeping sheep in the older states was $2.65 a head, while on the plains it was but $0.50. The former figure was probably too high (judging from other reports, between $1.00 and $1.50 would have been more nearly accurate for the average flock), nevertheless, the difference in favor of the plains was considerable. Pasturage was abundant on the prairies, while little or no protection was necessary for the flocks in winter. The rapid railroad development since the fifties had made the region beyond the Mississippi accessible, and as the lines spread out ahead of settlement a larger part of the population secured easy access to the eastern markets.[1] Once a flock was started, the chief item in the cost of its maintenance was pasturage, and on the prairies this was at a minimum. Free grazing land was still abundant in many sections, and after 1862 a homestead could be had for nothing; even if land were bought outright, it was cheap. "The prairie farmer," says a writer in 1864, " can commence operations without buying anything but his sheep. Or, if he does not choose to be a pure nomad, he can buy acres for less than the annual interest on acres of the ordinary grazing land of the older states." [2]

One difficulty, however, beset the western farmer, one which had appeared before [3] and which is typical of newly developing regions — the lack of capital. For many the important question was not so

[1] In 1862 the cost of shipping wool from Kansas to New York was two cents a pound. See *Country Gentleman*, vol. xx, p. 111.

[2] *American Agriculturist*, 1864, vol. xxiii, p. 223. The writer contrasts with this the situation elsewhere. "He who embarks extensively in sheep husbandry in the older states must buy a large amount of comparatively high priced land, clear up the forest, fence his land carefully, sow pastures and meadows, build barns for winter storage and shelter, or buy all these things before he is ready to purchase a flock of sheep to commence his business. This requires much capital." As we have seen, however, the question of raising sheep involved the cost and profit in raising other products just as much as the cost and profit in raising sheep.

[3] Cf. *ante*, page 143.

much that of maintaining a flock as that of getting the flock in the first place. To begin sheep-raising on any considerable scale required no small outlay, especially if one desired good stock. Reports like the following, from different counties in Iowa, well illustrate this point. "No very large flocks; farmers working into them as fast as their means permit." "Farmers who have had capital have turned their attention to wool-growing, regardless of price, paying $5.00 a head." "Sheep are beginning to be introduced by the more wealthy and enterprising." [1] As previously, the farmers in many cases overcame this difficulty by securing small bands of sheep on shares, agreeing to keep them for half the clip and half the increase or on similar terms, and thus eventually securing flocks of their own.[2] It is evident, however, that the farmers were too profoundly convinced of the superior advantages which the region offered the wool-grower to let this obstacle remain in the way very long. This conviction is admirably expressed in the following extract from the *Report* of the Illinois Board of Agriculture for 1864: "If there is any one branch of husbandry in which the state of Illinois should, and, as we believe, will become especially prominent it is the production of sheep and wool." [3] But the actions even more than the words of the farmers of the Middle West compel the belief that they were thoroughly persuaded that with them wool-growing had a great and permanent future.

The Far West.

It was found that at the close of the preceding period the Far West was the only part of the country where the sheep flocks seemed to have real prospects of future growth. Up to that time the chief cause for such little spread of the sheep industry as had taken place in

[1] Commissioner of Agriculture, *Report*, 1864, pp. 178–179.

[2] This method was a very common one, and has continued in use down to the present. Cf. *Sheep Industry*, p. 736; also *ante*, page 144.

[3] Quoted in *Sheep Industry*, p. 594. The *Report* continues: "We found this statement not simply on the facts that wool-growing here has been very profitable, that the soil and climate are peculiarly favorable, that the number of sheep and number of flock-masters have multiplied with great rapidity within a few years; but we add to these another consideration which is clearly seen and beginning to be felt with great force — woolen manufactures must be largely increased. The necessity exists and the facilities abound." For a laudation of the advantages of Kansas, cf. *Country Gentleman*, 1862, vol. xx, p. 111.

this section was the demand for mutton which arose from the mining camps. Although small quantities of wool had been shipped eastward from California, Oregon, and New Mexico before 1860, it was really the Civil War stimulus which first led the sheep husbandry of this region to make the production of wool its primary object.

This assertion finds support in the rise of a demand in the early years of the war for the best merino sheep for shipment to California. The editor of the *Country Gentleman* remarked, "California particularly seems to be awakened to the value of all kinds of improved stock. Every steamer now takes out more or less."[1] New Mexico had no full-blooded merinos till 1859.[2] In this section of the country, as in the Middle West, people were suddenly seized with the notion that with them conditions were ideal for the growing of wool. "If Oregon has a specialty," says a report of the Oregon Agricultural Society for 1862, "it is her preëminence as a wool-growing country. Until recently little attention has been paid to the matter of wool-growing, but it is now becoming one of the staple interests of the state."[3] The result of all this interest was that by the end of the war the clip of this region had more than doubled, and by 1867 had mounted to over 11,000,000 pounds.[4] Virtually all of this wool came from the three states, New Mexico, Oregon, and California, chiefly from the last named. Outside of these the stimulus to wool-growing was but little felt in this region.

The gradual spread of sheep to the other states of the Rocky Mountain group at this period was due, primarily, to the demand for mutton. The chief increase came in Nevada, where the rapid development of the mines furnished a steadily expanding market. The Mormon settlers in the eastern part of the state also increased the number of sheep.[5] A good many flocks were to be found in Utah, the source of supply being either New Mexican sheep or those driven across the plains from the states to the east. The chief market was the Mormon settlements, though many flocks fattened here were

[1] Vol. xv, p. 48. Cf. also p. 80, and vol. xvii, p. 113.

[2] *Sheep Industry*, p. 919.

[3] Quoted in *Country Gentleman*, vol. xxi, p. 336.

[4] The clip of California was 4,600,000 pounds in 1861. See *Hunt's Merchants' Magazine*, vol. xlviii, p. 105.

[5] *Census*, 1880, vol. iii, p. 1058.

afterwards driven to the mines. Some sheep were to be found in Arizona, and a few bands in southern Colorado, but elsewhere, notably into the more northern states, they scarcely penetrated. In short, apart from the comparatively small output of New Mexico, California, and Oregon, the Far West contributed nothing to the wool supply of the country, and except in these three states, the course of the wool-growing industry in this section, being determined largely by the local needs for mutton, remained uninfluenced by the events of the Civil War.

As one looks back over this account of the wool-growing industry of the country, the fact which must now stand out more clearly than ever is that the Civil War absolutely reversed the current of events which at its outbreak was shaping the industry. The decline which had prevailed throughout the main wool-growing sections of the country was suddenly stopped. In its place came a phenomenal advance — an advance which, though failing to recover fully the ground once lost in the East, yet in the Middle West carried the industry to a point of development unknown either before or since. But a sound economic justification for this advance has yet to be discovered.

The Situation in General Agriculture.

It was found that during the twenty years preceding the Civil War the course of the wool-growing industry was determined by the situation in general agriculture — by the relative profitableness of wool-growing and other agricultural pursuits. For the period now in review, this question of relative profitableness is greatly complicated by the abnormal events of war times, but a study of the problem offers hope of further light on the mysterious course of the sheep husbandry.

The decade and a half preceding 1860 had brought rather unusual prosperity and development to the agriculture of the country. The rapid extension of railroads gave to vast areas which had previously been unable to reach the water-ways easy communication with the markets, and, in spite of the great increase in production, the rise of the export trade in food-stuffs helped to maintain a generally high level of prices. The panic of 1857, though sharp, was of short duration, and did not seriously affect the agricultural community. In

1860, then, the Middle West was in the midst of a period of rapid development.[1]

The Homestead Act, offering free land to settlers, went into effect early in the war, and during the first two and a half years of its operation some 21,600 farms were taken up, chiefly in Minnesota, Michigan, Wisconsin, Kansas, Nebraska, and Iowa. Farm machinery, which was very rapidly coming into use, tended to offset the scarcity of labor due to the drain for the army. In this country the harvests of 1860, 1861, and 1862 proved to be unusually good,—in fact, the largest known up to that time, and, except for some damage to corn in 1863 and to wheat in 1864, the harvests continued satisfactory throughout the war.[2] The steady rise in prices, in the face of the fact that by the last of 1864 agricultural produce had more than doubled, furnished its usual stimulus, and as freight rates from Chicago to New York advanced but little during the war, in some cases even falling, the farmer gained there also.[3] Furthermore, the West, being a debtor section of the country, greatly profited by the opportunity offered to pay off its mortgages in depreciated currency.[4] Dr. Fite concludes that "in the middle and last part of the war the western farmers enjoyed vigorous prosperity; there was steady progress in the size of the crops, in the extent of the cultivated area, and in population; profits were normal in the middle of the struggle, and in the last part of it extraordinarily high." Though the war era as a whole was fairly prosperous it can hardly be called a period of great agricultural development, for in fact the relative increase in the chief crops during the decade 1860–70 was less than normal.[5]

[1] Fite, "The Agricultural Development of the West during the Civil War," *Quarterly Journal of Economics*, vol. xx, pp. 259–278. For a more detailed account see this article.

[2] The good crops, though the main cause, in a measure offset the low prices which prevailed from the autumn of 1860 to the summer of 1862.

[3] See Fite, *Quarterly Journal of Economics*, vol. xx, p. 270. For freight rates 1857–70, see *Report New York Produce Exchange*, 1872–73, pp. 392–396.

[4] Cf. D. A. Wells, *Recent Financial, Industrial, and Commercial Experiences of the United States*, p. 25.

[5] Sheep were the only stock to increase in numbers. Swine did not increase rapidly enough to keep up with the demand (cf. *N. Y. Produce Exchange Report*, 1873–74, pp. 386–389). The acreage of corn, oats, and wheat in ten states of the Middle West increased almost twice as rapidly between 1865 and 1870 as between 1862 and 1865. For elaborate tables see *Minnesota Bureau of Labor Report*, 1895–96.

A prominent factor in the prosperity of the time was the great advance in exports of agricultural products. The export trade in food-stuffs had steadily increased since 1846, but during the Civil War, it far exceeded any point attained before that time. This was partly due to the failure of the harvests in Great Britain in 1860, 1861, and 1862, and on the Continent in 1861, — just when our own crops were the largest, — but not wholly, for though the exports fell off slightly during 1864–65, they still remained far above the average for the years preceding the war. The extent of this increase for the chief commodities is shown in the following table: —

Average Annual Exports of Agricultural Products (in thousands).

	Wheat	*Wheat flour*	*Corn*	*Corn meal*
	bu.	bbls.	bu.	bbls.
1851–1860	5,525	2,892	5,149	240
1861–1865	27,661	3,959	10,523	235
	Butter	*Cheese*	*Bacon and hams*	*Lard*
	lbs.	lbs.	lbs.	lbs.
1851–1860	3,633	7,852	27,070	32,437
1861–1865	23,970	41,873	113,332	92,697

For the Middle West in particular, from which most of the exports came, the increased foreign demand was most opportune, for it served to offset the loss of the southern market following the outbreak of hostilities and the closing of the Mississippi.[1]

The bearing of two of the points mentioned in describing the influence of the general agricultural situation upon wool-growing deserves to be explained more specifically. The relative decline in freight rates between the Mississippi valley and the Atlantic coast worked in favor of the bulkier agricultural products and against wool, the cost of transportation being relatively insignificant for the latter. On the other hand, the scarcity of labor at this time tended to favor the stock-owner, for, relatively, labor was a less important item in the component costs of growing wool than in the component costs of the products obtained by cultivating the soil.

[1] The average receipts of grain and flour reduced to grain, over the Erie and Champlain canals at tidewater in New York was 30,000,000 bu. for the years 1851–60 and 60,000,000 for the years 1861–65 (see *N. Y. Produce Exchange Report*, 1872–73, p. 391). There was no such relative increase in the crops.

But the composite result of all the various factors is best registered by the market quotations of the different agricultural commodities. To get this result two tables have been constructed — the first to show the movement of currency prices of wool and the chief agricultural products during the years of the war, the second to show how the general level of prices at this period compared with that of the years just preceding.

Relative Currency Prices of Agricultural Products.[1]
(Basis: 100 = average for 1860.)

	1861	1862	1863	1864	1865
Ohio fine washed wool	80	93	145	166	153
Ohio medium " "	81	106	159	184	173
Ohio coarse " "	84	124	174	209	173
Average 3 grades of wool	82	108	159	186	166
Sheep's meat	92	99	116	150	158
Beeves' meat	95	89	110	154	196
Pork	76	58	77	154	217
Wheat	82	83	101	140	137
Corn	72	76	122	209	162
Oats	71	95	168	209	177
Average of five chief products	79	80	116	173	178
All commodities	97	114	153	209	209

It is evident from this table that during the three years 1861 to 1863 the relative changes in the price of wool and the prices of the most important agricultural products were very decidedly in favor of wool: it advanced far more rapidly than the others. Moreover, if we compare the price of either medium or coarse wool — and these two classes made up the greatest part of the domestic clip — the rise is even more striking. During 1864 and 1865, however, the situation was reversed, the other agricultural products advancing in price more rapidly than wool. We may further note that in 1862 and 1863 mutton showed a greater advance in price than did either pork or beef, though, like wool, it advanced less rapidly during the two

[1] In this table the figures for all commodities except the several grades of wool have been taken from Mitchell's *History of the Greenbacks*, pp. 433–434. The relative prices for wool are calculated from the quotations of Mauger & Avery.

following years. Finally, we see that the increase in prices generally was considerably greater and more rapid than the increase in either the average price of wool — except for the year 1863 only — or the average price of other agricultural products.

The second table, showing the average currency and gold prices during the Civil War as compared with those for the preceding decade, is even more instructive.

Relative Prices of Agricultural Products.[1]
(100 = *price for* 1860.)

	Ohio medium scoured wool	*Ohio fine scoured wool*	*Mutton*	*Beef*	*Pork*	*Wheat*	*Corn*	*Oats*	*Butter*	*Cheese*
1850–59	91	91	96	111	84	98	108	119	102	81
1861–65, currency	147	131	144	140	116	107	131	162	137	129
1861–65, gold	101	90	100	96	76	77	97	112	103	90
Ratio (%) of the Rise or Fall in Relative Gold Prices between 1861–65 and 1850–59 to the Relative Prices 1850–59.	10+	1–	4+	14–	10–	21–	10–	6–	1+	11+

The last line of figures in this table conveys the best comprehensive view of the general situation. It shows that during the Civil War the gold prices of wheat, corn, pork, and beef, the chief agricultural products of the North, were from 10 to 21% below the prevailing prices of the previous decade, and that the gold price of mutton and the average gold price of the two quoted grades of wool rose. Even fine wool shows but a slight decline, nothing like that which occurred in the case of these other agricultural products.[2] The only other products in the list which rose in price were the two dairy products, butter and cheese; and beef declined instead of advancing as did mutton. Probably, in the East, as a result of this change, dairying, with the added gain by factory methods in cheese-making which were then generally introduced, attracted some farmers, but to most sheep-raising looked still more promising.

[1] This table, somewhat different in construction from the preceding, is based entirely on data in the Aldrich Report.

[2] It will be noticed that there is no quotation here for coarse Ohio wool. Had that been available it would have shown an even greater advance.

Here at last we find some reasonable explanation for our puzzle. This at least affords some sound economic basis for the rush of the farmers after sheep at a time when the gold price of wool advanced so slightly. For, even if wool and mutton should fail to advance at all, a decline in the prices of other agricultural products might make the sheep husbandry relatively more lucrative.[1] And, as has previously been pointed out, since the land in the wool-growing sections of the country could be put to many different uses, the relative profitableness of these various uses determined the choice of one. Still, however accurate this explanation may be, it is only too clear that the excessive investment in sheep was not generally based on closely calculated and well-reasoned economic motives. The most that can be said is that, so far as such motives were the guide, the decline in the prices of the chief agricultural products, at the same time that the prices of wool and mutton were rising, furnishes the soundest and by far the most important single reason for the line of action actually chosen. But at best the reason is most inadequate.

The Period of Reaction, 1867–70.

The brilliant prospects which seemed to open before the wool-grower on the outbreak of the war were mainly based on the extra needs of the army and the scarcity of cotton. The advance in the prices of wool under the stimulus of an inflated currency appeared to confirm his high hope. On the surface all looked prosperous. Soon he became filled with a conviction that this seemingly fortunate state of affairs was destined to continue. When the war, which had given him his first stimulus, gave signs of coming to a close, he was still undaunted: he expected higher protection; his future was assured. And so the wool-grower serenely pursued his way. But a movement so inadequately backed by sound economic motives could not go on forever. Reaction was inevitable, and in 1867 it began, keeping on to 1870. The readjustment which then took

[1] This, of course, holds absolutely true only on the assumption that other things remain the same. If the fall in price in other agricultural products was due to a lower cost of production which did not at the same time affect wool similarly those products might still be just as attractive. Seriously to affect many lines of agriculture would involve a change so fundamental as to take some time. There is no evidence that such was the case here. The most important change of general influence, the scarcity of labor, tended to favor wool-growing.

place forms the conclusion of this episode in the history of wool-growing.

The Wool Market.

The great break in the wool market did not occur until after 1866. The highest currency prices for wool were reached, to be sure, during the last of 1864, but the decline which took place during 1865 was due to the falling premium on gold; the general level of gold prices for that year, in spite of the fact that the war closed in the middle of it, ranged higher than for any year of the war excepting only 1863. Moreover, although the decline began in 1866, the gold prices for that year averaged about as high as for 1864. The final sudden and precipitous drop came in the latter part of 1867, and carried gold prices below any point reached in the preceding twenty-five years. The appreciating standard only emphasized the drop as reflected in currency prices. The low level of gold prices which was reached toward the close of 1867 was maintained through 1868, but the two succeeding years brought a gradual recovery, and by the end of 1870 the market situation had become fairly normal once more. The average prices for the three worst years, 1867–69, with those of previous periods for comparison, were: —

Average Gold Prices of Ohio Washed Wool.

	Fine	*Medium*	*Coarse*	*Average 3 grades*
1852–61	51.00	43.48	37.65	44.04
1862–65	49.39	45.85	43.78	46.34
1867–69	38.52	36.10	32.67	35.76

It is evident that the reaction which carried prices to so low a level must have been a violent one. It was not confined to this country, however, for the London market was demoralized as well. But in London the crisis came about a year later — 1868–70 being the worst period — and was apparently, for the most part, but a reflection of the weak market of this country.[1]

The world's supply of wool at this time has been shown in the table for the earlier years of the decade.[2] It there appears that the absolute amount of the increase during the last five years of the decade was but half that for the first five, and the relative rate of

[1] For other quotations see Appendix.

[2] See page 164.

increase much less. Of the various countries Australasia alone continued the former rate of advance. In South America the increase was much smaller than before, while the United States stood out in striking contrast to both by remaining stationary. The increase in the world's supply was below the normal, but that did not serve to stave off a collapse in the market.

One depressing factor was the rapid increase in the supply of cotton which became available. In the United States the quantity produced did not attain the highest ante-bellum level until after 1870, but the consumption of the country had surpassed any previous figure as early as 1869.[1] In Great Britain the situation was even more favorable. The war had scarcely ended before the cotton supply was as great as ever, and from 1866 on, the total imports of cotton regularly exceeded the highest previous figure, while after that year, the amount consumed invariably surpassed all earlier records. The prices of the Liverpool market were still high, averaging 10¾*d.* for the years 1867–1870, though this was less than half the average war-time figure. It was not until after 1875 that prices returned to the normal level again.[2] It is thus evident that within two or three years after the close of the war the cotton manufacture had virtually recovered the ground lost during those difficult years, though relatively there was some loss, since thc decade failed to bring forth the usual growth. This recovery of the cotton manufacture, together with the assured lower level of prices in the near future, showed that the expanding market for consumption enjoyed by wool during the cotton famine had been replaced by an enforced contraction of its abnormally extended bounds. Undoubtedly the increased supply of cotton weighed heavily upon the wool market. But although the return of cotton was a depressing influence, it was too steady and continuous in its operation to explain the suddenness of the collapse in 1867.

This collapse had its origin in the American market. Hopes long sustained on too slender a foundation had brought over-production in the face of a contracting market. Prices fell steadily, the decline being further accentuated by the appreciating currency. To aggravate the situation came the enormous imports of wool and

[1] Hammond, *The Cotton Industry*, Appendix.

[2] For tables see Ellison's *Cotton Trade of Great Britain*, Appendix.

woolens that were rushed into the country in 1866 to escape the higher duties then expected. Under this accumulated weight of troubles the market broke. The bubble had been pricked. The reaction, once started, was complete. The previous high hopes of the wool-growers were only surpassed by the depths of despair into which all were now plunged. For the next three years the market went through the depressing process of readjustment to more normal conditions and saner ideas.

The London market at this time was largely influenced by conditions in America. During the Civil War, with the aid of the cotton famine, the world's market had sustained in a surprising manner the heavy increase in the wool clip from the Southern Hemisphere, in spite of the absence of any noticeable growth in the American demand for foreign wool. In 1866 the unusually heavy demand from the United States had served to postpone the reaction. Then came the slump in the American wool market, and the demand fell below normal. This, with the rising cotton supply, left the wool-market overburdened, notwithstanding the fact that the increase in the world's wool supply was less than normal. In looking back over the decade, however, one is greatly surprised that the break did not come long before. In the next few years the consumption of wool was readjusted to fit more normal conditions, and the declining rate of increase on the supply side brought that into closer conformity with the usual needs. By 1870 the equilibrium had about returned.

Imports and the Tariff.

At least a few sheep-owners had forebodings that the end of the war would bring a reaction in their industry. But apparently the majority saw no threatening features in the prospect, and certainly the way in which the prices of both wool and sheep were sustained after the war had actually ended lent support to their view. The more farsighted, however, took active steps to insure, so far as possible, their future prosperity. The means most readily available was the protective tariff. In the movement toward higher protection all sheep-owners gladly joined, for in whatever light they viewed the future of their industry, a higher tariff made it appear brighter.

Additional support was obtained from the manufacturers, ever keen to the advantage to be derived from an alliance with the powerful agricutural interests, and in this case desiring a voice in the matter lest their raw material be too highly taxed. The result was the famous Syracuse Convention of wool-growers and manufacturers, held in December, 1865.[1] The manufacturers hoped the growers would concede some reduction in the rates on at least the non-competing combing and carpet wools, and they were much taken aback at the growers' demand for an increase in the duty, on all unwashed wool but carpet wool, from 6 cents a pound to 20 cents a pound and 20% ad valorem.[2] After some discussion a compromise was arranged whereby the rates demanded by the growers were to be cut in halves, and the manufacturers were to receive a duty which, it was calculated, would compensate them for the increased cost of their raw material as well as for the 10% internal revenue duty, and would afford in addition about 25% net protection. The wool and woolens schedule of the tariff bill of 1866 was the outcome of this agreement. When that bill failed to pass, this schedule was brought in as a separate measure, and in 1867 was finally put through Congress in virtually the form agreed upon between the growers and the manufacturers. It eventually became one of the most important tariff acts in the history of the duties on wool and woolens, and established a level for the duties on wool which, except for one brief period of free wool, has remained substantially unaltered ever since.

Inasmuch as during the first few years of the operation of this tariff, conditions were so abnormal as to afford little idea of its actual effect, its provisions in detail will be given in the account of the following period, where the situation described affords better means of judging this point. Here it will be sufficient to note the extent of the imports during these few years.

The act went into effect in March, 1867. During the fiscal years 1868 and 1869 the imports of wool fell off heavily, reviving somewhat in 1870. The average for each of the three years was 32,600,000

[1] "There is good evidence to show that the whole movement was the work of a few energetic manufacturers of New England, engaged chiefly in producing carpets and worsted goods, and of some prominent breeders of sheep" (Taussig, *Tariff History*, p. 199. There is also further comment here). The proceedings are found in the *Transactions of the National Association of Wool Manufacturers*, 1865–66. Cf. also Special Commissioner of the Revenue, *Report*, 1866, pp. 441–460.

[2] *Ibid.*, p. 50.

pounds, of which 25,000,000 was coarse carpet wool. This is less than half the average annual importation during the Civil War, yet slightly above that for the three years just preceding the war. The average value was 15 cents a pound, as compared with 17 cents for the two preceding periods, the decline being due to the low level of prices which prevailed. The annual imports of manufactured goods during these years averaged $35,000,000 in value, an amount 50% above the average under the tariff of 1862, lower than that under the tariff of 1864, and about the same as that under the Act of 1857. The total amount of imported wool, raw and manufactured, was only slightly lower than under the tariffs of 1857 and 1862. Such importations under higher duties and in a period of depression certainly did not afford much encouragement to the sheep-owner, but it was still too early to judge as to the real effectiveness of the tariff. Such aid as it afforded at this time was largely of a negative character — in preventing the situation from growing still worse.

The Manufacture of Wool.

Since the general condition of the woolen manufacture at the end of the decade has received some notice in the treatment of the first part of the decade, a brief description of conditions during the years of reaction will suffice.

The woolen manufacturer as well as the wool-grower seems to have been undisturbed by the close of the war. The year 1865, says Mr. Bond, "was a very busy year with the woolen manufacturers. Nearly all were pressing their machinery to its utmost capacity, and many were running extra hours; some running a portion of their machinery night and day." [1] Confident that the tariff bill of 1866 would be passed, they increased their machinery. Some manufacturers of machinery estimated in 1868 that 2000 sets had been installed since 1864,[2] and the total number of sets in 1868 was figured at 6000,[3] as compared with 5000 in 1865.[4] The value of the manufactures of wool, calculated at $122,000,000 in 1864,[5] had risen to $156,000,000 in 1868.[6] Much the greater part of the increase at this

[1] *Bulletin*, vol. i, p. 80.
[2] *Ibid.*, p. 88.
[3] Special Commissioner of the Revenue, *Report*, 1869, p. xvii.
[4] *Bulletin*, vol. i, p. 59.
[5] *Ibid.*, p. 64.
[6] Special Commissioner of Revenue, *Report*, 1869, p. xvii.

time took place in the Middle West, the growth there being so marked as to attract considerable attention.[1] In 1869 the North Western Wool Manufacturers Association held an exposition in Chicago, and imperfect statistics for the previous year which were given at this exposition showed 557 establishments with 995 sets of machinery and $5,500,000 capital, figures which were asserted to be double those for four years previous.[2] In the older states, where the manufacture was chiefly located, it merely held its own up to 1868.[3]

At about that date the outlook changed, and the manufacturer entered upon dark days. Even before then his activity in running mills had not always meant a profitable business. Now rapidly falling prices bore heavily on him. "Many, from the decline in value of raw materials and wool consequent on the rapid fall of gold, lost a large portion of the profits they had before realized in a rising gold market." [4] Furthermore, the government was dumping great quantities of army supplies upon the market.[5] When prices failed to rise after the tariff of 1867 had taken effect, importers began to dispose of the heavy supplies of stock they had procured in 1866. In short, to quote the Special Commissioner of the Revenue,[6] "The woolen manufacture is characterized by a greater depression than that of any other branch of industry in the country with the exception of ship building, small profits accruing to a few, heavy losses to many, with numerous and constantly recurring failures." [7] The Commissioner was inclined to lay much of the blame for this upon the tariff of 1867, but such conclusions are hardly justified.[8] The tariff had doubtless helped to stimulate growth, but reaction was inevitable in any case.

[1] "The high tariff of 1867 led to a large increase of woolen mills, particularly in the West" (*Boston Board of Trade Report*, 1869). Cf. *Bulletin*, vol. i, p. 88.

[2] See Special Commissioner of the Revenue, *Report*, 1868, p. 3. See also *Bulletin*, vol. i, p. 11.

[3] Cf. *Bulletin*, vol. i, p. 88.

[4] *Boston Board of Trade Report*, 1866.

[5] For figures, see Commissioner of Agriculture, *Report*, 1871, p. 41.

[6] *Report* for 1869, p. xcvi.

[7] Cf. *House Report*, no. 72, 41st Congress, 1st session, p. 92: "One third of the woolen machinery of the country is said to be idle" [April, 1870].

[8] Cf. his *Report* for 1869. But see especially Wells's "Wool and the Tariff," a Letter to *The New York Tribune*, March 20, 1873 (pamphlet).

The fact that the woolen manufacture ended the decade under a heavy cloud should not be allowed to blind us to the point that it had made enormous strides during these years. It was more diversified in character, more strongly intrenched, and it more completely supplied the domestic needs than ever before.

The Growing of Wool.

No signs of reaction appearing in the wool market or in the woolen manufacture at the close of the war, it was but natural that the grower of wool should continue his onward march undisturbed. The conviction, which seems to have been indelibly stamped upon the minds of many by the Civil War period, that their section was predestined for a great wool-growing centre, continued unshaken. The prospect of higher tariff duties raised brighter hopes. The demand for the best stock was as strong in the fall of 1865 as it had been during the war, and the number of sheep in the country continued to increase till 1867. Then warning signs in the wool market caused a halt, and the reaction set in.

It was not until 1867 that the gold price of wool fell much below the Civil War level. Up to that year the flocks of all sections, with the exception of New England in 1866, had steadily increased. The year 1867, however, brought a decline in all but the granger group. The final and precipitous drop in the price of wool occurred near the end of that year, and the prices then reached held throughout the year which followed.

This final drop in the wool market in the face of the newly enacted tariff, with rates far higher than any known before, was of decisive fate, and the year 1868 marks the Waterloo of the sheep industry in the wool-growing regions of that period. From the blow which it then received it has never recovered. All the bright hopes and enticing illusions conjured up in the brain of the wool-grower during the preceding half-dozen years were completely shattered. The despair which succeeded quickly brought wholesale slaughter. Though 1867 had been bad, 1868 was yet worse. "In the whole history of the fluctuations in American industry," writes the Special Commissioner of the Revenue,[1] "there never has been a more discouraging and disastrous record than that presented by the Depart-

[1] *Report* for 1869, p. xcv.

ment of Agriculture for March and April, 1867, some seven pages of which are occupied with a detailed statement of the conditions of the sheep husbandry in 170 counties of 21 different states, in only one of which, Missouri, is there anything which indicates a condition of even moderate prosperity for this particular branch of industry." The general destruction which followed culminated in the latter part of 1868. It was estimated that 4,000,000 sheep were killed in that winter.[1] In the wool-growing sections of Ohio, from 10,000 to 40,000 were killed in each county, and "similar conditions prevailed in Michigan and other western states." [2] In New York culls were selling at from $.75 to $1.00 each. Some, to escape the slaughter, were driven across the plains to the Rocky Mountains. By 1869 it was estimated that the decrease since 1867 had been as great as one quarter.[3] After the winter of 1868–69 the reduction of the flocks still continued, though at a slower pace, and by the end of 1870 it had run its course. When the reaction then came to an end and the industry again reached rock bottom, it was found that the decrease in the loyal states east of the Rocky Mountains — the real wool-growing region of the period — was from 35,800,000 sheep in January, 1867, to 22,400,000 in 1871, a loss, that is, of over one third of the total.[4]

For these years of reaction, as for the years of sudden growth, some explanation, though again only a partial one, is to be found in the changes in price of the other products of agriculture.

[1] Commissioner of Agriculture, *Report*, 1871, p. 40.

[2] *Ibid.*

[3] Special Commissioner of the Revenue, *Report*, 1869, p. xcv.

[4] The estimates of the number of sheep made by the Department of Agriculture for the years previous to 1871 are not altogether trustworthy. A former statistician of the Department says, "It is not fair to go back of 1871, the earliest date for authentic statements of sheep and wool. Before that was a period of abnormal increase followed by sudden slaughter, when the machinery of statistical investigation was only partially in operation, and results uncertain" (*Senate Miscellaneous Documents*, no. 124, 53d Congress, 2d session, p. 46). The best data available have led me to accept the estimates for the years up to and including 1867 as reasonably accurate. The figures for 1868–70, however, were seriously in error, greatly underestimating the decrease which then took place. This fact was brought out by the Census of 1870, and the great drop of nearly one quarter in the Department's figures for 1871 was simply the correction of this error, and did not represent any reduction that actually took place in that year.

Relative Gold Prices of Agricultural Products.[1]

	Ohio medium scoured wool	*Ohio fine scoured wool*	*Mutton*	*Beef*	*Pork*	*Wheat*	*Corn*	*Oats*	*Butter*	*Cheese*
1850–59	91	91	96	111	84	98	108	119	102	81
1861–65	101	90	100	96	76	77	97	112	103	90
1867–70	71	79	97	129	105	114	95	135	127	126

Ratio (%) of the Rise or Fall in Relative Gold Prices between 1861–65 and 1867–70 to the Relative Prices 1861–65.

30−	12−	3−	34+	38+	48+	2−	21+	23+	40+

The reversal of relations in the relative price movements is here most striking, and far greater than that which occurred during the first part of the decade. Wool and mutton declined in price, yet, with the single exception of corn, every other important agricultural product advanced, and the advance was in every instance more than 20%. It was sufficient, in fact, in each case to carry the price level above that for the decade 1850–59. With many of the agricultural commodities this rise had come as early as 1865, when sheep were still being increased. Undoubtedly so noticeable an advance in the price of these other agricultural products hastened the movement to abandon sheep when the bottom dropped out of the wool market.[2] It is quite evident, nevertheless, that at this time, as before, it was a minor influence in the movement, for if the slight change in relative prices in 1861–65 had been sufficient to double the number of sheep, then the change of 1867–70, many times greater in extent, would have reduced them to but a fraction of their former number. The main factor in the reaction was the sudden abandonment of long-

[1] Cf. note to the similar table on page 192.

[2] "At that juncture [the close of the war] there was a remarkable revival in the stock business. . . . The people who had my sheep out on shares — I had at that time 6000–7000 — said to me: 'You won't compel us to keep these sheep now, when we can get $6 for pork and cattle.' I said, if they desired to do so to bring them back, and they brought them back, and they changed their occupation to the raising of cattle and pork, and I transferred those sheep to Colorado. . . . The dogs, low price of wool, and the cessation of the war, together with the fact that another industry promised larger returns, were the causes of the decline in the wool business." (J. B. Grinnell of Iowa, *Tariff Commission*, 1882, p. 1136.)

cherished hopes, in a situation which left no question as to their mistaken character.

A comparison of the number of sheep in the different sections of the country at the outset of this period, at the climax of the movement, and at the end of the reaction, gives an admirable survey of the whole episode.

Number of Sheep (in thousands).[1]

	New England	*Middle Atlantic*	*North Central*	*Central West*	*Total 4 groups*	*South*	*Far West*
1860	1,779	4,559	6,911	1,224	14,473	5,938	2,051
1867	3,276	9,314	18,648	3,662	34,900	4,470	. . .
1870	1,450	4,248	11,164	2,473	19,335	5,188	3,949

In what was at the opening of the war the great wool-growing section of the country (including the first four groups of the table), the stimulus of Civil War times by the year 1867 had brought an increase in the flocks of over 140%. The years of reaction which followed reduced those same flocks by 45%. Admitting the possibility of error in comparing Census figures with Department-of-Agriculture estimates, it is well within the limits of safety to say that the Civil War episode so affected the flocks that in the course of a single decade they were more than doubled and then were reduced by more than one third. The final outcome was a net increase of about one third.

Still more instructive, however, is the survey of this movement by groups of states. In the New England and Middle Atlantic groups of states, the number of sheep had approximately doubled by 1867, and then was more than cut in half in the three years that followed, the result being that these states ended the decade with fewer sheep than they had at the beginning. These two sections, in fact, did not go to quite such extremes in the rush for sheep as did the others, and proved far more ready to abandon them when the reaction set in. In the South, the flocks in 1867 still showed the effect of the war's ravages, and had not fully recovered in 1870. Were it not for the inclusion of Texas, where sheep were on the increase, the show-

[1] The figures for 1860 and 1870 are those of the Census; for 1867, the estimate of the Department of Agriculture. The North Central states include Ohio, Indiana, Illinois, Wisconsin, and Michigan; the Central West, Missouri, Iowa, Minnesota, Kansas, Nebraska, Dakota; the South, the Confederate States plus Kentucky and West Virginia. The Census figures for the Far West do not include range sheep.

ing would be much worse. For the Far West, satisfactory figures are not available, but such evidence as we have leads us to conclude that in the few states where growth had begun by 1860 the events of the period considerably stimulated the advance, and that the reaction was less felt in those states than in any other region — in fact, after the reaction set in, sheep were driven to this section from the eastward, and it is unlikely that there was any serious setback to the growth which had started. It was in the Middle West, however, that the craze for sheep secured the greatest hold upon the people. There, in both the North Central and the Central West group of states, the number of sheep tripled within seven years. There, too, the reaction was less severe upon the flocks than in the East, the reduction being about one third. As a result, the year 1870 found these states with about twice the number of sheep that they had held at the beginning of the decade.

In this summing up one fact is very striking. That the New England and Middle Atlantic states should have fewer sheep in 1870 than in 1860 was but natural, for there the flocks had been on the decline for two decades. Nor was it to be expected that the flocks of the South should have recovered from the war-time ravages so early as this. That the Far West would be sure to increase the number of its sheep was clear before the war began. The Central West states also were still in process of settlement, and were therefore reasonably sure to make some gain in their flocks. But the North Central states present a problem. For half a decade or more before the war the number of sheep in those states had been declining, yet after the reaction from the Civil War stimulus had passed we find the number double what it had been in 1860. For this net increase no satisfactory explanation is at hand.[1] There appears no reason to believe that the decline which had begun in about 1855 would have been replaced by such a growth had it not been for the Civil War stimulus, for the factors which brought about the decline were still existent and stronger than ever. The change in the relative prices of agricultural products during the first of the decade did not last, and was never sufficient to account in full for the course of events. One favorable factor was the increased price of mutton and

[1] In parts of Michigan and, to a less extent, of Wisconsin, the settlement of new sections would help to explain it.

the rising city markets of this section, but the fact that the region did not begin a general resort to mutton breeds of sheep until a whole decade later indicates that this was not of much influence. Furthermore, it might equally be argued against this view that dairying, favored by the new factory methods, the better means of transportation, the growing city population, and the general high level of prices for its products, offered even greater attractions. Everything thus points to the conclusion that in 1870 the sheep industry of the North Central states had not fully returned to normal conditions. It was in this section that the movement for sheep had been carried to the greatest extremes, and here apparently some of the fond hopes engendered by war times still lived.[1] It was thus in what was the centre of the wool-growing industry of the time that this Civil War episode had the greatest effect and most lasting influence. Elsewhere, by 1870, virtually all signs of the disturbing event had passed away.

Summary, 1860–1870.

To one who looks back over the history of wool-growing in the United States during the decade 1860–70 it must now be evident why these years have been set aside and their events called an episode. The period does not make a chapter in the natural development of this industry. Had it been omitted that development might have gone on almost without interruption. The course of the industry during these stirring times was not in the main governed by the factors which had controlled it before, nor, as will later appear, by such as controlled it afterwards. For this brief period peculiar and abnormal forces ruled. A tremendous upheaval took place. For the time being the whole course of the industry was reversed. But the vanishing of the unusual forces called a sudden halt to the new turn of events. Normal factors were once more in control. Another reversal followed. Readjustment then took place and eventually the industry resumed its old course, while, except in one section, hardly a sign of all the disturbance remained.

What were the abnormal factors which caused so much trouble?

[1] It might possibly be thought that the decrease in flocks before 1860 was due to an error in judgment which the greater experience with sheep during this decade showed to be a mistake. It will be seen that later events make this too improbable a hypothesis.

At the outbreak of hostilities it was evident that there would be a heavy increase in the demand for wool to meet the needs of the army and to take the place of cotton. Consequently, a big advance in the price of wool was expected. It came, and it lasted — lasted moreover till wool rose to over a dollar a pound. To be sure, other things rose as well, but not to quite the extent that wool did, especially during the first year or two of the war. The rush for sheep, once started, increased of its own momentum, gathering force upon the way. On the surface everything appeared favorable and went as had been expected. Increased tariff duties further fired the imagination. Careful calculation was then cast aside, and the movement soon degenerated into an unreasoning stampede, in utter disregard of either the close of the war or the facts which might have told how illusory were the hopes that guided the movement. Such were the factors which swayed the course of the industry during these eventful years.

But why were these hopes so illusory? It must certainly be admitted that at the opening of hostilities the outlook was such as to justify increased attention to sheep. Even then, however, the events of the previous decade should have cautioned the wool-grower to keep an eye on his new rivals in the Southern Hemisphere. But the most fatal error came when, after the passing of a year or two had given him an opportunity to study results under the new conditions — to analyze the situation and change his action accordingly — he failed to do so. As time went on his expectations rose higher and higher, and soon soared far above any contact with the hard earth of fact.

A careful examination of the situation would have shown him that the high prices which he was getting for wool were deceptive, — that in fact, on a gold basis they were but a trifle above the ordinary prices, and in the case of some grades were below them. He would have learned that the world's supply of wool was increasing at an unprecedented rate; that the increase in this country alone was so great as to prove sufficient for all the extra needs without an increased consumption of foreign wool; and that in the rest of the world the enormous output was constantly threatening to break the market, the use of wool in place of cotton and the American demand of 1865–66 alone serving to postpone the final collapse. To go on paying exorbitant prices for stock and extravagantly increasing his flocks in the face of such a situation betokened either pure ignorance or foolish recklessness. The one sound basis for any increase of sheep was the relative decline in the price of the other chief agricultural products, but this offered no justification for such extremes as were then indulged in.

No further comment is necessary on the way in which a large body of producers continued to increase the supply of a commodity with motives sadly deficient in economic basis, if indeed an economic basis were ever calculated at all. But it may be well to point out three or four facts of broader import that are clearly illustrated by this episode. It shows with what facility an agricultural pursuit of this character may be taken up and abandoned. For starting in this industry land was the only necessity that involved a large investment in what might fairly be called fixed capital, and since land is susceptible of a great variety of other uses, it is possible for the farmer to take up this branch of agriculture much more quickly and abandon it with much less loss than is the case with most industries. And this is a fact which it is important to bear in mind in connection with agricultural products generally. The history of the industry during these years also admirably brings out the evils which follow in the train of a depreciated monetary standard; the deceptive character of the price level, the misleading and unduly stimulating effect of rising prices, and the hardships which follow when they begin to fall. Most important of all, however, is the example afforded of the economic disturbance that follows in the train of war. We are wont to measure the cost of war by the expenditures for the army, for supplies, and so forth, the increase in the government debt, and possibly an estimate of property destroyed. But no account is taken of the changes in the industries and in the whole economic organization of a country which it may involve. This history but shows the results in a single pursuit. The process of adjusting an industry to new and abnormal conditions, and then readjusting it once more, is inevitably injurious and wasteful in the extreme. In the enormous reckoning of the economic costs of war such items must form no inconsiderable part.

CHAPTER VII

THE RISE OF THE FAR WEST, 1870–90

WITH the period upon which we now enter there began the movement which finally resulted in the transfer of the main seat of the wool-growing industry from the valley of the Ohio to the region of the Rocky Mountains. This was but another step in that westward expansion which had marked the course of the pursuit from the first of the century. Starting on its westward journey from the hill regions of the East after the thirties, the industry had settled upon the fertile plains of the Middle West. There its stay was extended for over a generation, its maximum growth being attained under the war-time stimulus. Now the onward march was resumed. This new move, however, brought it to a region far different from any it had hitherto known. In consequence there followed great, far-reaching, and permanent changes in the character of the industry: its economic organization was altered; its economic basis became fundamentally different. Many forces which had before largely moulded its course disappeared, and new ones took their places. By the end of the period the transfer was completed: thereafter the centre of the wool-growing industry of the country is found in the Far West. This rise of the Far West thus marks a new epoch in the industry's history.

The Wool Market and the World's Wool Supply.

At the opening of this period inflated currency prices still continued in the United States, and they did not finally vanish until the resumption of specie payment in 1879. But since most of the inflation had disappeared by the end of 1869, the worst of the depressing effects consequent on the appreciating standard were then a matter of the past. The three years preceding 1870 had been marked by the lowest level of gold prices for wool that the country had ever known. The world's market, though not greatly disturbed during the Civil War, was abnormally depressed during the years which immediately followed. As a result, the unnatural stimulus of the preceding period had been counteracted, so that by 1870 the market situation was more nearly normal than it had been for some time. This condition, however, was not destined to continue long.

The general tendency of prices in the world's wool market during the two decades now under review was downward. But the period is marked by two very sudden and spectacular advances in price, both of which were followed by a rapid decline.

The first of these, the most sudden and remarkable in the course of the century, began in 1871. Prices soared skyward throughout the year, and finally reached the maximum in the first quarter of 1872. During this rise the price of wool on the London market advanced from 50 to 100%, according to its grade, combing wool going rather higher than merino. In the United States the advance was about 75%. The three grades of Ohio wool reached the highest average price attained — 71 cents a pound, gold basis — since the beginning of the regular records in 1824. Only one grade, the fine wool, had ever been so high before, and the medium and coarse grades, especially the latter, were far above any previous record.[1] In the United States, the drop which followed was as precipitous as the rise had been sudden, and by the middle of 1873 prices had about returned to the level from which they started in 1870. The rapidity of the drop was largely due to the outbreak of the panic of this time. On the European market the rise was a little better sustained, and the decline which succeeded was more regular and longer drawn out, not fairly coming to an end until the middle of 1876. But in both Europe and this country, after the first reaction from the sudden rise, a steady but slow fall in prices continued until the middle of 1879, when about the same low level was reached that had prevailed in the years 1867–69.

The reason for this sudden rise does not appear upon the surface. The outbreak of the Franco-Prussian War at first depressed the market, but soon the demand for the army supplies was felt, and it was estimated that possibly 300,000,000 pounds of wool were used for this purpose.[2] Though the rise did not begin until the war

[1] The prices, gold basis, for April, 1872, are: fine, 72 cents; medium, 72 cents; coarse, 68 cents.

[2] London *Economist*, January 13, 1872, p. 36; quoted from Helmuth Schwartze & Company's circular.

was nearly over, evidently this drain had pretty well cleared the market. The European demand, which continued active after the close of the war, was then augmented by the unexpected appearance of enormous buying orders from the United States. The imports for the fiscal year 1872 reached an unprecedented amount, for it had suddenly been discovered, as the manufacture was reviving, that the sheep slaughter of the preceding years had reduced the domestic clip below the normal needs. At bottom, however, the real reason for the rise seems to have been a sudden realization that the world's demand had been advancing more rapidly than the supply. As the *Economist* put it, "The proportion of supply to consumption, which since 1865 has stood unfavorably to the grower, has this year [1871] been reversed and turned in his favor."[1] The rate of increase in the world's supply during the last years of the previous decade had been below the normal, thus serving to counterbalance the phenomenal advance of the earlier years. This with the rapidly increasing demand, augmented by the special factors of the early seventies, resulted in a shortage which brought on the sudden rise in price. The appearance of the panic of 1873 in the United States, with the following long-drawn-out industrial depression, together with the troubles in Europe at the same time, brought some falling off in the demand; and this, in conjunction with the more rapidly increasing supply, adequately explains the downward tendency of prices which lasted till 1879.

The situation as regards the world's supply during this period was as follows, in millions of pounds: —

Average Annual Output, Wool in the Grease.[2]

	United Kingdom	*Continent*	*North America*	*Australasia*	*Cape*	*River Plate*	*Others*	*Total*
1860–62	140	500	103	67	26	58	78	973
1869–71	150	485	170	172	46	209	90	1321
1874–76	162	460	203	248	49	228	110	1459
1879–81	147	450	275	293	55	245	112	1594
1884–86	135	450	343	407	56	342	121	1854
1889–91	140	450	317	527	95	326	174	2029

[1] January 13, 1872. Cf. *Boston Board of Trade Report*, 1872, pp. 102, 120; *Bulletin*, vol. xiii, pp. 348–349.

[2] Helmuth Schwartze & Co., *Annual Wool Review*. See note to similar table on

The increase during the decade ending with 1880 was 21%, as contrasted with 36% for the preceding decade, and proved to be about evenly divided between the two halves of the decade. By far the greater part of the increase came from two countries — Australasia and the United States, each of them contributing over 100,000,000 pounds. The phenomenal growth of the clip from the River Plate, the most noticeable growth in the previous decade, was not continued, the advance there being far below the normal. At this time also the flocks of the United Kingdom began to retrograde, and on the Continent the decrease which had started in the middle of the century continued.[1] The result was an increasing dependence of Europe on the output of the Southern Hemisphere, which, fortunately, proved adequate to the demands, and seemed not to be disturbed by the steady fall in the price of wool.

The second quick advance to interrupt this general decline in the wool market started in the latter part of 1879 and culminated in the first half of 1880. The rise was not nearly so great as that of 1872,[2] and was much more marked in this country than in England. The advance in this country had its origin in the sudden general revival in business at the time, and resulted in an unprecedented amount of imports, this in turn being the main cause of the rise in the London market. The reactionary drop, which followed within the same year, wiped out most of the advance, and was succeeded by several years of rather rapidly falling prices, culminating in 1885–86 at a point below that reached in the depression of 1868–69. A slight rise ensued, but from then on till 1890 the general level continued unusually low.

On the demand side of the market, conditions were fairly normal

page 164. The figures for North America for 1860–62 have been changed to agree with my previous estimate. For two other estimates of the world's wool production by countries, for 1887, see Ford's *Wool and Manufactures of Wool*, p. 14. For estimates of the number of sheep in the world in 1875, see Department of Agriculture, *Report*, 1875; for estimates of the number in 1888, see Ford, *op. cit.*, p. 471; for estimates of the number in 1892, *ibid.*, p. 467.

[1] In Germany the maximum number of sheep was reached in 1864, at 30,000,000; since then the decline has been steady, leaving about 10,000,000 in 1900. For figures and history see Mendelson, *Die volkswirtschaftliche Bedeutung der deutschen Schafhaltung um die Wende des XIXten Jahrhunderts*, p. 14.

[2] The average price of the three grades of Ohio wool was 56 cents as compared with 71 cents in 1872.

after the temporary disturbance in 1880, the only other difficulty being the comparatively slight setback brought on by the crisis of 1884.

On the supply side the prominent feature of the years 1880–89 was the unusually rapid increase in the world's wool clip, which was 27% for the decade. A glance at the table given on page 210[1] shows that the greater part of the increase came during the first half of the decade. The flocks of the United States, the River Plate region, and Australasia were then all multiplying at an unusual rate, the clip of the last two regions advancing 100,000,000 pounds apiece within these five years. During the latter half of the decade, however, the growth was much less rapid. Although the flocks of Australasia continued to increase as rapidly as ever, and the Cape and other countries showed more than usual progress, yet in both the United States and the River Plate region the clip actually declined. These changes on the side of supply offer a simple and adequate explanation for the general trend of prices during this decade. The unusually rapid increase in the supply during the first half of the decade was the cause for the rapid decline in prices at that time, while the heavy falling off in the rate of increase which followed shows the reason for the nearly stationary position in prices, with the slight tendency to rise, during the closing years of the decade.

Finally, it is important to know how the general level of prices at this period compared with the level at earlier periods. This is indicated in the following table: —

Average Price of Ohio Washed Wool.

	Fine	*Medium*	*Coarse*	*Average 3 grades*
1840–59	46.7	42.3	33.6	40.9
1860–69	46.1	43.1	40.1	43.1
1870–89	41.8	42.8	36.9	40.4

The Civil War decade, as was to be expected, shows a slightly higher range of prices than the other two periods. But the most interesting comparison is that of the period under review with the corresponding period of 1840–59. The general average of all grades for the two periods is substantially identical, and the same may be said of the price of the medium grade of wool. The only changes

[1] See complete table in the Appendix.

to be marked are the decline in the price of fine wool and the rise in the price of coarse wool. A striking instance of this change in relative positions is found in the fact that during the years 1878–89 medium wool sold for more than fine wool. An examination of the table of prices in the Appendix will show that up to 1861 the price of Ohio fine washed had invariably been above that of Ohio medium washed, and this situation continued to be the usual one from 1861 to 1878, though the difference in price between the two grades was far less than before. But after 1877 the fine wool is almost always found to be below the medium in price. Another point to be noted is that all three grades are much nearer one another in value than they had ever been before 1860.[1] One reason for this was the growing ability of the manufacturer, by means of improved machinery, to substitute one grade of wool for another.[2] A more important explanation is found in the fact that much of the increase in the world's wool supply during these years came from the fine-wool merino stock and was constantly improving in quality, while the more rapidly growing demand of these years, coming as it did from the manufacturers of worsted goods, was for a medium or a coarse grade of wool suitable for combing.

Imports and the Tariff.

The heavy increase in the world's wool supply, which poured in upon the market of this period, affected the American wool-grower mainly through the general lowering of prices under the pressure of that supply. How far the increased tariff duties helped to counteract this by preventing the foreign rival wools from invading the domestic market in competition with the native clip is the question next in order.

The tariff of 1867 went into operation in March of that year and

[1] This is strikingly brought out in the price chart in the Appendix, which shows the price of two of the grades of wool — fine and coarse.

[2] "A study of these records of imports shows that it is not indispensable quality or peculiarity of fibre, so much as cheapness, that controls importation. When manufacturers can practically blot out of existence the radical differences between carding and combing wool, so as to make combing wool of the very type of the clothing class, the merino, and drive from the market nearly all wools of English breeds, it is difficult to fix a limit to the substitutions and combinations that are possible." (Department of Agriculture, *Report*, 1889, p. 248.)

remained in force until July, 1883, except that from August, 1872, until March, 1873, the duties were lowered 10%, — an exception which, inasmuch as it had no appreciable effect, may safely be disregarded. As previously said, — when the detailed account of the bill was postponed, — the tariff of 1867 proved to be unusually important, as it became the model for all but one of the succeeding tariffs. It is commonly considered the first act in which the wool and woolens schedule was constructed on a scientific basis,[1] though in fact, this method had been foreshadowed in the tariffs of the Civil War period.

The scientific basis consisted in an attempt exactly to measure the increase in the cost of raw materials which the manufacturer had to pay because of the tariff, and then in levying a specific duty on manufactured goods to compensate him for that extra cost, while the protection which he received came through an additional ad valorem duty.[2] By this method, it was calculated that the cost of the raw material entering into a pound of cloth was enhanced about 50 cents by the tariff. In making this estimate it was assumed that it took four pounds of unwashed wool to make one pound of cloth. In a few cases where the shrinkage of wool was unusually heavy (as with the South American mestiza), this assumption was true, but in most cases the allowance was excessive. It is obvious that where an excess existed the so-called compensating duty was in part protective. The specific duty was not the same for every class of goods, though in most cases it was supposedly estimated at an amount to compensate for any increased cost due to the tariff. Among the notable exceptions to this general rule, the most striking was that of the worsted manufactures, the specific duty on which, as the manufacturers admitted, contained an element of protection, one third of it, in truth, being in excess of the necessary compensation. This was due to the fact that but two pounds of Canada wool were required for one pound of worsted cloth. The excuse advanced

[1] Cf. *Bulletin*, vol. xxv, p. 47. See also *supra*, page 167.

[2] Cf. Statement of the Executive Committee of the Wool Manufacturers' Association to the United States Revenue Commission, in *Transactions of the National Association of Wool Manufacturers*, 1865–66. Cf. also Special Commissioner of the Revenue, *Report*, 1866, and Taussig's *Tariff History of the United States*, pp. 201–216.

for making an exception in this case was that the worsted manufacture had sprung up under the combined effect of free wool, obtained through the Canadian reciprocity treaty, and a high duty (about 50%) on worsted goods, and that anything less than the protection thus given would kill it, the withdrawal of the reciprocity treaty having been a severe blow as it was.[1] It was also admitted that there was protection in the compensating duties on dress goods, as well as on the lower grades of woolen cloth, in which substitutes for wool or revamped wool were used to a greater or less extent.[2] The manufacturers declared that all the protection needed, after making these numerous exceptions, was 25% net. But since the 6% internal revenue tax on manufactures was still collected, 10% was added to compensate for that[3] and the ad valorem duties were placed at 35%. Yet when the internal revenue duty was repealed a year or two later no reduction in the ad valorem rate followed.

Raw wool imports under the tariff of 1867 were divided into three classes, the chief basis of classification being the breeds of sheep. Class I included the relatively short and fine fibred wool obtained from all sheep of merino stock. It was commonly called clothing wool from the fact that it comprised such wools as were put through the cards and used for making cloths and cassimeres. Very nearly all of the wool then grown in the United States would have come under this heading. Class II was wool from the English breeds of sheep. Being of comparatively long and fairly coarse fibre, it could be combed, whence it derived its name of combing wool. It was chiefly used in the manufacture of worsteds. Very little of this grade of wool was then grown in the United States, though the amount was increasing, being estimated at 2,500,000 pounds in 1871 and at from 5,000,000 to 8,000,000 in 1880.[4] Class III covered what were known as carpet wools, substantially all of them being

[1] See Statement to the United States Revenue Commission, in *Transactions of the National Association of Wool Manufacturers*, 1865–66, pp. 20–24.

[2] *Ibid.*, pp. 15–18, 24.

[3] The explanation advanced by the manufacturers for this discrepancy in rates was: "That the 10% is not more than an equivalent for the 6% revenue tax will appear from considering that the customs duty being levied on the foreign value and the internal tax on the home value, a larger percentage of the former than of the latter will be required to make a given sum" (*ibid.*, p. 13).

[4] *Bulletin*, vol. iii, p. 267; vol. x, p. 323.

used in the manufacture of carpets. They were the coarsest and poorest grades of wool from all parts of the world, and were raised chiefly in the semi-civilized countries. Outside of the backward flocks of Mexican sheep in Colorado and New Mexico, no wool of the sort was found in this country.[1] Physically, it was perfectly possible to grow it here, but economically it was not, since wool of a better grade bringing a higher price could be produced at about the same cost.

The duties levied were nearly the same for both Class I and Class II wool. If valued at 32 cents a pound or less, a duty of 10 cents a pound plus 11% ad valorem was paid; if valued at more than 32 cents, the duty was 12 cents a pound and 10% ad valorem. In Class III, wool worth 12 cents a pound or less paid 3 cents and the rest 6 cents. A duty of 12 cents a pound was placed on woolen rags, shoddy, mungo, waste, and flock. A further provision doubled the duty on any wool of Class I which was imported after it had been washed, and trebled the duty if it had been scoured. In Classes II and III no such surcharge was made on washed wool, but on scoured the triple rate was imposed. All wool of Class II and much of that in Class III came to the market washed. The absence of a double duty on this wool when it was imposed on Class I wool meant a relatively lower rate for the former, and was favorable to worsted and carpet manufacturers. The fact that no appreciable amount of such wool was to be obtained in this country at the time was advanced as a justification for the discrimination.

This provision for increasing the duty on wool that came in washed or scoured does not appear previous to the tariff of 1864. Before then, the rates had been so arranged that there was less incentive to reduce the weight of wool before importing it than was the case thereafter, when such a large proportion of the duty was in the form of a specific rate per pound. Now, as a matter of fact, the shrinkage in washing and scouring was more than counterbalanced by the double and treble duties, and hence the amount imported subject

[1] A leading carpet manufacturer declared the American production of carpet wool was uncertain, varying from 2,000,000 to 3,500,000 pounds (*Tariff Commission*, 1882, p. 2337). Another said: "90% of all wool consumed by our carpet mills is of foreign origin" (*ibid.*, p. 469). The United States, it was stated, used two thirds of the world's supply of this grade. For figures cf. *ibid.*, p. 2335.

to these surcharges has always been exceedingly small. They served, however, to prevent a practice which would have made it possible to evade the greater part of the intended duty.

A moment's glance at these rates will show that they meant a great increase in the protection afforded the wool-grower of the country. Under the tariff of 1864, when the wool duties were higher than they had been under either of the two previous tariffs, something more than half of the imports paid a duty of 6 cents a pound, most of the remainder paying 3 cents. Under the tariff of 1867 these rates remained the same as before for wool of Class III, but that was not the grade of wool grown in this country. The wool which competed with the domestic clip, and which had formerly come in on paying 6 cents duty, now had to pay about twice that amount. This was the same grade of wool, generally speaking, which during most of the Civil War was paying about 1 cent duty and, under the Act of 1857, came in free. Formerly the most prominent rivals of the American clip in the domestic market had been the cheap wools from South America and the Cape. Coming to market in poor condition and shrinking heavily, they had low values and entered under low rates of duty. Under the new classification, such wools had to pay the same rates of duty as others; while in actual effect the heavy weight duty made the charge on these wools much higher relatively than on those in better condition. In fact, it was the avowed intention of the framers of this act to levy duties that would exclude these wools from the domestic market altogether.[1] How successful they were we shall presently see. There can be no doubt, however, that this act was far more skillfully framed to secure the ends desired by the wool-growers than any previous tariff had been, and that the level of duties was decidedly higher than ever before.

The average annual importation of wool under this tariff for the years 1868–83 was 61,792,000 pounds; the average value 18 cents a pound. This did not vary greatly either in quantity or value from

[1] "It is well known, at least to those familiar with the circumstances connected with the legislation referred to, that the object sought by the wool-growers in the increase of the wool duties in 1867 was primarily to check the importation of the mestiza wools of the Argentine Republic, and secondarily those of the Cape of Good Hope, both, and especially the former, among the cheapest wools in the world." (*Bulletin*, vol. xiii, p. 96.)

the average for the Civil War decade, but the quantity was far in excess of anything before that decade, while the value was much above that for any period since the twenties. The imports under the three classes and their chief subdivisions were as follows, in thousands of pounds:—

Average Annual Imports of Wool, 1868–83.

Value	*Class I*	*Class II*	Value	*Class III*
32 cents or less	9,209	10,016	12 cents or less	22,481
Over 32 cents	607	1,496	Over 12 cents	10,244
Total	10,217	11,513	Total	33,220

The slight amount by which the total for each class exceeds the two subdivisions given indicates the quantity coming in washed (Class I only) or scoured under the double or triple duty imposed in such cases. The most striking feature of the table is the predominance of carpet wool, exceeding by 50% the imports of the two other classes combined.

The source of the greater part of this wool, so far as that is indicated by the country from which it was imported, was as follows:[1]

Average Annual Imports of Wool by Countries of Shipment, 1868–83.

	United Kingdom	*France*	*Russia*	*British N. Amer.*	*S. America*	*Africa*	*Australasia*
Thousands of lbs.	19,483	2,605	4,179	2,746	20,033	5,076	3,647
Av. value, cents	21	13	15	32	14	17	26

The average value of the imports from each country gives some indication of the class of wool coming from that source. So far as this and other available data enable one to judge, all of the wool from France and Russia, about a quarter of that from the United Kingdom, two thirds of that from the Cape, and over three quarters of that from South America was carpet wool.[2] Nearly half of that

[1] With the exception of the United Kingdom and France, the country of shipment was the country of origin. Imports from France included wool from Turkey or Northern Africa; imports from the United Kingdom included wool from Russia, South America, and Australasia.

[2] Statistics showing both the country of origin and the country of shipment begin

from Canada was combing wool. The remainder, composed of less than a quarter of that from South America and the United Kingdom, about a third of that from the Cape, and all of that from Australasia, was clothing wool. Most of the wool of this class imported from England was grown in Australia.

A comparison of the situation at this time with that in preceding years shows the greatest change to be the rise of the imports from Australia. Up to 1872 they had never reached 1,000,000 pounds, but in that year they suddenly jumped to 12,000,000, and from then on continued heavy, though not so high as in that year.[1] This wool, clipped from merino sheep, in many respects resembled the bulk of the domestic clip, but was in some ways superior. It came to market in good condition, did not shrink very heavily, and had a softness which led many American manufacturers to mix it with native wool to produce the better "feel" of foreign goods.[2] Its appearance in the domestic market at this time marked the advent of a serious rival for the American wool-grower.

The importation of wool from South America continued heavy, though below the figure for Civil War times: it now made up a third of the total, whereas before the Civil War it had made up over one half. Moreover, by far the greater part of it was the coarse carpet wool, the only Class I wool that came from there being the fine Montevideo clip, which was much superior to the ordinary mestiza wool. The mestiza proved to be so very generally barred out of the country by the heavy weight duties that little of it was imported under this tariff.[4] The decrease in the imports of wool from the Cape was

in 1882, and are thus available for the last two years of this period. They have largely influenced the above estimates.

[1] In 1872 the extra 10% duty on wool coming from countries to the east of the Cape of Good Hope and not imported directly was repealed, and thereafter much of this wool came through England, London then being the chief market for Colonial wool.

[2] Cf. Letter of Mauger and Avery, *Bulletin*, vol. xxiii, p. 256.

[3] "There has been of late years [about 1883] a large importation of wools from Australia, — a class unknown before 1867, — and these most nearly corresponding in quality with the best Ohio wools will be dangerous competitors to the latter wools under the new tariff." (*Ibid.*, vol. xiii, p. 107.)

[4] "Mestiza and Buenos Ayres wools are almost excluded by our tariff now on account of their heavy weight. We used to import from 20,000 to 30,000 bales of these wools before the present tariff [of 1867] was enacted; now we only import be-

even more noticeable. It is thus evident that the framers of this tariff had met with a considerable degree of success in their avowed intention to keep out these two cheap rivals. How much they gained by it seems doubtful, for apparently the result was simply to replace this wool, which had been the main foreign reliance of the country ever since the thirties, by another of somewhat finer grade and less shrinkage, but promising an equally effective rivalry.

Under this, as under previous tariffs, by far the larger part of the foreign wool entering the country to compete with the domestic clip came in the form of manufactured goods. The value of the average annual importations for the years 1868–83 was $38,900,000, a figure somewhat above the average for the preceding decade. The imports of all the different classes of goods, averaging over $1,000,000 in value, for the years 1868–83, were:—

Cloths	*Dress goods*	*Carpets*	*Shawls*	*Man'f's not otherwise specified*
$9,200,000	$18,700,000	$2,700,000	$1,300,000	$1,400,000

Alterations in the classification make exact comparison with imports under previous tariffs difficult, but it is clear that the only important change was the heavy increase in dress goods, the amount now being fully twice that for the decade preceding the war, and making up one half of the total imports of all manufactures. The imports of cloths, on the other hand, remained about what they had been for twenty years previous. All the other classes of goods, less than a quarter of the total, remained without much change, carpets showing a little advance.

The method of adjusting the duties on manufactured goods under the tariff of 1867 has already been described, but just how much protection these duties afforded is difficult to determine. The manufacturers declared that 25% net was all they wanted. It is very evident, however, that this tariff afforded them more than that. In the first place the additional 10% ad valorem given to compensate for the internal revenue tax was not removed after the tax was abolished. It is also clear that the specific weight duties which were

tween 1000 and 2000 bales yearly. In place of mestiza we use more Australian wools now, because they shrink only 54–55%." (Testimony of Gustav Schwab, wool importer, *Tariff Commission*, 1882, p. 472. Cf. *Bulletin*, vol. xv, p. 56; vol. xxv, p. 41.)

supposed to offset the duty on the raw material included an element of protection. This was especially true of the duties on the cheaper grades of goods, and resulted in a virtual exclusion of these goods from the domestic market.[1] On the classes of goods making up the great bulk of the imports — cloths and dress goods — the duties actually paid averaged 61% and 65% respectively of their value. If the total cost of the wool in a piece of goods never makes up more than half its value,[2] it is obvious that the net protection which this act afforded the manufacturer, as well as the wool-grower, was greater than any before granted.

Overabundant revenue and a demand for lower duties led to a revision of the tariff in 1883. Under the new act the rates on raw wool were slightly reduced. Both Class I and Class II wools paid a duty of 10 or 12 cents a pound as formerly, only now the line where the higher rate began was placed at 30 cents instead of 32 cents. The chief change was the dropping of the additional ad valorem duties of 11% and 10%. It is evident that this meant but a slight reduction — roughly 2 cents a pound — when compared with the rest of the duty, besides being in a measure offset by the lowering of the dividing line. Class III wool now paid 2½ cents a pound instead of 3 cents when valued at 12 cents or less, and 5 instead of 6 cents if above 12 cents. This reduction raised a great outcry from the wool-growers, who held it responsible for the decline in flocks which followed. Since prices were unusually low while this tariff was in force, the protection under the operation of the specific duty became relatively higher than ever before; but as this added nothing to the price which the grower obtained, it afforded him no satisfaction.[3]

The total average importation of raw wool under this tariff for

[1] Cf. *Bulletin*, vol. xxiii, p. 18.

[2] Mr. Whitman, long President of the Wool Manufacturers' Association, says: "I do not think any one has ever estimated the value of wool in a piece of goods at over one half the total value" (*Tariff Commission*, 1882, vol. ii, p. 2424).

[3] "The reduction in the wool duties in 1883 was so slight, that it did not equal the decline in prices which preceded it, nor the decline which has followed it. Being specific in form the duty on wool continues to be protective; and in most cases it is proportionately higher to-day than it was under the Tariff of 1867, or than it has ever been in the history of the United States." (*Bulletin*, vol. xx, p. 151. Cf. *ibid.*, pp. 148–150; vol. xiii, pp. 237–238; vol. xiv, p. 271.)

the years 1884–90 was 102,000,000 pounds. The average value was 14 cents a pound, 4 cents lower than under the tariff of 1867, but this difference is mainly to be explained by a lower price level. The figure for the imports of raw wool far exceeded anything previously known, the increase over the figures for the preceding tariff being 66%. The amounts coming in under each class were as follows, in millions of pounds:[1] —

Class I	*Class II*	*Class III*	
Unwashed	*Unscoured*	*Unscoured*	
Value 30 *cents or less*	*Value* 30 *cents or less*	*Value* 12 *cents or less*	*Value over* 12 *cents*
19.2	5.8	59.6	15.4

This shows that the imports of clothing wool and carpet wool were twice as great as under the previous tariff, while the imports of combing wool fell off nearly one half. The decline in combing-wool imports was due partly to the fact that lustrous fabrics went out of fashion, and partly to an increasing use of merino wools for combing purposes. As a result of these variations, carpet wool came to make up three quarters of the total. Thus almost all of the increase in imports which took place was in a non-competing grade of wool.

Beginning with this period, statistics show the country of production of virtually all the wool imported.[2] The following table gives all the important sources of supply for each class, in thousands of pounds: —

Average Annual Imports of Wool, 1884–90.

Class I			*Class II*
South America	*Australasia*	*British Africa*	*United Kingdom*
5,523	12,785	1,558	5,232

Class III						
France	*Russia*	*Turkey*	*United Kingdom*	*South America*	*China*	*British E. Indies*
2,353	17,566	15,358	9,827	12,093	4,236	8,781

[1] The imports of Class I and Class II wool valued at over 30 cents averaged but a few hundred thousand pounds each.

[2] In fact, the figures show the country of production of all the wool imported into Boston, New York, and Philadelphia, which made up 95 to 98% of the total.

Australasia clearly had gained ground very rapidly and become by far the most serious rival that the American wool-grower had in his domestic market. Australian wool had come to take the place of that formerly obtained from the River Plate and the Cape, the imports from these two regions having fallen off, especially in the case of the latter. Turning to carpet wool, we find that Russia was the chief single source of supply, while the British East Indies and China now first appear as important contributors. The heavy increase in the imports of this class of wool led to renewed complaints on the part of the wool-growers that it really competed with a considerable portion of the domestic clip and was constantly used in place of that. Though the growers had exaggerated notions as to the amount, it seems to have been the case that a small proportion of the carpet wool imports — say 5 to 10% — did enter into other things than carpets. Some was used in felt boots, some in horse blankets, and at the time when rough cheviot was in vogue some of the cheviot wool from Great Britain was used for that fabric. This could take the place of a small fraction of the domestic clip — that from the few Mexican sheep and perhaps some of the skirtings from others. For the wool-grower generally, however, the effect was extremely slight.[1]

Although the tariff of 1883 was passed as the result of a general demand for a lower level of duties, yet in the case of manufactures of wool, the reductions made proved in actual operation to be more nominal than real. The chief lowering of rates came in the specific duties. As these were to compensate the manufacturer for the duty on his raw material, the slight reduction made in the duty on raw wool was logically followed by a lowering of the duty here. In some cases the reduction in the duty on manufactured goods more than offset the lowered duty on the raw material. Another change by which the manufacturer suffered was the lowering of the basis of the estimate for the compensating duty from four to three and a half pounds of wool per pound of finished cloth, which, though more nearly correct, still afforded additional protection in many cases. The ad valorem rates generally remained unaltered. Some rather striking exceptions were the advances made in the rates on the higher

[1] Cf. *Tariff Commission*, 1882, p. 2528; *Tariff Hearings*, 1890, pp. 155–156 and 217–224; *Bulletin*, vol. xviii, p. 333–335; *ibid.*, vol. xx, p. 171.

grades of cloths and dress goods, which formed the largest part of the imports. On the other hand, there was a considerable reduction in the duties on some of the cheaper grades of goods; but the previous duties on these had been prohibitive, and the reduction was not sufficient to have any practical effect.[1]

The average annual imports of manufactures under this act were valued at $45,000,000, on which the duty paid was 67% of the value. Though the imports of manufactures exceeded any previous figure, they did not increase so rapidly as did the raw material. The figures for the average annual imports of the chief classes of goods were as follows, in millions of dollars:—

Cloths	*Dress goods*	*Carpets*	*Knit fabrics*	*Yarns*	*Man'f's not elsewhere specified*
11.2	17.5	1.4	1.9	1.6	5.8

Cloths show a slight increase and yarns first begin to reach an appreciable figure under this tariff. The heavy increase under the heading "manufactures not elsewhere specified" was due to an error on the part of the manufacturers' representative in drawing up the schedules, an error whereby worsted coatings were let in under this heading at a lowered rate of duty.[2]

We are now in a position to form some judgment as to the effect of the wool and woolen duties upon imports for the period as a whole. The following table shows the total amount of competing wool entering the country under each tariff, in millions of pounds, and also the ratio of the domestic clip to foreign wool of all grades.[3]

Av. for years	*Domestic clip*	*Imports of competing wool, classes I & II*	*Imports, wool in form of man'f's*	*Total imports*		*Percentage of domestic clip*	
				Competing wool	*All grades*	*Competing wool*	*All grades*
1868–83	211	21	116	137	178	65	84
1884–90	314	26	135	161	237	51	75

[1] For a fuller discussion of these duties, cf. Taussig, *Tariff History*, pp. 239–242; and *Bulletin*, vol. xiii, pp. 1–13, 89–128.

[2] Cf. *Bulletin*, vol. xiv, pp. 295–310; vol. xxviii, pp. 130–133, 174–177; Taussig, *Tariff History*, p. 243.

[3] As Class III wool does not seriously compete with the domestic clip it is omitted. Similarly, a part of that imported in the form of manufactured goods might be excluded, but the amount is so small as to be negligible. The figures for the domes-

According to these statistics the American wool-grower was more than holding his own, was in fact making substantial gains in his control over the domestic market. Were the period to be further subdivided, it would be found that the domestic clip reached its strongest position in about the year 1884, before it stopped increasing and before the imports began their rapid advance. It is evident that the new high level of duties on wool which went into effect with this period failed to prevent a rise in the imports of foreign wool, the total imports in all forms being higher than ever before. On the other hand, the domestic clip was increasing at a greater rate than the imports. Consequently the native wool supplied a much larger proportion of the domestic consumption than before. The contrast in this respect is most striking when this period is compared with *ante bellum* days. During the years for which we have fairly accurate statistics of imports, the imports of wool in all forms were from over one to over one and one half times the amount of the domestic clip.[1] The Civil War decade is the period of transition. From the close of the war until the admission of wool free of duty, assuming the larger basis of three pounds of wool per dollar of value for manufactured goods, the imports of foreign wool were only 75 to 84% of the domestic clip.[2] In short it was during this

tic clip are those of Mr. Lynch and Mr. Truitt. The imports of wool in the form of manufactures are calculated on the basis of three pounds of wool per dollar of value.

[1] This statement is on the generally accepted assumption that a dollar's worth of manufactured goods contains three pounds of wool. The following table shows the situation.

Percentage of All Imports of Wool, Raw and Manufactured, to the Domestic Clip.

1830	1840	1850	1860	1870	1880	1890	1905
101	113	131	158	114	60	86	88
169	142	149	201	115	68	96	

In constructing this table the figures for the amount of wool imported represent an average for five-year periods centering in 1830, etc. The first line is computed by using my own estimates of the domestic clip for years previous to 1870 and the usual trade figures since; the second line by using the estimates of the Department of Agriculture, which I believe to be too low for the earlier period. A calculation assuming two pounds of wool per dollar of manufactures somewhat decreases the proportion of imports during the period before 1860, though showing the same general tendency.

[2] 84%, 1868–83; 75%, 1884–90; 78%, 1891–93. The figures in the preceding footnote table show an even smaller proportion in the years about 1880.

period that the country came nearer to supplying its own need for wool than it had at any time since the first of the century or ever has since.

The chief measure of the benefit which the tariff confers upon the American wool-grower is the increase in the price at which it enables him to dispose of his clip. The operation of the new, heavy, weight duties makes the question of the amount of this increase a most difficult one to answer. Ordinarily the mere fact that a commodity is imported and the duty paid may be taken as evidence that the price of the article in this country is raised to the full extent of the duty. This, however, presupposes that the article produced here and the one imported are identical in quality. Yet it would be difficult to find another commodity which varies in so many respects as do different clips of wool. Fineness, elasticity, length, and strength of fibre, working quality, and shrinkage all enter into the question. Each separate fleece even may be sorted into six or eight different grades. It is obvious, then, that the effects of a system of duties like ours are neither simple nor easily analyzed.

A comparison of prices in the two countries is the simplest and most direct method, but clearly not easily made. Inasmuch as the events of the following period, when wool was for a while admitted free, afford the best opportunity for making such comparisons, this question will be taken up more fully in connection with those events. For the present period it is sufficient to note that a comparison of prices for the two grades of wool which most closely resembled one another shows that during these years the American wool remained from 8 to 11 cents a pound higher than its foreign rival.[1] Thus it ranged slightly below the duty, which ran from 10 to 12 or more cents a pound. To what extent this difference between the duty and the additional price was due to a difference in quality and shrinkage and to what extent it might have been caused by an overabundant supply of the domestic clip it is not easy to determine.[2] It is known, however, that the practice of importing only the best

[1] *Bulletin*, vol. xxii, p. 114. For a chart showing the course of London prices from 1866 to 1890 and the price of a corresponding grade of American wool, with comment, cf. *ibid.*, vol. xxi, p. 362.

[2] The difference between the price of Australian average and that of fine Ohio fleece on a scoured basis averaged 33½ cents for the years 1871–90. See page 287.

portion of the fleece, which became very general at a later period, had already begun, and this tended to lessen the actual protection.[1] Moreover, it seems unlikely that the domestic supply of any grade was so great as to depress it below the duty price. The heavy imports of Australian wool were sufficient proof that such was not the case with fine wool, and it is probable that it was not with the medium grade, though the supply of that grade came nearer to meeting the domestic needs than did any other. Furthermore, the previous facts seem inadequate to explain the discrepancy. We may therefore conclude that the growers got nearly the full benefit of the duty, which meant more protection than they had ever enjoyed before.

But just how far this last fact was causally related to the great increase in the number of sheep and the growing control over the domestic market still remains to be determined.

The Manufacture of Wool.

The chief statistics covering the growth of the manufacture of wool for this period are shown in the following table, based on the Census returns:[2] —

	Number of establishments	*Capital*	*Value of product*	*Consumption of wool, in condition purchased*
1860	1673	$42,000,000	$80,000,000	95,000,000 lbs.
1870	3456	132,000,000	217,000,000	220,000,000 "
1880	2689	159,000,000	267,000,000	296,000,000 "
1890	2489	296,000,000	337,000,000	373,000,000 "

In these two decades the manufacture enjoyed steady growth, but, as was to be expected, nothing like the phenomenal advance of

[1] Cf. *Bulletin*, vol. xvii, p. 204. A resolution of the Wool-Growers' Association complained that in effect the duty actually paid was but little over half the rate fixed by the Act of 1883 for such wools, when in the condition in which American unwashed wools were usually sold in the market. This, however, exaggerated the situation.

[2] Obviously numerous allowances must be made in interpreting such a table. A decrease in the number of establishments does not mean a decline in the industry. The value of the product varies with good or bad years. The census year 1870 was poor; 1880 was good. In 1870 the inflated currency was a misleading factor, though having less influence on the value of the product, then depressed, than on the amount of invested capital, much of which was put in under inflated prices.

the Civil War decade. Having been somewhat overextended in 1870, it would naturally show less progress in the succeeding ten years than in the decade beginning with 1880.

The growth in relative strength of the American manufacturer in his competition with foreigners for the domestic market is made clearer by the following table:—

	1850	1860	1870	1880	1890
Per capita value domestic m'f'gs	$2.07	$2.57	$5.65	$5.33	$5.39
Per capita value net imports of m'f'gs[1]	0.80	0.98	1.07	0.63	0.74

This brings out very vividly the remarkable progress which the manufacturers of the country had made after 1860 in securing the domestic market. In 1890 the per capita consumption of American manufactures of wool was more than twice what it was in 1860, whereas the per capita consumption of foreign goods had declined one quarter. The ground which the American manufacturer gained during the war decade had been relatively more than maintained, while his foreign rivals had been falling behind. It was plainly necessary for the manufacturer to secure the domestic market if the grower of wool was to do so. This exclusion of foreign manufactures was, then, an essential step towards the exclusion of foreign raw wool. We may therefore conclude that during the years 1870–90, so far as the tariff on manufactures was concerned, it operated in a manner to favor the wool-grower.

The progress of the manufacturers was due in part to developments on the technical side of the industry, though probably to a less extent than in earlier days. The most radical improvements in the machinery for the manufacture of wool had been introduced before 1860, and thereafter the main advance was simply through

[1] These figures are the average for five-year periods centering in 1850, etc. The paper currency somewhat exaggerated the value of domestic manufactures in 1870. It should be noted that these two series of figures are to be compared with one another relatively. To compare them absolutely would require an increase in the value of the imports of manufactures by the amount of the tariff duties. Owing to the rising rates of duty such a correction would slightly lessen the decrease in consumption of foreign manufactures.

improvements in that already existing. The chief innovation of these years was the general adoption of the self-acting mule, which took place about 1870. Down to the close of the Civil War, spinning had commonly been done on hand-jacks. The introduction of the self-acting mule increased the production per spindle 40–60%, and decreased the cost per pound fully 50%. Its adoption is said to have completed the development of the woolen manufacture.[1] Then, too, at about this time, American looms, especially the Crompton and Knowles open-shed fancy looms, won a well-earned fame by a steady advance in speed and productivity.[2] Further, the general introduction of the great improvements in combing-machines which had been made in Europe during the fifties greatly facilitated the growth of the worsted manufacture.

The sheep-owner was concerned not only with the growth of the wool manufacture generally, but also with the question as to which branches of the manufacture were growing, and whether or not they were those which employed the grade of wool that he produced. In some branches the domestic manufacturer had a virtual monopoly of the market, as in flannels and blankets, in cloths which, being of mixed material, held a smaller amount of wool than others, — the duties on these being prohibitory,[3] — and to a less extent, in knit goods and carpets. The Census returns for the value of the product in the three branches that made the greatest progress during these years were as follows, in millions of dollars: —

	Worsted	*Carpet*	*Hosiery and knit goods*
1860	$3	$7	$7
1870	22	21	18
1880	33[4]	31	29
1890	79	47	67

The worsted manufacture far exceeded all others in the rate of its growth. In 1860 it just barely existed, "but up to 1865 it developed

[1] North, in Davis's *New England States*, vol. i, p. 220.

[2] Cf. *Bulletin*, vol. ix, p. 46.

[3] Cf. *ibid.*, vol. xxv, pp. 47–48.

[4] Some worsted goods made in woolen mills were returned in the Census of 1880 as woolen goods. The amount is estimated at $12,000,000 in value, which should be added to the above. See *ibid.*, vol. xiv, p. 282.

with a rapidity that has scarcely any precedent in the history of American manufactures."[1] By 1870 it had become fairly important, and by 1890 was a close second to the woolen manufacture, long the leading branch. The relative progress of these two main branches may be judged from the following figures, with the fact in mind that worsteds are made from wool which is combed and woolens from that which is carded.

	1870	1880	1890
Number of cards	9224	7581	8198
Number of combs	261	518	855

While the number of cards declined,[2] the number of combs more than tripled. There was also growth in the variety of worsted fabrics put out. In 1861 the manufacture of worsted braids had been started at Pawtucket. Soon after the war, the manufacture of bunting was established, and in the eighties came the first plush manufacture.[3]

Worsted fabrics had been rapidly coming into more and more general use ever since the first of the century, a development which, as has been seen, wrought great changes in the wool manufacture of Great Britain. In the United States, however, up to the time of the Civil War, the worsted branch of the industry had never secured a start, and the only result of the increased use of such goods had been to increase the imports. One consequence was that the country fell behind in the technical appliances for this branch of the manufacture; another was the comparative absence of a strong demand for protection for worsteds. Since neither the wool-growers nor the manufacturers were particularly interested in excluding this class of goods, in nearly all the tariffs antedating the Civil War worsted goods had been either subject to comparatively low duties or admitted free.

[1] Special Commissioner of the Revenue, *Report*, 1866, p. 58.

[2] The decrease in cards did not mean an absolute decline in that branch, as the capacity of cards — and also of combs — was increasing.

[3] North, in Davis's *New England States*, vol. i, p. 242. Some idea of the relative importance of the different fabrics in this branch of the industry may be gained from the fact that in 1886 the number of combs in the worsted manufacture, besides those in carpets, were: braids 20, alpacas 28, ladies' dress goods 134, men's wear worsted coatings 119, spinning mills making yarn for the trade generally, principally for worsted coatings, 262. See *Bulletin*, vol. xvi, pp. 304–306.

The rapid advance which afterwards took place was the outcome of a combination of favoring circumstances. The initial impulse came from the admission of Canadian combing wool free under the Reciprocity treaty with that country, though the manufacture of delaines, using merino wool and cotton, had begun a little earlier. By the end of the Civil War, under the peculiarly favorable tariffs enacted during that struggle, a good start had been made.[1] In the Act of 1867, which came at a most opportune time, the worsted manufacturer was especially guarded, the arrangement of the compensatory duty and the admission of Class II wool in washed condition without extra duty both being provisions of considerable advantage.[2] Throughout the existence of the Act of 1883 the manufacturers were struggling to secure a rectification of the error by which worsted coatings came in at reduced rates, but without success until a few months before the McKinley bill became a law in 1890.[3] Imports increased somewhat, but the manufactures did not suffer greatly, and the tariff must be given great credit for its influence in building up the industry at this period.

The only other important factor was the improvement of machinery which made possible the very general introduction of American wool into worsted coatings. Up to 1867 combing wool or worsted had never been used in the United States in cloths or fabrics for the ordinary wear of men, but only in stuffs or thin unfelted fabrics such as women's dress goods and linings. But when an American representative at the Paris Exposition of 1867 found that the French were combing fairly long merino wool, he suggested that Americans try the medium Ohio wool for this purpose. In 1869 appeared the first worsted coatings manufactured in the United States, and they

[1] The statement of the Special Commissioner of the Revenue (*Report*, 1866, p. 58) that "an almost complete annihilation of the worsted manufacture followed the abrogation of the Reciprocity treaty with the maintenance of the same duty on woolens and the 5% internal revenue duty besides" is an exaggeration. Such depression as followed was chiefly due to an abnormal situation in the industry generally. The abrogation of the treaty did remove an advantage, however, and the worsted manufacturers put this forward as a reason for particularly favorable treatment in the compensating duties under the tariff of 1867. Cf. *supra*, pages 214–215.

[2] Cf. *Senate Miscel. Doc.* No. 15, 55th Congress, 1st session.

[3] A Resolution of Congress on May 10, 1890, directed the Secretary of the Treasury to classify as woolen cloths all imports of worsted cloth. Cf. *Bulletin*, vol. xx, p. 184.

were made of American wool of merino stock.[1] The goods immediately met with great popularity, and not only began at once to displace the fancy cassimeres which had formerly driven out the broadcloth, but greatly increased the opportunity to expand the market for worsted manufactures. The grade of wool which was thus employed came to be used in other worsted fabrics as well, the rapid improvements in combing-machines making this feasible. "In old times," says Mr. Bond, "combs required a four inch staple of strong wool, while now [1887] a one and one half inch staple is enough, and the finest merino can be spun into worsted yarn."[2] This enabled the manufacturers to use for worsteds a large part of the domestic clip, chiefly that from states east of the Mississippi river. In the growth of the worsted manufacture which took place during these years this wool at once came into general use. In fact it was to just the fabrics in which this wool could be used, frequently in combination with cotton, that the worsted manufacturers of this country chiefly turned. Goods requiring the long coarse wool clipped from such breeds as the Lincoln, Leicester, or Cotswold were still mainly imported.

How great an effect all these developments had upon the wool-grower may be judged from the fact that the consumption of wool by this branch of the manufacture rose from 3,000,000 pounds in 1860 to 100,000,000 in 1890. At the time of the war it was declared that "American spinners go to Canada for all their combing wool,"[3] and the manufacturers estimated that not over 300,000 pounds of combing wool was produced in the United States.[4] In 1871 the total consumption of delaine[5] and combing wool by the worsted manu-

[1] Cf. *Bulletin*, vol. x, p. 329; vol. xvi, p. 101.

[2] *Report on Wool and Manufactures of Wool*, 1887, p. xlii. Mr. Bond concluded that with this machinery it was possible to comb all the wool grown in the country east of the Mississippi, a small portion of the California, Texas, and Southern, a good deal of that from Colorado and New Mexico, and five eighths of the other western wool (p. xli).

[3] Commissioner of Agriculture, *Report*, 1864, p. 509. *Transactions of the National Association of Wool Manufacturers*, 1865–66, Statement of Facts Relative to Canada Wools and the Manufactures of Worsteds.

[4] Special Commissioner of the Revenue, *Report*, 1866, p. 57. Though the Commissioner thought this an overestimate, it impresses me as the reverse.

[5] Delaine wool, clipped from merino sheep, was fairly fine, with a staple of three to five inches, of uniform quality, and having strength, soundness, and softness, but no lustre.

facturers was 14,500,000 pounds, of which 7,500,000 was the long combing wool from English breeds of sheep and the rest delaine. Of this amount, all the delaine was native wool, but only 2,500,000 pounds of the other.[1] The growing demand was denoted "unprecedented," and it was reported that the production of combing wool was on the increase, though "limited to populous districts where there is a demand for mutton and to countries where there is an improved agriculture."[2] By 1880 the consumption of combing wool of English breeds was estimated at from 10,000,000 to 20,000,000 pounds, of which this country produced from 5,000,000 to 8,000,000.[3] In 1886 it was asserted on good authority that, if the merino wool suitable for the comb were added to the clip of English breeds, the total for the country would be 60,000,000 pounds.[4] Of the total amount of wool consumed by the worsted manufacturer in 1890, about two thirds was of domestic origin, but by far the larger part of this came from merino sheep.

It is obvious that this turn of events meant a great deal for the many owners of merino sheep, and in 1870 this breed formed four fifths of all the sheep in the country. In fact it was commonly said at the time that the changes which made it possible to use certain grades of merino wool in the manufacture of worsteds raised the price of such wool by 25%.[5] Here we find one of the chief reasons which tended to put the price of Ohio medium wool above that of Ohio fine. It is also obvious that the facility with which Ohio medium could be used for worsted fabrics made it a rival of the combing wool from the English breeds of sheep. This explains why during these years foreign combing wool has been treated as a competitor of the domestic clip, though it had not been such before.

Another branch of the wool manufacture which made notable progress during these years was that engaged upon carpets. Between 1860 and 1870 it tripled, and between 1870 and 1890 it doubled. This industry was greatly advanced by the American inventions in carpet looms, but it was especially favored by the tariff of 1867.

[1] *Bulletin*, vol. iii, pp. 265–267.

[2] Commissioner of Agriculture, *Report*, 1871, pp. 190–200.

[3] *Bulletin*, vol. ix, p. 111; vol. x, p. 323.

[4] *Ibid.*, vol. xvi, pp. 210, 304–306. For an estimate of the shrinkage and quantity of various grades of combing wool produced in each state, see *ibid.*, p. 207.

[5] *Ibid.*, p. 106.

The growers maintained that the arrangement of duties whereby washed carpet wool was admitted at the same rate as unwashed operated to favor the manufacturer in the same way that the similar arrangement for combing wool in Class II did,[1] and that it injured the market for domestic carpet wool. But imported wool of the third class rarely took the place of the domestic clip, and never in the carpet manufacture. There, out of 55,000,000 pounds of wool used in 1890, but 2,000,000 was of domestic origin.[2] The domestic clip of carpet wool was exceedingly small, and was produced under such conditions that neither the tariff nor the growth of the carpet manufacture had much influence over it.

The third of the leading branches of this industry to enjoy a rapid advance during these years was the manufacture of hosiery and knit goods, which was surpassed in rate of growth by the worsted manufacture alone. Unlike the others it owed little to the tariff, for its progress appears to have been mainly a result of successful mechanical inventions and the increasing use of cotton as a raw material. American inventiveness had been unusually early and successful in this field. The application of power to knitting twenty years before it was made in England, the invention of the circular knitting machine and automatic machines for making fashioned hosiery goods, had by the time of the Civil War laid a strong foundation upon which to build.[3] From that period on the use of cotton became more and more important. Starting in 1860 with a consumption of 3,000,000 pounds of wool and about 4,000,000 pounds of cotton, the raw material used thereafter was as follows, in millions of pounds: —

Consumption by Hosiery and Knit Goods Manufacture.[4]

	Foreign wool	*Domestic wool*	*Cotton*	*Cotton yarn*	*Wool yarn*
1870	0.2	5.3	11.4	2.1	2.2
1880	0.4	8.1	20.1	8.3	4.5
1890	3.7	18.9	32.4	32.2	10.5

[1] Cf. pages 214, 223 and references.

[2] *Census*, 1890. This does not include wool bought in the form of yarn.

[3] Cf. *Transactions of the National Association of Wool Manufacturers*, 1865–66. The Condition and Necessities of the Knit Goods Manufacture; *Bulletin*, vol. ix, p. 49.

[4] Bureau of the Census, *Bulletin* No. 74, pp. 78–79. The figures for wool give the amount in condition purchased; those for yarn indicate the amount purchased outside of the mill.

By 1890 cotton, it will be seen, had far outdistanced wool. But it is also evident that to whatever extent wool was used in this branch of the manufacture it was pretty sure to be domestic wool, the medium staple, strength, and fineness of which made it particularly well adapted to the purpose. In so far, then, as the growth of the hosiery and knit goods manufacture increased the demand for wool rather than for cotton, it was of especial benefit to the domestic wool-grower, but it is clear that this increase was never very great in amount.

The demand for wool arising from the growing manufactures of the time was partly offset by the devices adopted for prolonging the useful life of the wool fibre. Wool once used was revamped and appeared again in such second-hand forms as shoddy, mungo, and wool waste.[1] Increased attention to waste products, new methods of preparing such material, and improved machinery which made it possible to put it to better uses, constantly augmented the consumption of these substitutes, and at the same time decreased by so much the demand for raw wool.[2]

In summarizing the situation as to the way in which the domestic wool-grower met the needs of the manufacturer, one would say that the chief deficiency was the lack of carpet wool. But economic conditions were such that the manufacturer could not expect the grower to turn to that. After this the crying need was for medium wool suitable for combing. "If a majority of the cloth manufacturers were to-day asked what wool to produce they would say that produced by a cross of full-blooded merino and full-blooded South-

[1] These forms are described as follows: "Shoddy is made chiefly from combed wool, and is the worked up waste of goods that have not been milled or felted, such as stockings, flannels, blankets, soft merinos, etc., also from hard spinning waste," and looser waste treated on the Garnett machine. "Mungo is made from hard spun and felted cloth, and generally from any and all cloths for men's wear into the fabrication of which no cotton has entered. It is of very short fibre, by reason of the tension required to pull it apart. . . . Wool extract is made from fabrics or wastes which have either linen or cotton in them. It is manufactured by carbonization" (*Bulletin*, vol. xxi, p. 341).

[2] In 1880 D. A. Wells estimated that 41% of the raw material that went into the wool manufactures of the country was not wool (see *Bulletin*, vol. xxi, p. 342; cf. Springer's *Report*, 1892, p. 18). In 1890 of the total amount of scoured wool and shoddy used in the manufactures of wool, exclusive of the hosiery and knit goods, shoddy made up 22% (see *Census*, 1900, vol. ix, p. 95).

down, which would be a typical medium wool."[1] There was complaint that the growers of the country were too generally given to one grade — about three quarters blood merino — whereas the tendency in manufacturing was towards lower grades, so that one half and one quarter blood wools were relatively scarce. Proof of this is found in the rise of medium wool above fine wool which took place at this time. On the other hand, the superfine wool employed by the manufacturers, though small in amount, was chiefly imported. It was estimated that not over 10,000 pounds of such wool were grown in the whole country, though before 1850 it had been relatively plentiful.[2] It is worthy of note that those branches of the wool manufacture of the country which largely employed raw material, either wool or cotton, of domestic origin have always been the strongest.

The Rivalry of Cotton.

The rise of the cotton manufacture, as has previously been pointed out, cut into the market for wool. In fact, during the first half of the century, cotton had offered what was probably the most serious competition that the woo -growers of the world had to face. The scarcity of cotton during the Civil War decade put a sudden stop to this tendency. It is now time to inquire whether the tendency revived after that episode had passed.

At the opening of the period we are considering the price of cotton was still above the normal, and it was not until after 1875 that it returned to the usual level. The average New York price, gold basis, for middling upland cotton for the years 1870–75 was 16.3 cents a pound, the Liverpool price 9.15 pence. For the years 1876–90 the quotations averaged 10.9 cents and 6.07 pence respectively. As this was a fair price there was no inducement more than the usual one, so far as cost was concerned, to substitute cotton for wool.

[1] Commissioner of Agriculture, *Report*, 1871, p. 190. Pages 189 to 190 give a detailed description of the different grades of wool used in the various fabrics. For a more minute account of the various grades of wool and the kind of wool clipped from different breeds of sheep, see Michigan Board of Agriculture, *Report*, 1900, pp. 214–216.

[2] *Bulletin*, vol. x, p. 319. In 1879 the secretary of the manufacturers' association declared that "the only valid objection which can be urged against the existing wool tariff" was that the duty on wool failed to stimulate the domestic supply of superfine wool (*ibid.*, p. 6).

The growth of the manufacture of cotton is shown by the following Census figures:—

	Number of establishments	*Capital*	*Value of product*	*Consumption of cotton*
1860	1091	$98,000,000	$115,000,000	422,000,000 lbs.
1870	956	140,000,000	177,000,000	398,000,000 lbs.
1880	756	208,000,000	192,000,000	750,000,000 lbs.
1890	905	354,000,000	267,000,000	1,117,000,000 lbs.

If this table be compared with the corresponding one for the manufactures of wool it will be found, on contrasting the years 1860 and 1890, that the rate of growth of the woolen manufacture was considerably greater than that of the cotton manufacture. But a comparison of the years 1870 and 1890 shows the rate of growth for this period to be more nearly equal, though the cotton manufacture somewhat leads. This gives further evidence of the great set-back that the cotton manufacture received through the war, the effects of which, as this shows, had not been entirely overcome two decades later.

The growth of the cotton manufacture, however, does not exactly measure the success of cotton in its rivalry with wool, for the consumption of the former was increasing at a still greater rate than that of the latter. The total consumption of the two fibres at different dates was as follows, in millions of pounds:[1]—

	1860	1870	1880	1890
Wool	194	343	390	412
Cotton	444	431	798	1193

This gives a rather better clue to the relative increase in consumption of the two fibres, and makes out the situation considerably more favorable to cotton. While the consumption of wool increased 200% between 1860 and 1890, that of cotton increased over 250%. If we

[1] Based on a table in the *Census* of 1900, vol. ix, p. 12. The original table includes cotton used in the wool manufactures, but makes no allowance for imports of wool or cotton in the form of manufactured goods. In the case of wool, I have added to the Census figures an estimate of the imports of wool in manufactures, taking the average imports for five-year periods centering in the Census years and assuming $1 in value to be the equivalent of 3 pounds of wool. The imports of manufactures of cotton remained virtually unchanged. Though the exports increased in amount, the total was negligible.

compare 1870 and 1890, we find that wool increased but 20% and cotton over 175%, which shows that this fibre was at least making up for the set-back it had received in the preceding decade. Moreover, no small part of this increase came in the wool manufacture itself, where the consumption of cotton rose from about 4,000,000 pounds in 1870 to nearly 160,000,000 in 1890, a rate of increase about five times as great as that of wool itself.

Nor was this situation peculiar to the United States, though the rate of increase in the use of cotton appears to have been somewhat greater here than elsewhere.[1] In Great Britain the general tendency in regard to both fibres was very similar, as the following table shows:—

Consumption of Raw Wool and Cotton in Great Britain.[2]

	1866	1870	1880	1890
Cotton, million cwts.	8.0	9.6	12.3	14.8
Wool " "	2.8	2.9	3.3	3.8

It is thus clear that although the cotton famine gave a severe check to the growing consumption of cotton, it was only a temporary one. But it is also evident that, after the scarcity had completely disappeared, cotton did not gain ground over its rival at anything like so rapid a rate as it had during the first half of the century.

The Growing of Wool.

Having surveyed the various factors affecting the demand side of the domestic wool market, we can now turn with a clearer understanding to the supply side and see how the wool-growing industry itself fared during these two decades.

Before entering upon a detailed examination of the course of the industry in different sections of the country, we may first briefly summarize the situation for the country as a whole. According to

[1] The following table from the *Census* of 1900 (vol. ix, p. 6) shows the consumption of cotton, in thousands of bales, for the five years ending with 1830, '40, '50, '60, '70, 80, and for the year 1890.

	1830	1840	1850	1860	1870	1880	1890
Great Britain	711	1156	1458	2265	2369	2924	4140
Continent	411	629	776	1490	1842	2455	4277
United States	130	255	553	813	875	1543	2983

[2] British Board of Trade, *Charts for St. Louis Exposition.*

the Census of 1870 the number of sheep in the country was 28,000,000. This did not include sheep on the range. In 1880 the Census returned 42,000,000, including 7,000,000 on the range; and in 1890, 41,000,000 in all. The figures of the Commissioner of Agriculture were 32,000,000 for 1871, and 41,000,000 and 44,000,000 for the last two dates. Probably these are more nearly correct.[1] Both sets of figures show an advance of about 36%, virtually all of which occurred during the first decade. But the most interesting point is that the flocks of the country steadily advanced up to 1884, when they attained the unequaled total of 51,000,000 head, an increase of nearly two thirds. Then a decline set in, resulting in a loss of about half the number gained.

The figures for the total production of wool naturally show a closely corresponding movement. Starting at 146,000,000 pounds in 1871, the clip rose to a maximum of 337,500,000 in 1884 and fell to 309,000,000 in 1890.[2] It is thus clear that the clip increased more

[1] Most of the discrepancy between the two is found in the returns for the Pacific and Rocky Mountain states, where the Census presumably was defective.

[2] These are the trade estimates of Mr. Lynch and Mr. Truitt, adopted, as previously noted, as the most reliable. The Census figures vary very considerably, being 100,000,000 in 1870 and 165,000,000 in 1890, but are unquestionably far too low. The Commissioner of Agriculture's figures are nearer those of the trade. The following comment of the *Census* of 1870 (vol. iii, pp. 73–74), upon the figures for the wool clip generally, are important. "Censuses have been severely criticised by 'the trade' on account of the low average clip per head reported throughout the country and more especially in certain states. It is doubtful whether the average yield of wool as shown by the ratio between the number of sheep returned in the Census and the number of pounds of wool returned will ever reach the average weight of fleece as reckoned by the trade. This is due, in part, to the fact that the average taken by the wool brokers for the purposes of this comparison is the average under favorable conditions. Still it must be admitted, as the result of candid investigation, that the figures of the trade have been much nearer the truth than those of the Census in the great majority of states. In certain of the states, however, notably those of the South, issue must be taken with the statements of the trade. . . . In some of the Southern states a large portion of the sheep owned are not kept with a view to the wool product and are actually not sheared. So general is this as to reduce the aggregate clip in those states more nearly to the figures of the Census than the trade. In all states, however, where sheep are kept in considerable numbers for the sake of the wool crop and in northern and western states generally, there is no doubt that the return of wool in previous Censuses has been partial and the average weight, therefore, brought below the facts of the case." This, it is explained, is because (1) all wool used in "Domestic Manufactures" is properly excluded in order to avoid a duplication of

rapidly, and decreased less rapidly, than the number of sheep. This was due to the improvement in the breed of sheep, especially in the West, following the introduction of the comparatively heavy-fleeced merino.

The period, as a whole, thus shows a considerable net gain in the wool-growing industry, though it ends with a very decided and most significant falling off in the flocks. In fact, as will later appear, the maximum attained during this period marks the highest point ever reached by the sheep industry in the history of the country. The steadily increasing weight of the fleece served to prevent any serious decline in the total clip, and in one later year the record of 1884 was slightly exceeded, but the number of sheep was never again so great as in that year.[1]

The East.

Originally, as we have seen, the East was the centre of the wool-growing industry of the country, but after the thirties it was forced to surrender this title to the Middle West, while its flocks steadily dwindled until at the outbreak of the Civil War they were about half the size of twenty years earlier. At the opening of the period under review, the reaction which followed the war had left the industry at a very low ebb, lower, in fact, than in 1860. The course of the industry in the New England and Middle Atlantic states during these years is shown in the following table, which gives the number of sheep, in tens of thousands, for each year: —[2]

	1871	1872	1873	1874	1875	1876	1877	1878	1879	1880
New England	138	131	143	141	144	145	141	140	144	152
Middle Atlantic	412	400	407	399	395	386	379	344	410	417
Total	550	531	550	540	539	531	520	484	554	569

value; (2) the clip of many small flocks is so slight that no return of it is made; (3) butchers buying sheep and selling wool on the skin make no return of it; (4) some spring lambs are returned as sheep, thus reducing the average yield; (5) some of the returns are on the basis of clean wool. The second and third of these reasons are by far the most important. An examination of the agricultural schedules of Iowa for 1860 showed 2416 farms with 24,067 sheep, 8% of the total in the state, for which no production of wool was returned.

[1] The recent figures of the Department of Agriculture are misleading. Cf. note of page 298.

[2] Estimates of the Department of Agriculture.

	1881	1882	1883	1884	1885	1886	1887	1888	1889	1890
New England	157	138	138	138	128	124	123	127	123	122
Middle Atlantic	429	383	384	379	349	308	296	283	276	277
Total	586	521	522	517	477	432	419	410	399	399

During the first half of the period a halt took place in the steady decline in the flocks which had prevailed for some time previous to 1860. The higher prices which succeeded the unusually low level of 1867–70, and especially the stimulus of the two sudden advances in 1872 and 1880, gave renewed hope. In both groups of states, however, the maximum was reached in 1881, and in neither case did the increase over the figures for 1871 amount to 200,000. Then followed a decline, though not very marked until after 1884, when the lower level of prices set in. In 1890 the number of sheep was probably lower than at any time since the War of 1812 had come to a close. Thus, although for the country as a whole this period brought a decided gain in the industry, for the East it brought a loss.

In New England the sheep industry suffered less than in the Middle Atlantic states, presumably because it had already fallen so low. The change most noticeable here was a rapidly growing tendency towards making the raising of lamb and mutton the chief object, while the wool clip was becoming purely secondary. In Maine, in 1890, fully 50% of the sheep were of the English breeds, 25% were merinos or grade merinos, and 25% common.[1] In Massachusetts sheep were kept almost exclusively for their meat; in fact, in 1890 only about 5% had merino blood.[2] As early as 1875 it was announced that "the keeping of large flocks of sheep in this state

[1] Figures giving the number of sheep for each breed are to be found in the *Census* of 1890, vol. iii, p. 236. Cf. *Sheep Industry*, pp. 337–342.

[2] *Ibid.*, p. 249. The state *Census* made the following returns:—

	Saxony	*Merino*	*Others*
1865	3126	55,428	110,888
1875	1631	14,456	42,686
1885	1215	5,307	48,618

J. S. Grinnell enumerates as causes for the decline in the number of sheep: the increased imports of wool, the introduction of shoddy, the increased number of sheep brought in from the West, the increase of the dairy industry, destruction by dogs, and decay of fences. *Agriculture of Massachusetts*, 1891, p. 116.

principally for wool is undoubtedly impracticable. Our farmers can't compete with the cheap and rich lands of the West. . . . But in the increased market value of mutton and ease of transportation eastern farmers have an advantage which can be turned to valuable account."[1] It was found that by raising sheep for lamb and mutton the farmer could best dispose of many of his coarser products, such as turnips and hay, without risk of prices falling below a paying standard. A small flock, too, would use up much produce otherwise wasted, and sheep always aided in fertilizing the fields. The new high price level for mutton and lamb which had come in just before the war was well sustained, and the price of the combing or delaine wool clipped from mutton breeds of sheep was also high. Had it not been for these advantages, combined with that of a near-by market for mutton, many other flocks would have been annihilated. As it was, circumstances were not sufficiently favorable to prevent them from declining.

Even Vermont, the old-time stronghold and famous breeding-ground of merinos, was invaded by the mutton-producing sheep. In 1890 nearly one half the sheep there were of English blood, the Southdown predominating. Along with this movement towards mutton sheep came renewed interest in the French or Rambouillet merino, first introduced in the fifties, but later overshadowed by the Vermont merino. The Rambouillet grew a good, fine, delaine wool and produced better mutton in greater amount than any of the other merinos. The Vermont breeders of fine-wooled sheep, however, still found a good market for their high-grade stock so long as the flocks of the West continued to expand. The high reputation of this stock continued unrivaled. At the Centennial Exposition, out of thirteen first-class awards nine went to the breeders of Vermont. Between 1877 and 1881 over 1200 sheep a year were shipped from Middlebury, the centre of the chief stock-breeding county of that state, to other parts of the country.[2] The majority of these went to Ohio, Texas, and Michigan, but many went farther west. A few years later Vermont was sending sheep to Argentina, the Cape, and Australia. The stock-breeders, however, made up a relatively small portion of the total number of sheep-owners. And here, as elsewhere

[1] *Agriculture of Massachusetts*, 1874–75, pp. 112–113, 118.

[2] *Sheep Industry*, p. 321.

in New England, the ordinary flocks were either abandoned or devoted to the raising of mutton.

In the Middle Atlantic states most of the sheep were in New York and Pennsylvania, and it was in these two states, of course, that the heaviest decline took place. In New York also the general movement towards mutton set in. Rams of English stock, especially Cotswolds, were obtained and crossed with the merinos. About this time, too, the practice became common of sending sheep from the West to the central and western sections of the state to raise lambs and to be fattened for the market. Flocks were all small, the general run having but 30–50 sheep, and they were really only incidental to general farming.

It was in Pennsylvania that the flocks suffered most at this time. The southwestern corner of that state, long noted for its superfine wool, produced a good proportion of all the Saxony wool grown in the country. The market conditions at the time were, however, particularly unfavorable to this grade, and there was much complaint from the growers of that section about not being able to obtain a "fair" price for their clip. There, to a greater extent than in New York, those who were dissatisfied, instead of turning their attention to mutton, gave up sheep altogether.[1] It is thus evident that, in the Middle Atlantic states as a whole, the general tendency was the same as in New England, simply a continuation, after a temporary halt, of the retrograde movement which had begun before the war.

The South.

At the beginning of the period now in review the flocks of the South had not altogether recovered from the war-time devastation. The general course of events for the whole period is sufficiently outlined in the table which follows. Texas, however, is omitted from this table, for inasmuch as the conditions in that state were entirely

[1] Considerable information on the situation here is to be obtained from the testimony given before the Tariff Commission of 1882. One grower declared that a duty of $1 a pound would increase the quantity of fine wool somewhat, but that not many would grow it even then. "I may say it is pride *alone* that has kept this wool in this country for forty years. The amount has been growing less and less every year. There is only one flock of what our breeders would term a pure-blooded flock of that kind in the United States, and that flock is about to be separated because there is no money in keeping it" (*Tariff Commission of* 1882, pp. 2147–2148. Cf. pp. 1994–1996, 2113–2117).

different from those in the rest of the South and almost exactly like those in the Far West, it seems better, for the purposes of this chapter, to group it with the states of the latter section.[1]

Number of Sheep (in tens of thousands).

	1871	1875	1880	1885	1890
Kentucky, Tenn., W. Va.	186	162	246	222	182
Rest of South omitting Texas	178	178	230	268	239
Total	364	340	476	490	421

The three states of Kentucky, Tennessee, and West Virginia, the only section of the South that could be said to be engaged in wool-growing on a commercial basis, end this period about as they began it, after having at one time made a gain of one third. Considering the unusually backward position at the very start, this failure to make any permanent headway shows that influences similar to those which were felt among the northeastern states were at work here as well.

The same tendency toward mutton sheep is also to be noted. West Virginia, when separated from Virginia, took many of the best flocks with her. There, especially in the Pan-handle district, merino sheep predominated, and many fine-wooled flocks derived from stock in the neighboring sections of Pennsylvania and Ohio were to be found. But Kentucky and Tennessee had been among the first to adopt the long-wooled Lincoln, Cotswold, and Leicester breeds. The rich blue-grass region was admirably adapted to them, and these states with Missouri and, later, Oregon were long the main domestic source of supply for combing wool. Thus, when a growing demand for this wool and good mutton appeared, they had a favorable start upon which to advance.[2]

The figures for the rest of the South tell a different tale. There the growth made after 1871 is more than maintained to the very end of the period. Most of this gain was simply recovery from war-time ravages, — for even in 1890 these flocks had not quite returned to the level of 1860, — but the very fact that there was a recovery

[1] From 1880 on to 1893 Texas held more sheep than all the rest of the Southern states put together.

[2] For more information on the conditions here, see *Tariff Commission of 1882*, vol. ii, p. 1267, but especially Killebrew's *Sheep Husbandry*. Extensive inquiry led the latter to put the annual cost of keeping sheep in Tennessee at about 80 cents a head (p. 177).

instead of a still further decline must be attributed to the conditions under which sheep of this section were kept. As the main purpose was simply to supply the household or local wants and not the distant market, the flocks were not affected by the low prices prevailing in the world's market, which in the older wool-growing states were playing such havoc among the sheep.

This organization on the basis of a household or local economy tended to favor the sheep in another way. Sheep in the South were mainly to be found either in the hill country or in the pine woods regions where the whole system of agriculture was non-commercial in character and hence remained unaffected by outside influences. The farmer raised various products in such proportion as befitted the needs of his household. As those needs were not likely to vary, there was no incentive to turn his attention to one product at the expense of another. Consequently such things as the growing export trade in food stuffs or the rising demand from urban centres for dairy produce or meat, — things which in other sections of the country were making different branches of agriculture relatively more profitable, — produced no effect upon the wool-growing sections of the South.

It was this same system which was in no small manner responsible for the general scarcity of sheep that had existed in the South from the first, and still continued. In spite of apparently favorable physical conditions, the flocks failed to make any advance. The host of curs which infested the country, the devotion to cotton or tobacco in one section, the narrow household economy and the backwardness of the people in other sections, and a variety of minor causes previously mentioned, all contributed towards this result. The course of events in the South, except in three northern states, had nothing to do with the general situation in the wool-growing industry, and is mainly of interest for the negative light which a study of the conditions there, especially the economic organization of the industry, throws, by way of contrast, upon the history of the industry elsewhere.

The Middle West.

Some little time previous to 1860 the centre of the wool-growing industry of the country had crossed the Allegheny Mountains and located in Ohio and the neighboring states. Through the varied experiences of the Civil War and on into the period now under review; this region continued to be the main seat of the industry.

In the two groups of states into which the region naturally subdivides itself for a view of the industry, the course of events was as follows: [1] —

Number of Sheep (in tens of thousands).

	1871	1872	1873	1874	1875	1876	1877	1878	1879	1880
North Central	1229	1213	1251	1264	1190	1172	958	920	929	938
Central West	368	356	351	347	340	331	338	235	250	282
Total	1597	1569	1602	1611	1530	1503	1296	1155	1179	1220

	1881	1882	1883	1884	1885	1886	1887	1888	1889	1890
North Central	968	976	1112	1111	1076	1033	975	894	918	895
Central West	304	308	344	354	347	392	368	330	330	294
Total	1272	1284	1456	1465	1423	1425	1343	1224	1248	1189

Knowing that the number of sheep in the country increased during these two decades, it is naturally with some surprise that one finds by a moment's glance at this table, that the number of sheep in the Middle West, the centre of the whole industry, actually declined by almost one third. The general trend here corresponded with that in the East. This decline was the beginning of one part of the movement which ultimately transferred the centre of the industry to a new location amid the Rocky Mountains.

For the North Central states, however, there is one exception to the assertion that the general course of events resembled that to the eastward. In the older states, when the upward movement in the number of sheep, which began in the later seventies, finally culminated in 1881, the maximum then reached was considerably higher than the number with which the period had begun. In the Middle West no such rise took place. In fact, except for 1873 and 1874, there never was a year after the opening of the period in 1871 when this

[1] Department of Agriculture figures. The first group includes Ohio, Indiana, Illinois, Wisconsin, and Michigan; the second, Missouri, Iowa, Minnesota, Kansas, Nebraska, and Dakota.

section of the country held so many sheep as it did then. That year had been preceded by a period of the most ruthless slaughter, yet in spite of the high tariff and better prices it was followed, not by recovery, but by still further decline.

The explanation for this peculiar course of events is to be found in the history of the preceding decade. We have here the sole remaining trace of the effects of the Civil War episode. In studying that period, we found that, in the reaction which followed the rush for sheep, fairly normal conditions were restored in every section of the country but the North Central states. There the flocks were still larger than could reasonably be accounted for. The failure of this section to show any growth in the years between 1871 and 1884, when in other parts of the country the flocks were being augmented, was simply due to the further reduction required for a proper readjustment of the industry. At the same time it gives further proof of the correctness of the conclusions expressed in regard to the preceding period.

Ohio was the leading wool-growing state of the country. It had been among the chief agitators in the movement to secure the tariff of 1867, and had expected great results if the bill were passed.[1] The results which it actually obtained, however, were most disappointing. The flocks did for a year or two rise a trifle above the figures for 1871, though they never recovered the position held when the bill was passed. In 1871 the number of sheep in the state was 4,600,000, and after declining to 3,700,000 in 1878 it finally rose to 5,000,000 in 1883, a net increase of 9%, but only to fall off again to 3,900,000 in 1890. The most that can be said is that the flocks of this state were kept at a point somewhat above that reached at the opening of the war, though not so high as that held in 1854. The heavy decline which set in after 1884 left the state at the end of the period with no more sheep than it had had a full generation before.

In 1885 the Ohio Wool-Growers Association reported, after inquiry among some hundred flock-owners, that a calculation based on the average cost of grain, hay, labor, the price of land, and the rate

[1] The memorial of the wool-growers and manufacturers asking Congress for the tariff of 1867 said: "We will engage that the sheep husbandry will increase and be remunerative, while the woolen manufactures will expand and diversify, affording a market for raw material and rescuing the people from dependence on foreign lands for their clothing."

of interest for the previous ten years showed the cost of well-washed Ohio fine middling or combing wool to be 39⅓ cents a pound.[1] At this time the farmer actually received for his clip about 5 cents a pound less than the price obtained in the seaboard markets, this difference being the amount required to cover the middleman's charges.[2] With the drop in prices which occurred after 1883, the wool-growers of Ohio declared they were actually realizing less than 30 cents a pound for their wool, which meant a loss of 10 cents a pound or 60 cents per sheep.[3] Still others announced that at the existing price of wool the grower lost at least 5 cents a pound on his clip, "in other words, even at the unremunerative prices of grain and hay, our wool-growers by sacrificing their flocks and marketing their grain would gain over the present price of wool an amount equal to from 5 to 8 cents per pound on all wool produced. Thus it is that our shepherds by thousands are fleeing to other occupations."[4] The low price of wool was very commonly connected by the growers with the slight reduction in duties under the tariff of 1883, and that act came in for a generous share of violent denunciation. These statements as to cost are of value, not because there is any reason for faith in their accuracy, but because many sheep-owners believed them to be fairly correct and acted accordingly.

The same falling off in the number of sheep that took place in Ohio appeared in the neighboring states. At no time during the eighties did any of the three states Illinois, Indiana, and Michigan

[1] *Senate Executive Documents*, No. 72, 49th Congress, 1st Session, pp. 227–228. It is obvious that this does not include all the items properly to be considered. This statement was approved by the President of the National Wool-Growers Association, only he maintained that the cost was still greater. Cf. *Tariff Commission of* 1882, pp. 2154–2157. Similar estimates were constantly appearing in agricultural papers. I have previously expressed my doubts as to the possibility of getting any really accurate figures of this character. The problem of cost-accounting where the industry was carried on as a part of general farming, which was the usual case, became altogether too complicated a task for any but experts.

[2] Joseph Walworth, long the buyer for one of the largest mills, says: "The expenses of buying in some sections are 2 cents per pound, owing to the heavy expenses of travel and the cost of collecting the wool. And in the best states the local commission for buying is 1 cent per pound. It is a well-established fact that it costs 5 cents per pound between the price paid the farmer and the price realized in Boston or New York to enable the operator to come out without a loss" (*Bulletin*, vol. ix, p. 110).

[3] *Senate Executive Documents*, No. 72, 49th Congress, 1st Session, p. 227.

[4] *Ibid.*, p. 224.

have as many sheep as in 1871. The first two, where the decline was most noticeable, ended the period with scarcely half the number they began with. Wisconsin and Michigan fared slightly better, losing only about one-fourth of their sheep. In fact, Michigan was the only state north of Mason and Dixon's line and east of the Mississippi, which did not hold fewer sheep in 1890 than in 1880. The explanation in this case as in that of Maine, the only state in the same region having more sheep in 1890 than in 1871, is that many parts of the state were still being settled and were not of a character especially adapted to cultivation.

During this period there appeared, for the first time in the North Central states, a general movement towards mutton sheep. The movement did not gain much headway until after 1880, but from then on it advanced rapidly, being closely connected with the drop in the price of wool. At the opening of the period, fully 90% of the sheep in Ohio were of merino stock; in 1886, scarcely 50%.[1] In 1883 about 75% of the Wisconsin sheep were merinos; in 1890, only 50%.[2] At the latter date they made up hardly one eighth of the flocks in Illinois.[3] This change in the proportion of merino stock was as much due to the sending of merinos to the butcher as to the introduction of English breeds. Among the latter the Southdown, and later the Shropshire, were the favorites, though the larger and coarser-wooled Cotswold was sometimes preferred. These mutton breeds, needing to be kept in small flocks and requiring more care and richer feed than the merinos, fitted in very well with the more diversified farming which was slowly being introduced at this time.

Across the Mississippi, in the states of the Central West, the general outcome was much the same as in the North Central group. Wool-growing, as we have seen, never had much of a foothold on the open prairie. It was not until the Civil War episode that many of the farmers of this section paid serious attention to sheep. After that had passed there was even less reason than before for keeping them. The railroads were opening the country ahead of the main influx of population. The settler no longer needed to be self-sufficing.[4] He had a growing market for the grain for which his land was so admirably adapted, and the abundant transportation facilities which

[1] *Sheep Industry*, p. 563. [2] *Ibid.*, p. 651. [3] *Ibid.*, p. 600.
[4] Cf. Taylor, *Agricultural Economics*, pp. 52–54.

enabled him to ship it, also enabled him to purchase such supplies as he did not produce himself. It was not strange, then, that in the older states like Missouri and Iowa the flocks should suffer heavy losses, these losses in the case of the latter state amounting to three quarters of the total. In the newer states, on the other hand, as the population increased with the great wave of settlement which passed over this region after 1870, there was an increase in the flocks. Thus Kansas, Nebraska, and Minnesota held many more sheep in 1890 than in 1871. With the completion of the transcontinental lines and the settlement of the territory west of the Missouri, the live-stock industry arose. Cattle came first, as a rule, and "sheep followed within two or three years." [1] Before the period had ended, many bands of sheep were being driven to these states from the Far West to be fattened for the market. Sheep did not reach Dakota in any number until the time of the Black Hills gold excitement in the early seventies, but after that they steadily increased. In all these states, however, the growth in the number of sheep, compared with the increase in population, was very slight. In fact, it proved insufficient to offset the decline in the two older states, and the total for the group shows a net decrease.

Having covered all the states which furnished the main wool supply of the country at the opening of this period, we have now to turn to the section where the great increase, which we know took place but have thus far sought in vain, actually occurred.

The Far West.

The dominating feature of the wool-growing industry in the era now under consideration is the rise of the Far West. As yet, we have hardly had occasion more than to mention this section. In 1860 its wool was an insignificant factor in the market, and even the Civil War stimulus did not bring the noteworthy development of the industry there that it did elsewhere.[2] The first step in the great advance which characterizes these years was taken when the railroads stretched across the continent, and, in connecting the Atlantic and Pacific, first made accessible this vast area, nearly one half of

[1] Cf. *Census*, 1880, vol. iii, p. 1009.

[2] In 1867, Lynch's figures credited this section with about 15,000,000 pounds of wool in a total clip of 137,000,000. By 1870 it had doubled (see Ford, *Wool and Manufactures of Wool*, p. 42).

the country in extent. The Union and Central Pacific railroads, which passed through the centre of the section, were opened in 1869, just before the period began. The Atchison, the Southern Pacific, and the Northern Pacific, opening the northern and southern sections, were soon started and were completed in the early eighties. Thereafter, progress was rapid. From this time on the Far West becomes the centre of interest in our study of the wool-growing industry.

In this section the industry was not at all what it was in the states we have previously been dealing with. In the first place it was a range industry — wholly independent of any general farming. Usually the sheep were the sole interest of their owner. Sometimes, they were kept along with other stock, but sections where they were in any way connected with the cultivation of the soil were few and far between. The practice almost invariably followed throughout the rest of the country — of making sheep-raising either a dominant or, what was far more likely, a subordinate part of general farming — did not exist here. As time went on, and cultivation of the soil began in the comparatively few spots of this region where it was possible, there appeared a very limited number of localities for which this assertion would not hold, but the sheep found in those localities were negligible when compared with the vast flocks on the great ranges. In the second place, in most of this region adequate transportation facilities preceded the rise of the wool-growing industry, and afforded easy access to large markets. This fact made possible the large scale of production which characterized the range industry, and it also explains why the stage of household or local economy, which so influenced the industry in the earlier-settled parts of the country, never really developed here.[1] Since the economic basis of the industry was therefore fundamentally different from that in the rest of the country, the factors which determined the course of its development were materially altered. We are thus afforded an opportunity to study the industry in a new and still more varied light.

As economic conditions differed in different parts of the Far West, it is necessary here, as elsewhere, to divide the region into groups

[1] The early flocks in New Mexico, California, or among such pioneer settlements as were started by the Mormons, and those kept to supply the local market for mutton at the mines furnish an exception to this general statement. The statement must be taken in a relative sense.

of states according to their environment. The eight Rocky Mountain states make up one group, and the three states along the Pacific another. For this period Texas has also been included in this section, since the situation there was essentially the same as in the rest of these states. The statistics for the three divisions are as follows:

Number of Sheep (in tens of thousands).

	1871	1872	1873	1874	1875	1876	1877	1878	1879	1880
Texas	113	123	123	133	144	169	282	367	456	514
Pacific Coast	405	415	453	524	531	746	814	763	804	891
Rocky Mountain	151	173	221	265	292	306	322	327	343	401
Total	669	711	797	922	967	1221	1418	1457	1603	1806

	1881	1882	1883	1884	1885	1886	1887	1888	1889	1890
Texas	602	685	787	795	755	680	476	452	465	475
Pacific Coast	867	868	870	923	894	908	921	894	747	763
Rocky Mountain	542	535	775	869	992	911	865	951	978	1182
Total	2011	2088	2432	2587	2641	2499	2262	2297	2190	2420

It was said at the outset that during these years the number of sheep in the country increased, yet, except for the slight gain in the South, every group of states thus far examined has shown a heavy falling off among the flocks. In 1871 there were 25,000,000 sheep in all the country excepting the Far West; but by 1890 the number had been reduced to 20,000,000. It was only through an increase of nearly 300% which took place in the Far West that the day was saved. Starting with 6,690,000 sheep in 1871, the flocks of this region multiplied till the maximum of 26,000,000 sheep was attained in 1885, and they ended the period with 24,200,000.

A brief glance at the table suffices to show that this increase in numbers was the result of two main movements. In Texas and the Pacific Coast states the flocks increased with great rapidity up to 1884, the former showing the remarkable growth of 600%, the latter a gain of 140%. A heavy loss followed, however, amounting in Texas to nearly one half by the end of the period. In the Rocky

Mountain states, on the other hand, although there was a slight decline after 1885, it was soon made up for, and in 1890 the number was considerably higher than ever before. The varied conditions in the different divisions and the causes for the differences in the course of the industry in each, we now take up in more detail, especially since this region has till now remained almost unnoticed.[1]

The increase of sheep in Texas which began just prior to 1860 was temporarily stopped by the war. That disturbing event once passed, the advance was renewed and, under the stimulating influences of a heavy influx of population and the construction of railroads, was pushed with vigor. The so-called "native" sheep of the region furnished a hardy and excellent stock upon which to build. Crossing them with merino rams, which were rapidly introduced at the time, brought about a marked improvement in the clip, originally of an inferior grade. The merino, too, was well adapted for traveling in the large flocks which were the rule here, — sometimes reaching the enormous proportions of from 10,000 to 50,000 or more, — and it throve on the pasturage of the arid range. Of such land from five to fifteen acres a head was the general estimate of the amount required.

The cost of keeping sheep on the range was undoubtedly much lower than in the East. The Department of Agriculture, after hearing from over a thousand sheep-owners, estimated the cost of keeping sheep in the northern and eastern states at $2.65 a head and on the plains at only $0.50.[2] The first figure is probably too high for the average flock, but the difference was undoubtedly considerable, and the cost of shipping to the eastern market was relatively slight, varying from 1 to 3 or 4 cents a pound. The range was free to all, and it usually afforded sufficient pasturage throughout the year. This reduced one of the chief items of expense, that for land, to almost nothing. Shelter in winter was seldom provided, and the labor item where sheep were kept in such immense flocks was relatively small.

In spite of all these advantages, however, the number of sheep in Texas soon began to decline. This was partly due to the low price

[1] A full account of the conditions in this section up to 1880 is found in Gordon's Special Report, *Census* of 1880, vol. iii.

[2] *Bulletin*, vol. ii, p. 577.

of wool which prevailed after 1884, but even more to the continued influx of a farming population that began to cultivate the soil. The free range rapidly disappeared, and land rose in value to a point where the sheep-owners who carried on the business independently of general farming — as the majority of them did — could not afford to keep it, but sold out and went to still unoccupied parts. In the sections of Texas where cultivation was possible, such a movement had begun before the end of this period, just as it had in other states at earlier periods.[1]

On the Pacific Coast the course of events was rather similar. Washington, the last of the coast states to be entered by sheep, had few flocks till after 1880; then the number slowly increased to 1890. They were driven into the state from Oregon and were mainly found in the southeastern corner. In Oregon, where sheep had been introduced much more widely at an early date, they were far more numerous. They first reached the fertile section of the state to the west of the Cascade Mountains. In time much of this land came to be used for the cultivation of wheat, and though many farmers still kept smaller flocks in connection with their wheat fields, others moved eastward to the more arid range country between the Cascades and the Rockies, where their sheep in turn began to displace the cattle. Between 1870 and 1880, when the cattle of Washington and Oregon increased over four times, the sheep increased sixteen times.[2] In Oregon, as well as in Washington, the flocks kept on increasing till 1890. The grade of sheep found in Oregon was good, probably a third being three-quarter blood. The large proportion of stock of English breeds, more numerous here than anywhere else in the Far West, was particularly noticeable. But this stock was largely confined to the richer and moister soil to the west of the Cascades, and was generally kept in connection with wheat-raising.

The great mass of the sheep on the Coast, however, were to be found in California. Here the maximum growth of the wool-growing

[1] "About 1855 almost the entire area of Texas was one vast unfenced feeding ground for cattle, horses, and sheep. During the last twenty years [1865–85] a great change has taken place. About half the area of the state has been taken up and is now cultivated as farms. The range and ranch portion of the state is also to a considerable extent settled by farmers, especially the eastern and southern portions." (Nimmo, *Report on the Range and Ranch Cattle Business*, p. 3.)

[2] Cf. *Census*, 1880, vol. iii, pp. 1079–1086.

industry was attained earlier than in any other state of the section, the decline setting in after 1880. Most of the flocks were located in the central and southern parts of the state, especially on the vast ranches of the south. The industry soon became so extended that in years of drought heavy losses were met with. This happened in 1863, 1864, 1871, and 1877, some 2,500,000 sheep having been lost during the last of these years alone.[1] In consequence, large numbers were driven out of the state, the exodus between 1877 and 1880 amounting to nearly 100,000 a year. Most of these sheep went northward to Idaho and Montana, or eastward to Arizona and New Mexico. But, as in Texas, the onward march of the tiller of the soil proved an even more serious menace. The scarcity of range which followed the taking up, fencing in, and cultivation of the free lands soon began to be felt. As early as 1880 the Census reported: "The tenure of land in California has been changing from free ranging to ownership or lease, especially since 1870. There is but little good government land now to be had in California. The subdivision and sale of the valuable agricultural lands of the larger ranches all through California is a feature of the times."[2] Along with this went the gradual abandonment of the high-grade merino sheep — which in 1880 composed nearly three quarters of the flocks — and the adoption of mutton breeds, especially in connection with wheat-raising, which at this time was rapidly becoming prominent in the central part of the state. A little later, with the great improvements in transportation facilities, came the quick rise of the fruit industry, which meant still another rival for the sheep. Thus the period ends with the wool-grower abandoning his flocks or else hastening to the eastward, where nature did not offer such a tempting variety of possible uses for his land.

In the process of settling and developing this country the Rocky Mountain states were the last to be reached. Thus it happened that the section of the country which under the present economic organization and system of agriculture seems better fitted to be a permanent home for sheep than any other was the last which they entered.

New Mexico presents an exception to this assertion. It was one of the oldest sheep regions in the country, for flocks had been brought

[1] Cf. *Census*, 1880, vol. iii, p. 1036.

[2] *Ibid.*, p. 1030. Cf. *Bulletin*, vol. vi, p. 3.

there from the early Spanish settlements. Yet, for all their early location, it was not until after 1860 that they exercised any material influence upon the sheep industry or the wool market of the rest of the country. For many generations they had simply furnished the necessary supply of mutton and wool for the inhabitants of the locality. Occasionally a little wool had been carried out over the Santa Fé trail or a flock driven to the New Orleans market, but such exports had never become important. In time, however, there had developed in this section a race of sheep admirably adapted to the conditions of these arid regions and well fitted to become the basis of a flourishing industry. For this reason New Mexico, either di-ectly or indirectly, became the chief source of supply when wool-growing began to assume importance in this section. New Mexico was "the mother of the sheep industry of the Rocky Mountains."[1] At the time of the gold discoveries many sheep had been driven from here to California to furnish a supply of mutton, as they were later driven to Nevada and Colorado when the mines of those states were opened. At first the demand upon the New Mexican sheep was to supply this need for mutton, but later they were sought as a foundation for flocks kept primarily for the sake of wool. New Mexican ewes were crossed with merino rams brought from the East, producing a hardy offspring with wool of a medium grade. The drain for these purposes was particularly heavy between 1870 and 1880. At a still later period flocks were driven from New Mexico northeastward to Kansas or Nebraska, where they were fattened for the Chicago market. Arizona, in spite of its position between two states that had kept sheep from an early date, was slow in taking up the pursuit. Frequent Indian raids made it a hazardous undertaking, and it was not until nearly 1880 that any number of sheep were to be found there. At that time many were driven in from the overstocked ranges of southern California, but the northern part of the state, where they were brought in by the Mormons, became the chief seat of the industry.

In the tier of states just to the north, Utah easily led, both in the size of her flocks and in priority of introduction. Sheep were first brought to this state by the Mormons, under whose careful husbandry they rapidly multiplied. Further additions were acquired

[1] *Sheep Industry*, p. 918.

from flocks crossing the plains to the western mines. Here, as elsewhere in the Rockies, when the range became well stocked, the sheep which were pastured in the river valleys during the winter and spring were driven to the mountains for the summer. The mountain ranges usually had a capacity considerably in excess of that of the valley ranges. By the middle of the seventies the sheep began to encroach upon the cattle lands, and soon they came into complete possession of some of the best valleys. The flocks were chiefly located in a section running north and south through the middle of the state and to the west of the Wahsatch mountains.

In Nevada sheep had been first introduced with the rush to the California gold mines in the fifties. The Truckee meadows and neighboring valleys in the western part of the state became a favorite feeding ground for flocks that were later driven to these mines. In the sixties the opening of the Nevada mines afforded a good local market for mutton. Soon the eastern part of the state was entered by Mormons, who brought their flocks with them. Before 1880 the range was fairly well stocked and sheep were being driven to the more abundant pasturage in Wyoming and Montana, though the number in the state continued to increase up to 1890, when the maximum was reached.

Colorado had few sheep before 1870. Her flocks were of Mexican stock, and were mainly located along the southern border. Improved merinos were rapidly brought in both from the East and California. With the development of the mines came a good market for mutton, and in time Colorado lamb acquired a reputation in the East.[1] Under this stimulus the flocks continued to increase until after 1890.

The northern tier of states in the Rocky Mountains was the last region to be reached by the sheep industry of the country in the course of its development. Although a railroad was put through here at about the same time as in the southern tier, still transportation facilities were not so abundant as in the south. Furthermore the northern states did not have the flocks to start with that the southern states had, nor did they during this period develop any such extensive mines as were being opened in the middle section of states. Finally, settlers were slower in reaching these northern states. It

[1] Cf. Montana Board of Agriculture, Labor and Industry, *Report*, 1900, pp. 257–258.

thus happened that when sheep were eventually brought in, it was mainly for the purpose of growing wool. The flocks here did not attain any appreciable size until about 1880. At that time they were coming in chiefly from the Pacific Coast as a result of the exodus from California. Many stopped in southern Idaho, and others advanced to southwestern Montana. In Wyoming most of the sheep were located in the southern part of the state, being driven in from Utah or Colorado. The clip from these states was mostly of a medium grade of merino wool, which as time went on steadily improved through the introduction of full-blooded merino rams. The number of sheep in all three of the states rapidly increased throughout the period, for here the range was not overstocked, and up to the very end still offered room for great growth. In fact, as will shortly appear, these were the only states which afforded an opportunity for appreciable expansion in the period which followed.

Finally it is to be noted that this growth resulted in the transition of the centre of the wool-growing industry from the Middle West, where it had been located since the forties, to the Far West. In 1871 the Middle West contained 16,000,000 sheep, over one half of the total in the country, and the Far West some 6,500,000, or about one fifth. In 1890 the Middle West held less than 12,000,000, which was something over one quarter of the total, while the Far West possessed 24,000,000, or over one half.[1] The year 1884 may be said to mark the turning point. In this year the number of sheep in the country reached the highest figure ever attained and the number in the Far West for the first time made up more than half of the total for the whole country.[2]

The General Situation in Agriculture.

How important a factor in the history of wool-growing the competition of other branches of agriculture might be was first clearly

[1] Even if Texas be omitted, this section then held 19,500,000. The Far West, excluding Texas, first surpassed the Middle West in the number of its sheep in 1880.

[2] This is the chief among a number of reasons which might lead one to choose a date about 1884 instead of 1890 as the dividing point between the different periods. Of all such cases this has been the most difficult one to determine, the arguments for both being very evenly balanced. When all sides of the question were considered, however, the year 1890 was deemed the more satisfactory.

brought out in the period 1840–60. It now remains to be seen what influence was exerted from this side during the years 1870–1890.

One of the chief methods of tracing influences of this sort is through the variations in the prices of agricultural products. These variations for the chief of the products are indicated in the following table:—

Relative Gold Prices of the Chief Agricultural Products.[1]

	Ohio washed fleece wool				*Mutton*	*Beef*
	fine	*medium*	*coarse*	*average*		
1840–59	86	89	83	86	83	93
1870–89	77	90	91	86	126	133
% increase or decrease	11—	1+	10+	0	52+	43+
	Pork	*Wheat*	*Corn*	*Oats*	*Butter*	*Cheese*
1840–59	71	87	95	109	91	75
1870–89	86	92	85	100	147	122
% increase or decrease	21+	6+	11+	8—	62+	63+

Despite the great changes that took place in the wool-growing industry of the country between the years 1840–59 and the years 1870–89 there was no marked change in the price of wool. The average prices of the three chief cereals also show but slight variations between these two periods, though crops were increasing at a very rapid rate,—much faster, indeed, than the population.[2] With the three kinds of meat, however, the situation was quite the reverse. Pork, beef, and mutton all showed a great advance in price, though pork gained much less than either of the others. But the most striking change of all is the rise of over 60% in the price of the two dairy products, butter and cheese. The dairy industry, as has previously been pointed out, was a particularly dangerous rival of the sheep, and this unusual rise in the price of its products together with that in

[1] 100 = the price in 1860. The table, except the prices of wool, is based on the figures of the Aldrich Report. Mutton prices are only for such years as are given in the Report. Wool prices are those of Mauger and Avery. For a chart showing the relative prices of the important products for each year from 1840 to 1890 see Appendix.

[2] Cf. table on page 260.

the price of beef far more than offset the advance in the price of lamb or mutton, and undoubtedly became a potent force operating against the sheep. In the sections of the Middle West where grain was raised to feed stock, the advance in the price of beef made cattle quite as attractive as sheep, and similarly, though to a less degree, swine found favor.

It will now be of interest to see the changes which actually took place in the general agriculture of this period. Since it was only in the East and the Middle West that agriculture had much influence on the sheep industry, our chief attention will be given to those sections, though a glimpse will first be taken at the situation in the country as a whole.

United States Farm Products per Capita.[1]

	Sheep	*Wool*	*Farm acreage*	*Neat cattle*	*Swine*	*Corn*	*Wheat*	*Oats*
1850	0.94	2.26	12.5	0.77	1.31	25.5	4.35	6.35
1860	0.72	1.94	13.0	0.81	1.07	26.7	5.58	5.55
1870	0.74	2.63	10.6	0.62	0.65	20.0	7.55	7.42
1880	0.84	3.10	10.7	0.79	0.99	35.1	9.12	8.14
1890	0.65	3.08	9.9	0.92	0.91	34.2	7.55	13.05
1900	0.52	3.68	11.0	0.69	0.83	35.5	8.77	12.57

In proportion to the population, sheep, it is evident, were decreasing before the end of the period, although the wool clip increased. Hogs and cattle were increasing. But the most noticeable change evinced is the great per capita increase in the cereal crops. The years 1870–1890, particularly the first decade, brought one of the most rapid expansions in general agriculture that the country ever experienced, the fifties alone being at all comparable in this respect.

The following tables show the course of events in the states, once

[1] Based on Census returns. As has previously been noted, the Census figures for wool are too low. If, instead, we use the trade estimates and take the average of five-year periods centering in 1870, etc., we have the following more accurate figures for the four dates from 1870 to 1900: 4.26, 5.12, 4.98, and 3.85. In the case of the cereals some allowance has to be made for variations of the crop. The table with the following survey covers somewhat more than the period under review, for it deals in broad movements, thus making it desirable to cover the whole question at once. Doing so also saves some needless repetition in treating other periods.

the centre of the wool-growing industry, where the pursuit was particularly affected by the general agricultural situation:—

North Atlantic and North Central States.

Farm Products per Acre of Farm Land.

	Sheep	*Wool*	*Neat cattle*	*Dairy cows*	*Swine*	*Corn*	*Wheat*	*Oats*
1850	.131	.350	.144	.031	.095	2.38	0.64	0.87
1860	.085	.260	.073	.030	.091	2.82	0.71	0.84
1870	.095	.375	.066	.030	.065	2.52	1.14	1.21
1880	.068	.352	.079	.031	.111	5.02	1.32	1.29
1890	.061	.295	.111	.043	.150	6.21	1.31	2.72
1900	.030	.238	.074	.031	.112	5.32	1.24	2.20

The basis of farm acreage, which has been adopted for this table, is the most satisfactory one available for a comparison of the relative growth or decline of different branches of agriculture. The number of sheep per acre of farm land declined between 1850 and 1860, and the point at which it was left in 1870, after the Civil War stimulus and its reaction had passed, was below that of 1850, while in the succeeding years it became steadily smaller and smaller. On the other hand, from 1870 on neat cattle, dairy cows, and swine were all increasing in proportion to the farm acreage, the most rapid advance coming between 1880 and 1890. Wheat showed a slight gain after 1870, and both corn and oats more than doubled their proportion. Thus, if we accept the farm acreage as a unit of measure for the agricultural products, we find that between 1870 and 1890 all of these products were increasing relatively, four out of the six nearly doubling, and that sheep and wool alone declined.

A more exact idea of the tendencies in certain typical states is obtained from the following figures, which show the situation in Vermont and New York, the great wool-growing states of the first part of the century, when the East was supreme; in Ohio, the centre of the industry during the middle of the century; and in Illinois and Iowa, two prairie states typical of the chief grain-raising section of the Middle West. To show the exact relative changes more clearly an index number for each has been adopted, the basis of 100 being the average for the six census years.

Index Number of Agricultural Products per Acre of Farm Land.

	Sheep	Wool	Neat cattle	Swine	Corn	Wheat	Oats
			Vermont.				
1850	195	140	101	105	118	176	78
1860	140	124	104	79	85	138	119
1870	102	117	85	66	90	136	110
1880	71	87	100	79	99	94	108
1890	60	82	108	155	91	47	105
1900	31	48	102	132	117	11	81
			New York.				
1850	185	133	103	147	106	139	85
1860	128	114	99	119	109	83	102
1870	100	109	97	64	84	111	98
1880	73	93	103	86	123	98	98
1890	72	77	102	106	78	76	109
1900	44	74	97	84	100	93	110
			Ohio.				
1850	119	71	103	95	78	58	62
1860	94	65	110	96	85	54	62
1870	126	119	90	70	74	93	97
1880	109	128	104	108	109	136	98
1890	95	113	103	122	106	110	142
1900	58	104	88	113	148	149	142
			Illinois.				
1850	176	110	97	104	61	72	35
1860	88	58	97	78	70	106	29
1870	145	136	85	68	64	106	65
1880	79	112	96	107	131	149	78
1890	71	90	128	127	121	117	177
1900	45	90	94	118	154	56	215
			Iowa.				
1850	174	111	54	62	43	61	24
1860	79	54	58	51	57	92	25
1870	174	155	70	48	60	207	57
1880	57	94	115	134	151	138	86
1890	57	71	175	149	139	30	203
1900	60	116	128	154	150	73	207

The tables indicate that sheep and wool were steadily and rapidly losing ground in these states at the same time that all the other products were gaining. The only instance of a loss at all comparable with that of sheep is the case of wheat in Vermont. The most marked gains were in the cereal crops of the states in the Middle West, the changes generally being much less noticeable in the East. Neat cattle and swine usually showed some gain until the very last decade.

From another angle we get a different view, less blurred by diversity of conditions, and the most exact of all. In order to study the situation in the regions best suited for sheep, in one or two typical states those counties have been chosen which, at the Census when the number of sheep in the state was at its maximum, had over 50 sheep per square mile.[1]

Relative Agricultural Products of Sheep Counties.

Index number 100 = figure for 1870.

	Sheep	*Dairy cows*	*Farm acreage*	*Improved land*	*Swine*	*Wheat*	*Corn*	*Oats*
				Ohio.				
1850	78	51	86	71	115	61	77	52
1860	71	103	88	90	128	38	110	62
1870	100	100	100	100	100	100	100	100
1880	99	113	109	120	186	160	153	104
1890	78	111	101	121	199	123	158	143
1900	49	115	105	121	186	114	195	144
				Iowa.				
1860	33	66	77	55	78	32	89	20
1870	100	100	100	100	100	100	100	100
1880	52	142	113	140	226	100	200	246
1890	71	205	113	152	218	25	178	390
1900	56	167	120	156	233	9	209	324

[1] For California, the basis of 100 is for the year 1880. The figures for the cereal crops in that state represent the acreage planted, not, as with the others, the number of bushels. The great changes in the county lines make figures for earlier dates impracticable in the case of California and Iowa. Vermont, typical of the East, is omitted here, since, every county but one having over 50 sheep per square mile, the table for the whole state is sufficient. There were some changes in the Census classification under the heading "dairy cows" in 1900, but the probability of serious error is slight. If anything it tends towards a trifling reduction of the number that year.

California.

	Sheep	*Dairy cows*	*Farm acreage*	*Improved land*	*Swine*	*Wheat*	*Corn*	*Barley*
1880	100	100	100	100	100	100	100	100
1890	53	155	106	100	96	123	87	124
1900	35	45	146	93	91	114	53	183

In Ohio and Iowa the farm acreage increased steadily, but the improved land grew even faster, and the more rapid growth of the cereal crops as compared with the farm area indicates that it was for these products that much of the land was being cultivated. The rise of the figures for dairy cows while sheep declined would lead one to conclude that some of the land still kept for pasturage was given over to the former.

All of these tables point in the same direction. Agriculture was steadily advancing, though most of the growth was in the valley of the Mississippi. Yet the flocks of the East and of the Middle West were declining. In their case the decline after 1870 was not only steady, but also universal. This situation, moreover, did not extend to any of the other chief agricultural products. The dairy, the keeping of hogs, and the cultivation of the soil for the purpose of raising grain were nearly everywhere on the increase. The growing attractiveness of these other pursuits was driving out the sheep.

In the Far West, with its newly developing sections and vast arid areas, the situation was different, and on the whole much simpler. The following table sufficiently indicates the trend of events in typical states of this section; it is based on index numbers (100 = the average for the four census periods) so as to show the relative decline or advance of the different pursuits:—

	Texas.				*California.*			
	Sheep	*Neat cattle*	*Farm acreage*	*Improved acreage*	*Sheep*	*Neat cattle*	*Farm acreage*	*Improved acreage*
1870	28	58	32	21	83	61	58	61
1880	145	81	63	90	165	78	85	104
1890	169	141	89	148	101	164	109	119
1900	57	120	217	140	51	107	147	116

	New Mexico.				Utah.			
	Sheep	*Neat cattle*	*Farm acreage*	*Improved acreage*	*Sheep*	*Neat cattle*	*Farm acreage*	*Improved acreage*
1870	24	8	46	59	5	22	9	22
1880	152	49	34	98	41	75	42	79
1890	96	230	43	109	153	156	85	104
1900	129	112	278	135	201	148	262	195

	Montana.			
1870	0	5	4	11
1880	16	64	11	35
1890	137	215	55	122
1900	246	116	330	232

In all of these states the farm acreage was increasing, a phenomenal advance being made in the decade following 1890, which was due to the taking up and enclosing of the range as farm land became scarce. At the same time improved land was increasing (except in Texas and California for the last decade), though at a much slower rate. Both California and Texas show a falling off, too, in sheep and cattle, but sheep decreased first and to a much greater extent. The figures for the sheep counties of California, given for comparison in the preceding table, tell much the same tale. In that state, evidently, cultivation of the soil was a minor element in the causes that led to the abandonment of sheep. In the Rocky Mountain region, the sheep proved more successful and were driving out the cattle, the decline among the latter starting everywhere after 1890, when sheep were still increasing in most of the states. The amount of land suitable for cultivation was so relatively insignificant in this section that the cultivator of the soil had practically no influence over the fate of the sheep industry.

In fact, the only serious rival of this industry on most of the great ranges of the Far West was the cattle business. It is said that the possibility of using this arid section as cattle range was really not discovered until 1864. About 1860, Texas cattle were still being slaughtered simply for their hides and tallow.[1] With the rise of the

[1] Nimmo, *Report on Range and Ranch Cattle Business*, pp. 3–4. One of the best sources of information. For further references see Gordon's Special Report in the *Census* of 1880, vol. iii; *Report of the Public Lands Commission*, 1905; Commissioner of Corporations, *Report on the Beef Industry;* Montana Bureau of Agriculture, Labor, and Industry, *Reports*, especially 1902, pp. 137–145; *Ohio Agricultural Report*, 1900, pp. 450–454.

beef-packing industry, which came during the seventies, and the growth of the export trade, the cattle business rapidly advanced. Steers, which in 1868 were selling at $4.50 a head, rose in a few years to $15.00 or $18.00 a head. Starting in Texas, the business soon extended over the rest of the region. At first Texas was looked upon as the breeding ground and the more northern range as a maturing and fattening section. Between 1866 and 1884 some 5,000,000 head of cattle were driven north from Texas. Others were driven eastward from the Pacific Coast states, and soon the Rocky Mountain section was well stocked, the northern tier of states, where hostile Indians delayed the beginning of the pursuit until after 1876, being the last to be occupied. By 1885 half the beef product of the country came from west of Chicago.[1] Sheep generally followed closely on the trail of the cattle, and the annals of the region recount many a desperate struggle between cattle-herders and sheep-drivers for possession of the open range. In this conflict the sheep-owner had something of an advantage in that sheep could graze where cattle could not, and when pastured on good land, sheep grazed it so close as to leave nothing for cattle.

This view of the actual course of events in agriculture shows a situation which clearly cannot be fully accounted for by the changes in prices which were found to have occurred. The heavy increase in the per capita supply of the chief cereals, which took place without any very marked change in prices, is one of the things that need further explanation.

The rapid growth of the European demand for our agricultural products helps to explain many of these difficulties. This demand, which first appeared at the time of the Irish famine, steadily increased through the fifties and the Civil War decade; nor was there any diminution during the years that succeeded. How very rapidly this increase took place is shown by the table which follows.

Average Annual Exports (in thousands).

	Wheat	*Wheat flour*	*Corn*	*Corn meal*	*Butter*	*Cheese*
	bu.	*bbls.*	*bu.*	*bbls.*	*lbs.*	*lbs.*
1851–60	5,525	2,893	5,149	240	3,633	7,852
1870–89	74,157	6,351	50,351	320	15,646	100,171

[1] For figures showing the growth of the packing business, see page 312.

	Beef[1]	*Bacon and Ham*	*Lard*	*Pork*[1]
		lbs.	*lbs.*	
1851–60	83	27,852	32,437	185
1870–89	105,000	409,000	249,000	68,000

It was this ever-expanding European market which made possible the great increase in the grain crops without a serious drop in prices. And it also had no slight influence in raising the price of beef and pork products in the face of an increasing per capita supply. The mutton and lamb of this country, however, found no European market. Such rise as took place in these products was almost entirely due to the domestic demand. Finally it should be borne in mind that it was during these years that the shipment of fresh meat, made possible by improvements in facilities for transportation, first began to assume some magnitude. These improvements included the introduction of refrigerator cars and also changes which furthered a reduction in freight rates and thus affected not only meat but all agricultural produce.

The decline in freight rates proceeded most rapidly during the first of this period. About 1870, when the chief trunk lines secured a through route to Chicago, a series of fierce rate wars broke out which within a very short time resulted in a general reduction of rates. Those on grain were soon cut in half.[2] In the inland rates the most rapid decline came in the years 1873–76, but in the ocean rates not until 1880–85.

This unusual decrease in the cost of transportation facilitated shipments for inland consumption as well as for export. It of course

[1] In the case of beef and pork, the figures for 1851–60 are in barrels, and for 1870–89 in pounds.

[2] *Freight Rates on Wheat per Bushel.*

	Chicago to New York			*New York to Liverpool*
	Water	*Lake and rail*	*All rail*	*Steamer*
	cents	cents	cents	pence
1868	23	29	43	$6\frac{15}{16}$
1875	11	15	24	$8\frac{7}{16}$
1880	12	16	20	$5\frac{8}{16}$
1885	6	9	14	$2\frac{3}{16}$
1890	6	8	14	$2\frac{7}{16}$

(*Statistical Abstract.*) The Chicago-New York rates are in currency, and hence somewhat exaggerate the drop previous to 1880.

tended to favor all the bulkier agricultural products of the Middle West, while bringing greater pressure of competition to bear upon the farmers of the East. Had the increased amount of produce which the lower cost of shipment enabled the western grower to pour upon the eastern market resulted in any appreciable drop in prices, this lower cost might not have meant any gain to the grower; but such does not appear to have been the case. The new supply either displaced eastern produce or was absorbed by the European demand.

Lower cost of transportation, however, as has previously been shown, was of almost no benefit in the case of a product of such relatively slight bulk, in proportion to its value, as wool. The result, then, was to make wool-growing relatively less profitable than before in those sections where the other agricultural products, more favored by the reduction in rates, could be grown. This applied to all of the Mississippi valley, not to mention the arable section of the Far West, which previous to this period had had virtually no transportation facilities. Unquestionably the reduction was no slight factor in the tendency away from sheep and towards grain which was so marked during these years. Conversely, however, it is clear that in the East some of the greater relative advantages for bulkier products which had previously been enjoyed because of the nearness to market now ceased to exist. But though this would serve to weaken one force which had tended to operate against wool-growing in that section, it at the same time tended to strengthen the position of the dairy. Moreover, the favor which it lent to wool was more than counterbalanced by the new competition which arose on the opening up of the cheap sheep range of the Far West. This but further illustrates how, under a commercial agriculture, wool-growing as an independent pursuit, when compared with other agricultural pursuits, has a relatively stronger tendency to gravitate toward the localities most distant from the market.

We thus see in the general agricultural situation forces which played no mean part in bringing about the transfer of the main seat of the sheep industry from the Middle West to the Far West.

Summary, 1870–1890.

What conclusions can now be drawn from this study of the factors which affected the wool-growing industry of the country during the two decades 1870–1890? Let us briefly summarize the chief facts brought out.

In the world's market, prices tended downwards throughout the period. The main cause of this decline was the great increase in the world's production of wool, chiefly in the supply from the United States, the River Plate, and Australasia. Athough the general trend was downward, the average price in the United States was the same as for the similar twenty-year period ending in 1860, the finest grades of wool being slightly lower, the coarser grades a little higher. This level of prices was in part sustained by the high protective duties on both raw wool and manufactures which began with the period. Under this tariff, not only did the growth of manufactures attained during the Civil War period suffer no diminution, but the advance continued, though at a much slower pace. It was especially marked in the worsted, carpet, and knit goods branches of the industry. Thus, in spite of increased imports of goods, the American manufacturer gained a far stronger hold on the domestic market than he had ever had before. Although there was also an increase in the imports of raw wool, chiefly after 1883, it was not in proportion to the increase in the American clip. During this period, therefore, the native wool came nearer to supplying the needs of the domestic market than at any previous period since the first of the century. Cotton once more resumed its attacks upon the historic domain of wool, but progressed less rapidly than theretofore. Under these conditions, the wool-growing industry in the country as a whole enjoyed a marked growth. In fact, it was during this period that the flocks reached the highest point which they ever attained, and although the years following 1884 brought a falling off, yet the end of the period showed a large net gain. What were the main causes to which this growth is to be attributed?

Our previous analysis has shown that the growth for the country as a whole was the net outcome of very divergent developments in different sections. In the East the increase in flocks which took place between 1870 and 1880, though not great, was the very opposite of the tendency which had dominated the situation for twenty years previous to the outbreak of the Civil War. This increase occurred, moreover, at a time when the price of wool was about the same as in the decade following 1850, and when the general trend of events was tending to make other farm products relatively more attractive. What is the explanation? Some credit must be given to the steadily increasing weight of the fleece, and some to the growing market for lamb and mutton. The greater competition of the West in other farm products also tended to make cultivation of the soil less attractive to the eastern farmer. But apparently the chief explanation is to be found in the new hopes engendered by the high tariff duties introduced at this time and by the two very conspicuous advances in the price of wool which mark the period. This was made more clear when the drop in prices which followed 1880 quickly dissipated those hopes. Flocks were rapidly abandoned, and by 1890 such as still remained were kept mainly for lamb and mutton. The dairy and other agricultural products won the day, and in the end ruled the course of the wool-growing industry in this section.

At the great centre of the pursuit in the Middle West the situation was essentially similar. The absence here of such a decrease in sheep as appeared in most regions is explained by the failure to react completely after the Civil War episode. This is shown by the rapidity of the decline when it finally set in. Yet, in spite of the fact that the general trend of events in the agriculture of the section was even more unfavorable to sheep than in the East, not to mention the lower price for wool after 1880, the flocks were not reduced below the level for 1860. It would thus appear that even at this time there were here many flocks that owed their continued existence to prolonged hopes aroused by the Civil War and the subsequent increase in tariff duties as well as to the inertia gathered from long-standing practice.

In the Far West the sheep-owner began with mutton as his main object and then turned to wool. The industry swept over the region with the wave of settlers which poured in when transportation facilities made these states accessible, a movement so dominant as more than to offset the decline which appeared in some parts consequent on increased cultivation of the soil. In most of the Far West, cultivation was impossible and sheep were well able to hold their own against the only other serious rival, cattle. Thus it proved to be a section peculiarly well adapted, both physically and economically, to wool-growing, and it offered better prospects for the future of the industry than any other part of the country.

In drawing our conclusions as to the influence of the tariff during these years, it is thus clear at the start that the higher level of duties introduced at this time kept the price of wool from falling quite so low as it otherwise would have done, and hence was not without influence on the number of sheep in the country. Nor was it without influence, aside from the actual effect on prices, through the added encouragement it gave to the grower. In the East, nevertheless, it proved powerless to prevent a decline in the flocks when other branches of agriculture became more attractive. Obviously, too, as mutton and lamb rather than wool became the chief aim of the flock owner, protection for wool became a matter of less and less moment and influence. In the Middle West it was among the important aids in sustaining his hopes, but there also it was unequal to the task of counteracting the growing attractiveness of other lines of agriculture. In the Far West, wool-growing had not materially developed in earlier years when prices were even higher than the tariff was able to maintain them at this period. In succeeding years, when wool was on the free list and an industrial depression seemed to leave the wool-market without a bottom, the flocks of this region still went on increasing. The only possible conclusion is that, in the great development of the industry in the Far West during this period, the tariff was among the least of the causes. The most that can be said is that it somewhat hastened it.[1]

Nor does this study bear out the common assertion that the decline in the number of sheep after 1884 was due to the reduction of duties in the tariff of 1883. The fact that in 1884 the country held the greatest number of sheep in all its history was the fortuitous result of a combination of several quite varied movements. Of these, three main movements can be distinguished. It happened that this date was just before the more rapid decline of the sheep in the East and Middle West, that it was in the middle of the great advance in the Rocky Mountain region, and, most important of all, that it came almost at the culmination of the rather phenomenal movement which so suddenly increased the number of sheep in Texas and California, and within a few years reduced them with equal rapidity. The last

[1] It might be pointed out that, if it be granted that the tariff caused the rise in the Far West, then it was in a measure responsible for the decline in the East, which was in part the result of lower prices under pressure of the increased world's supply, — an increase towards which this country contributed its full quota.

two movements were simply stages in the process of settling and developing these states. In California the decline began before the tariff of 1883 was enacted, and both there and in Texas the movement was far greater than could be accounted for by the comparatively slight changes in the protective duties which that tariff brought. In the older states, especially in the Middle West, the reduction of the wool duty, even though slight, may have had a discouraging effect, and hence may have led to the abandonment of some flocks a bit sooner than would otherwise have been the case. The most that can be said about the tariff is that it may have shifted by a year or two the date when the decline of the flocks began. Under the forces then operating upon the industry, this turn to a downward path was sure to come at about this time. The drop in prices, moreover, was world wide; it had started before the enactment of the tariff of 1883, and was far greater than could possibly be explained by any changes caused by that act. Thus it was only a chance combination in the complex working out of many factors which happened to place the decline from the maximum number of sheep and the tariff of 1883 in such close chronological connection. The case is an admirable illustration of the fallacious reasoning constantly met with in tariff discussions. It should stand as a warning against the danger of employing *post hoc propter hoc* arguments when dealing with economic problems that involve such an intricate combination of factors.

If the tariff was only a very minor factor in determining the course of events for the country as a whole, what, are we to conclude, were the chief forces? The answer must have become evident before now. In the East and the Middle West the flocks were slowly giving way under the combined pressure of lower prices, resulting from increased production in the Far West and the Southern Hemisphere, and the growing relative attractiveness of other lines of agriculture, the latter being the more influential factor of the two.[1] But the loss in all

[1] The drop in the price of wool of course made this relative advantage much greater. Emphasis is placed on the competition of other agricultural products rather than on the drop in wool for the reason that if it had been impossible to use sheep lands for any other purpose, the fall in the price of wool would eventually have led to a decrease in the value of land, and thus in time have brought readjustment on the old basis of profit. It was just because the land could be used for other purposes that its price was maintained or raised so as to make it economically impossible to keep sheep upon it.

the old wool-growing sections of the country was far more than counterbalanced, indeed was almost hidden from sight, by the great growth of the industry in the Far West. This growth was simply a natural step in the development of a section which from an economic point of view was particularly well adapted to this industry. These years in the country's history witnessed the final march in that great process of developing and settling the West which so influenced that history during the nineteenth century. The rise of wool-growing in this region was but one phase of the great westward movement. Inasmuch, therefore, as this growth was so rapid and extensive as completely to outweigh all other tendencies in the rest of the country, and even to cause the transfer of the main seat of the industry to this section, we conclude that the dominating factor in the history of wool-growing during the period 1870–1890 was the opening of the Far West, the final step of this general westward movement.

CHAPTER VIII

FREE WOOL AND THE END OF THE WESTWARD MOVEMENT, 1890–1907[1]

IN 1890 the geographer of the Census wrote: "At present the unsettled area has been so broken into by isolated bodies of settlement that there can hardly be said to be a frontier line."[2] The steadily advancing line of settlers which had slowly pushed forward over the Alleghany Mountains and down the valley of the Ohio or along the Gulf to the Mississippi, and then across the plains, had finally been met by the thin line which started eastward from the Pacific Coast. With that meeting, the frontier may be said to have disappeared, and with its disappearance one of the great eras in the economic history of the country came to an end. Throughout the nineteenth century, the process of opening and settling the West had been the most important factor in the country's history. In looking back, as we presently shall, over the whole course of the industry, we shall find that if there is a factor which more than any other affords a key to the understanding of the history of the wool industry during the past hundred years, it is this same thing, — the development of the West. In the sheep industry, the final effects of the movement did not come to an end until the beginning of the twentieth century. There as elsewhere are found many signs which indicate that the last decade of the nineteenth century was a period of transition marking the close of one era in the history of the country and the opening of a new one. The period now under review is the last under the old conditions. The important consequences that follow from the new conditions will appear as we proceed.

This period is also of special importance from the point of view of one interested in the protective tariff. The unusual series of changes in tariff legislation, — three acts in less than a decade, —

[1] A note at the end brings the chapter to 1910. The substance of this chapter appeared in an article in the *Quarterly Journal of Economics*, vol. xix, pp. 610–647.

[2] *Census*, 1890, vol. vi, p. xxxiv.

but especially the change which admitted raw wool free of duty for the first time since the early years of the nineteenth century, afforded new opportunity to judge of its effectiveness. This brief experience with free wool in the midst of the long era of high protection is unusually interesting and illuminating.

The World's Market and Prices.

The low level in the price of wool which was reached in 1885, after the long decline following 1870, continued with little change till 1891. Then the downward movement was renewed, but did not gain much headway until the spring of 1893.[1] With the outbreak of the panic of that year came a sudden drop, the price of Ohio wool falling between 7 and 10 cents a pound in the course of the year. The unusually severe and long-drawn-out business depression which followed, together with Cleveland's election and talk about free wool, only increased the decline, which continued until the Wilson tariff put wool on the free list. The final enactment of this bill in August, 1894, had little effect, its expected passage and the general business depression having previously made allowances for it. London prices, though not participating in the drop incident to the panic and the free wool scare, were also on the down grade, and during these years ranged lower than for any equal length of time since the first years of the century.[2]

Though abroad the increased American demand brought a rise that began about the middle of 1895, in the United States prices fluctuated about the low level reached at the close of 1894 until 1897. The table which follows indicates the situation under free wool, and, for purposes of comparison, at earlier and later periods.

[1] A pop-gun bill putting wool on the free list passed the House of Representatives in April, 1892, but had little effect, the Senate never taking it up for action.

[2] "There has never been such a low yearly average for colonial wool" (Helmuth Schwartze & Co., *Annual Wool Report*, 1892). "That wool has fallen to a lower level than ever in the year of free wool for the United States points to the conclusion that production is ahead of the world's requirements, such as they have shown themselves in recent years" (*ibid.*, 1894). The *Bradford Observer's* review for 1894 said English wools were at the lowest prices ever known, and declared that New Zealand, Australia, and the River Plate region did not care whether the world wanted their wool, as it wanted their mutton, so the supply of wool was not regulated by the demand (quoted in *Bulletin*, vol. xxix, p. 75). See the two tables of London prices in the Appendix.

Average Price of Ohio Washed Wool.

	Fine	Medium	Coarse
1840–59	46.7	42.3	33.6
1885–90	32.8	35.5	31.1
1895–96	17.9	20.2	18.4
1901–07	31.2	34.3	30.1

During the period of free wool, prices were over one third lower than during the years 1885–90, when the new price level first appeared. In 1897, on the restoration by the Dingley tariff of the old duty on wool, along with the stimulus of reviving business and the movement which lifted the prices of all commodities, the quotations for wool quickly advanced to a point slightly below the level which prevailed before 1893. Then — except for a sharp rise and fall in the latter part of 1899, which originated in Europe and was chiefly due to the fear of a scarcity of merino wool — there came a gradual rise ending, in 1905, at a point a trifle above the level around 1890. From this point there has been no marked change. Abroad, the skyrocket speculative rise of 1899[1] was followed by a drop almost to the low point of the middle nineties, after which there came an upward movement until 1905. Since 1901 the general level of prices has been from 17 to 25% below that maintained in the period 1870–89, and still farther below that for the years 1840–59. It is thus clear that the low level of prices ushered in during the middle eighties was something more than a temporary phenomenon. In spite of fluctuations, that general level remains substantially unaltered, and at present it bids fair to continue so.

An examination of the world's wool supply during the period under review enables one to understand most things in the fluctua-

[1] The speculative dealing in futures is, in the case of wool, a comparatively new phenomenon. Because of the difficulty in establishing uniform grades of wool and in classifying the fleece, dealing in futures has been much less common than with many commodities. These difficulties have, in a measure, been overcome by taking for the basis of sale what is known as wool tops, this being wool scoured, combed, and graded so as to be ready for spinning to a given number of yarn. In the latter part of 1899 the majority of the sales in the top markets on the Continent, mainly at Roubaix, assumed a character purely speculative. The price movements abroad at this time were reflected in a modified form in the United States. For some further account see *Bulletin*, vol. xxx, pp. 374–377, and vol. xxxi, pp. 289–314.

tions of the market quotations.[1] The following table shows the situation in detail.

World's Wool Supply, Wool in the Grease[2] *(in millions of pounds).*

	United Kingdom	*Continent*	*North America*	*Australasia*	*Cape*	*River Plate*	*Others*	*Total*
1880–89	135	450	319	395	64	313	130	1807
1890	138	450	322	511	91	272	160	1944
1891	148	450	320	592	102	330	179	2121
1892	153	450	346	644	88	369	175	2225
1893	151	450	361	632	91	360	164	2209
1894	142	450	338	659	73	376	174	2212
1895	135	450	307	730	84	439	197	2342
1896	136	450	285	646	96	464	186	2263
1897	139	450	272	660	83	496	204	2304
1898	139	450	280	608	96	513	181	2267
1899	140	450	285	593	92	520	181	2261
1900	141	450	301	514	46	398	175	2025
1901	138	450	316	600	73	532	143	2252
1902	136	450	329	579	83	493	170	2240
1903	133	450	300	512	80	517	203	2195
1904	132	450	305	513	70	444	215	2129
1905	131	450	309	597	78	456	228	2249
1906	130	450	312	638	81	438	263	2312
1907	131	450	311	787	108	460	251	2498

The most prominent fact brought out by this table is that the year 1895 marks the culmination of the continued and rapid rise in the world's wool supply which had started in the preceding period. The point attained at that time was not again surpassed until 1907, the intervening years showing a slight falling off in the supply. The year of the greatest output coincides, then, with the end of the downward movement in prices which had prevailed for so long, and the subsequent rise with the period of stationary supply.

The chief cause of this retrograde movement was the unusually severe series of droughts which occurred in Australia, beginning in

[1] For a recent estimate of the number of sheep in all the chief countries of the world see Department of Agriculture, *Year Book*, 1907, pp. 698–701.

[2] From the *Wool Circulars* of Helmuth Schwartze & Co., of London. Cf. footnote to similar table on page 164.

1895.[1] The year 1892 found 106,000,000 sheep in Australia, but by 1903 the flocks had been reduced to 54,000,000.[2] The heaviest losses came in the seasons of 1894–95 and 1901–02, and fell mainly upon New South Wales. The improvement in the fleece has since resulted in bringing the clip of 1907 above the previous high record, although the number of sheep is not so large as before. The opinion prevails that under present conditions the flocks are not likely to rise far above the former level very soon, and such increase as may be expected will have to come mainly through the gradual opening of the interior of that continent and the slow process of improving the fleece.[3]

The gap in the world's supply following the decline in the Australian clip was for a few years partly filled by the increased production of the River Plate region, but even there the last decade brought no advance. The output from South Africa and North America showed no permanent alteration during this period. The increase in Russia fairly offset the decline in the flocks of western Europe. Thus, for the time being, no progress was made.

Another matter of importance in the world's wool market during recent years has been the change in the character of much of the wool coming to market. The tendency to decrease the supply of merino wool and to replace it by medium grades from cross-bred sheep, which has been noted in this country, is also to be found in other parts of the world. The movement appears to have had its start with the rise of the frozen mutton trade, which began about

[1] For a detailed account of Australian conditions in the early nineties see *Special Consular Report* No. 55, on Australian Sheep and Wool.

[2] Figures from the *Annual Wool Reports* of Helmuth Schwartze & Co. New Zealand did not suffer during these years, the number of sheep there, at the two dates given, being 18,000,000 and 19,000,000 respectively. The distribution of the flocks in Australia in 1907 was as follows, in millions: Queensland, 14.9; New South Wales, 44.1; Victoria, 12.9; South Australia, 6.7; Tasmania, 1.7; West Australia, 3.3; New Zealand, 21.0.

[3] "One cannot expect to see the production of Australia go on increasing at the same rate as of recent years. Firstly, the country is being split up into small holdings wherever dairying and agriculture pay better than sheep; secondly, the dangers of overstocking are too recent to be forgotten, and lastly, it will require better means of communication before the desert country in the far interior can be taken up for sheep." (*Wool Report*, Wenz & Co., Rheims. Quoted in *Bulletin*, vol. xxxvii, p. 350.)

1882, on a small scale, in both Australasia and Argentina.[1] The decline in the price of wool which was then taking place gave it an added impulse, especially as the finer wool of the pure merino declined below the medium grades of wool from the mutton sheep.[2] Wool in general sank so low that the growers gladly turned to raising sheep for mutton as a method for securing additional income from their flocks. Rams of the various English breeds were imported and crossed on merino ewes, the offspring generally proving acceptable as mutton and bearing the cross-bred wool, finer than that of the pure-bred English sheep, but coarser than pure merino.

Since 1890, and especially since 1895, the supply of this grade has begun to assume great proportions. More than once the prospective scarcity of merino wool has, as in 1899, seriously alarmed the market. In 1889, of the total imports of wool into Europe and North America from the British Colonies and the River Plate, 17.2% (on the clean wool basis) was cross-bred wool. In 1895 the proportion was 31.7%, and by 1904 it had risen to 51.8%,[3] but in 1907 it fell off to 45%. The main increase in this supply has come in the output from the River Plate region, where at present this grade makes up about 80% of the total. Nearly all of the Australasian cross-bred wool comes from New Zealand, the conditions there being more favorable for mutton sheep, and it does not as yet form any considerable portion of the clip from Australia, that still consisting primarily of merino wool.[4] The full significance of such a large increase of cross-bred wool will be understood when it is remembered that the clip of Australasia and the River Plate region represents fully one half of the world's wool supply. This change in the quality of the product of the chief competitors of the United States might

[1] Gibson, *History and Present State of the Sheep Breeding Industry in Argentine Republic*, pp. 35–43.

[2] See table of prices in the Appendix.

[3] From the *Annual Wool Review* of Helmuth Schwartze & Co. A part of this increased percentage was due to the effect of the droughts on the output of Australia, which furnishes the greater part of the merino wool. The decline that followed is explained by the recovery from the droughts. Cf. *Journal of the Royal Statistical Society*, vol. lxv, pp. 505–509.

[4] For the years 1902–07 the average annual quantity of Australasian wool catalogued in London was 816,000 bales, of which 363,000 bales were cross-bred, and of these 315,000 came from New Zealand.

have been of some relief to the wool-growers of the country had not similar circumstances, to be considered later, brought about a corresponding change here. Formerly both were growing merino wool; now both give more attention to cross-bred, and the relative situation remains essentially unchanged.

Imports of Wool and the Tariff.

The outcry raised by the wool-growers after the passage of the tariff of 1883, and their arguments ascribing to that act the decline in the number of sheep which then took place, were favorably listened to when Congress again took up the question of a revision of the tariff. In the McKinley tariff of 1890, which took effect on October 6th of that year, the growers secured what was virtually a restoration of the duties of 1867, under which the flocks had multiplied so rapidly. It was hoped that this would restore the prosperity of the earlier years. Under the new law the duties on wool of the first two classes were made purely specific in form. Class I wool paid 11 cents a pound unwashed, twice as much if washed, and three times as much if scoured. Class II wool paid 12 cents a pound in both washed and unwashed condition, and three times this amount when scoured. The duty of Class III wool still remained ad valorem in form, being fixed at 32% if valued at 13 cents or less, and 50% if above that. As previously, both unwashed and washed carpet wool came in at the same rate, which was trebled for scoured wool.

When the Democrats again came into power and undertook to scale down the tariff barriers, the most striking and almost the only important innovation of a free trade character which they made was to put raw wool upon the free list. The Wilson bill was passed August 1, 1894, and took effect as regards raw wool on the 28th of that month, as regards manufactured goods on the first of the following year, thus allowing the manufacturers some time to dispose of the goods made from wool upon which a duty had been paid before the reduction took place. How great a change free wool meant will be understood on recollecting that this commodity had been aided by protective duties almost from the very first, — duties which, since the Civil War at least, had invariably been maintained at a high level.

The Republicans, on reacquiring the reins of government under President McKinley, felt called upon to restore the more serious breaches in the tariff wall made during the previous administration, and on July 24, 1897, the Dingley tariff became law. Under this act the duties on wool of Class I and Class II were the same as under the McKinley tariff. The duty on carpet wool was made specific in form: 4 cents a pound if valued at 12 cents or less, 7 cents if valued above that, — a slight increase over the previous rate.[1]

The following table gives a general survey of the imports of wool under each tariff since 1867.

Average Annual Imports of Wool by Classes (in millions of pounds).[2]

	Class I	*Class II*	*Class III*
1867–83	9	10	33
1884–90	20	6	75
1891–93	40	5	99
1895–97	141	21	117
1900–07	59	11	102

The most significant record in the table is the column giving the imports of Class I wool. This is the class which most closely resembles the domestic clip, and the table shows a constant increase (the free wool period excepted) in the imports under the successive tariffs, the amount having tripled in the short interval since 1890. The enormous increase in the imports of this class under the free wool schedule, though of course much greater than if such were the normal state of the tariff, makes it evident that it is this grade which feels the duty most. The imports of Class II, also a rival wool, have risen but slowly, and, except under the tariff of 1867, have always been

[1] "These duties [of the Dingley tariff] in their ad valorem equivalent are higher [because of the lower price of wool] than under any previous tariff in our history" (North, *Bulletin*, vol. xxvii, p. 236). For a criticism of the tariff from the wool-growers' point of view, see *Ohio Agricultural Report*, 1897, pp. 658–662.

[2] A few grades of wool were transferred from Class III to Class I by the Act of 1897. In most comparisons under the Dingley tariff, a period beginning two or three years after the act went into force is taken, as the enormous imports of the free wool period could not be worked off all at once. The fiscal year 1891 includes three months under the previous tariff. The average annual importation, 1900–07, of Class III wool valued at over 12 cents a pound, and thus coming in under the higher of the two rates of duty for that class, was 18,600,000 pounds. The proportion paying this rate has increased of late years, but the great bulk of wool in the class is still of the lower value. For a complete table showing the imports of each class by years, 1867–1907, see Appendix.

relatively small in amount. In Class III wool there has been a steady though not rapid advance. This wool, unlike that of the two other classes, was but little affected by the free wool era, a fact which adds strength to the conviction that this class of wool is not produced to any extent in the domestic clip, and which also seems to indicate that the tariff on it is virtually a duty for revenue. Finally it is to be noted that the average total imports of all classes for the period 1900–07 show an increase over the imports under the tariff of 1883 of 70%, and over those under the Act of 1867 of 231%.

A division of the imports of each class by countries of production shows the situation under the existing tariff, and for purposes of comparison under the tariff of 1883, as follows, in thousands of pounds: —

Average Annual Imports by Classes and Chief Countries of Production.[1]

	Class I			*Class II*	
	Argentina	*Uruguay*	*Australasia*	*Turkey*	*United Kingdom*
1884–90	967	3,933	12,785	800	5,232
1900–07	22,334	2,625	33,817	1,138	7,548

	Class III					
	Russia	*Turkey*	*United Kingdom*	*Argentina*	*China*	*Br. E. Indies*
1884–90	17,566	15,358	9,827	8,187	4,236	8,781
1900–07	19,724	13,613	14,547	8,209	26,235	8,623

The table affords a good indication of present tendencies in the import trade. The most noticeable change depicted is the enormous increase in recent years of the imports of Class I wool from the River Plate region. From Uruguay and Argentina together, the imports are now over 400% greater than they were about twenty years ago; from Argentina alone, they are greater by 2200%. It will be remembered that when the new high level of duties was introduced during the Civil War period, the wool which it avowedly set out to exclude was this self-same South American product. At the time the effort met with some success: there was a falling off in the imports of River Plate clothing wool, the heavy specific duty proving too high for the wool of this grade in the condition in which it then came to

[1] Cf. footnote to similar table on page 222.

market. That situation continued substantially unaltered down to about 1894, the imports of such wool under the McKinley Act being even smaller than under the preceding tariff. The change came with the period of free wool, and was due to several causes: partly to the better chance then given our manufacturers to test this wool; partly to the great improvement which in the course of time had taken place, not only in the grade of the wool, but also in the condition in which it came to market; and partly to the fact that the increased demand for coarser wool made it possible to use the clip from these regions, much of which was cross-bred, to supplement the diminished Australian supply. It is evident that the statement commonly made, that the tariff of 1867 shut out this South American wool, does not hold true under the present tariff, in spite of the duty's being relatively higher. The River Plate region is once more a very formidable rival for the American grower.

The only other country that furnishes a large quantity of Class I wool is Australasia. The total supply from this source considerably exceeds that from South America. Although there was a steady advance in the imports from Australasia up to the middle of the nineties, drought stopped further increase, and for the last seven years the imports have averaged the same as under the McKinley tariff.

By far the larger part of Class II wool comes from the United Kingdom, as is but natural in view of the fact that this class is composed of wool from the English breeds of sheep. Except Turkey no other country sends any amount worthy of mention. The recent rise in the imports of this grade is due to the growing preference for coarser goods and worsteds.

As regards Class III, the table shows that China has made such wonderful progress in recent years that it is now the chief single source of supply for this wool. China, in fact, is the only country which, during the period we are considering, showed any marked capacity for increasing its output — a point of no little significance for the future. Inasmuch as carpet wool is mainly grown among the less civilized peoples of the globe, the march of progress, except where it opens new countries, tends to decrease the available supply. For the present, however, there are no signs of scarcity.

If we now put together these facts as regards the imports of wool and the changes which, as we have seen, have taken place in the world's wool supply, it becomes evident that for the present the most dangerous rivals of our wool-growers are to be found in Australasia and Argentina. Eventually some of the countries that now produce only carpet wool may improve their product, and there are still regions, notably Central Asia, to which we can confidently look for a further supply of carpet wool. For the more distant future, the most promising prospect of any considerable increase in the world's supply is found in Asia. As for the more immediate future, Australasia, as has been seen, is not likely to become much more dangerous than she has been, but an increasingly serious rivalry will probably come from Argentina. That country grows almost as much wool as Australia, yet most of her sheep are in one province. As cultivation increases, the number in that province will decline, as it has done in some sections of Australia. But the unoccupied territory in Argentina seems to afford greater opportunities for the further extension of the industry than does the island continent, since the vast areas to the south and west of Buenos Ayres are still comparatively undeveloped.[1]

The extent to which our wool-grower is protected against foreign wools by the tariff duties is a question often asked, but most difficult to answer. The chief complications in this problem have been caused by the varying shrinkage of wool in the processes of washing and scouring, and by the practice of skirting the fleece. It was partly because of its heavy shrinkage that South American wool was for a long time virtually prohibited by the tariff; and it is generally agreed that no Australian wool is imported into this country that shrinks much more than 52%.[2] American wool similar in other respects to Australian wool shrinking 52% shrinks from 60 to 80%, averaging perhaps 66%. Other things being equal, what a manufacturer is

[1] Cf. Department of Agriculture, *Year Book*, 1904, pp. 272–284; *Bulletin*, vol. xxxv, pp. 213–220; Bureau of Animal Industry, *Bulletin* No. 48; *American Sheep Breeder*, February–March, 1905.

[2] "American purchasers are confined to wools of the lightest shrinkage on account of the duty, and these purchases will not average to shrink more than 50 to 53 per cent. . . . The condition of Ohio wool has been growing heavier of late years, correspondingly decreasing the yield when scoured, while the Australian wools have as steadily improved in condition." (Letter of Mauger and Avery of Boston, in Aldrich Report. *Senate Reports*, 2d Session, 52d Congress, vol. iii, part 1, pp. 384–388. See also *House Document* No. 338, 54th Congress, 2d Session, p. 1366; *Bulletin*, vol. xxviii, p. 137.)

willing to pay for his wool is of course determined by the amount of clean wool he obtains from it. Clearly, the American buyer can afford to pay more for Australian wool shrinking 52% than he can for otherwise similar American wool shrinking over 60%, or even for Ohio fine washed shrinking 55%. Thus the duty of 11 or 12 cents a pound on these Australian wools (the improvement in the Argentina wools has frequently secured a similar result there) does not give protection of an equal amount to the American product.[1]

A similar effect comes from the practice known as skirting the fleece, resorted to in both Australia and South America, though heretofore more complained of in regard to the former country. As has already been said, the wool found on a single fleece varies considerably in both fineness and shrinkage. In skirting the fleece, the coarser wool and that holding most dirt — such as comes from the belly, breech, and legs — is cut off, leaving simply the best and cleanest part of the fleece. A foreign fleece improved in this manner is of course worth more to the manufacturer than is an otherwise similar American fleece. A well-known American buyer says: "I know of no class of wool grown in the United States, which is sold in the fleece, that does not need 2 cents per pound added to the price paid in the fleece to make it equal to all Australian wool and all New Zealand wool and most of the English and Irish wools as they come to market. It takes the above 2 cents a pound to make our wool equal in condition as wool before estimating shrinkage." [2]

[1] Probably the possible gain is somewhat neutralized by centering the demand of the American buyers upon these low-shrinkage wools, thus slightly raising their price.

[2] Letter of the late Mr. Joseph Walworth, for forty-two years buyer of the Pacific Mills, Lawrence, Mass. He adds for illustration an actual transaction showing that an American wool which sold in Boston at 20 cents actually cost per scoured pound 7 cents more than a similar grade of South American wool which sold there at the same time at 21 cents, duty paid. See *Bulletin*, vol. xxxi, p. 381.

On this point the late Judge Lawrence, formerly president of the National Wool-Growers' Association, said, "Australian merino unwashed, as heretofore imported, will sell at from 5 to 7 cents a pound more than our Ohio washed merino, because of the less shrinkage of the foreign wool and the value added to it in the skirting, and because of the special demand for a soft wool of that particular lustre, which, however, adds nothing to its utility, but, nevertheless, subtracts from the protective benefit of the wool tariff, leaving the protective benefit of a tariff of 12 cents a pound at less than 7 cents in competition with skirted Australian unwashed merino" (*House Document* No. 338, 54th Congress, 2d Session, p. 1358). An estimate made by Mauger & Avery, based on the prices of 1891, showed that Ohio washed wool was enhanced, because

Further indication that this practice of skirting serves as a loophole is found in the attitude of the manufacturers toward what is known as the "skirting clause" of the tariff, a clause which makes particular exception for skirted wool in admitting it at the same rate of duty as unskirted.[1] The manufacturers secured the insertion of this clause in the McKinley Act, and in spite of the vigorous protests of the growers, who asked for a duty of at least 3 cents a pound additional on skirted wool, they also secured its retention in the Dingley Act. There can be little doubt that through this practice of skirting the growers again fail to obtain the full benefit of the nominal duty.

Attempts have been made to throw some light on this subject by a comparison of prices here and abroad, and the period of free wool gave an added opportunity to secure data; but the results have been, at best, unsatisfactory. To find two clips of wool that are exactly alike has proved impossible. Those most frequently compared have been Ohio fine washed and Port Phillip (Australian) average grease. But of these the latter, because of its superior softness, will probably sell in a free market a bit higher than the Ohio wool. During the free wool period this Australian product sold in London at a price sometimes a little below, sometimes a little above, the Boston price of the American wool; but at that time the market conditions in this

of the duties and charges, $11\frac{8}{10}$ cents. A similar estimate, based on the quotations of July 1, 1893, showed the price to be raised but 6 cents (see *Bulletin*, vol. xxiii, pp. 252–263; cf. *ibid.*, vol. xxvi, p. 130). It is evident that only an estimate covering a period of several years could be at all satisfactory.

For further references as to skirting, see *Bulletin*, vol. xxvii, pp. 127–132, 155–162, 282–288; *Tariff Hearings*, 1889–90, pp. 217–224; *Tariff Hearings, House Document* No. 338, 54th Congress, 2d Session, pp. 1374–1378, 1588–1596; *Senate Miscellaneous Document* No. 35, 53d Congress, 2d Session, pp. 325–326; *Senate Miscellaneous Document* No. 17, 54th Congress, 2d Session, p. 36; *Ohio Agricultural Report*, 1894, pp. 609–610.

[1] The text of this clause (Section 383) in the Act of 1890 is most suggestive, and runs as follows:—

"The duty upon wool of the sheep or hair of the camel, goat, alpaca, and other like animals, which shall be imported in any other than ordinary condition, or which shall be changed in its character or condition, for the purpose of evading the duty, or which shall be reduced in value by admixture of dirt or any other foreign substance, or which has been sorted or increased in value by the rejection of any part of the original fleece, shall be twice the duty to which it would otherwise be subject: Provided that skirted wools as now imported are hereby excepted" (*United States Statutes at Large*, vol. xxvi, p. 595).

country were abnormal. If we leave out the period of free wool, the quotations for the years since 1890 show a difference between the prices of these two grades of wool varying from 3 to 11 cents, the average difference being about 8 or 9 cents. The duty, it will be remembered, is 11 cents on Class I (clothing wool), 12 cents on Class II (combing wool).[1]

During the events which led to the repeal of the duty on wool all grades of our domestic wool fell in price together, and to virtually the same extent; and on the reimposition of the duty they all rose again. There is little evidence that there is now any important grade of our domestic clip of which the supply is so large as to depress the price below the possible limits of the protective duties. We import nearly all grades of wool; and though the imported wools do not exactly correspond in all respects to our own, one being a bit better for this purpose and another for that, it is improbable, with the advance that has been made in adapting wools to varied uses, that the difference in quality between any important grade of domestic and at least some grade of foreign wool is so great as permanently to prevent one from competing with the other. The steady decrease of the difference in price between different grades of wool strengthens the evidence as to the correctness of this assertion.

It thus appears that, although the difference between the price of the most important competing wools here and abroad is less than can be accounted for if the tariff protects to the full extent of the duty, there is little reason to believe, in view of the character of our imports, that the failure of the domestic wool to advance in price is caused by any pressure of competition at home. Other causes seem sufficient to explain this discrepancy. It is reasonable to conclude that, because of the better condition in which the wool of our only really serious competitors comes to market, the specific weight duties do not, indeed, raise the price of American wool by the nominal amount of the duty, but that the price is raised, under normal

[1] The President of the National Association of Wool-Growers declared that this operated so as to give but 4 cents a pound net protection (see *Ohio Agricultural Report*, 1897, p. 662). Freight rates from London to Boston would add from ½ to 1½ cents a pound. Much is imported direct, and the rates from Australia to Boston and London do not greatly differ. Freight rates from the western plains to Boston are still higher, generally from 2½ to 3 cents a pound (cf. *Bulletin*, vol. xxv, pp. 112–113; vol. xxvii, p. 365).

market conditions, to the full amount of the protection possible and actually given by these duties. To that extent the wool-growers do benefit by the tariff.

There yet remains for consideration the importation of wool in the form of manufactured goods, a matter especially deserving of attention because of the remarkable change which occurred, as is indicated by the following table, in the period under review.

	Av. annual value of imports of manufactures of wool	*Average rate of duty paid*	*Estimated av. annual imports of wool in form of manufactures of wool*
1884–90	$45,000,000	67%	135,000,000 lbs.
1891–93	38,000,000	91%	114,000,000 lbs.
1895–97	47,000,000	49%	141,000,000 lbs.
1900–07	19,000,000	91%	57,000,000 lbs.

The amount of wool imported in the form of manufactures of wool can only be estimated in a very rough manner, but, accepting the generally used basis of 3 pounds of wool to a dollar in value, we find such a drop under the present tariff as cannot but be of decided importance to the wool-grower. The full significance of this change is better realized when it is stated that in only two years since 1850 (in 1862 and 1894) have the imports of manufactures of wool been so low in value as they have averaged for the whole decade since the Dingley Bill went into force. Or, continuing our calculations on the above basis, up to the time when the McKinley Bill went into operation, there had been, since the beginning of the records in 1822 but three years (1863, 1880, and 1886) in which the imports of raw wool exceeded the imports of wool in the form of manufactures, whereas in every year since (except 1894) the case has been exactly the reverse.[1]

This change is so notable as to deserve more detailed inquiry as to its cause. It is a point of some significance that on the question of excluding manufactures of wool the interests of both the wool-grower and the wool-manufacturer, usually so diverse, happen to coincide.

[1] Some allowance should properly be made for the higher price of wool and the more expensive methods of manufacture of the earlier days; but this does not seem sufficient to detract seriously from the general significance of this assertion. Furthermore, this explanation would have much weight only if we were to go back for a long period, whereas the decline has been comparatively recent.

The growers have at times opposed higher duties on woolen goods, not because they would not have been glad to exclude these goods, but only in order to force from the manufacturers the concession of higher rates on the raw product. The manufacturers, on the other hand, generally admit that in being deprived of free wool they suffer a handicap, perhaps better realized now than ever before.[1] Apparently, they only consent to duties on wool (though some declare for free wool in any case) because of political necessity, fearing that, unless these be granted, they cannot obtain protection for their own product.[2] The growers have evidently felt that they could safely leave the care of protecting woolen goods to the manufacturers, and certainly the results have entirely justified this expectation.

That the decline in imports, as we may most naturally suppose, is due to heavier protection, further examination seems to substantiate. After the enactment of the tariff of 1890, the duties paid on the imports of manufactures of wool showed higher ad valorem rates, and the total value of these imports fell off somewhat. Under the tariff of 1897 the duties paid indicate the same percentage of value as under the Act of 1890; yet the amount of these goods imported, as shown both by the value and by the quantity (where such comparison is possible), has undergone a very marked decline when compared not only with the figures under the McKinley Act, but also with those under the Act of 1883. Thus in the two classes of

[1] "For the first time in the history of the organization [1897] the Association [of wool manufacturers] found it necessary to take a positive stand in opposition to the rates of duty on wool urged by the wool growers" (*Bulletin*, vol. xxviii, p. 28). "It can do no possible harm to have it known and understood, and not denied or concealed, that free wool is the ideal condition of an unhampered and progressive wool manufacture; that when the wool manufacturers consent to a wool duty they consent to a sacrifice which is real, tangible, and troublesome to a degree that outsiders cannot fully understand" (S. N. D. North, long secretary of the manufacturers' association, *ibid.*, vol. xxxv, p. 46. Cf. *ibid.*, vol. xxvii, pp. 122–127, 234; vol. xviii, p. 191; vol. xx, p. 90; vol. xxx, pp. 308–312; vol. xxxiii, pp. 4–7). Another point sometimes urged is that the duty on wool, by throwing an increased supply of wool on the European market, so depresses its price there that foreign manufacturers can more easily undersell American manufacturers (cf. *Tariff Hearings*, 1889–90, pp. 167–174). D. A. Wells used to advance a similar argument (cf. Special Commissioner of the Revenue, *Report*, 1869; *Bulletin*, vol. xxiii, p. 52). The point is of doubtful value, and in any case the effect is too slight to be susceptible of measurement.

[2] Cf. *ibid.*, vol. xx, pp. 3–9, for statement of the president of the manufacturers' association on this point.

goods which make up two thirds of the total value of the manufactures, and in which by far the greater share of this decline occurred, we have the following outcome: —

	Average annual imports of cloths		*Average annual imports of women's dress goods*	
	Pounds	*Value*	*Square yards*	*Value*
1891–93	14,000,000	$13,000,000	82,000,000	$17,000,000
1900–07	5,000,000	5,000,000	39,000,000	8,000,000

There was also a decrease in nearly all the other classes, the only instance of any considerable increase being under the heading "carpets," in this case, apparently, in the class of Oriental rugs. Heavier protection has been secured in some instances by higher rates of duty, but probably with more effect by adopting new dividing points in the valuation and by changes in classification; with the result that what little foreign competition remains has been shifted to a grade of goods even higher than before. The growing use, in many products, of cheaper substitutes for wool, together with the continuance of the old compensating rates which assumed an all-wool basis, has quietly but steadily increased the actual amount of protection received. Undoubtedly, too, the American manufacturers learned much during the period of free wool, from a better acquaintance with foreign wools as well as from the necessity of meeting more severe competition from abroad, and hence are now better prepared to cope with their European rivals than formerly. But it is equally certain, as they themselves readily admit,[1] that the Dingley Bill affords them greater protection than any previous tariff.

The actual effect which the duties on manufactures have upon the grower deserves a little closer attention. When the present system of

[1] In the September, 1897, issue of the *Bulletin*, vol. xxvii, p. 258, Mr. S. N. D. North, then secretary of the National Association of Wool Manufacturers, wrote: "So far as the most critical examination can now detect, there is no weak spot in the woolen schedule. . . . Our belief is that it will be found in practical operation to be the most perfect woolen schedule which has ever been enacted." That this belief proved to be correct is indicated in an address by the same gentleman before this association (though he was no longer its secretary) in 1905, when he said: "The present wool and woolens schedule, whatever its defects, is, on the whole, as satisfactory to wool-growers and to wool manufacturers alike, as any that has ever been enacted. . . . So long as the wool and woolens schedule remains as it is, you are safe" (see *ibid.*, vol. xxxv, pp. 46, 47).

duties was adopted in 1867, the specific weight duties on goods were supposed to compensate the manufacturers for the duty on their raw material and were adjusted on the supposition that the price of wool was raised to the full extent of the duty. Here, it may at first appear, the wool-grower benefits to the full extent of the duty; and so he probably does, as far as the imports of goods are concerned. But, on further consideration, it is clear (even if we grant the estimate of 3½ pounds of wool to 1 pound of cloth to be, as a rule, not excessive) that, just so long as the duties on raw wool do not actually protect to the full amount of the tariff, these full protecting duties on the manufactures are unable to give a particle of additional aid. The manufacturer may gain, but not the grower; for before the price of domestic wool rises to the full extent, as estimated for the compensating duty, the former will turn abroad for his raw material.

The actual extent of the competition which the tariff permits, so far as that can be determined by the amount of foreign wool imported, is as follows, in millions of pounds: —

	Av. net imports of wool, Classes I and II [1]	*Av. imports of wool in form of manufactures*	*Total av. imports competing wools, raw and manufactured*	*Av. domestic wool supply*
1884–90	26	135	161	321
1891–93	45	114	159	329
1895–97	153	141	294	272
1900–07	73	57	130	294

These figures indicate that, although the imports of raw wool of the grades competing with our own have been advancing in spite of the duties, yet if the imports in the form of manufactured goods be taken into account, the total shows a falling off as compared with that which prevailed under either the tariff of 1883 or that of 1890. We now manufacture a greater proportion of the foreign wool consumed in this country than formerly, and since about 1880, the proportion of foreign wool in the total consumption has increased.[2] But the total amount of competing wool consumed has slightly decreased;

[1] As carpet wool does not seriously compete with our domestic wool, it is omitted. Similarly, a part of that coming in as manufactures might be excluded, but the amount is so small as to be negligible. The figures for the domestic production are the estimates of Mr. Lynch, of Mr. Truitt, and of the manufacturers' *Bulletin*.

[2] See table on page 225.

and, although the American product has not advanced, yet during this period it has fairly held its own against the foreign invader.

With a steadily growing population the continuance of this situation is impossible. There has already been a decline in the per capita consumption of wool, but this cannot go on indefinitely. The figures for the last three years, 1905–07, already show a heavy advance in the imports of competing raw wool,[1] and every circumstance points to the conclusion that this is only the beginning of a tendency which will inevitably continue to grow in importance. In short, the United States seems destined to rely more and more on foreign countries for its supply of wool.

The Manufacture of Wool.

If one were to judge from the decline in imports of goods which took place during these years, the period would seem to have brought great growth for the woolen manufacture. The actual course of events, as shown by the Census figures, was as follows: —

Manufactures of Wool.[2]

	Number of establishments	*Capital (millions)*	*Value of product (millions)*	*Per capita value of product*	*Per capita value of imports of m'f'gs*
1890	2,489	$296	$338	$5.39	$0.74
1900	2,335	392	392	5.16	0.20
1905	2,292	477	518	6.23	0.24

It is evident from the table that the manufacture of wool did in truth make very substantial progress, in spite of the fact that the period saw one of the most severe industrial crises in our history. As the last two columns show, the domestic manufacturer gained at an unusual rate over his foreign rivals, probably greater than at any other period except the Civil War decade, so that at the end, out of the total consumption of manufactures of wool but 6–8% was of

[1] During the years 1905–07 the average net imports of Class I and Class II wool were 107,000,000 pounds, double the average for the years 1900–04. The average imports of wool in the form of manufactured goods increased to 63,000,000 pounds.

[2] This includes hosiery and knit goods. The value of imports is the average for five-year periods. As the census year of 1900 was a poor one, and 1905 was good, the gain in the latter years is exaggerated. The rising prices also tended to magnify the real growth.

foreign origin.[1] Under such circumstances we may fairly say that the domestic manufacture has reached the point where it virtually supplies the American demand, and is more firmly intrenched than ever before.[2]

An idea of the growth of the different branches of the manufacture, and their relative importance as consumers of wool, can be obtained from the following table.

Consumption of Scoured Wool in Wool Manufactures (in millions of pounds).[3]

	Worsteds	*Woolens*	*Carpets and rugs*	*Hosiery and knit goods*	*Felt goods*	*Wool hats*
1890	54	100	36	17	4	3
1900	103	89	38	13	6	2
1905	139	102	32	14	8	1

As in the preceding period, the branch of the manufacture which grew most rapidly was that engaged upon worsteds.[4] These years, in fact, witnessed the greatest growth experienced by this branch since it first became fairly established. The result was that by 1900 it led all other branches of the industry, surpassing the manufacture of woolen cloth both in the value of its product and in the amount of wool consumed. The lead which it then secured has since been still further increased.

This was but the outcome of the preference for worsted fabrics which, as we have seen, had been steadily growing since the beginning of the century.[5] Here we find the reason why in the face of the

[1] This estimate is obtained by increasing the dutiable value of the imports 75–100% in order to put them on a level for comparison with the protected domestic goods.

[2] A significant event — the first appearance of the modern industrial combination in the textile industry of the country — was the formation in 1899 of the American Woolen Company. Since then its capacity has nearly doubled, so that it now includes about thirty properties.

[3] Bureau of the Census, *Bulletin* No. 74, pp. 92, 108; *Census*, 1890, Manufactures, part iii, p. 129; *Census*, 1900, vol. ix, p. 186.

[4] In this connection the particularly favorable treatment afforded the worsted manufacture by the tariff should not be overlooked.

[5] The greater increase in this demand has come from the male population, and is well illustrated by the changes which have taken place in their apparel. Formerly it was all preferably broadcloth, then worsted coatings grew in favor, and now fashion favors worsteds for the frock coat and dress suit.

great increase in the supply of medium or cross-bred wool suitable for combing, which occurred during this period, the price of this grade was so steadily maintained. Such a preference, moreover, provided it continue, will be of no little benefit to the sheep-owner of the country if, as we shall soon learn seems to be the case, he is destined to become primarily a producer of mutton; for it means that the wool clipped from his sheep will sell at so much the better price for being of this grade. It will also be favorable to the consumer, for it is evident that, under the conditions which will increasingly prevail in the more advanced countries, growing wool upon mutton sheep must be the more economical method and thus produce the cheaper wool.[1]

After the worsted manufacture, the two branches of the industry which made the most rapid progress during the preceding period were those engaged in the production of carpets, and of hosiery and knit goods. In the years following 1890 the former made little advance, but the growth of the knit goods branch was quite phenomenal — over 100% as measured by the value of the product. Yet, with all this growth, it was most remarkable that the amount of wool consumed increased less than one quarter as fast. The gain in the output was made possible only by the increased use of cotton, the consumption of which rose over 300% during the succeeding decade and a half. Moreover, it was just the possibility of using the cheaper fibre, cotton, that was one of the chief causes of the growth. The result of cotton's steady invasion of the manufacture of hosiery and knit goods is that at present this manufacture uses four or five pounds of cotton for every pound of wool. Hereafter hosiery and knit goods can hardly be classified under the head of "manufactures of wool."[2]

The general situation as regards the raw material used in the manufactures of wool is shown in the following table, which, for the sake of comparison, gives some figures for an earlier date.

[1] It is quite possible that the growing demand for this grade of wool can be explained largely on economic grounds, *i. e.* by the possibility of thus supplying the need for wool at the lowest cost.

[2] It was in final recognition of this fact that the Census of Manufactures for 1905 put it under a separate heading. Cf. Bureau of the Census, *Bulletin* No. 74, p. 96.

Raw Material Consumed (millions of pounds).[1]

	Wool in condition purchased		*Wool yarn purchased*	*Cotton and cotton yarn*	*Animal hairs and noils*	*Shoddy*
	Foreign	*Domestic*				
1870	47	173	2	40	no data	20
1890	114	259	11	159	27	62
1900	140	272	10	280	36	38
1905	154	347	16	309	46	43

One of the most striking phenomena in the course of events affecting the industry of wool-growing is the falling off in the per capita consumption of wool which appeared during this period. Up to 1890, according to the Census figures, the per capita consumption of wool had increased in every decade since 1840, when the figures began, yet in 1900 it dropped back nearly to the point reached in 1850, and in the Census of 1905 it was but a trifle higher.[2] The phenomenon, moreover, is not limited to this country. Thus there proves to have been a slight falling off in the consumption of the United Kingdom,[3] and the most authoritative figures available indicate that the decline is general over both Europe and North America.[4]

[1] Bureau of the Census, *Bulletin* No. 74, pp. 79, 131. This includes hosiery and knit goods.

[2] *Ibid.*, p. 107. The figures follow: —

Per Capita Consumption of Wool (in pounds).

1840	1850	1860	1870	1880	1890	1900	1904
4.49	5.58	6.80	7.93	8.52	8.75	5.97	6.22

A part of the decline in 1900 is due to abnormally small imports of woolens. If the average for the five years previous be taken, the corrected result is 6.93. A similar conclusion is reached by the late H. G. Kittredge, former editor of the *Textile American*, who adds: "No effort on the part of wool-growers to tax woolens can turn from their course the currents of trade or coerce manufacturers to use their products more freely at a consequently higher price" (*Bulletin*, vol. xxxii, p. 75).

[3] British Board of Trade, *Charts for the St. Louis Exposition*. Based on figures of Helmuth Schwartze & Co.

[4] Helmuth Schwartze & Co., *Wool Report*, March 8, 1904. Commenting on the situation, it says: "The diminishing or stationary production of wool since 1895 has greatly reduced the average available per head of population, and its place has no doubt been taken by the largely increased production of cotton. The change is particularly striking in the United States, where during the seven years 1887–93 the actual consumption of raw wool (including the equivalent of imported manufactures) was over 8½ pounds per head, in the succeeding eight years, 1894–1901, it was still over 7½ pounds on the average, while during the last two years it was barely more than 6½

The explanation, of course, is found in that insidious form of competition which has done so much to undermine the market for wool. Wool is an expensive fibre, and the manufacturer is constantly on the lookout for any method that promises an opportunity to employ a cheaper substitute. Whether the substitute be cotton, cow's hair, vegetable fibre, or shoddy makes no difference so long as it possess the saving grace of cheapness. The competition between the manufacturers in their efforts to undersell one another inevitably leads to a greater use of these less expensive substitutes. The movement has, moreover, been greatly facilitated of late by improved methods of employing them, and has been further spurred on by the demand of the public for less expensive fabrics. The revamping of wool in various forms has so increased the length of its useful life that a smaller supply performs a greater amount of service than formerly. Nor, from the social point of view, is the tendency to use cheaper material necessarily to be deprecated. The term shoddy has malodorous associations, but the real objection to the product is not so much that it is used as that its use is concealed. The effective utilization of substitutes for wool undoubtedly enables many a consumer to satisfy his needs at a lower cost than would otherwise be possible.

But the most dangerous rival of wool is cotton. Ever since the beginning of the century, except for the decade 1860–70, the consumption of cotton in this country has been growing at a faster rate than that of wool. The increase was especially noticeable in the decade following 1890.[1] The same tendency, moreover, is seen in Great Britain.[2] Not only are cotton goods rapidly gaining in popular favor,

pounds per head." Their figures, which follow, give for Europe and North America the quantity of clean wool, per head of population, at the disposal of the industry for average periods. This does not specifically state the quantity actually consumed in the form of manufactures, but it may be said to represent that with fairness.

1861–70	1871–80	1881–90	1891–1900	1901–07
2.26	2.43	2.57	2.76	2.64

(*Wool Circular*, March 17, 1908.) Cf. also the manufacturers' *Bulletin*, vol. xxxii, p. 75.

[1] *Per Capita Consumption of Cotton in Cotton Manufacture.*

1860	1870	1880	1890	1900
13.6	10.5	15.0	18.0	24.2

(*Census* of 1900, vol. ix, p. 12.)

[2] *Ibid.*, p. 6; cf. British Board of Trade, *Charts for the St. Louis Exposition.*

while woolens remain nearly stationary, but, as the situation in the hosiery and knit goods industry shows, cotton is invading the very home of wool. In fact the use of cotton in the "manufactures of wool" is increasing faster than that of wool itself.[1]

Doubtless one of the chief reasons for this tendency was the low price of cotton which prevailed during the decade 1890–1900. Wool also was unusually cheap during this period, but the fall in cotton was proportionately greater. The average price of upland middling cotton for the decade 1881–90 was 10.8 cents a pound, and, although this was lower than for any like period since the forties, the average for the decade 1890–1900 was but 7.6 cents. All this helps us to comprehend why the decline in the world's wool supply at this time failed to result in a greater advance in the price of that staple. Since 1900 the price of cotton has once more averaged about 10 cents (which is probably nearer its normal level), and the Census of Manufactures for 1905 notes that the years between these two dates saw no appreciable increase in its consumption. Since a permanent lower level in its price is hardly to be expected, it is unlikely that the substitution of cotton for wool will proceed quite as rapidly as before. Still, although there are other substitutes struggling with cotton for the same field, we may be sure that just so long as one pound of cotton costing 10 cents can possibly be used in the place of two or three pounds of wool (allowing for shrinkage) costing from 10 to 35 cents per pound, the wool-grower will continue to suffer from this rivalry.[2]

[1] Cf. table on page 295.

[2] Much of the blame for this is frequently put upon the tariff. Even some strong protectionists agree to this. Thus Stanwood (*American Tariff Controversies*, vol. ii, p. 169) says: "It is a consequence of the enhanced price [resulting from the tariff] that the consumption of woolen goods has never had, and cannot have, an expansion like that which has taken place in cotton, in sugar, in iron, and in many other articles. Wool and woolens are always the strongest arguments of the free trader, and the most difficult to answer." S. N. D. North says: "The increased duty raises the price of wool and results in decreased consumption per capita. Modern mechanical ingenuity has made it impossible for 50 cent wool to maintain the old proportional relationship with 6 cent cotton in the consumption of fibres for clothing" (*Bulletin*, vol. xxx, p. 312). For an argument that the duty on wool does not increase the use of shoddy, see Dodge, *Sheep and Wool*, Department of Agriculture Report, No. 66, p. 44. This pamphlet contains a brief history of the industry from the point of view of a protectionist. Unquestionably the increased price resulting from the tariff does tend to lower the consumption, but it is by no means the chief cause of the decrease.

The Wool-Growing Industry.

The Old Wool-Growing Centres.

It was found that at the close of the preceding period the flocks of virtually all the states in the East and the Middle West were on the decline. The passage of the McKinley tariff in 1890 evidently revived the drooping hopes of the flock-owners, for in spite of the downward trend of prices there appeared an increase in the number of sheep in all parts of these two great sections excepting New England. Yet the rise was but slight, and in many states did not even last through 1892, while the year 1893 brought a heavy decline all around, as is to be seen in the following table:—

The Number of Sheep, 1890–1907 (*in hundreds of thousands*).[1]

	1890	1891	1892	1893	1894	1895	1896	1897	1898
New England	12	12	12	9	7	6	6	5	5
Middle Atlantic	27	27	28	33	29	23	19	17	17
South	76	78	78	76	66	60	54	49	46
North Central	102	104	110	124	107	92	74	65	65
Central West	27	26	31	37	35	30	28	26	27
United States	443	434	449	472	435	399	364	347	356

	1899	1900	1901	1902	1903	1904	1905	1906	1907
New England	5	5	5	5	5	5	5	5	5
Middle Atlantic	17	17	18	20	16	16	17	17	18
South	42	41	43	34	33	34	34	34	32
North Central	68	69	74	79	67	62	61	68	69
Central West	28	28	32	30	31	29	29	30	29
United States	369	402	419	421	392	383	386	385	389

[1] These figures are taken from the *Bulletin* of the wool manufacturers. For the years 1890–93 they are the same as those of the Department of Agriculture. Except for these years and 1901 (when they are for January 1) they give the number on April 1. About one and one half million of the decline between 1893 and 1894 is due to this change. The North Central states include Ohio, Indiana, Illinois, Wisconsin, Michigan, West Virginia and Kentucky, — the wool-growing centre of the East. The South includes Virginia, North Carolina, South Carolina, Georgia, Florida, Alabama, Mississippi, Louisiana, Texas, Arkansas, and Tennessee; the Central West, Minnesota, Iowa, Missouri, North Dakota, South Dakota, Nebraska, Kansas, Oklahoma, and Indian Territory.

The estimates of the Department of Agriculture for the years since 1900 appear erroneous. At the time it was announced that the figures for 1901 were withheld pend-

Then followed the régime of free wool under the Wilson tariff, together with severe industrial depression, and about two fifths of the sheep were disposed of. The losses fell heaviest upon the states where sheep had been most numerous, and in some cases amounted to one half of the flocks. It is, however, surprising that the restoration of the former tariff under the Dingley Act of 1897, and the upward price movement consequent on renewed prosperity, were able to stimulate only the most meagre increase in the number of sheep, an increase which culminated in 1901–02. Since then there has been a slight decline. But the most striking and significant fact of all is that in the New England, Middle Atlantic, North Central, and Southern states, as here grouped, — sections that include states long famous for their flocks, — there were in 1905, after eight years of as high protective duties on wool as the country has ever known, *fewer sheep than at any time throughout the period when prices in the world's market were at the lowest level in years and wool was admitted into the country free of duty.*[1]

The explanation for this outcome is simply the familiar one which has been encountered again and again throughout these regions where the sheep lands could generally be used for a great variety of purposes, the one which of late years has so largely determined the course of the industry there, — the competition of other products of

ing revision when the Census returns should come in. The Census showed 40 million sheep and 21 million lambs, or a total of sheep *and lambs* of 61 million. When the Department of Agriculture published its delayed estimates for January 1, 1901, the figures showed 59 million sheep, — an increase of nearly 18 million over their figures for 1900, and of 19 million over the Census returns for seven months previous. This is incredible. Other available data fail to substantiate it, and certainly there was no such increase in the domestic wool supply as this would entail. The most obvious explanation is that the figure of the Department, through some error, included *lambs* as well as sheep. This practice of including lambs in the Department's estimate of the number of sheep in the country appears to have been continued ever since, and is a constant source of error.

[1] It should be noted, however, that the last figures available, those for 1907, show that in the Middle Atlantic and North Central states the flocks at that time were a trifle above what they were in January, 1897. This, however, does not impair the strength of the above assertion, which means substantially that a high tariff absolutely failed to raise the flocks of these sections above the point reached when wool came in free. There has been an increase in the clip as a result of the improvement in the fleece, but even under free wool, so long as sheep are kept at all, such an improvement would take place. For condition in 1910 see note, page 315.

agriculture which, under the prevailing economic conditions, were becoming relatively more and more attractive.

Some conception of the nature of these other products of agriculture to which the farmer turned may be gathered from the following table, which covers all the important wool-growing states in these sections of the country.

Percentage of Increase or Decrease of Farm Products, etc., 1890–1900.

Counties with Fifty or More Sheep per Square Mile in 1890.

	Sheep	*Dairy cows*	*Improved land*	*Total farm area*	*Wheat acreage*	*Corn acreage*	*Oats acreage*	*Hay and forage acreage*
Ohio	36−	2+	0−[1]	3+	35+	23+	6−	1−
Michigan	39−	5+	8+	5+	19+	31+	15−	6+
Indiana	19−	4+	7+	5+	3+	25+	13−	2−
West Virginia	45−	11+	13+	8+	12+	9+	53−	5−
Kentucky	19−	3+	4+	2+	44+	26+	70−	19+
Pennsylvania	41−	8+	1−	2+	23+	12+	8−	3−
New York	36−	8+	2+	3+	27+	34+	13+	5+
Vermont	51−	22+	25+	8+	78−	35+	30−	3+

Counties with Less than Fifty Sheep per Square Mile in 1890.

	Sheep	*Dairy cows*	*Improved land*	*Total farm area*	*Wheat acreage*	*Corn acreage*	*Oats acreage*	*Hay and forage acreage*
Ohio	21−	5+	17+	8+	53+	16+	14−	3+
Michigan	12+	40+	50+	44+	61+	134+	12+	16+
Indiana	6−	3−	11+	1+	14+	25+	7−	6+
West Virginia	13−	8+	24+	2+	33+	26+	43−	6+
Kentucky	27−	1−	20+	3−	65+	14+	48+	2−
Pennsylvania	40−	0+[1]	0+[1]	6+	14+	19+	11−	2−
New York	34−	4+	4−	3+	10+	33+	14−	5−
Vermont	39−	15+	15+	7+	79−	52+	27−	0+[1]

These tables, based on the Census, show that the total farm area increased in every case but one, and that, except in Pennsylvania, New York, and Vermont, the improved land increased more rapidly than the total farm area. Evidently farming was not on the decline. The

[1] Less than 1 per cent decline or increase.

number of sheep, on the other hand, fell off in every case but one,[1] and the losses were, as a rule, proportionally greater in the sheep counties. From this it seems reasonable to infer that, where sheep were most numerous, the flocks presumably the largest, and the industry specialized in, there sheep-raising proved more unprofitable than where the flocks were smaller and kept as incidental to general farming. In the sheep counties in every case, and in the other counties in every case but two, there was an increase in the number of dairy cows. Moreover, this increase was proportionately greater in those very counties where the losses in sheep were the heaviest,—certainly strong presumptive evidence that it was the dairy business which was driving out wool-growing, especially when we remember that in these states the land used for one of these pursuits is, as a rule, equally well suited to the other.

But the dairy is not the only rival of the sheep, for the figures indicate in every instance a considerable rise in the corn acreage, and in every state but Vermont a similar tendency towards wheat. The hay and forage area has remained fairly stationary. The absolute figures would show that a small part of the extension of the wheat and corn acreage could be accounted for by the decrease in oats, and still more by the increase of that portion of the improved land which had been included in or replaced by a part of the new farm area. Yet, when allowance is made for the amount of the improved land which is turned to still other purposes, the tables would seem to show (and general observation bears this out) that some of this land has been diverted from the use of sheep.[2] The causes leading to these changes are most instructive.

The years when wool was free happened to be unusually trying ones for the farmer, as well as for industry in general.[3] Nearly all

[1] This exception represents an abnormal condition, including, as it does, the northern part of Michigan, which was undergoing a rapid development at the time.

[2] In the case of wheat, at least, it is perfectly possible for both sheep and wheat to increase together; but there is no indication that such was the case here.

[3] The rise of the demand for free silver and the Populist movement but reflected the general discontent. The index numbers for farm products for the years 1894–97 were 95.9, 93.3, 78.3, and 85.2 respectively, 100 being the average for 1890–99. The index numbers for all commodities for the corresponding years were 96.1, 93.6, 90.4, and 89.7. For this and other prices for this period, see *Bulletin of the Department of Labor*, No. 75.

farm products were low in price, but wool and mutton naturally suffered most. It was then that the possibilities in the raising of other farm products were most vividly brought to the notice of the wool-grower, for almost anything seemed to pay better than sheep. And since in the general drop in prices cattle and dairy produce suffered less than other farm products, the farmer, where conditions were favorable, naturally turned to them. Such, for instance, seems to have been the case in Vermont, eastern New York, southeastern Ohio, West Virginia, and Wisconsin. On the other hand, where the soil offered better opportunities for cultivation, he turned to grains: in western New York, northern Ohio, and Kentucky, to wheat; and in the belt extending westward from Ohio, to corn, accompanied by the feeding of stock, notably hogs, and frequently also by the dairy. When the period of distress had passed, and the Dingley tariff offered the stimulus of protection to revive the stricken industry, the response of the Eastern wool-growers was but faint. Some increased their flocks only to give them up again soon afterwards. Still more seemed content to let the change to other farm products remain permanent. After long and costly experience they had learned a lesson.

The burden of that lesson was that economic conditions had changed. There *had been* a time when conditions in the region centering about Ohio were admirably adapted to the industry of growing wool. As early as 1855, however, there were some indications that these conditions were passing away. Then came the abnormal and artificial stimulus during and following the Civil War, and the real state of affairs was hidden from view. With the vanishing of this stimulus the situation grew worse, while the wool-grower battled against his impending fate. But when the inertia, the characteristic conservatism, and the spell of these earlier years were at last broken through, and the truth was sharply revealed to him by the period of free wool, he at last became convinced. In this revelation he saw that, as the means of communication and transportation had improved, and new regions had been opened and developed, there had appeared, both here and abroad, lands economically better fitted for wool-growing than his, while on the other hand his own acres were well suited to the raising of other commodities in the production of which these new lands were unable to compete. In effect, the change was a step in advance — a step already too long delayed — towards a better and more nearly world-wide division of labor.

In this division of labor, as it now appears arranged, there are other things for which this section of the United States is economically better fitted than for the growing of wool. Preëminent among these is the raising of corn. The great corn belt of our country stretches from central Ohio westward to eastern Nebraska, including a part of Kansas and northern Missouri. Probably no other region of equal area on the earth is so well adapted, by both climate and soil, to the raising of corn. Along with the corn there naturally goes the feeding of stock, especially cattle and hogs, and the closely related dairy. This stock may even include sheep — as it already has done to a limited extent — provided they can easily be shipped in. In most cases, however, neat cattle prove more profitable.[1] May we not predict that the growth of this belt in the more immediate future will be in this direction? Those parts better suited for wheat are at present able to compete with the world, but since their relative advantage does not seem so great as that of the corn lands, their future is perhaps less certain. That sheep will play any prominent part in it seems unlikely.[1]

In the districts unsuited for the plough, the outlook for the sheep is not much better. Though sheep can be kept where dairy cows cannot, the pasture of the East will keep either; and so long as there are many regions which support the dairy cow either with difficulty or not at all, the chances are that in the competition between the two for the better pasture here the sheep will be worsted. Further, the dairy secures an additional hold on these eastern states because it has more to gain from being near the centres of population than has the sheep industry. We are thus led to conclude that in this section of the country the growing of wool, as an independent industry, is doomed. At present there is little prospect here for sheep, except as incidental to general farming. The general farmer can easily keep

[1] "The small farmers who have taken up lands and made homes for themselves in Texas and elsewhere in the newer portions of the United States have found it more profitable to keep neat cattle than sheep, and farmers throughout the country have had the same experience, hence the decrease in sheep in farming sections." (L. G. Powers, *Bulletin*, vol. xxxii, p. 78.)

[2] The small flocks of sheep frequently kept in connection with wheat are incidental, and the purpose for which they are kept is to raise mutton or lamb and improve the land rather than to grow wool.

a small band (though it must be mainly for mutton and lamb): it incurs almost no additional expense, makes use of much that would otherwise be wasted, and helps to improve his fields. Such has long been the economic basis of most of the English flocks, though even among them a steady but slow decline has been going on. As the grain fields become less fertile and farming becomes more diversified, the opportunities for flocks so kept may be greater; but, to find the sheep industry carried on separately and with any independence, we must look elsewhere.

The Far West.

By 1890 the main seat of the wool-growing industry had been transferred to the Far West. The rise of the pursuit in this section had been the most important item of its history in the period preceding that date, and during the years under review this was the only section where the industry showed substantial growth. The progress of events here in this period can be traced in the following table:—

The Number of Sheep in Western States, 1890–1907 (*in hundreds of thousands*).[1]

	1890	1891	1892	1893	1894	1895	1896	1897	1898
No. Rocky Mount'n[2]	34	36	37	44	46	47	52	57	63
So. Rocky Mount'n[2]	83	80	78	72	70	73	70	70	73
Pacific Coast	76	68	72	74	70	64	59	56	57

	1899	1900	1901	1902	1903	1904	1905	1906	1907
No. Rocky Mount'n	75	90	109	121	116	116	120	118	116
So. Rocky Mount'n	80	97	91	85	80	76	78	75	76
Pacific Coast	51	50	43	42	41	41	42	41	41

In the group of Pacific Coast states there was a steady decline in the number of sheep from the first of the period to the last, largely a reflection of the situation in California. The assertion made of the older wool-growing states, that they hold fewer sheep under the high duties of the Dingley tariff than at any time under free wool, may also be made of this group. In the group designated as the Southern Rocky Mountain states the flocks decreased under the McKinley

[1] See note to corresponding table for the rest of the country, page 298.

[2] The Northern Rocky Mountain states include Idaho, Wyoming, and Montana; the Southern Rocky Mountain states, Nevada, Utah, Colorado, Arizona, and New Mexico.

Act, remained about stationary under the régime of free wool, and have made no substantial and permanent gain since.

In the Northern Rocky Mountain states, on the other hand, a rapid advance took place, — an advance so determined that even the terrors of free wool could not check it. In fact, beginning with April 1, 1894, and ending April 1, 1897, there was a gain in the number of sheep in Idaho every year, and in Montana, Arizona, Nevada, Wyoming, and Colorado in every year but one.[1] *All of these states ended the period of combined industrial depression and free wool with more sheep than they had at the beginning* — a fact which cannot but lead one to raise the question how necessary the protective tariff is for the wool-growers of this section.[2] On the reimposition of the duties and the return of prosperity the advance became more rapid, and in Montana, Idaho, and Wyoming attained such a rate of growth that the flocks doubled within the next four years. In 1902, however, the maximum was reached in these northern states and, as the decline had already started to the southward, it became general, though but slight, throughout the Far West.

The chief reason for the stationary or retrograde situation of recent years seems to be the fact that the range, under present conditions, has reached its full capacity. The best information comes from the Report of the Public Lands Commission of 1905.[3] Out of 1400 replies received from stockmen of the region in answer to a series of questions sent out by the Commission, 921 declared that the carrying capacity of the range had decreased as compared with former years, and only 276 gave a contrary answer. In reply to the question what had caused this decrease, by far the greater number said over-stocking.[4] Other reasons given were drought, excessive sheep grazing, methods of handling the range, premature grazing, and settlement. The replies, says the Report, "show very plainly that under present

[1] This assertion is based on the figures of the wool manufacturers' *Bulletin*. According to the estimates of the Department of Agriculture, there was a gain *every* year from January 1, 1894, to January 1, 1898, in Montana, Arizona, Nevada, Wyoming, Colorado, and Idaho. See the *Year Books* of the Department.

[2] Cf. *Bulletin*, vol. xxxi, p. 72.

[3] *Senate Document* No. 189, 58th Congress, 3d Session. This also contains an admirable large map of the whole region which very clearly shows the location, extent, and character of the grazing lands.

[4] *Ibid.*, pp. 6–7, 11.

conditions the greater portion of the public grazing lands are not supporting the number of stock they did formerly. . . . On the whole it seems very evident that the free range system has been a destructive one and that the situation is one that demands grave consideration. Where the carrying capacity is reported increasing, it is mostly due to fencing pastures." [1] The commission, summarizing the situation, says the letters show that "under the present system the pasturing value of the ranges has deteriorated and the carrying capacity of the lands has greatly diminished; that the present condition of affairs is unsatisfactory; that the adoption of a new system of management would insure a better and more permanent use of the grazing lands; that a certain improvement in range conditions has already been brought about by range control on the forest reserves; and that the great bulk of the western stockmen are definitely in favor of government control of the open range." [2] It is thus clear that under existing conditions no appreciable increase is to be expected from the flocks of the Rocky Mountain section — the present centre of the industry.

In all this, the point which it is of the utmost importance to understand is that, with the filling up of the northern tier of states in the Rocky Mountain section, the period when the wool-grower of the country could turn to new and yet unoccupied lands has at last come to an end. Heretofore that possibility has always existed; for the future it is eliminated. By the close of the nineteenth century the sheep had traversed this country from shore to shore, having entered at one time or another almost every nook and corner of its vast area. Some localities afforded congenial surroundings, and there they lingered; others proved hostile, and from these they soon moved on. Looking back over the course of the industry during that century, we see that the regions of growth have always been in the newly settled sections; the current of advance has constantly carried the industry westward. Ever since it arose, such growth as took place came through the opening of new regions, and it has been upon the

[1] *Senate Document* No. 189, 58th Congress, 3d Session, p. 9.

[2] *Report of the Public Land Commission*, 1905, p. xxii. Cf. *Bulletin*, vol. xxxii, pp. 347–353; vol. xxxiii, pp. 397–400. The former says nearly all available land in Texas had been leased or fenced prior to 1900 and so devoted to farms. Very few range sheep remain in the state.

growth from these sections that the country has had to depend to offset the decline (in some cases hastened though not primarily caused by the advance) which was constantly going on in the older sections. The northern group of Rocky Mountain states held the last large area of unoccupied land, and with the filling up of the range in these states — with the end of the westward movement — there disappears from the scene of action a factor which, as will soon appear, has had a greater influence over the course of this industry than any other.[1]

This at once raises the question as to the future of the wool-growing industry in the Far West. The importance of such a question must now be clear. At present that region holds nearly two thirds of the country's sheep. The survey of the situation in the older wool-growing states which were formerly the main seat of the industry indicates that there is little prospect of any very marked change in the East or the Middle West. It has just been pointed out that there are no new regions within the country to which resort can be had. Our study of the past history of this industry and the forces which were then and are now operative in moulding its course would thus lead us to the conclusion that, for so far ahead as we can now see, the main seat of the wool-growing industry will continue to be located in the Far West. Such being the case, it is essential to inquire what are the future prospects in this section.

That the past has seen a great deal of unnecessary waste on the free range is only too true. The methods that have been pursued there afford an admirable illustration of the reckless extravagance and lack of foresight which has characterized so much of the industrial history of this country. Following the policy which for the moment was cheapest has too often proved but a mistaken economy in the long run. Undoubtedly, less wasteful methods would in many cases make possible a considerable increase in the stock-carrying capacity

[1] Were the author writing upon this subject at some more distant time, he would make the date 1900–1902 mark the beginning not only of a new period, but of a great epoch in the history of the industry. The passing epoch covered the nineteenth century, and was dominated by the westward movement. The dawn of the twentieth century will prove, as he believes, to mark the opening of a new era in the whole economic history of the country, as well as in the history of growing wool. But under the existing circumstances it hardly appeared advisable to start on a new period of so brief duration and so void of important events as the few years which have since elapsed.

of the Far West. But this, like most plans for bettering similar situations, will usually involve increased expense in keeping sheep. One reason why the cost has been so low in the past is that no account has been taken of the natural wealth of the range which was being steadily exhausted, and no depreciation fund was set aside. Here, as in so many cases in the history of American agriculture, dividends have been paid out of capital. But as in this instance the capital happened to be the property of the government, it was a long time before any objection was raised. At last, however, the country has wakened to the necessity of looking to the future and of preserving a little of what is left of our rich heritage of natural resources, though the fundamental principle involved in the policy of their conservation—that is, that ordinarily it involves increased cost for the present generation for the benefit of future generations — does not appear to be fully realized.

The policy of establishing forest reserves, one of the first steps in this new movement, has been pushed so rapidly of late that over 100,000,000 acres are now included within their limits. This has considerably reduced the range area, and although, under reasonable regulations, stock is permitted to graze within many of these reserves, the government has recently charged a fee for the privilege, averaging about 8 cents a head for sheep for the summer season, and 14 cents for the year-long season.[1] In more recent years a great many individuals or companies have bought and fenced large tracts, or at least such water rights as secure virtual control over large tracts. While this also involves additional expense, the more far-sighted policy adopted under private ownership secures greater economy in the use of the range. However, it will probably tell more in favor of the cattlemen than the flock-owners. Undoubtedly the carrying capacity of the range can be augmented under careful management. The chief question is whether this management would involve such extra expense as to make competition impossible between this country and newer lands in foreign parts which, perhaps, are being exploited in the same way as the range originally was here.

Another factor tending to decrease the available pasturage is the conversion of the land to cultivation. We have seen that in other sections of the country this has proved to be the most serious obstacle

[1] Cf. *Bulletin*, vol. xxxvii, p. 327.

against which the sheep had to contend. What are the prospects here?

The dominating factor is the water supply. Although the soil is generally fertile, and sometimes exceptionally good, yet the lack of water is in most places an insuperable difficulty. There are, however, a large number of comparatively small strips which it has been found possible to cultivate, and the farming area is gradually being extended. In part this is the result of more scientific methods of cultivation brought about by the admirable work of the Department of Agriculture, the agricultural colleges, and the experiment stations in giving instruction in dry farming or in introducing new plants suited to the arid region.[1] In part it is due to the extension of irrigation. But the amount of grazing land which can be irrigated is comparatively slight. Some estimates have gone as high as 50,000,000 or more acres, but the more trustworthy are much lower. Even the vast projects which the reclamation service has under way or projected, involving the expenditure of millions, are not calculated to irrigate much over 5,000,000 acres.

Frequently, moreover, these cultivated strips prove a boon to the wool-grower, for the crop which they produce enables him to maintain a larger flock. Alfalfa has been found especially valuable for this purpose, growing luxuriantly in this soil and being excellent fodder for sheep. It is said that land irrigated and planted with alfalfa will support ten times as much stock as before.[2]

After all these possible inroads upon the grazing land have been allowed for, there still remains a vast stretch of territory suitable only for stockraising. The extent of such public grazing lands as estimated by the Public Land Commission is over 300,000,000 acres, an area approximately one fifth of the United States. In the words of the Commission, "The great bulk of vacant lands throughout the West are unsuitable for cultivation under the present known conditions of agriculture, and so located that they cannot be reclaimed by irrigation. They are, and probably always must be, of chief value for grazing."[3]

[1] Macaroni wheat, for example, is said to occupy some 10,000,000 acres formerly used for pasturage.

[2] Cf. *Century Magazine*, July, 1906, p. 436.

[3] *Report*, p. xx. Elwood Meade says: "If every drop of water which falls on the

This leads us to a point of the most vital importance when considering the future of the industry. It was not until this far-western region was opened that the wool-grower at last found a place where he could feel fairly secure before the ever advancing march of cultivation, which had driven him nearly across the continent from the Atlantic and later threatened a like attack from the side of the Pacific. Here he first reached soil upon which the cultivator could not venture, — land too arid for farming, yet suitable for sheep. It is here alone, then, if anywhere in this country, that the business of wool-growing as an independent pursuit can have any future.

The bearing of these conclusions upon the question of the relation of the tariff to the future of the industry must now be plain. Since this region, under the conditions which seem likely to prevail in the country, is economically better suited for wool-growing than any other section, it follows from the character of the region and of the pursuit as there carried on that the actual direction which the industry takes in the future will be determined to a greater extent than formerly by the competition it meets with in its own line of production, and less by the competition of general agriculture. Serious domestic competition in its own line of production is highly improbable. We, therefore, conclude that, in the future of the independent wool-growing industry of the United States, the competition of foreigners will play a greater part than ever before. Hence we may infer that in the future the tariff, potentially at least, may be a factor of relatively greater importance in determining the course of the industry than it has been in the past.

There yet remains to be spoken of a tendency which is destined to be of the utmost importance in moulding the future of the industry, one which will doubtless modify the importance of the tariff, the tendency towards mutton. In 1890 it was estimated that fully 50% of the sheep east of the Mississippi river were of mutton breeds.[1] These sheep are best kept in smaller flocks, besides requiring richer pasture and greater care than the ordinary merino — conditions

mountain summits could be utilized it is not likely that more than 10% of the total area of the arid west could be irrigated, and it is certain that because of physical obstacles it will never be possible to get water to even this small percentage" (*Irrigation Institutions*, p. 3).

[1] For figures in 1893 see *Bulletin*, vol. xxv, p. 110.

which that region was well prepared to meet. It was found that, as a part of general farming, a small flock could be kept with very little additional cost, and a good market for the mutton was at hand. Then the raising of spring lambs proved especially profitable, the practice being to buy western ewes in the fall, cross them with a mutton ram, sell the lambs early in the spring, and fatten the ewes for slaughter later. Feeding his grain in this manner has frequently proved the farmer's most profitable way of marketing it. That these advantages are generally recognized is indicated by the fact that now fully 80% of the sheep of that region are of mutton breeds.[1] Thus mutton and lamb, not wool, will probably continue to be the chief object in keeping sheep in that section of the country, for few regions where sheep are kept are so well adapted to the mutton breeds. We have already found that sheep-raising there is but a part of general farming. Now, it seems, wool-growing is but incidental to the raising of lamb and mutton.[2]

Turning to the West, we find that even here wool no longer holds undisputed sway as against mutton. The introduction of mutton rams has proceeded so rapidly that in 1900 it was estimated that 30% of the wool grown in this section came from mutton sheep.[3] This tendency is more general in the northern and central states than in the more barren and dryer districts farther south.[4] The demand from the granger states, to which most of the western sheep are sent to be fattened for market, for "feeders" has much to do with this. With the increasing demand for mutton, the advantages to be gained will certainly lead the sheep-raiser, where possible, to give more of his attention to the meat-producing qualities of his flock, and less to the fleece. In brief, wool-growing as the main object in sheep-

[1] *Census* of 1900, vol. v, p. cciv. These include the French (Rambouillet) merino and delaines — the mutton breeds of the merino race — as well as the English breeds, the most popular of the latter being the Shropshire and Southdown. For a detailed statement of the proportion of each breed in the flocks of Ohio see *Ohio Agricultural Report*, 1902, pp. 30–36.

[2] John E. Russell of Massachusetts says: "I should keep my sheep first for lambs, second for mutton, next for improvement of my pastures and the manure; then if I got anything from the wool so much the better" (*Agriculture of Massachusetts*, 1891, p. 139).

[3] Department of Agriculture, *Report*, No. 66, p. 19.

[4] Cf. Montana Board of Agriculture, Labor and Industry, *Report*, 1900, pp. 262, 594.

raising, having already virtually disappeared from the East, seems destined to play a less and less important part in the West. It therefore appears that the domestic wool supply is likely to depend less on the wool market than on the market for lamb and mutton.[1]

Summary, 1890–1907.

As we look back over this period and view the varied experiences through which the industry passed, the fact which stands out with greatest prominence is that for the first time in the history of wool-growing, we have a period when the industry failed to progress. The retrograde movement which began during the last few years of the preceding period continued into this. Although, by grace of an improvement in the fleece which has now brought the average weight up to nearly seven pounds, the amount of wool grown decreased but slightly, the number of sheep declined to about three quarters of the maximum for the preceding period. Unquestionably the industry lost ground.

What were the chief facts in the case?

For the period as a whole the general level of prices in the world's market was abnormally low. This seems to have been the result of an unusually rapid increase in the world's wool supply during the earlier years, while a falling off in the consumption of wool prevented a more rapid rise when the supply failed to advance. In the United States the situation was aggravated by a severe and long-drawn-out industrial depression, on top of which came the abolition of the protective duty on wool. During the last half of the period, however, under the aid of the restored tariff, rising prices, and a period of extraordinary prosperity, wool quotations regained the level of the latter eighties, though still below that which prevailed during most of the century.

The decline in the number of sheep which took place during these

[1] The number of sheep slaughtered in the five chief western markets and the number received at the four chief eastern markets were as follows, in thousands: —

	1870	1875	1880	1885	1890	1895	1900	1903
East	2771	2289	2489	3284	3274	4224	3074	3252
West	315	270	306	989	1620	3995	5075	6164

The figures for the West cover but two cities in 1870, three in 1875, and four in 1880. Commissioner of Corporations, *Report on the Beef Industry*, p. 8.

events was the resultant of two tendencies, which, for most of the period, were working in opposite directions. The falling off in the East and the Middle West, which began in 1893 and continued throughout the period of free wool, cut down the flocks between one third and one half; nor was there any recovery of the lost ground with the later return of both prosperity and protection. Along the Pacific coast the record is one of almost unvarying decline. The only section of the country to show an advance was the Rocky Mountain region. At first the growth there was slow, but later it increased in speed, finally culminating in 1902. Being largely confined to the northern tier of states, it proved insufficient to counterbalance the heavy decline in the rest of the country.

To what extent was the tariff a factor in determining the course of the industry?

A marked feature of the period in connection with the tariff was the heavy decline in the imports of manufactures of wool. Whereas in all previous history much the greater part of the wool coming into the country to compete with the domestic clip had come in the form of manufactured goods, this was no longer the case after 1894. The manufacturers clearly made great gains and secured a far stronger hold on the domestic market than they had ever had before, partly because of the experience they had acquired during the period of free wool, partly because of the greater protection afforded by the tariff. To infer from this that the domestic wool-grower necessarily gained thereby would, however, be a mistake. The actual outcome was that wool was imported in the raw state instead of in the form of manufactures. Although, during most of the period, the native product held its own in the domestic market against the foreign rival, yet the events of the closing years indicate that the struggle will prove a losing one. In spite of the high tariff the country will have to rely more and more upon foreign lands to supply its need for wool. The chief measure of the benefit which the wool-grower derives from the tariff is the extent to which it raises the price of wool. Here it is unquestionable that the grower does gain, though the way in which the tariff actually operates makes the amount of aid received less than the nominal duty would seem to indicate. In fact, the combination among the wool-growers and manufacturers to support the protective tariff, judged by the results obtained as the tariff actually works out, has proved, generally speaking, to be of much greater advantage to the manufacturer than to the grower.

Even such aid as the growers got does not appear to have been of very fundamental importance in determining the course of the industry during this period. In the East and the Middle West the low level in the world's prices would certainly have brought some decline in the flocks after 1893. Yet there can be no doubt that the greater part of the decrease which took place must be charged to the removal of the duty on wool. It was responsible for the larger part of the drop in price, and aside from all effect upon the market, the action in itself must have discouraged many flock-owners who appear to have been engaged for years in a desperate and losing struggle with fate. The most illuminating fact of all was that, after the high tariff had been restored, while prosperity reigned throughout the land and the price of wool fluctuated above the level of 1890–92, — a time when many of the flocks had actually increased, — there still was no sign of an attempt to fill the thinned ranks. The number of sheep remained substantially unchanged at the level reached under the combined pressure of free wool and hard times. Thus while the free wool tariff must be set down as the more immediate cause of the decline in the flocks of this region, the permanent obstacle to the replacing of the losses was that factor which has been becoming ever more pervasive — the competition of other lines of agriculture. It was the violent shock given by the removal of the protective duty which first awakened many a flock-owner to a full realization of the true state of affairs. He soon saw where his best interests lay, and the flocks which had vanished did not return.

In the Far West the situation was simpler. Along the Pacific coast the steady decline was due to advancing cultivation or diversion of the land to other purposes. The change was largely due to the normal development of that region, and was one in which the tariff had little part. In the Rocky Mountain section the course of the industry was mainly determined by the process of opening the country and stocking the range. This process still continued during the period of hard times and free wool, though at a slower rate. The final filling up of the range by 1902, when the westward movement came to an end, was doubtless somewhat hastened by the high tariff. Where the wool-growing industry was on an independent economic basis and strictly commercial in character, as was the case in this region, the tariff was of greater influence than where it was carried on as a part of general agriculture. But even here its rôle was a minor one. Still it may be said that for the country as a whole the influence of the tariff at this time was rather greater than in most periods.

We conclude as regards this period that, since the decline in the older sections of the country more than counterbalanced the growth that took place in the Rocky Mountain states, and since that decline, though more immediately caused by the free wool tariff, was made permanent by the superior attractiveness of other agricultural pursuits, this last, among all the conflicting factors which shaped the course of the industry, may fairly be chosen as that which dominated.[1]

[1] The passage of a new tariff law and the lapse of something over a year since this manuscript was finished and submitted in the competition for the Wells Prize make it desirable that, as it passes through the press, advantage be taken of the chance to add a note concerning the events of that period. A brief note will suffice, for the whole thing may be summed up in the statement that the situation remains substantially the same as it was during the years 1905–07, described above.

During the years 1908 and 1909 the price of wool maintained the same average as during the three preceding years, 1908 being marked by a decline, which was offset by the rise that followed in 1909. The price of mutton continued at its previous high level. The result has been a slight increase in the number of sheep, the total number, according to the estimates of the manufacturers' *Bulletin*, being 40,311,548 in 1908, and 42,293,205 in 1909; while the production of wool in the country increased in these two years to 298,294,750 pounds and 311,138,321 pounds respectively. This means that so far as the number of sheep and the amount of wool is concerned the United States in 1909 is just where it was in 1902, the industry now having recovered from the slight losses which followed that year. In the rest of the wool-growing world the only important feature is the increase in the Australasian clip, the decline in the flocks during the long series of droughts having been more than replaced. The imports of raw wool into the United States have continued to be as large in amount as during the years 1905–07, the decline to 126,000,000 pounds in 1908 having been offset by the importation of 266,000,000 pounds in 1909, this latter being the largest total on record, except for one of the years under free wool. In the case of the imports of manufactures of wool also there is no change, the figures for the two years 1908 and 1909 being $19,400,000 and $18,100,000 respectively. The course of events generally has only tended to bear out the previous suggestion that the future domestic wool supply was likely to depend less on the wool-market than on the market for lamb and mutton.

On turning to the revision of the tariff under the Act of 1909 we find that the combined power of the manufacturers of wool and the growers of wool proved so strong that the House bill contained but one important modification of the previous law, a slight reduction on the cheaper grades of carpet wool. This was later thrown out, so that the act as finally passed made no alteration in the duties on raw wool as fixed by the Act of 1897. In fact, in the whole schedule relating to wool and woolens the only modifications worthy of mention are a reduction in the duty on wool tops, which had particularly benefited certain manufacturers, and a fractional cut in the rates levied on certain grades of women's dress goods. Under the tariff of 1909, as in other respects, the situation remains unchanged.

CHAPTER IX

GENERAL CONCLUSIONS

THE purpose of this study, as announced at the outset, has been to examine the history of the wool-growing industry in this country, with a view to finding out what influences have shaped its development, and, especially, to what extent it has been affected by the tariff. It was believed that such a study would help us to determine what should be the future policy of the nation towards this industry, and it was hoped that the investigation would throw light on certain aspects of broader problems in the economic history of the United States.

First of all let us briefly summarize the main facts in the history of the industry.[1] Sheep, after a hard struggle on an inhospitable shore, had finally secured a firm foothold before the close of the seventeenth century. Wherever found among the colonists, and they were broadly scattered, they were kept to supply the household with as much wool as was required by the family and no more. The growing of wool was merely a part of the prevailing household economy. For over a century this situation remained unaltered. The number of sheep increased with the increase in population, but the nature of the industry did not change, and its growth was dependent simply on the extent of settlement and the number of the inhabitants. In 1800 the growing of wool in the United States was in character the same household industry that it had been in 1675. Even in later years examples of the industry carried on on the household basis were always to be found, as they are in the upland regions of parts of the South to-day. As the country developed and settlers streamed westward, this household industry was the typical frontier form. But in later years it became steadily less and less important, and by the time general settlement reached the arid section of the Far West it had virtually disappeared.

It was not until the rise of manufacturing outside of the household

[1] Since the chapters have each been summarized, the conclusions here may be stated very briefly and limited to those of the most general character.

that the industry came to be established on a commercial basis. The first quarter of the nineteenth century saw the situation thus revolutionized. The new-born country, having attained its political freedom, was then striving for economic independence. In this struggle the growing of wool began to play its part in the development of a broader national economy. The change of wool-growing from a household industry to one of broader character, though comparatively sudden, did not take place in a moment. It was not until towards the middle of the century that the transformation was fairly general, being finally brought about by the wonderful advance in the methods of transportation. The beginning of the change came through the shutting off of our foreign commerce by legislation and war. Then that part of the population which had previously depended on England for their cloth had to find some other source of supply; and since they were unable to meet these needs themselves, factories rose to satisfy them. With the growing of wool to supply the factories, the industry began to assume a commercial character.

During the years immediately following the War of 1812, the fate of the commercial part of the industry hung very largely upon that of the manufactures of the country, which in turn was strongly affected by the situation in English manufactures. Once the domestic manufactures were fairly established, and an adequate home market obtained and made more secure through protection, the industry made good progress, and during the thirties the sheep flocks reached their maximum growth in the eastern states. At the same time the rapid settlement of the Mississippi valley brought about the gradual extension of the industry to that section, though until 1840 it was essentially local in character. In the first part of the following period the sudden drop in the prices of the chief agricultural products of the Middle West, the only ones extensively raised for the market, led the farmers there to give more attention to sheep, and it was then that they began to send wool to the eastern markets. Another change in relative prices soon reversed the situation, though not until the sheep had increased to such numbers as to make this region the centre of the industry; a result due partly to a decline among the flocks of the East consequent on rising competition from the West or from South America, and partly to the greater attractiveness of other agricultural products.

Then came the Civil War, which introduced new and unfamiliar factors, — the scarcity of cotton, the inflation of the currency, the confusing effects following therefrom, and the mistaken course of action based upon them. For the time being, the normal course of development was completely reversed. But a phenomenal growth in the world's wool supply, together with a senseless rush to increase flocks in the face of an unfavorable turn of affairs, counteracted the expected deficiency, and soon brought on the inevitable and disastrous reaction, with its wasting process of readjustment to more normal conditions. This marked a distinct and separate episode in the industry's history; it had no lasting results except in one section of the country, and it formed no part of the industry's regular course of development.

By the time the effects of this disturbance had passed, the westward movement had stretched across the vast plains to the Pacific coast and Rocky Mountain sections, thus marking the beginning of a new era for the industry. The rapid growth which followed this new step governed the course of events for the time being, and by 1890 had resulted in the transfer of the main seat of the industry to still another region. In part this transfer was caused by the decline in the flocks of the older states, due to the low prices in the world's market consequent on the rapidly increasing supply and to the growing attractiveness of other lines of agriculture. In the closing years of the century the last-named factor reasserted its supremacy, aided by the shock of a period of free wool; and, opportunity for further expansion in the Far West finally coming to an end, our history closes with the industry in a new position, no longer quite able to maintain its ground.

As we look back over this history, that which must impress us most strongly is the great variety of the influences which at one time or another have affected the course of the industry. The same factor has never been the ruling one for any two successive periods. The spread of population, the rise of manufactures, the relative changes in the prices of agricultural products and the competition of other farm pursuits, the abnormal conditions of war with its distorting inflation of the currency, the opening of the Far West, and again the greater relative profits in other lines of agriculture, — each in turn seems for a period to have controlled the situation. The supremacy of each was constantly threatened, and in any case was of but brief duration. And yet we have not mentioned a number of minor forces which also aided, though to a lesser degree, in determining the course of events. The question as to what is the cause of a particular turn of affairs in such an industry is by no means so simple as many try to make out.

But there has been another force, lying so far beneath all those which for the moment seemed to dominate that its significance in the comparatively brief periods of time into which our study has been divided was hardly recognizable. Its far-reaching influence can only be appreciated now that we are able to survey all these periods as a whole. The clue to it is found in the slow, sure march of the centre of the industry. Starting on the Atlantic coast it has steadily moved towards the West. On crossing the Alleghanies and descending to the valley of the Mississippi, it was forced to halt by the abnormal conditions engendered by the Civil War. Once that had passed, the advancing tide of settlement swept the industry on its westward way and eventually placed it among the arid uplands of the Rocky Mountain region. This steady march of the industry across the continent was but a part of that westward movement — the settlement and development of the West — which has shaped the course of American economic history throughout the nineteenth century. If, then, we seek one key to the whole story of this industry, it is here, in the westward movement.

But the mere opening and settlement of the West is not of itself sufficient to explain the outcome. Another fact must be noted to make the explanation complete. "The West" in this country has been synonymous with "the frontier," and when we say that the wool-growing industry kept pace with the westward movement we imply that it has had a close connection with the industrial life of the frontier. This sort of connection, however, is by no means limited to the United States. Our examination of the sources of the world's supply has made it plain that the growing of wool as an independent industry on a commercial basis has steadily gravitated towards the outposts of civilization — it has become more and more a pursuit of the frontier. True, much wool is obtained from some of the most advanced and thickly populated countries; but it is not for the sake of the clip that the sheep are kept, and the constant tendency in these countries is towards a reduction of the flocks. In the most progressive parts of Europe the number of sheep has steadily decreased in the same manner as in the older sections of the United States. As a result the world has come to rely more and more upon the newer and undeveloped regions, such as Argentina, Australasia, Central Asia, and the western part of the United States.

The reason for this frontier character is clear. Among the various uses to which land can be put it is of greater relative importance for most pursuits to be near the centres of population than is the case with wool-growing. The greater demand from these other pursuits for the more favorably situated land thus makes it cheaper for wool-growing to be carried on in the more distant regions; for the greater cost of transportation thus involved is, in the case of wool, a relatively insignificant matter. In earlier times, under household or purely local economy, such a segregation on distant frontier lands was not feasible. This result was only made possible by the improvements in transportation and the expansion of the market which brought about a territorial division of labor more nearly world-wide in its scope. A development of this character was something which the mere settlement of the unoccupied lands of the West could never have accomplished, though it could not well have taken place without such settlement. It happened that, as things actually worked out in the United States, both the westward movement and the general evolution of industry tended to drive sheep-raising to the same location. The frontier and the section economically best fitted for wool-growing under the existing territorial division of labor chanced to coincide.

The significance of the second factor — the general evolution of industry — has been emphasized in the course of the present study because our historians, in their growing recognition of the potency of the West in American history, have almost completely ignored the real importance of this other force. The reason is probably to be found in the fact that the great influence of the West in shaping the course of events is what chiefly distinguishes the history of the United States during the nineteenth century from the history of most of the great civilized nations of Europe. Among the latter it would appear — so far as it is possible to generalize broadly as to the effect of the two factors — that their relative importance was reversed. In Europe the influence of the newly developing lands was great, but that of the general evolution of industry was greater. In American history, the fundamental importance of the latter must not be overlooked, though the former may be considered the more important. Working together as they did, they cannot well be separated. If one seeks to know what were the most deep-seated, far-reaching, and fundamental forces at work determining the course of the wool-growing industry of the United States, they are to be found in these two movements.

Having thus drawn our conclusions as to the factors which were most active in determining the course of the wool-growing industry in this country, we may next turn to the point which has received special attention in our study and inquire to what extent the tariff controlled the development of the industry.

We have already made much progress towards a conclusion on this point by excluding the tariff from the list of influences which, during any one period, could be considered to have dominated the situation. There was not a single one of the periods into which the history of the industry has been divided when we did not find some one influence, or possibly some half-dozen, more potent than the tariff. At best the tariff was of minor importance. But if not at any time the controlling force, how far did its power extend?

The period after the War of 1812, when the manufacturing industry was struggling so desperately to make secure the slight foothold it had gained, was the time when the aid of the tariff was most needed, and when the situation was such that its influence might have proved the greatest. It is true that the imports of raw wool during those years were insignificant; but the exclusion of manufactures by the tariff meant a distinct stimulus to that part of the wool-growing industry which was then on a commercial basis, — a stimulus coming at a crucial period in its development. Doubtless the duties were of some aid. But the peculiar situation of English manufactures at this period, and the consequent repeated sale of English goods on the American market at ruinous prices, nullified in great measure the gain which might otherwise have been secured. In the decade following 1830 the absence of these disturbing elements gave the tariff a more favorable chance for action. But at best it was a minor factor in the final outcome.

From 1840 till the Civil War it was still less important — less, indeed, than during any other period in the course of the century. The expansion which at that time took place was due to the opening of a vast area of free land where sheep-raising could be carried on at a minimum expense, and to an unfavorable turn in the market for the other chief products of the same region. But as soon as the railroads, with the aid of the canals, gave better access to the rising European market for agricultural produce, it again became more profitable to raise wheat, corn, pork, and beef, for which the section was so admirably adapted. In the Southern Hemisphere, in the meantime, rivals were fast appearing that were destined to become the most severe competitors of American wool-growers.

During the Civil War decade the tariff was of some prominence, not so much because of what it accomplished directly as for the hopes it aroused and the indirect results which followed. On the other hand, its influence was weakened by the unusual number of new elements which complicated the situation. In the succeeding period it was of less importance, the main growth of the industry being due to the final step in the westward movement. That this movement was at best only hastened by the tariff was made sufficiently plain during the period of free wool. The subsequent decline in the older states during the last period, though more immediately due to the shock of free wool, became permanent through other forces, and it was made clear that, where the growing of wool was incidental to general farming, the tariff was reduced to a very negligible quantity.

In short, the most that can be said for the tariff is that, by raising the price of wool above that in the world's market, it has somewhat increased the number of sheep in the country, chiefly since the war and during the time after the rise of the industry in the Far West, where the basis was independent of general farming. But though the tariff has meant a greater number of sheep than would otherwise be kept, our study points to the conclusion that the increase thus brought about is but a relatively small proportion of the total. The assertion, frequently met, that the very existence of the sheep industry of the country depends on the duties finds no substantiation in the facts of history.

As for the future, there seems at least a chance that the tariff may play a more prominent part than heretofore. Present tendencies point to a decline in sheep-raising as an independent industry mainly for wool. Mutton will increasingly become of first importance, and wool secondary. In the East, where sheep promise to be incidental to general farming, and wool subordinate to mutton, the basis of the industry will be such that the tariff on wool can be of but comparatively slight moment. In the West, which offers far larger possibilities and a more independent basis, the competition of the foreign grower is likely to become more serious, and there, in the main seat of the industry, protection can do much more for the wool-grower. Still, in that section also, just so far as mutton becomes the main object in place of wool, to that extent the weight of this foreign rivalry will be lessened, the security of the industry strengthened, and the influence of the tariff diminished.[1]

It must now be plain that the grossest exaggeration has characterized general discussion and reasoning in regard to the connection between the tariff and the wool-growing industry. Indeed, one of the most valuable conclusions to be reached by a study of this chapter of our economic history is that the tendency to overestimate the power of the tariff, either for good or for evil, is almost universal. For this tendency the almost perpetual presence of the tariff in the political arena is, no doubt, mainly responsible. In discussions upon the subject an attempt is invariably made to simplify the situation by leaving out of consideration the numerous other factors, and then applying the argument *post hoc, propter hoc.* This method is employed on both sides of the question: free traders and protectionists alike are guilty. It must be admitted that the wool-growing industry is unusually complicated, and that the neglect of other factors is in this case peculiarly misleading. But there is no lesson that can be applied to the tariff which would be productive of more good than the one to be drawn from the situation here exemplified. The importance of the tariff as a factor in the industrial history of the country has too long been grossly magnified.

From the conclusion that the power of the tariff to affect the course of the wool-growing industry has in the past proved very

[1] This tendency, combined with the very conceivable advent of a time when the country imported mutton extensively, might eventually lead to a situation where a higher duty on mutton (it is two cents a pound under the Act of 1897) became as important for the domestic wool-grower as the duty on wool.

slight, it does not necessarily follow that such power as it has should not be exercised. Whether the maintenance of the industry in this country is worth the cost involved is a question upon which we do not here attempt to pass judgment. The advisability of the adoption of free trade or protection involves broad problems of economic principle and public policy such as would carry us rather beyond the subject in hand.[1] But assuming that the policy to be followed is determined, that it is deemed best to maintain the wool-growing industry and to protect it against foreign competition, let us see what light a study of the history of the industry throws upon the methods to be adopted and the line of action to be followed in order to secure the end desired.

To reach this end, two things are essential. First there must be a thorough understanding of all the forces which exert an influence on the industry; secondly, there must be sufficient power in the duties to counterbalance the rivalry, of whatever sort, which all the other forces may develop. This being the case, a bare outline of the situation that would confront us may be suggested.

As the newer lands of the world are opened and developed and transportation facilities are improved, the territorial division of labor will become more nearly world-wide, especially among industries largely dependent upon natural resources. In the United States the situation is such as to render any marked advance in the wool-growing industry improbable,[2] and a gradual decline likely. Experience indicates that the power to prevent this is not to be found in the present tariff. If the industry is to be maintained in a position of the same relative importance as formerly, a higher tariff will be necessary. A tariff which simply offsets such advantages as the foreign wool-grower may have in relatively cheaper cost of production is not sufficient. The foreign fleece is by no means the only rival of the American: equally serious competitors are found at home, in the greater relative profits of other lines of agriculture. The very advantages and great natural resources of the country thus become an obstacle. Therefore, if the lands of the wool-grower prove to be par-

[1] For the best statement of this problem from the point of view of a protectionist see Lewis, *Our Sheep and the Tariff*.

[2] Unless it be through the slow process of increasing the weight of the fleece, which, so long as the sheep exist, will take place anyway.

ticularly well adapted for something else, and it is still deemed best that his sheep be not abandoned, he must have a duty such as will make wool at least as profitable as that other product for which his land is so well adapted. The greater the superiority of the land, — the better fitted it becomes for other things, — the heavier must be the duty. To some this may appear to make the cost of protection high, but as the history of the old wool-growing centres shows, it is a cost which the adoption of this policy involves. It does not necessarily condemn the policy: it is simply one of the things to be weighed in the balance against such advantages as the maintenance of the industry may secure to the country.

Even then there still remain the many forms of competition which, through the process of substitution, lessen the consumption of wool. There the difficulty which confronts us when we try to understand all the forces in operation is made plain. The higher the tariff raises the price of wool the greater will be the extent to which other fibres are substituted for it. Against such rivalry the tariff is impotent.

In drawing this study to a close it seems worth while to mention one or two matters suggested by the history of wool-growing which are of a more general character.

The course of the wool industry brings out a characteristic of many agricultural pursuits, one of considerable importance in understanding the economic forces that govern them. Wool is the economist's classic example of a by-product.[1] He who picks up a text-book on the subject will learn that the grower has to consider the price of the other products of the sheep in order to determine the price at which he can sell his wool or whether he can keep sheep at all. In many cases, however, the raising of sheep is itself a by-product of general farming. Here there at once arises before us a most intricate mass of interdependent factors, all of which should be taken into account by the farmer in determining the size of his flock. His calculation must include the cost and the selling price not only of wool, lamb, and mutton, but also of wheat, corn, beef, pork, butter, cheese, and various other farm products. In consequence, the factors which may determine the course of an agricultural pursuit are greatly mul-

[1] The term joint-product might also be used here. The line between the two is not easily drawn.

tiplied. Though not without influence under a single-crop system, this applies more particularly to general farming, and the increasing introduction of intensive cultivation with rotation of crops renders the situation more complex than ever. The fact that under a system of general agriculture so many crops are largely in the nature of by-products is one of the chief elements in this complexity. The fact that most agricultural land can be used for a variety of purposes is another. The fact that agricultural pursuits, as at present carried on, involve as a rule an investment of specialized capital so small that a change can be made from one product to another with little or no loss, is still another. The result is a large increase in the number of factors which may enter into the question of the profitableness of any particular product, and a greater instability of any one agricultural crop. In studying the economic history of any product of agriculture one must constantly bear in mind the special complexity of the problem and the peculiar basis of the industry.

This point, moreover, is closely related to the final one, to which, as we venture once more to insist, too much attention cannot be given. If there is one truth brought out by this analysis of the history of wool-growing and its connection with the tariff which is of broader application and more fundamental importance than any other, it is that most economic problems are complex. And if there is one evil which more than any other warps the judgment of the mass of people in regard to such problems it is the constant ignoring of this complexity. There is always a tendency to pick out one factor: to put the finger on this and say that it is the sole cause or the only element which enters into the question. The wish thus to reduce a problem to one or two terms is natural, but the complex questions arising in the intricate interdependent mechanism of modern industrial organization do not permit of any such easy method of solution. It leads inevitably to failure. Once this fact is recognized, the first and most essential step towards a final and satisfactory solution of these difficult problems will have been taken.

APPENDIX

BIBLIOGRAPHY

NOTE. — The best source of information in the nature of a detailed narrative account of the history of wool-growing in the United States is the *Special Report on the Sheep Industry*, 1892, edited by Salmon. A government publication of some thousand pages, it contains an enormous mass of material, especially on the history of the industry in the East. It is poorly digested and written and of little value except as a source for the narrative. As to these facts, so far as it has been possible to determine, it is reliable. Ford's *Wool and Manufactures of Wool*, 1894, also a government publication, is a very complete compilation of statistics relating to sheep, wool, the tariff, and imports, and includes much data for foreign countries as well. Taussig's *Tariff History of the United States* is the authority on the various tariffs. The text of all the tariffs can be found in *Tariff Laws, 1789–1897*, a government document compiled by R. G. Proctor. The best general account of the history of the woolen manufacture in this country is by S. N. D. North in the *Bulletin of the National Association of Wool Manufacturers*, vols. xxix–xxxiii. This same *Bulletin*, started in 1869, contains a mass of valuable material especially in connection with tariff legislation, and the *Annual Wool Review* issued in recent years is the most satisfactory summary of American conditions. The best reports on the London wool market are those of Helmuth Schwartze & Co. The Congressional tariff hearings contain a mass of evidence on the question of the relation of the tariff to wool-growing and manufacture. The files of the agricultural papers are hardly as serviceable for the purposes of a study of broad character as one might expect. They have been chiefly utilized for the earlier years, when other sources of information were not available. Nor have the agricultural reports of the different states proved as valuable for one approaching it from this point of view. Had there been a chance to give more attention to the general agricultural situation they would have been employed more extensively. W. D. Lewis' *Our Sheep and the Tariff* is the most serious existing study of the same subject. It is comparative rather than historical in character, laying special emphasis on the relative costs in different countries, and written from the standpoint of a protectionist.

The following titles cover most of those consulted: —

American Agriculturist. New York, 1847–96.
American Husbandry. London, 1775.

American Sheep Breeder. Chicago, 1881–.
Andrews. *Report on the Trade and Commerce of the British North American Colonies and the Great Lakes.* Washington, 1853.
Bagnall. *History of the Textile Industry in the United States.* Cambridge, 1893.
Bailey. *Cyclopedia of American Agriculture.* New York, 1907–09.
Baines. *History of the Cotton Manufacture.* London [1835].
Bard. *A Guide for Young Shepherds.* New York, 1811.
Barton. *Sketch of the Commerce of the Great Lakes.* Buffalo, 1847.
Batchelder. *Introduction and Early Progress of the Cotton Manufacture in the United States.* Boston, 1863.
Benton and Barry. *A Statistical View of the Number of Sheep and an Account of the Principal Woolen Manufactories.* Cambridge, 1837.
Bischoff. *History of the British Woolen Manufacture.* London, 1842.
Bishop. *History of American Manufactures.* Philadelphia, 1864.
Blodget. *Economica.* Washington, 1806.
Bolles. *Industrial History of the United States.* Norwich, 1878.
Boston Board of Trade Reports. Boston, 1855–.
British State Papers, Calendar of, Colonial and West Indies. London, 1860–.
British Board of Trade, Charts for the St. Louis Exposition. London, 1903.
Brothers. *Wool and Woolen Manufactures of Great Britain.* London, 1859.
Bruce. *Economic History of Virginia in the Seventeenth Century.* New York, 1896.
Burnley. *History of Wool and Wool-combing.* London, 1889.
Callender. *Early Transportation and Banking Enterprises. Quarterly Journal of Economics*, vol. xvii. Boston, 1903.
Chicago Board of Trade Reports. Chicago, 1857–.
Commissioner of Corporations. *Report on the Beef Industry.* Washington, 1905.
Country Gentleman. Albany, 1853–.
Coxe. *A View of the United States of America.* Philadelphia, 1794.
Coxe. *Arts and Manufactures of the United States*, 1810. Philadelphia, 1813.
Connecticut, Public Records of the Colony of. Hartford, 1850–90.
Dodge. *Sheep and Wool, Department of Agriculture Report*, No. 66. Washington, 1900.
Dzialas. *Entwickelung der Schafhaltung.* Stargard i. Pomm., 1898.
Economist. London, 1843–.
Eggleston. *Agriculture of the Colonies. Century Magazine*, 1884. New York, 1884.
Ellison. *Cotton Trade of Great Britain.* London, 1886.
Evans. *Exports and Imports.* Washington, 1884.
Fite. *Agricultural Development of the West during the Civil War. Quarterly Journal of Economics*, vol. xx. Boston, 1906.
Ford. *Wool and Manufactures of Wool.* Washington, 1894.

Gallatin. *Report, American State Papers, Finance*, vol. v. Washington, 1859.
Genesee Farmer, Rochester, 1848–64.
Gibson. *History and Present State of the Sheep Breeding Industry in Argentine Republic*. Buenos Aires, 1893.
Gordon. *Report on the Live Stock Industry. Census*, 1880, vol. iii. Washington, 1883.
Graham. *Statistics of the Woolen Manufactories in the United States*. New York, 1845.
Gregg. *Commerce of the Prairies*. New York, 1845.
Hall. *Statistics of the West*, 1836. Cincinnati, 1836.
Hammond. *Cotton Industry*. New York, 1897.
Hayes. *Memoirs Relating to the Wool Industry*. Boston, 1872.
Hazard. *United States Commercial and Statistical Register*. Philadelphia, 1840–42.
Helmuth Schwartze & Co. *Annual Wool Reviews* and *Circulars*. London, 1869–.
Hibbard. *History of Agriculture in Dane County, Wisconsin*. Madison, 1904.
Hildreth. *Pioneer History of the Ohio Valley and North West Territory*. Cincinnati, 1848.
House of Commons, Report on Wholesale and Retail Prices. London, 1903.
House of Lords, Report on the Wool Trade, 1828. London, 1828.
Howells. *Recollections of Life in Ohio*, 1813–40. Cincinnati, 1895.
Hunt's Merchants' Magazine. New York, 1839–70.
Illinois State Historical Society Publications, No. 9. Springfield, 1904.
Iowa Historical and Comparative Census. Des Moines, 1883.
Industrial Commission, Report of the. Washington, 1900–02.
James. *History of the Worsted Manufacture in Great Britain*. London, 1857.
Johnson. *Wonder-Working Providence of Sion's Savior in New England*. Edited by W. F. Poole. Andover, 1867.
Journal of the Royal Statistical Society, vols. i, xxii–xxiv, xxxiii, lxv. London, 1839–.
Kalm. *Travels in North America*. London, 1770.
Killebrew. *Sheep Husbandry*. Nashville, 1880.
Lee. *Exposition of the Evidence*. Boston, 1832.
Lewis. *Our Sheep and the Tariff*. Philadelphia, 1890.
Livingston. *Essay on Sheep*. New York, 1809.
Lord. *Industrial Experiments in Colonial America*. Baltimore, 1898.
Massachusetts Agricultural Repository and Journal. Vols. iii–x. [Boston], 1813–32.
Massachusetts Agricultural Societies, Transactions. Boston, 1845–.
Massachusetts, Agriculture of. Boston, 1837–.
Massachusetts Bay in New England. Records of Governor and Colony. Boston, 1853.

Massachusetts Bureau of Labor, Report, 1885. Boston, 1885.
Massachusetts State Census. Boston, 1838–.
Mead. *Irrigation Institutions*. New York, 1903.
Mendelson. *Die Volkswirtschaftliche Bedeutung der deutschen Schafhaltung um die Wende des neunzehnten Jahrhunderts*. Jena, 1904.
Michaux. *Travels to the Westward of the Alleghany Mountains*. London, 1805.
Michigan Board of Agriculture, Reports. Lansing, 1863–.
Minnesota Bureau of Labor Report, 1895–96. St. Paul, 1896.
Mitchell. *History of the Greenbacks*. Chicago, 1903.
Mitchell. *Gold Prices and Wages under the Greenback Standard*. Berkeley, 1908.
Morrell. *The American Shepherd*. New York, 1845.
Montana Board of Agriculture, Labor, and Industry, Reports. Helena, 1893–.
Mudge. *Report on Wool and Manufactures of Wool*. Washington, 1887.
National Association of Wool Manufacturers, Bulletin. Boston, 1869–.
National Association of Wool Manufacturers, Transactions, 1865–6. Boston, 1867.
New England Farmer. Boston, 1849–63.
New York Agricultural Society, Transactions. Albany, 1842–.
New York Chamber of Commerce Reports. New York, 1859–.
New York, Documents Relating to the Colonial History of; Callahan ed. Albany, 1858.
New York Produce Exchange Reports. New York, 1873–.
New York, Society for Promoting Useful Arts in the State of, Transactions. 1794–1819.
New York State Census. Albany, 1826–.
Niles' Register. Baltimore, 1812–49.
Nimmo. *Report on the Range and Ranch Cattle Business*. Washington, 1885.
North. *History of the New England Woolen Manufacture*, in Davis, *New England States*, vol. i. Boston, 1897.
North. *The Wool Book*, 1895. Boston, 1895.
Ohio Archæological and Historical Publications. Columbus, 1893–.
Ohio State Board of Agriculture, Reports. Columbus, 1847–.
Peck. *Guide for Emigrants*. Boston, 1831.
Pitkin. *Statistical View of the United States*. New Haven, 1835.
Prairie Farmer. Chicago, 1841–.
Proceedings of Meeting of Wool-growers of Woodstock, Vermont, 1826.
Proctor. *Tariff Laws*, 1789–1897. Washington, 1897.
Quandt. *Die Niederlausitzer Schafwollindustrie*. Leipzig, 1895.
Randall. *The Sheep Husbandry in the United States*. New York, 1881.
Randall. *The Fine Wool Sheep Husbandry*. New York, 1863.
Ringwalt. *Development of Transportation Systems in the United States*. Philadelphia, 1888.

Rushworth. *The Sheep*. Buffalo, 1899.

Salmon. *Special Report on the History and Present Condition of the Sheep Industry in the United States*. Washington, 1892.

Shaw. *Sheep Husbandry in Minnesota*. St. Paul, 1901.

Semple. *American History and its Geographic Conditions*. Boston, 1903.

Senkel. *Wollproduktion und Wollhandel im xix. Jahrhundert*. Tubingen, 1901.

Seybert. *Statistical Annals*. Philadelphia, 1818.

Sheffield. *Observations on the Commerce of the American States*. London, 1784.

Southey. *The Rise, Progress and Present State of Colonial Sheep and Wools*. London, 1851.

Stanwood. *American Tariff Controversies*. Boston, 1903.

Stanwood. *History of the New England Cotton Manufacture*, in Davis, *New England States*, vol. i. Boston, 1897.

Sterns. *The Foreign Commerce of the United States*, 1820–1840. *Journal of Political Economy*, vol. viii. Chicago, 1900.

Stewart. *The Domestic Sheep*. Chicago, 1900.

Swift. *History of Middlebury and Addison Co., Vermont*. Middlebury, 1859.

Switzer. *Report on Internal Commerce of the United States*, 1887, Pt. 2. Washington, 1888.

Taft. *Some Notes on the Introduction of the Woolen Manufacture into the United States*. Providence, 1882.

Taussig. *Tariff History of the United States*. New York, 1898.

Taussig. *The Duties on Wool and Woolens, Quarterly Journal of Economics*, vol. viii. Boston, 1894.

Taylor. *Agricultural Economics*. New York, 1905.

Tooke. *History of Prices*. London, 1838–57.

United States Census Reports. Washington, 1791–.

United States Census, Digest of Accounts of Manufacturing Establishments. Washington, 1823.

United States Commerce and Navigation Reports. Washington, 1822–.

United States Consular Reports. Washington, 1880–.

United States Special Consular Report, No. 55, *Australian Sheep and Wool*. Washington, 1892.

United States Department of Agriculture, Reports. Washington, 1890–.

United States Department of Agriculture, Year-Books. Washington, 1895–.

United States Commissioner of Agriculture, Reports, Washington, 1863–89.

United States Patent Office, Reports on Agriculture. Washington, 1839–62.

United States Commission on the Public Lands. Washington, 1905.

United States Finance Reports, 1845, 1863. Washington, 1851, 1863.

United States Special Commissioner of the Revenue, Reports. Washington, 1867–70.

United States Report on Wholesale Prices, Wages, and Transportation. Washington, 1893.

United States Congressional Annals, Register of Debates, Globe, and Record. Washington, 1825–.

United States Forty-First Congress, 1 ses. *House Rept.* No. 72. Washington, 1869.

United States Forty-Ninth Congress, 1 ses. *Senate Ex. Doc.* No. 72. Washington, 1886.

United States Fifty-Third Congress, 2 ses. *Senate Miscel. Doc.* No. 124. Washington, 1895.

United States Fifty-Fifth Congress, 1 ses. *Senate Miscel. Doc.* No. 15. Washington, 1897.

Ure. *Philosophy of Manufactures.* London, 1861.

Vickerman. *Woolen Spinning.* London, 1894.

Wallace. *Rural Economy and Agriculture of Australia and New Zealand.* London, 1891.

Watson. *History of Agricultural Societies on the Modern Berkshire System.* Albany, 1820.

Weeden. *Economic and Social History of New England.* Boston, 1890.

Wells. *Recent Financial, Industrial and Commercial Experiences of the United States.* New York, 1872.

Wells. *Wool and the Tariff.* New York, 1873.

White. *Memoir of Samuel Slater.* Philadelphia, 1836.

Youatt. *Sheep.* New York, 1848.

STATISTICAL TABLES

TABLE I

Number of Sheep and Amount of Wool Produced in the United States, 1840–1907.

THE number of sheep is based on the Census figures 1840–1860, on the estimates of the Department of Agriculture 1867–1893, and on the figures of the wool manufacturers' *Bulletin* since then. The first column of figures for the wool clip, believed to be the more accurate, is based on my own estimates for the years previous to 1862, the figures of Tichenor and Tingle (see *ante*, p. 176) 1862–1867, the figures of Lynch and Truitt 1868–1891, and the manufacturers' *Bulletin* since then. The second column gives the estimates of the Department of Agriculture. Since 1895 the Department has accepted the estimates of the *Bulletin*.

(*The figures are to the nearest thousand.*)

	NUMBER OF SHEEP	POUNDS OF WOOL PRODUCED	
		TRADE FIGURES	DEPT. OF AGRICULTURE FIGURES
1840	19,311	45,000	35,802
1850	21,723	60,000	52,517
1860	22,471	80,000	60,265
1861		92,000	
1862		106,000	
1863		123,000	
1864		142,000	123,000
1865		155,000	142,000
1866		160,000	155,000
1867	39,385	168,000	160,000
1868	38,992	177,000	168,000
1869	37,724	162,250	180,000
1870	40,853	163,000	162,000
1871	31,851	146,000	160,000
1872	31,679	160,000	150,000
1873	33,002	174,700	158,000
1874	33,938	178,000	170,000
1875	33,784	193,000	181,000

	NUMBER OF SHEEP	POUNDS OF WOOL PRODUCED	
		TRADE FIGURES	DEPT. OF AGRICULTURE FIGURES
1876	35,935	198,250	192,000
1877	35,804	208,250	200,000
1878	35,740	211,000	208,250
1879	38,124	232,500	211,000
1880	40,766	264,000	232,500
1881	43,577	290,000	240,000
1882	45,016	300,000	272,000
1883	49,237	320,400	290,000
1884	50,627	337,500	300,000
1885	50,360	329,600	308,000
1886	48,322	323,031	302,000
1887	44,759	302,170	285,000
1888	43,545	301,876	269,000
1889	42,599	295,779	265,000
1890	44,336	309,475	276,000
1891	43,431	307,102	285,000
1892	44,938	333,018	294,000
1893	47,274	348,538	303,153
1894	43,502	325,211	298,057
1895	39,949	294,297	309,748
1896	36,464	272,475	
1897	34,784	259,153	
1898	35,672	266,721	
1899	36,905	272,191	
1900	40,268	288,637	
1901	41,921	302,502	
1902	42,184	316,341	
1903	39,284	287,450	
1904	38,342	291,783	
1905	38,621	295,488	
1906	38,541	298,915	
1907	38,865	298,295	

TABLE II

Number of Sheep in the United States, by States, 1840–1900.

Census returns. In 1850 and 1900 lambs were specifically excluded, at other Censuses probably a few lambs were included in the returns. For 1860 the figures do not include 1,505,810 sheep not in the Census returns but estimated as unenumerated, since there are no such estimates for 1840, 1850, and 1870. The figures for 1880 and 1890 include the estimated number of range sheep reported separately. For discussion of the Census figures see *Census* of 1900, vol. v, p. ccxiii.

(*The figures are to the nearest thousand.*)

	1840	1850	1860	1870	1880	1890	1900
Maine	649	452	452	435	566	370	252
New Hampshire	617	385	311	249	212	132	65
Vermont	1,682	1,014	752	580	439	334	182
Massachusetts	378	189	115	79	68	51	34
Rhode Island	90	44	33	24	17	11	7
Connecticut	403	174	117	84	59	38	23
Total New England States	3,820	2,258	1,780	1,450	1,326	937	563
New York	5,119	3,453	2,618	2,182	1,715	1,529	939
New Jersey	219	160	135	120	117	55	26
Pennsylvania	1,768	1,822	1,632	1,794	1,777	1,612	959
Delaware	39	28	19	23	22	12	7
Maryland	258	178	156	130	171	132	112
Dist. of Columbia	1			1			
Total Middle Atlantic States	7,404	5,642	4,559	4,249	3,802	3,341	2,043
Virginia	1,294	1,310	1,043	370	497	495	392
North Carolina	538	595	547	463	462	402	209
South Carolina	233	286	234	125	119	79	52
Georgia	267	560	513	419	528	440	259
Florida	7	23	30	27	57	98	103
Alabama	163	372	370	242	348	386	229
Mississippi	128	305	353	233	288	452	236
Louisiana	98	110	181	119	136	186	169
Texas		105	753	714	3,652	4,264	1,440
Arkansas	42	91	203	161	247	244	169
Tennessee	742	812	773	827	673	541	308
West Virginia				552	675	785	573
Kentucky	1,008	1,102	939	937	1,000	937	716
Total Southern States	4,521	5,667	5,939	5,189	8,679	9,311	4,855
Ohio	2,028	3,943	3,547	4,929	4,902	4,061	2,648
Indiana	676	1,122	991	1,613	1,101	1,081	1,011
Illinois	396	894	769	1,568	1,037	923	629
Wisconsin	3	125	332	1,069	1,337	985	986
Michigan	100	746	1,273	1,986	2,189	2,400	1,626
Total North Central States	3,203	6,831	6,912	11,165	10,566	9,450	6,900

	1840	1850	1860	1870	1880	1890	1900
Minnesota			13	132	268	399	359
Iowa	15	150	259	855	455	547	658
Missouri	348	763	937	1,352	1,411	951	664
Oklahoma and Indian Ter.					55	17	61
Kansas			18	109	630	401	180
Nebraska			2	23	247	209	336
Dakota and North Dakota				2	85	136	450
South Dakota						239	507
Total Central West	363	913	1,230	2,474	3,152	2,899	3,216
Montana				2	279	2,353	4,215
Idaho				1	117	358	1,965
Wyoming				6	450	713	3,327
Colorado				121	1,091	897	1,353
Utah		3	37	60	523	1,937	2,553
Nevada				11	231	273	568
New Mexico		377	830	619	3,939	2,474	3,334
Arizona				1	467	515	668
California		18	1,088	2,768	5,727	3,373	1,725
Oregon		15	86	318	1,368	1,780	1,961
Washington			10	44	389	265	558
Total Far Western States		414	2,052	3,952	14,282	14,939	22,229
Total United States	19,311	21,723	22,471	28,478	42,192	40,876	39,853

TABLE III

World's Wool Supply (Wool in the Grease), 1850–1907.

(In millions of pounds.)

From Helmuth Schwartze & Co., Wool Circulars. Cf. note to similar table, *ante*, p. 253. The figures for North America have been left as in the original table.

	PRODUCTION OF			IMPORTS FROM				
	UNITED KINGDOM	CONTINENT	NORTH AMERICA	AUSTRALASIA	CAPE	RIVER PLATE	OTHERS	TOTAL
1850	130	470	90	39	6	19	36	790
1860	140	500	110	60	26	43	76	955
1861	140	500	110	70	27	62	78	987
1862	140	500	110	72	26	69	80	997
1863	145	500	110	77	32	89	93	1046
1864	145	500	110	99	38	100	101	1093
1865	150	500	125	110	33	137	86	1141
1866	150	500	149	115	38	166	109	1227
1867	157	500	172	135	39	182	89	1272

	PRODUCTION OF			IMPORTS FROM				
	UNITED KINGDOM	CONTI-NENT	NORTH AMERICA	AUSTRA-LASIA	CAPE	RIVER PLATE	OTHERS	TOTAL
1868	166	495	189	156	39	211	93	1349
1869	156	490	174	158	42	218	84	1322
1870	150	485	176	175	43	197	69	1295
1871	145	480	159	183	52	211	116	1346
1872	156	475	173	185	58	224	132	1403
1873	165	470	188	192	49	248	113	1425
1874	167	465	191	229	49	225	105	1431
1875	162	460	206	248	51	220	116	1463
1876	156	455	211	267	46	239	108	1482
1877	152	455	221	284	46	248	103	1509
1878	152	450	224	278	45	245	122	1516
1879	153	450	246	288	51	226	108	1522
1880	149	450	277	308	60	256	133	1633
1881	139	450	303	332	53	254	96	1627
1882	129	450	313	357	57	296	109	1711
1883	128	450	333	366	52	302	96	1727
1884	132	450	350	408	52	322	106	1820
1885	136	450	343	385	50	356	110	1830
1886	136	450	335	429	66	348	147	1911
1887	134	450	315	418	69	292	163	1841
1888	134	450	315	471	87	329	161	1947
1889	133	450	309	478	93	375	184	2022
1890	138	450	322	511	91	272	160	1944
1891	148	450	320	592	102	330	179	2121
1892	153	450	346	644	88	369	175	2225
1893	151	450	361	632	91	360	164	2209
1894	142	450	338	659	73	376	174	2212
1895	135	450	307	730	84	439	197	2342
1896	136	450	285	646	96	464	186	2263
1897	139	450	272	660	83	496	204	2304
1898	139	450	280	608	90	513	181	2267
1899	140	450	285	593	92	520	181	2261
1900	141	450	301	514	46	398	175	2025
1901	138	450	316	600	73	532	143	2252
1902	136	450	329	579	83	493	170	2240
1903	133	450	300	512	80	517	203	2195
1904	132	450	305	513	70	444	215	2129
1905	131	450	309	597	78	456	228	2249
1906	130	450	312	638	81	438	263	2312
1907	131	450	311	787	108	460	251	2498

TABLE IV

Imports of Wool and Manufactures of Wool, 1822–1907.[1]

(In thousands.)

YEAR	IMPORTS OF WOOL.		IMPORTS OF MANUFACTURES
	pounds	value	value
1822	1,715	387	11,752
1823	1,673	340	7,953
1824	1,300	355	8,124
1825	2,147	569	12,017
1826	2,638	449	8,657
1827	3,331	408	8,866
1828	2,453	491	8,842
1829	1,494	239	7,193
1830	669	96	5,900
1831	5,622	1,288	13,197
1832	4,042	698	10,440
1833	950	240	13,713
1834	591	317	7,444
1835	7,290	1,088	19,151
1836	12,687	1,270	24,637
1837	10,407	893	10,410
1838	6,968	532	13,130
1839	7,925	699	21,024
1840	9,898	846	10,808
1841	15,006	1,091	12,943
1842	11,420	797	9,689
1843[2]	3,612	262	2,971
1844	14,077	872	11,751
1845	23,896	1,708	13,578
1846	16,630	1,154	12,778
1847	8,488	562	13,664
1848	11,400	864	18,405
1849	17,869	1,177	16,779
1850	18,695	1,690	19,620
1851	32,007	3,847	22,358
1852	18,343	1,931	20,611

[1] For the years 1825–28 and 1858–61 the quantity of wool imported is based on estimates. The figures for 1855–68 and 1872 include a small estimated amount of wool imported on the pelt.

[2] Nine months only.

YEAR	IMPORTS OF WOOL		IMPORTS OF MANUFACTURES
	pounds	value	value
1853	21,616	2,678	31,819
1854	20,228	2,834	37,904
1855	18,918	2,164	27,754
1856	16,835	2,191	35,582
1857	18,463	2,613	35,289
1858	29,937	4,354	29,534
1859	33,201	5,117	37,295
1860	26,282	5,336	43,141
1861	32,057	5,119	30,430
1862	44,031	7,219	15,639
1863	75,121	12,716	21,524
1864	91,250	16,262	33,349
1865	44,420	7,947	21,929
1866	71,277	10,837	58,719
1867	38,158	6,246	46,502
1868	25,467	4,030	32,489
1869	39,275	5,600	34,628
1870	49,230	6,743	34,490
1871	68,058	9,780	43,839
1872	126,507	27,206	52,408
1873	85,496	20,433	51,075
1874	42,939	8,250	46,883
1875	54,901	11,071	44,609
1876	44,642	8,247	33,209
1877	42,171	7,156	25,701
1878	48,449	8,363	25,230
1879	39,005	5,034	24,355
1880	128,131	23,727	33,911
1881	55,964	9,703	31,156
1882	67,861	11,096	37,361
1883	70,575	10,949	44,274
1884	78,350	12,384	41,157
1885	70,596	8,879	35,776
1886	129,084	16,746	41,421
1887	114,038	16,424	44,902
1888	113,558	15,887	47,719
1889	126,487	17,974	52,564
1890	105,431	15,264	56,582
1891	129,303	18,231	41,060
1892	148,670	19,688	35,565
1893	172,433	21,064	38,048
1894	55,152	6,107	19,439

YEAR	IMPORTS OF WOOL		IMPORTS OF MANUFACTURES
	pounds	value	value
1895	206,033	25,556	38,539
1896	230,911	32,451	53,494
1897	350,852	53,243	49,162
1898	132,795	16,783	14,823
1899	76,736	8,322	13,832
1900	155,928	20,260	16,164
1901	103,583	12,529	14,585
1902	166,576	17,711	17,384
1903	177,137	22,152	19,546
1904	173,742	24,813	17,733
1905	249,135	46,225	17,893
1906	201,688	39,068	23,080
1907	203,847	41,534	22,321

TABLE V

Imports of Raw Wool by Classes, 1867–1907.

Imports for Consumption (in thousands of pounds).

Note. — It should be borne in mind that the imports for consumption, representing the amount imported for immediate consumption and that withdrawn from warehouses, is not the same as the total general imports. This explains the discrepancy which frequently appears to exist between the sets of figures found in different places. Statistics for total general imports showing the division by classes are not given in the Statistics of Commerce and Navigation for the years preceding 1884. After that the total for each class is given, but not the subdivisions under each, these being obtainable only in the tables showing imports for consumption. Consequently the practice usually followed by the Government and others using these statistics, and the one, therefore, which has been followed in this study, is to use the imports for consumption when dealing with imports by classes or their subdivisions and general imports when dealing with total imports.

YEAR	CLASS I	CLASS II	CLASS III
1867	1,270	150	36,263
1868	4,551	1,931	18,096
1869	2,512	4,533	27,650
1870	6,530	2,752	29,351

YEAR	CLASS I	CLASS II	CLASS III
1871	5,960	17,665	26,550
1872	16,871	41,155	36,289
1873	6,029	49,540	28,642
1874	2,398	27,087	27,308
1875	13,117	7,769	30,799
1876	8,643	3,149	28,465
1877	9,294	2,509	28,310
1878	9,916	3,028	26,856
1879	5,229	1,709	33,163
1880	26,785	13,266	59,320
1881	20,609	4,421	42,385
1882	13,489	2,318	47,208
1883	11,546	1,373	40,130
1884	20,703	4,474	62,525
1885	13,472	3,891	50,782
1886	23,321	4,872	79,716
1887	23,195	9,703	81,504
1888	16,952	5,568	74,710
1889	22,973	6,651	96,556
1890	21,387	7,662	80,851
1891	26,520	6,973	85,895
1892	38,641	5,421	90,560
1893	35,403	7,035	133,197
1894	7,860	1,334	36,530
1895	106,516	14,722	144,488
1896	117,533	12,992	98,121
1897	200,485	37,949	110,814
1898	18,122	3,865	48,345
1899	9,583	2,160	65,644
1900	19,369	9,910	98,970
1901	35,806	7,334	81,722
1902	55,203	6,745	98,487
1903	46,667	13,738	119,245
1904	39,927	13,659	108,133
1905	76,769	21,922	112,595
1906	93,488	16,387	109,619
1907	91,504	12,077	92,453

TABLE VI

Average Annual Imports of Wool and Manufactures of Wool under each Tariff Act, 1821–1907.[1]

YEAR	WOOL		MANUFACTURES OF WOOL
	pounds	average value	value
1821–24	1,563,071[2]	$0.23	$8,767,417
1825–28	2,642,752	.18	9,595,877
1829–32	2,957,530	.18	9,183,124
1835–41	10,026,343	.09	16,014,052
1844–46	18,133,812	.06	12,703,059
1848–57	19,437,763	.11	26,612,642
1858–60	29,807,197	.17	36,657,412
1862–64	69,800,978	.17	23,514,616
1865–67	51,288,915	.16	42,384,064
1868–83	61,792,356	.18	38,931,772
1884–90	101,639,993	.14	45,732,135
1891–93	150,136,046	.15	38,224,825
1895–97	262,598,798	.14	47,398,961
1900–07	178,855,189	.16	18,588,774

TABLE VII

The Tariff Duties on Wool, 1789–1907.

DATE OF ACT OF CONGRESS	DATE OF TARIFF	RATES OF DUTY
July 4, 1789	July 4, 1789	Free
Apr. 27, 1816	July 1, 1816	15% ad valorem
May 22, 1824	July 1, 1824	Value not exceeding 10 cents a pound, 15% Value exceeding 10 cents a pound, 20%; after June 1, 1825, 25%; after June 1, 1826, 30%
May 19, 1828	July 1, 1828	4 cents a pound and 40%; the ad valorem rate to be 45% from July 1, 1829, and 50% from July 1, 1830

[1] The averages do not invariably include *all* years under each tariff. The years omitted were marked by abnormal features caused by a change in the tariff.

[2] The figures for raw wool cover 1822–24 only.

DATE OF ACT OF CONGRESS	DATE OF TARIFF	RATES OF DUTY
July 14, 1832	Mar. 3, 1833	Value not over 8 cents a pound, free Value over 8 cents a pound, 4 cents a pound and 40% ad valorem
Mar. 2, 1833	Jan. 1, 1834	Duties of the preceding act in excess of 20% to have one tenth of such excess taken off every two years till Jan. 1, 1842, when one half the residue to be deducted, and the remaining half after June 30, 1842
Aug. 30, 1842	Aug. 30, 1842	Value not over 7 cents a pound, 5% Value over 7 cents a pound, 3 cents a pound and 30%
July 30, 1846	Dec. 1, 1846	30% ad valorem
Mar. 3, 1857	July 1, 1857	Value not over 20 cents a pound, free Value over 20 cents a pound, 24%
Mar. 2, 1861	Apr. 1, 1861	Value less than 18 cents a pound, 5% Value 18 cents and not over 24 cents a pound, 3 cents a pound Value over 24 cents a pound, 9 cents a pound
June 30, 1864	July 1, 1864	Value 12 cents or less a pound, 3 cents a pound Value over 12 cents a pound and not over 24 cents, 6 cents a pound Value over 24 cents a pound and not over 32 cents, 10 cents a pound and 10% ad val. Value over 32 cents a pound, 12 cents a pound and 10% ad valorem
Mar. 2, 1867	Mar. 2, 1867	Class I, clothing wool Value 32 cents a pound or less, 10 cents a pound and 11% ad valorem Value over 32 cents a pound, 12 cents a pound and 10% ad valorem Washed wool, twice the regular duty Class II, combing wool Value 32 cents a pound or less, 10 cents a pound and 11% ad valorem Value over 32 cents a pound, 12 cents a pound and 10% ad valorem Class III, carpet wool Value 12 cents a pound or less, 3 cents a pound Value over 12 cents a pound, 6 cents a pound All classes, scoured wool, treble the regular duty

DATE OF ACT OF CONGRESS	DATE OF TARIFF	RATES OF DUTY
June 6, 1872	Aug. 1, 1872	All duties reduced 10%
Mar. 3, 1875	Mar. 3, 1875	Duties of Act of Mar. 2, 1867 restored
Mar. 3, 1883	July 1, 1883	Class I, clothing wool Value 30 cents a pound or less, 10 cents a pound Value over 30 cents a pound, 12 cents a pound Washed wool, double the regular duty Class II, combing wool Value 30 cents a pound or less, 10 cents a pound Value over 30 cents a pound, 12 cents a pound Class III, carpet wool Value 12 cents a pound or less, 2½ cents a pound Value over 12 cents a pound, 5 cents a pound All classes, scoured wool, treble the regular duty
Oct. 1, 1890	Oct. 6, 1890	Class I, clothing wool 11 cents a pound If washed, double the regular duty Class II, combing wool 12 cents a pound Class III, carpet wool Value 13 cents a pound or less, 32% Value over 13 cents a pound, 50% All classes, scoured wool, treble the regular duty
Aug. 1, 1894	Aug. 28, 1894	Free
July 24, 1897	July 24, 1897	Class I, clothing wool 11 cents a pound If washed, double the regular duty Class II, combing wool 12 cents a pound Class III, carpet wool Value 12 cents a pound or less, 4 cents a pound Value over 12 cents a pound, 7 cts. a pound All classes, scoured wool, treble the regular duty

TABLE VIII

Prices of Fleece Wool.

Prices of Fine, Medium, and Coarse Washed Clothing Ohio Fleece Wool in the Eastern Markets at the Beginning of January, April, July, and October, from 1824 *to* 1907.

(Figures of Mauger & Avery, New York.)

YEAR	JANUARY			APRIL			JULY			OCTOBER		
	Fine	Medium	Coarse	Fine	Medium	Coarse	Fine	Medium	Coarse	Fine	Medium	Coarse
	cents	cents	cents	cents	cents	cents	cents	cents	cents	cents	cents	cents
1824	68	53	40	70	46	31	55	40	30	60	40	30
1825	60	43	32	60	42	33	50	41	32	50	42	36
1826	55	43	38	52	46	41	37	30	26	43	37	32
1827	36	32	28	45	34	30	37	31	25	43	32	25
1828	42	30	25	44	36	28	48	38	33	48	40	32
1829	54	45	35	45	35	32	46	36	32	37	30	27
1830	40	35	30	50	38	32	60	50	40	70	60	48
1831	70	60	48	70	60	50	75	65	50	70	60	50
1832	65	55	44	60	52	42	50	42	30	50	40	30
1833	55	41	33	63	53	38	61	54	40	65	55	45
1834	70	60	48	67	56	44	60	50	40	62	50	40
1835	63	50	40	65	60	45	63	56	42	65	60	45
1836	65	60	45	68	62	47	70	60	50	70	60	50
1837	72	63	48	68	56	46	52	52	36	49	40	31
1838	50	42	35	50	42	35	46	36	30	56	48	37
1839	56	48	38	56	48	38	57	48	40	60	55	44
1840	50	45	38	49	43	36	45	39	33	46	38	33
1841	52	45	35	53	46	37	50	44	34	48	42	33
1842	48	42	35	46	40	32	43	37	30	38	31	25
1843	35	30	25	33	28	25	35	30	26	36	32	26
1844	37	30	26	43	36	30	45	37	32	50	40	33
1845	47	40	31	45	38	32	40	36	30	38	35	28
1846	40	35	30	38	33	28	38	32	27	36	30	22
1847	45	40	30	47	40	31	46	40	31	47	40	30
1848	45	38	30	43	37	30	38	32	28	33	30	24
1849	33	30	23	40	36	30	40	35	28	42	36	30
1850	47	40	33	45	37	30	45	37	30	46	40	35
1851	46	40	33	50	44	36	47	42	37	45	40	35
1852	43	38	34	42	36	33	45	38	33	50	42	37
1853	58	56	50	62	56	50	60	53	48	55	50	48
1854	53	47	42	57	52	46	45	37	30	42	36	30

YEAR	JANUARY			APRIL			JULY			OCTOBER		
	Fine	Medium	Coarse	Fine	Medium	Coarse	Fine	Medium	Coarse	Fine	Medium	Coarse
	cents	cents	cents	cents	cents	cents	cents	cents	cents	cents	cents	cents
1855	40	35	32	43	35	32	50	40	33	52	41	36
1856	50	38	35	57	45	38	55	42	36	60	55	45
1857	58	50	42	60	56	45	56	50	40	38	30	25
1858	40	33	27	42	35	30	43	37	30	56	41	36
1859	60	52	45	60	46	37	56	40	35	60	50	42
1860	60	50	42	52	45	40	55	50	40	50	45	40
1861	45	40	37	45	37	32	38	30	22	47	48	50
1862	48	50	50	46	45	43	48	47	45	60	60	63
1863	75	68	70	80	85	80	75	70	65	85	80	76
1864	80	78	76	78	77	72	100	100	90	103	95	100
1865	102	100	96	80	80	75	75	73	65	75	75	65
1866	70	65	50	65	60	48	70	67	60	63	60	56
1867	68	53	50	60	55	50	55	49	45	48	46	40
1868	48	43	38	50	48	45	46	45	43	48	48	45
1869	50	50	48	50	50	48	48	48	47	48	48	46
1870	48	46	44	48	47	46	46	45	43	48	48	44
1871	47	46	43	50	52	47	62	60	55	63	62	58
1872	70	72	66	80	80	76	72	70	65	66	60	57
1873	70	68	65	56	53	48	50	48	44	54	53	47
1874	58	54	47	56	56	47	53	53	46	54	54	47
1875	55	56	47	54	52	46	52	49	46	48	50	42
1876	48	52	42	46	49	40	38	35	31	45	40	33
1877	46	43	36	45	40	33	50	44	37	48	44	36
1878	44	45	38	40	43	35	36	36	32	35	37	32
1879	34	35	32	34	34	31	37	38	34	41	43	38
1880	50	55	48	55	60	52	46	48	42	46	48	42
1881	47	49	43	40	44	37	42	44	36	43	46	36
1882	44	46	37	42	45	34	42	45	34	42	45	34
1883	40	43	33	44	44	37	39	41	33	39	40	34
1884	40	40	34	38	38	34	35	34	30	35	34	30
1885	34	33	29	32	32	28	32	31	28	33	35	32
1886	35	36	32	33	34	30	33	33	29	35	38	34
1887	33	38	34	33	37	33	34	37	34	32	36	34
1888	31	35	33	31	34	33	29	33	31	31	34	31
1889	34	38	33	33	37	31	35	39	32	33	37	31
1890	33	37	29	32	36	29	33	37	29	33	37	31
1891	33	37	31	32	37	31	31	35	29	31	35	30
1892	30	35	31	29	34	31	28	34	30	29	33	29
1893	29	33	29	30	32	31	24	26	25	23	24	21
1894	23	24	21	21	23	20	20	21	18	19	21	19

YEAR	JANUARY			APRIL			JULY			OCTOBER		
	Fine	Medium	Coarse	Fine	Medium	Coarse	Fine	Medium	Coarse	Fine	Medium	Coarse
	cents	cents	cents	cents	cents	cents	cents	cents	cents	cents	cents	cents
1895	17½	20	19	16½	20	18	18	21	19	18	21	19
1896	19	21½	19	19	21	18	17	18	17	18	19	18
1897	19	21	19	21	22½	20	21½	23½	21	27	29	25
1898	29	30	26	29	29½	25½	28	29	24½	28½	30	24½
1899	26½	29	24	25½	28	24	29	31½	27	31	33½	29
1900	35	36½	31½	32¼	35½	30½	28½	31½	27½	26½	28½	26½
1901	27	29	26	25	27	24½	25	26	22	25	26½	23
1902	25½	26½	24	25	26½	24	26	26¾	25	28	28½	25½
1903	30	31	27	29½	30½	26	31½	31½	27	32	31½	28
1904	33½	32½	29½	33½	32½	29½	32½	32½	30½	32½	33½	31½
1905	34	35	36	34	36	36	36	39	36	35	35	34
1906	34	38	36	34	38	36	33	37	36	34	38	33
1907	34	39	36	34	38	36	34	36	35	35	38	34

Prices of Same, 1862–1878, reduced to a Gold Basis.

	cents	cents	cents	cents	cents	cents	cents	cents	cents	cents	cents	cents
1862	47	49	49	45	44	42	42	41	39	47	47	49
1863	52	47	48	53	56	53	57	54	50	58	54	51
1864	51	50	49	45	45	42	39	39	35	50	46	48
1865	47	46	44	54	54	51	53	51	46	52	52	47
1866	50	41	36	51	47	36	46	44	40	42	40	38
1867	50	39	37	44	40	36	39	35	32	33	32	27
1868	34	31	27	36	34	32	32	31	30	34	34	32
1869	36	36	35	37	37	36	35	35	34	36	36	35
1870	39	37	36	42	41	40	39	38	36	42	42	39
1871	42	41	38	45	47	42	55	53	48	55	54	51
1872	64	66	60	72	72	68	62	61	56	58	52	50
1873	62	60	57	47	44	40	43	41	38	49	48	43
1874	52	48	42	49	49	41	48	48	41	49	49	42
1875	48	49	41	47	45	40	45	42	40	41	42	35
1876	42	46	37	40	43	35	33	31	27	41	36	30
1877	43	40	33	42	37	31	49	41	34	46	42	35
1878	43	44	37	39	42	34	35	35	31	34	36	31

TABLE IX

Prices of English Wools, 1790–1901.

Lincoln is typical of the English long wool and Southdown of short wool. Based upon tables in the *Journal of the Royal Statistical Society*, vol. i, pp. 56–57; vol. xxxiii, pp. 514–521; vol. lxv, p. 504; and North's *Wool Book*, 1895, pp. 63, 67. It has been impossible to find any one table covering the whole period. After 1811 prices are for Lincoln half hog, and after 1837 for Down ewe and wether.

YEAR	SOUTHDOWN	LINCOLN	YEAR	SOUTHDOWN	LINCOLN
	pence	pence		pence	pence
1790	16	8	1821	16	14
1791	17½	8½	1822	18	12
1792	24	10	1823	18	11¼
1793	14½	7	1824	18	12
1794	16¼	7¾	1825	12	17½
1795	19½	8	1826	12	13
1796	19½	8½	1827	10	11½
1797	18	9	1828	9	11
1798	18½	7¾	1829	8	10
1799	24	9	1830	12	9
1800	21½	9½	1831	14	12
1801	21½	12½	1832	12	13
1802	23½	12	1833	16	14
1803	22½	12	1834	19	15½
1804	24	13½	1835	18	15½
1805	31½	14¼	1836	20¼	16
1806	25½	13½	1837	16	13½
1807	24	9½	1838		14
1808	25	9½	1839		17
1809	36	13½	1840	15¼	14
1810	25	13½	1841	13½	12½
1811	25	11½	1842	12	11
1812	26	12½	1843	11¼	10
1813	28	14	1844	12¾	16
1814	30	19	1845	13½	13
1815	22	22	1846	13	13
1816	22	16	1847	12½	12
1817	24	15	1848	11½	11
1818	24½	22	1849	11	10
1819	18	16½	1850	11¾	11
1820	18	16½	1851	12½	12½

YEAR	SOUTHDOWN	LINCOLN	YEAR	SOUTHDOWN	LINCOLN
	pence	pence		pence	pence
1852	12	13⅝	1877	17	16¼
1853	15¼	16	1878	15¼	15
1854	17¼	15½	1879	12	12½
1855	12¾	13	1880	15	15⅛
1856	15	16	1881	14	12⅜
1857	18½	20½	1882	15	11¼
1858	14½	15⅝	1883	12⅜	10
1859	18¼	18⅝	1884	11¾	10
1860	18½	20⅓	1885	10⅝	9⅞
1861	18¼	19½	1886	11	10
1862	17	20½	1887	11½	10½
1863	20	22⅝	1888	10¾	10⅜
1864	21¾	27⅜	1889	11⅜	11
1865	23¼	25¾	1890	12	11
1866	21½	23½	1891	11¾	9¾
1867	17	18⅞	1892	11½	8¾
1868	14	17½	1893	11¼	10¼
1869	14¼	18⅙	1894	10⅞	10⅛
1870	13½	16¾	1895	10½	12
1871	17¾	21⅜	1896	10¼	11½
1872	21½	25⅝	1897	9⅝	9⅝
1873	18½	24½	1898	9	8¾
1874	17¼	20¾	1899	9⅜	8¼
1875	18¼	19¾	1900	10	7⅞
1876	16	17¾	1901	8¼	6⅞

TABLE X

Prices of Colonial and River Plate Wool in the London Market, 1860–1902.

(*Wholesale and Retail Prices.* Report to the House of Commons, 1903, pp. 52–56.)

YEAR	PORT PHILLIP Good average		AUSTRALIAN CROSS-BRED Greasy average	CAPE FLEECE Eastern average	RIVER PLATE, BUENOS AYRES Greasy average	EAST INDIA, CANDAHAR Best white
	Greasy	Scoured				
	pence	pence	pence	pence	pence	pence
1860	15.			18.5	9.5	14.
1861	13.			16.0	8.0	14.0
1862	14.			17.0	8.2	15.0
1863	14.			17.5	8.0	16.0
1864	13.			16.0	7.2	16.0
1865	15.			17.0	8.0	15.2
1866	13.			16.0	7.5	14.5
1867	11.			12.5	6.2	12.5
1868	11.			13.0	6 0	11.7
1869	10.			10.5	5.5	11.0
1870	9.5			11.0	5.2	11.5
1871	14.0			17.0	8.2	17.7
1872	15.4	27.7		17.5	8.7	18.5
1873	15.2	26.7		15.5	7.4	16.5
1874	14.6	26.2		16.1	7.5	14.7
1875	13.5	24.7		15.1	7.9	14.2
1876	12.5	22.8	11.6	13.0	6.7	12.7
1877	12.1	22.1	10.5	12.2	6.4	11.3
1878	11.9	21.9	10.2	11.5	6.2	10.5
1879	11.7	21.1	10.0	11.1	6.4	10.6
1880	13.8	24.2	12.4	12.6	7.6	13.4
1881	11.9	22.2	10.5	11.4	7.0	11.7
1882	12.5	22.7	9.7	11.6	6.7	11.9
1883	12.3	22.1	8.9	11.2	6.7	11.2
1884	11.6	21.2	9.6	10.4	6.2	9.9
1885	10.0	18.7	9.6	8.9	5.1	9.0
1886	9.8	18.0	9.2	8.9	5.3	9.9
1887	10.1	18.1	9.8	8.9	5.6	9.7
1888	10.3	18.4	9.4	8.6	5.6	9.2

YEAR	PORT PHILLIP Good average		AUSTRALIAN CROSS-BRED Greasy average	CAPE FLEECE Eastern average	RIVER PLATE, BUENOS AYRES Greasy average	EAST INDIA, CANDAHAR Best white
	Greasy	Scoured				
	pence	pence	pence	pence	pence	pence
1889	11.5	20.3	10.3	10.1	6.2	9.0
1890	10.6	18.8	10.1	9.5	6.0	9.4
1891	9.8	18.0	10.1	8.7	5.4	8.5
1892	8.5	15.4	9.0	7.7	4.8	8.1
1893	8.6	15.7	9.6	7.7	4.7	7.9
1894	8.0	14.7	9.0	7.3	4.2	7.6
1895	8.5	14.8	8.9	7.0	4.1	7.7
1896	9.4	16.2	9.0	7.5	4.5	8.0
1897	9.2	15.4	8.6	7.1	4.3	8.1
1898	9.7	17.2	7.6	8.1	4.9	7.1
1899	12.4	22.2	8.5	11.0	6.9	6.9
1900	11.6	20.8	8.4	9.7	5.3	8.1
1901	9.6	17.2	5.9	7.0	4.6	7.7
1902	11.5	19.7	6.3	8.3	5.2	7.9

TABLE XI

Relative Average Annual Prices of Agricultural Products in the New York Market, 1825–1860.

Calculated from Tables of Prices in the Report of the Secretary of the Treasury for 1863.

(100=average price, 1825–1860.)

100=	BEEF $9.74 @ bbl.	BUTTER 16.05¢ @ lb.	PORK $14.62 @ bbl.	CORN 70.93 @ bu.	WHEAT $1.3175 @ bu.	COMMON WOOL 30.59¢ @ lb.	MERINO WOOL 43.13¢ @ lb.
1825	90	95	94	78	68	110	133
1826	94	105	78	109	71	98	115
1827	93	106	89	86	75	82	90
1828	94	60	92	74	93	82	86
1829	95	86	86	80	94	70	80
1830	92	84	90	79	81	72	91
1831	87	87	95	98	90	90	124

100 =	BEEF $9.74 @ bbl.	BUTTER 16.05¢ @ lb.	PORK $14.62 @ bbl.	CORN 70.93 @ bu.	WHEAT $1.3175 @ bu.	COMMON WOOL 30.59¢ @ lb.	MERINO WOOL 43.13¢ @ lb.
1832	97	97	92	96	96	90	110
1833	96	98	100	104	91	103	114
1834	94	89	94	93	80	99	113
1835	103	109	112	128	93	110	125
1836	114	122	154	134	135	140	136
1837	139	113	144	147	135	142	132
1838	151	125	146	119	146	100	89
1839	152	119	132	122	94	126	120
1840	134	109	101	80	80	91	91
1841	92	75	76	88	90	88	103
1842	76	73	58	84	86	63	74
1843	74	54	68	78	75	67	71
1844	58	63	63	71	74	98	84
1845	85	84	85	77	79	88	81
1846	77	81	74	96	82	77	75
1847	117	100	98	121	104	84	82
1848	101	100	76	90	88	85	80
1849	120	94	74	89	95	96	84
1850	93	95	73	88	97	103	93
1851	91	89	96	87	82	116	99
1852	110	120	118	95	84	105	92
1853	96	113	110	100	106	134	114
1854	112	122	94	121	166	106	98
1855	118	137	110	140	185	97	86
1856	97	135	127	99	133	109	104
1857	127	134	150	114	127	120	114
1858	108	116	116	114	101	98	90
1859	78	119	112	122	109	124	114
1860	53	105	123	104	113	120	114

INDEX

INDEX

QUARTERLY PRICES, OHIO FINE AND COARSE W

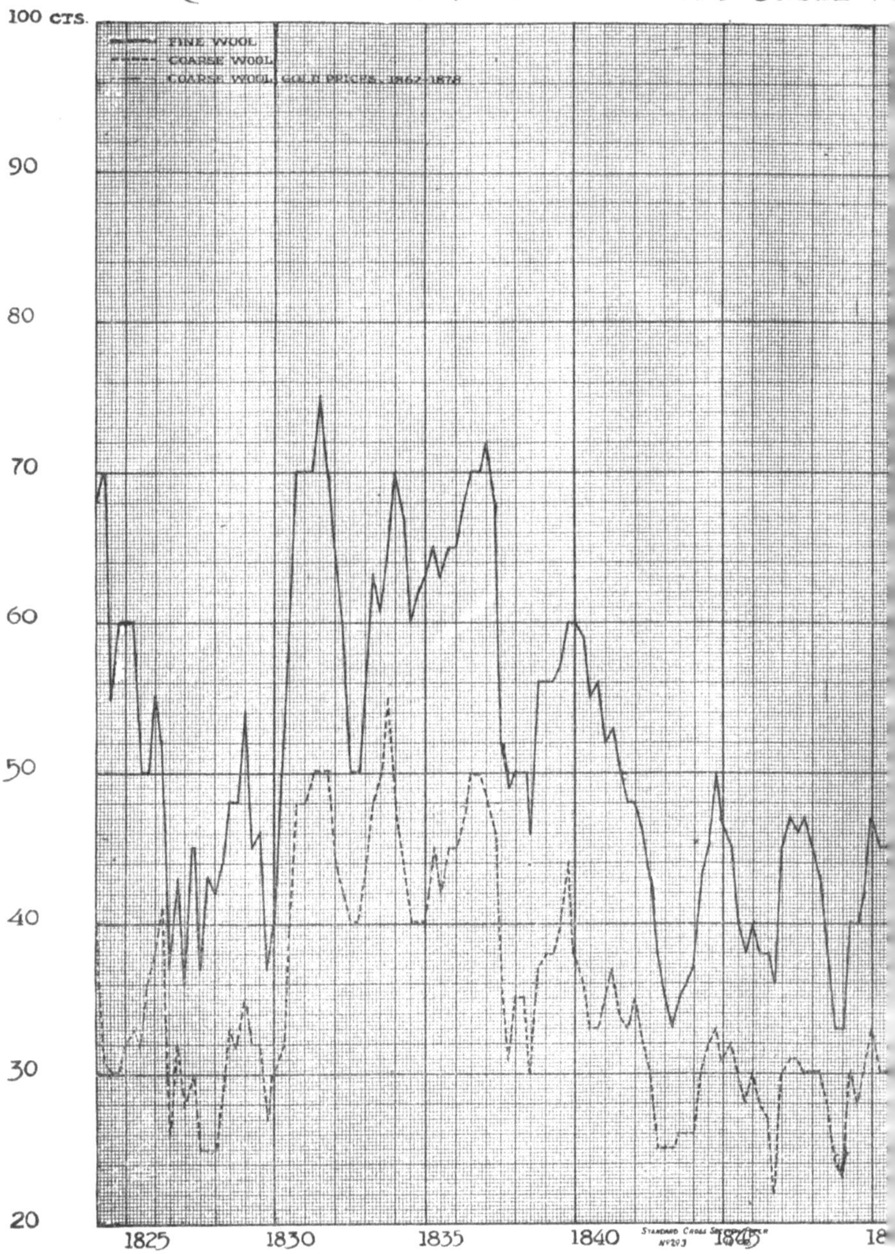

Note the general downward tendency in prices for the period as a whole, also the
the Civil War, as well as the drop in prices following the admission of wool free of
the early thirties, the extremely low prices during the early forties, and the recovery

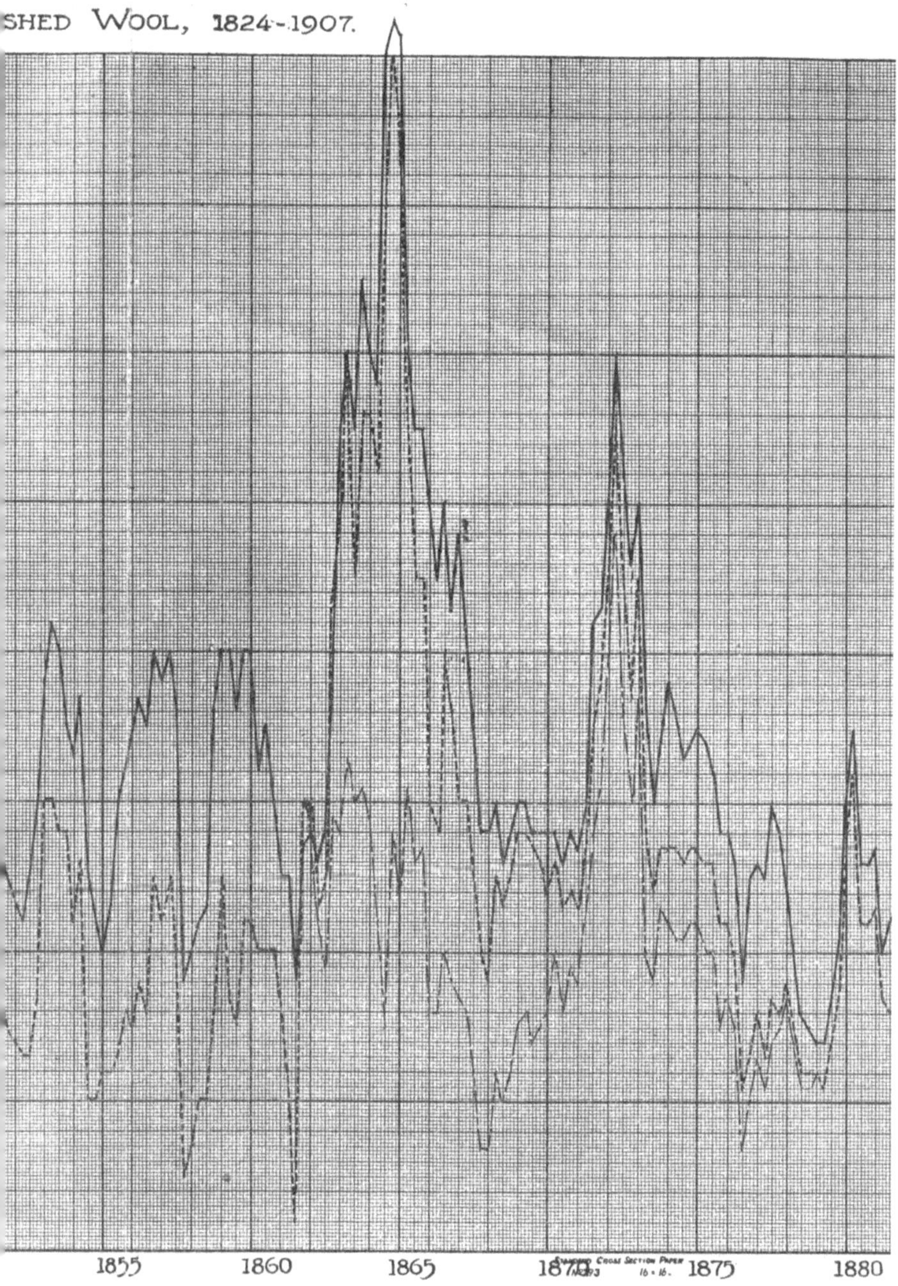

CHART I

QUARTERLY PRICES OF OHIO FINE AND COARSE WASHED WOOL, 1824–1907

ady decrease in the difference in price between the two grades of wool. The chart also makes ve
y under the Wilson tariff of 1894. From the chart, too, one gets the best idea of the importanc
r 1850, or such features as the phenomenal advances in 1872 and 1880, and the new low level of

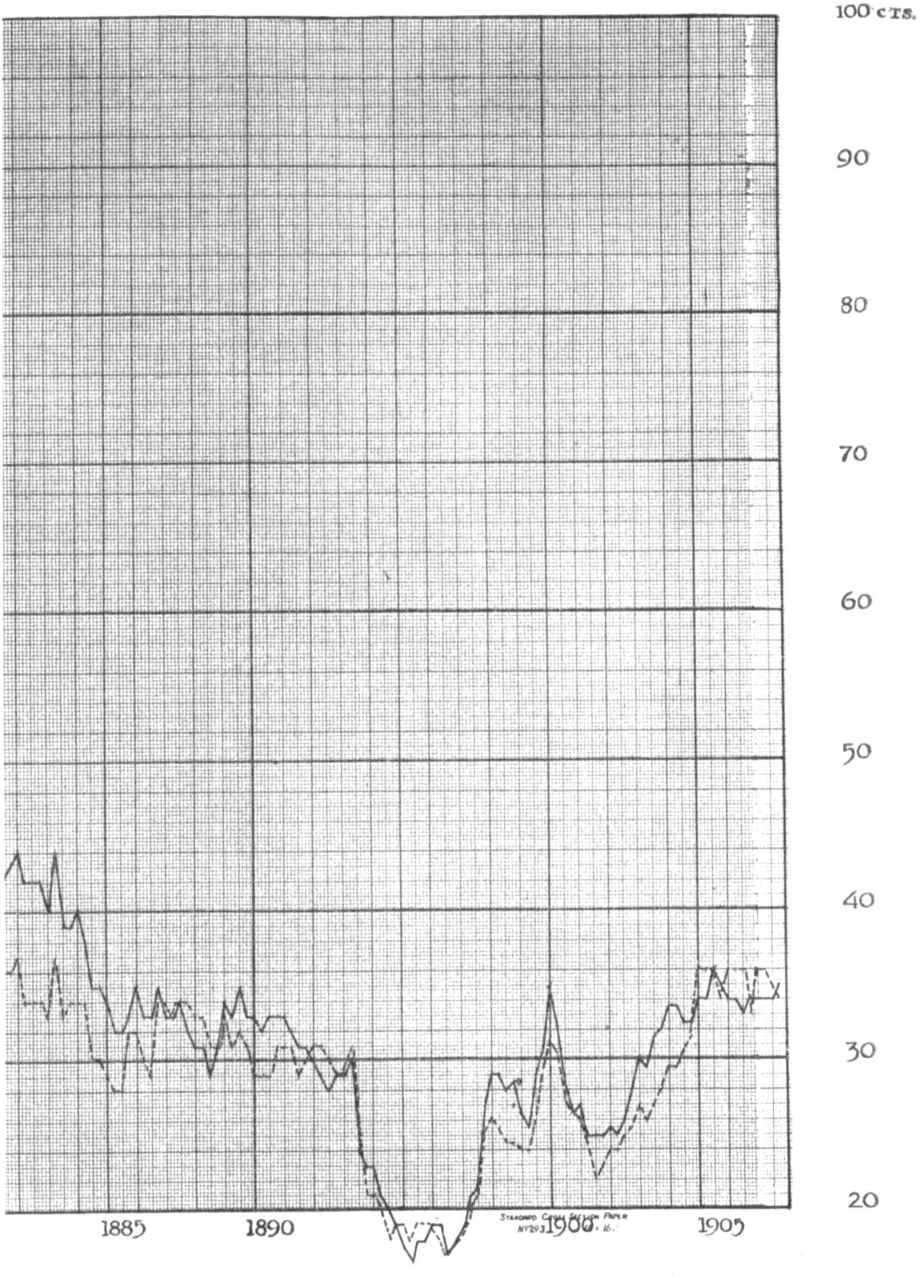

ery clear how gold prices failed to rise above the previous level during the period of
e of the fluctuations in prices at other periods, such as the abnormally high prices of
prices which set in after about 1884. The quotations are those of Mauger and Avery.

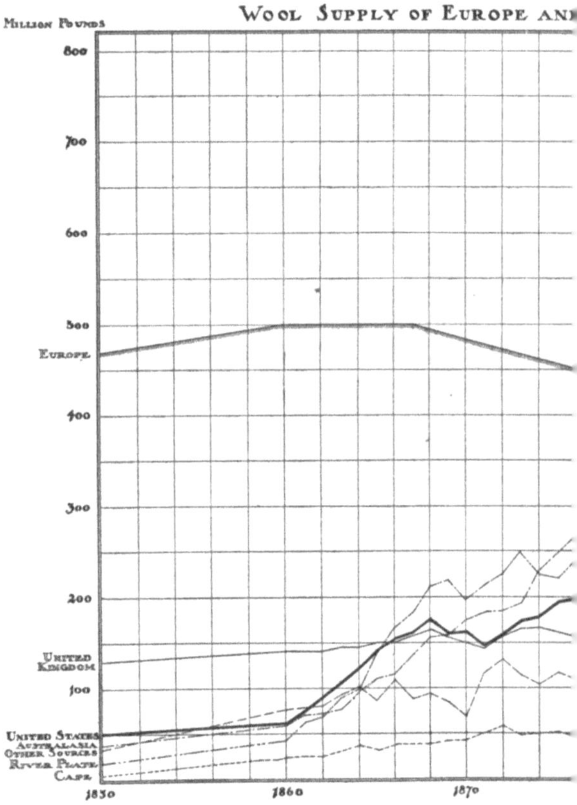

C

WOOL SUPPLY OF EUROPE

Note the declining or stationary wool clip of Eu
increase in the output of the United States and the
out the stationary condition of the American clip
rapidly, and in addition conveys a good impression
of the world's wool supply at the present. Attent
since 1891 and the slowly rising importance of th
Helmuth Schwartze & Co. See footnote, page 164.

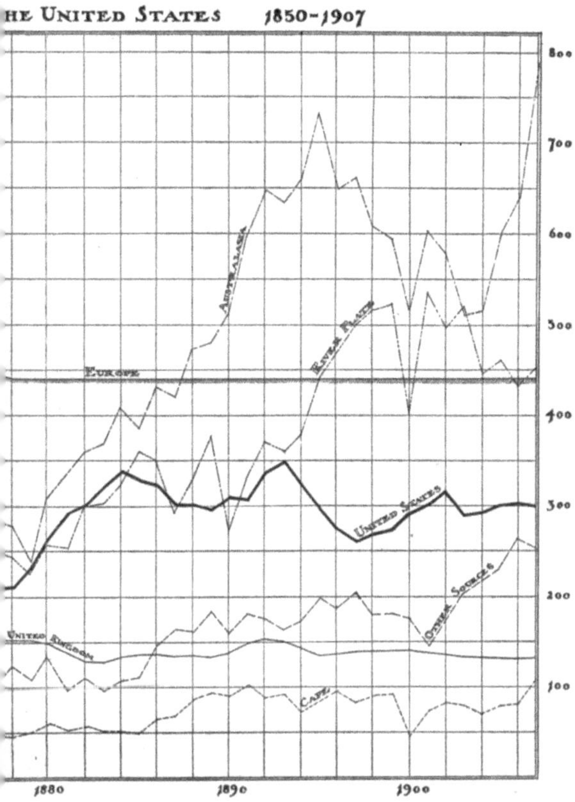

ART II

THE UNITED STATES, 1850–1907

e and the United Kingdom as contrasted with the rapid
ntries of the Southern Hemisphere. The chart also brings
er 1884, while Argentina and Australia were advancing so
he relative importance of the various countries as sources
may also be called to the stationary position of the Cape
"other sources" of the wool supply. Based on figures of

Relative Annual Average Gc

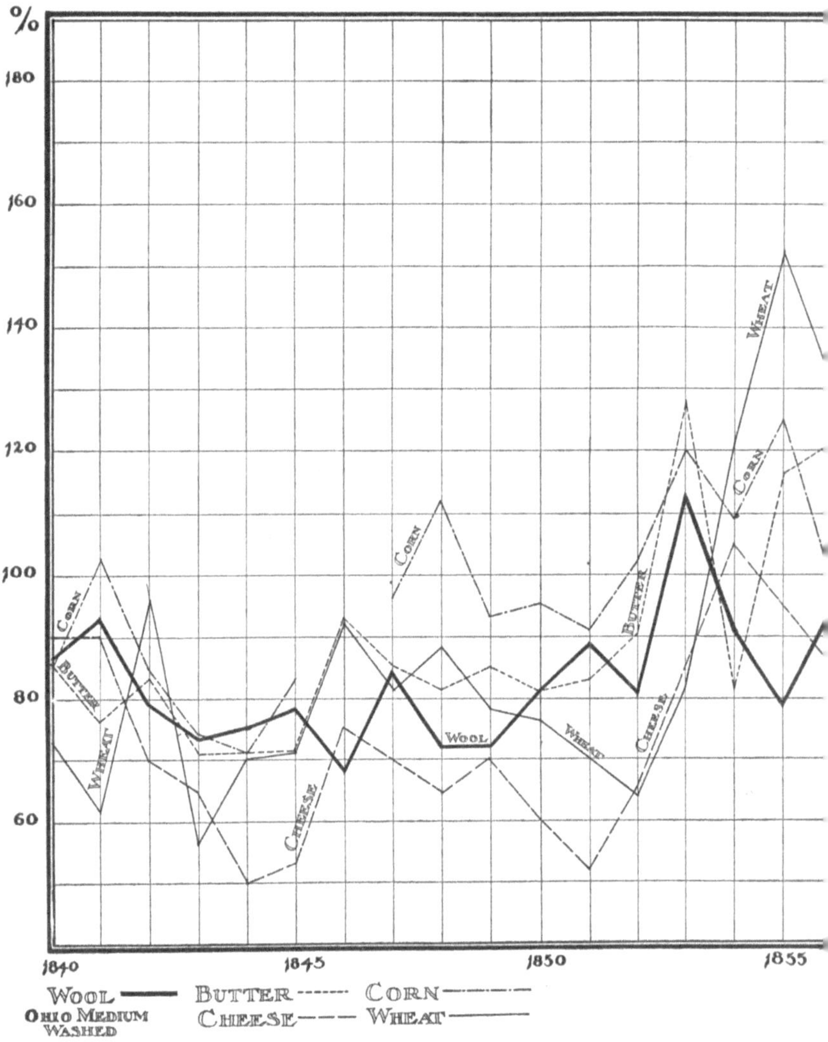

RELA

This chart is designed to bring out the relative changes which took place in the
and consequently does not indicate the absolute prices, which for such a purpose a
which the absolute prices of those years bore to the absolute price in 1860. Except

Attention may be called to the way in which the chart brings out the relatively h
products, particularly the dairy products. The situation as regards relative prices d
other periods. Other points deserving of notice are the low price of wool after 186
generally high level of dairy produce which began to appear in the fifties and was
any one time is influenced by factors not peculiar to the particular commodity or i

D PRICES OF WOOL AND OTHER AGRICULTUR

BASIS: 100 = PRICE IN 1860

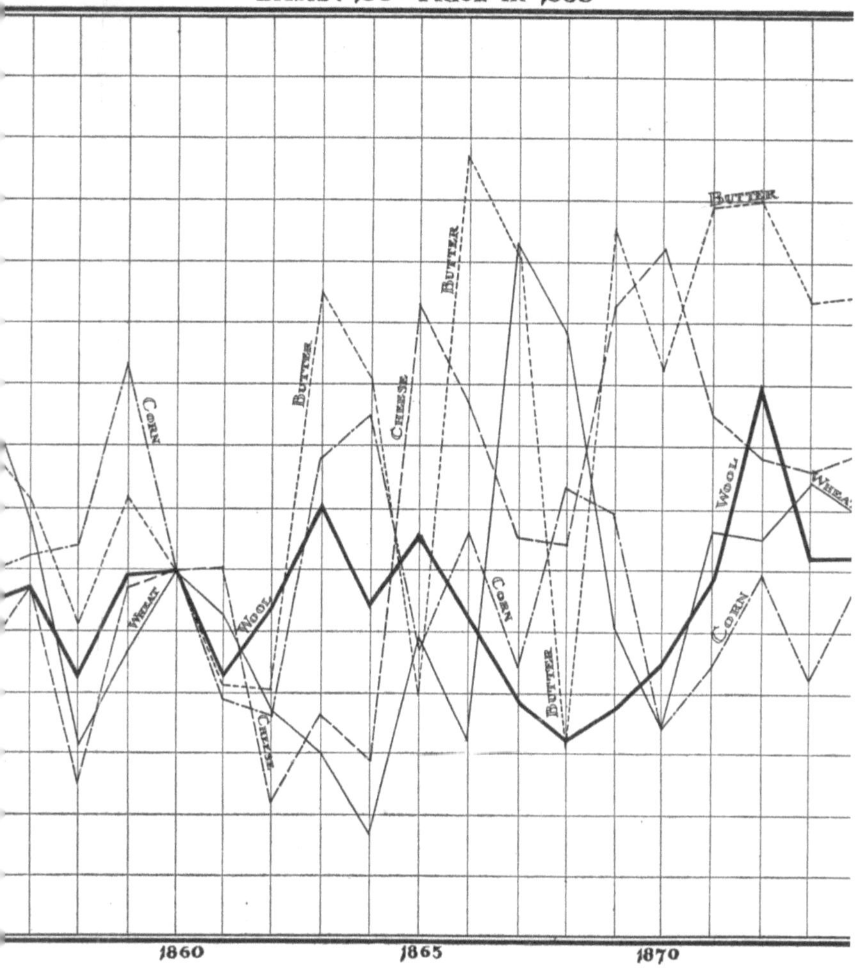

CHART III

E ANNUAL AVERAGE GOLD PRICES OF WOOL AND OTHER AGRICULTURAL PRODUCTS, 18

ces of agricultural products — a point of the utmost importance in determining the direct
of little significance. In carrying this out the price in 1860 is taken as the basis and is eq
wool the prices are those of the Aldrich Report; wool prices are based on figures of Ma
er prices of wool in the early forties (up to about 1845), and the relatively low prices in the
g the Civil War is also made plain; the chart shows not only the changes of the different
he two sudden advances and declines in 1872 and 1880, the generally lower level prevail
manently maintained after about 1868. On the other hand, the general waves of fluctuatio
stry but common to all.

AL PRODUCTS. 1840–1890.

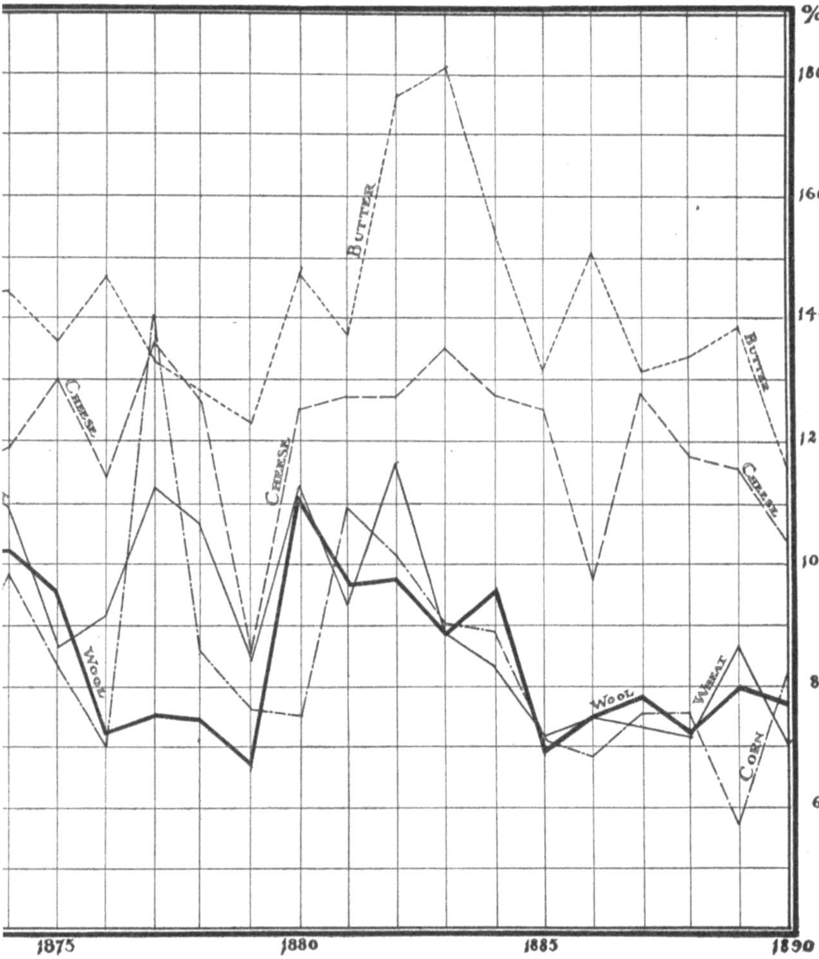

40–1890

ion in which the farmer turned his efforts and the kind of crops which he produced—
qual to 100%. The figures for the other years simply represent the ratio or percentage
nger and Avery.

fifties (especially after 1854), when compared with the prices of the other agricultural
prices during the war but also the relation of war prices on a gold basis to those of
ing after the middle eighties, the drop during the period of free wool, and, finally, the
n in which all commodities participate give some notion as to what extent the price at

NUMBER OF SHEEP BY GROUPS OF STATES AT CENSUS PERIODS.

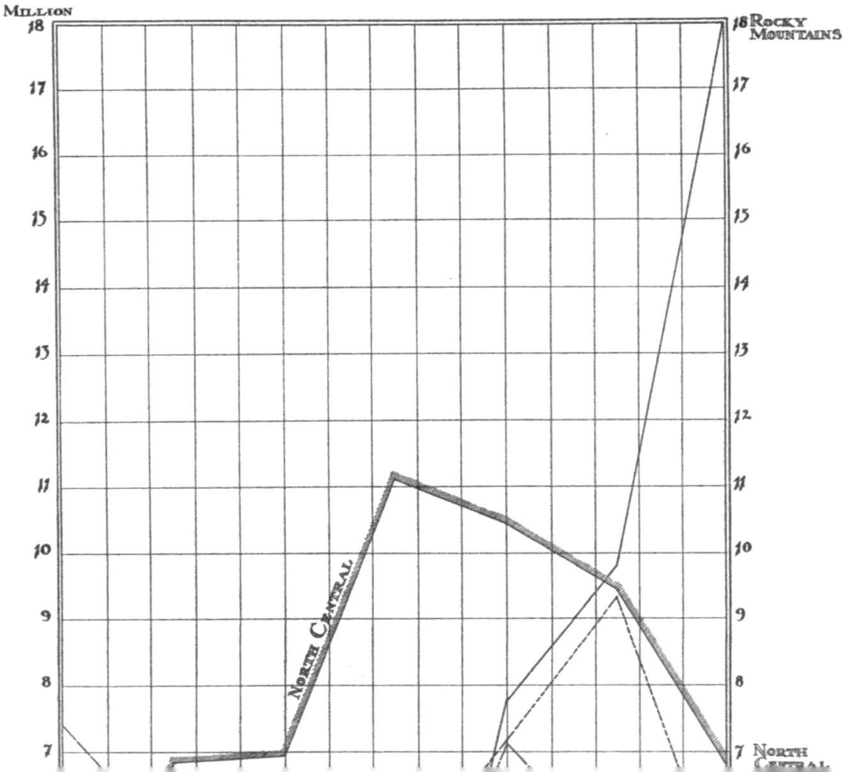

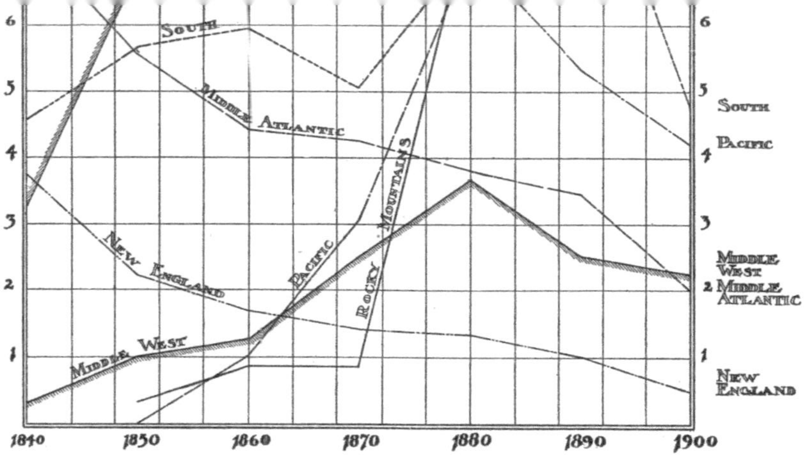

CHART IV

THE NUMBER OF SHEEP BY GROUPS OF STATES AT CENSUS PERIODS, 1840–1900

Note especially the very different tendencies which appear in the various groups at the same time, and also those which appear in the same group at different times. Note, too, the time at which the flocks begin to fall off in each section; in the New England and Middle Atlantic states from 1840, in the North Central states after 1870, the Pacific states after 1880, and the South after 1890, while in the Rocky Mountain states, on the other hand, there is only a constant growth. The chart thus brings out the steady westward movement of the centre of the industry and also indicates what a great variety of factors must have been shaping its course in the country as a whole.

The Riverside Press
CAMBRIDGE . MASSACHUSETTS
U . S . A

Bei Fragen zur Produktsicherheit wenden Sie sich bitte an:
If you have any questions regarding product safety,
please contact:

Walter de Gruyter GmbH
Genthiner Straße 13
10785 Berlin
productsafety@degruyterbrill.com